Fifteenth-Century English

Fifteenth-Century English Dream Visions

AN ANTHOLOGY

Julia Boffey

OXFORD
UNIVERSITY PRESS

This book has been printed digitally and produced in a standard specification in order to ensure its continuing availability

OXFORD
UNIVERSITY PRESS

Great Clarendon Street, Oxford OX2 6DP

Oxford University Press is a department of the University of Oxford.
It furthers the University's objective of excellence in research, scholarship,
and education by publishing worldwide in

Oxford New York

Auckland   Cape Town Dar es Salaam   Hong Kong   Karachi
Kuala Lumpur Madrid Melbourne Mexico City   Nairobi
New Delhi Shanghai Taipei Toronto
With offices in
Argentina Austria Brazil Chile Czech Republic France Greece
Guatemala Hungary Italy Japan South Korea Poland Portugal
Singapore Switzerland Thailand Turkey Ukraine Vietnam

Oxford is a registered trade mark of Oxford University Press
in the UK and in certain other countries

Published in the United States
by Oxford University Press Inc., New York

© Julia Boffey 2003

ISBN 978-0-19-926398-1

Acknowledgements

This anthology has a long history, and I have appreciated help from many people in the course of its preparation. I am grateful to a number of libraries for permission to consult manuscripts and books in their possession, and to library staff for much information and practical help. My debt to previous editors of all the texts included in the volume is incalculable, and will be evident (if not always specified as fully as would be just) throughout the notes and apparatus. Colleagues and students in the School of English and Drama at Queen Mary, University of London, have provided support and stimulus during the completion of the work, and London medievalists more generally (especially the members of the London Old and Middle English Research Seminar) have constituted an invaluable scholarly advice line. Material relating to some of the texts edited here has been presented in the form of papers at conferences and at other meetings, and I am grateful to the audiences who listened, questioned, and commented. Specific debts are too numerous to list here in full, but I should especially like to thank Charlotte Brewer, for advice on editorial and other matters, Mary Worthington, for patient and meticulous copy-editing, and Tony Edwards, for information and support at all stages.

Contents

Abbreviations

A & A	Chaucer, *Anelida and Arcite*
Aen.	Virgil, *Aeneid*
AL	*The Assembly of Ladies*
AN&Q	*American Notes and Queries*
BC	Skelton, *The Bouge of Court*
BD	Chaucer, *The Book of the Duchess*
BL	British Library
Bodl.	Bodleian Library, Oxford
Boece	Chaucer's translation of Boethius's *De consolatione Philosophiae*
CA	Gower, *Confessio Amantis*
CFMA	*Classiques français du Moyen Age*
Chau R	*Chaucer Review*
Cl T	Chaucer, *The Clerk's Tale*
CT	Chaucer, *The Canterbury Tales*
CUL	Cambridge University Library
De cons	Boethius, *De consolatione Philosophiae*
EC	*Essays in Criticism*
EETS	Early English Text Society
ELN	*English Language Notes*
ELR	*English Literary Renaissance*
EM	*Early Music*
E S	extra series
ES	*English Studies*
Fkl T	Chaucer, *The Franklin's Tale*
FL	*The Floure and the Leafe*
Gen Prol	Chaucer, the *General Prologue* to *The Canterbury Tales*
HF	Chaucer, *The House of Fame*
JEGP	*Journal of English and Germanic Philology*
JMRS	*Journal of Medieval and Renaissance Studies*
Kn T	Chaucer, *The Knight's Tale*
KQ	James I of Scotland, *The Kingis Quair*
LGW	Chaucer, *The Legend of Good Women*
LGWP	Chaucer, the Prologue to *The Legend of Good Women*

LR	Charles of Orleans, *Love's Renewal*
M Ae	*Medium Aevum*
ME	Middle English
MED	*Middle English Dictionary*
Mer T	Chaucer, *The Merchant's Tale*
Mil T	Chaucer, *The Miller's Tale*
MLN	*Modern Language Notes*
MLQ	*Modern Language Quarterly*
MLR	*Modern Langue Review*
NPT	Chaucer, *The Nun's Priest's Tale*
N S	new series
N & Q	*Notes and Queries*
OED	*Oxford English Dictionary*
O S	ordinary series
PF	Chaucer, *The Parliament of Fowls*
Phys T	Chaucer, *The Physician's Tale*
PLL	*Papers on Language and Literature*
PQ	*Philological Quarterly*
RR	Guillaume de Lorris and Jean de Meun, *Le Roman de la Rose*
Romaunt	Chaucer (?), *The Romaunt of the Rose*
SAC	*Studies in the Age of Chaucer*
SATF	Société des Anciens Textes Français
SB	*Studies in Bibliography*
SP	*Studies in Philology*
Sq T	Chaucer, *The Squire's Tale*
SSL	*Studies in Scottish Literature*
STC	*Short Title Catalogue* (see bibliography: Pollard & Redgrave)
TC	Chaucer, *Troilus and Criseyde*
TG	Lydgate, *The Temple of Glass*
TLF	Textes littéraires français
TSLL	*Texas Studies in Language and Literature*
WB Prol	Chaucer, the Prologue to *The Wife of Bath's Tale*
WBT	Chaucer, *The Wife of Bath's Tale*
YES	*Yearbook of English Studies*

Note on Editorial Policy

The aim in these editions has been to preserve as much as possible of the flavour of the original texts while at the same time presenting them in clear and comprehensible forms. ME thorn (þ) and yogh (ȝ) have been modernized in the texts, as appropriate, and -u, -v, -w, -y, -i, -j have been regularized when this will aid understanding; expansion of abbreviated forms of final-e has also taken account of comprehensibility as well as metrical considerations. The textual notes to each poem explain the principles of transcription and collation which have been followed, and indicate the range of problems specific to each text. Punctuation and layout are editorial. Titles of Middle English Works (e.g. *The Parliament of Fowls, Winner and Waster*) are generally cited in modern spelling.

Introduction

THE GENRE OF THE DREAM VISION

The late medieval taste for poems in the form of dreams responds to an extensive and significant tradition of writing of which examples can be cited from the Bible, from the Greek and Latin classics, and from the late antique and early medieval periods.[1] Interest in the prophetic or symbolic potential of dreams is especially marked in ancient and classical writings (as in, for example, the biblical dreams interpreted by Joseph in Genesis, chapter 41; John's dream as recounted in The Book of Revelation; the dream of the underworld in Book VI of Virgil's *Aeneid*), and the body of Latin scholarship in which such dreams were discussed and categorized continued to be influential in the Middle Ages. Macrobius, whose commentary on the dream of Scipio dates from the fifth century, was still widely read and cited ten centuries after his death.[2] The enduring interest in dreaming was demonstrated in various ways. Some medieval writers experimented creatively with narration of fictional dreams, others wrote about the different categories of dream and possibilities for interpreting them, and still more considered the physical causes of dreams, relating them to theories about the balance of bodily humours.[3]

The poets whose works are collected in this volume (Lydgate, James I of Scotland, Charles of Orleans, Skelton, and the anonymous author of *The Assembly of Ladies*) draw productively on all these strands of interest, making sometimes explicit, sometimes covert, reference to aspects of the different traditions concerning dreams which they recognized as influential. At the same time they exploit to the full the liberating possibilities that writing a dream can hold open, and the extraordinary variety of figurative discourse that the form permits. For writers in English, furthermore—still in the fifteenth century a relatively new literary language—the composition of dream poetry

[1] The tradition is outlined by Spearing (1976).
[2] See e.g. Chaucer's *Parliament of Fowls*, lines 29–84, and Charles of Orleans, *Love's Renewal*, lines 106–9. The commentary is translated by Stahl (Macrobius 1952), and, in extracts, by Brewer (1960).
[3] See Kruger (1992).

offered a notable opportunity for reflection on their own creative practices, particularly in relation to the inescapably dominant models of Chaucer's poems. The texts collected in this volume thus gesture in various ways towards Chaucer's literary experiments with dreams in *The Book of the Duchess*, *The Parliament of Fowls*, *The House of Fame*, and the Prologue to *The Legend of Good Women*.

MEDIEVAL DREAM VISIONS

For Chaucer, as for the Middle Ages more generally, the most influential late classical experiment with the form of the retrospectively narrated vision was probably Boethius's *De consolatione Philosophiae* (The Consolation of Philosophy), written in 524–5.[4] Boethius (*c*.480–*c*.525) became a consul in Rome and chief of staff to King Theodoric before suddenly falling from favour after accusations of treason. He was imprisoned at Pavia in northern Italy and executed there, but was able before his death to write the *Consolation*, a treatise in prose and verse which recounts a vision in which the dreamer while in prison is visited by Lady Philosophy, and learns through dialogue with her the means to confront and rationalize his misfortunes. The *Consolation* engaged interest throughout the Middle Ages, prompting influential commentaries by Nicholas Trevet and Remigius of Auxerre, and translations into French by Jean de Meun and into English prose, first by King Alfred (*c*.892) and later by Chaucer himself.

Boethius does not draw special attention to the boundaries between 'real' and visionary worlds in his treatise; he begins the *Consolation* with some lines of lament for his misfortune, and introduces what constitutes the 'dream' simply by recounting that 'I saw, stondynge aboven the heghte of myn heved, a womman of ful greet reverence by semblaunt' (Chaucer's *Boece* I, pr. 1, lines 3–4)[5] and recalling some of Philosophy's supernatural features. That the *Consolation* might be counted a dream is made more explicit in some of the opening illustrations to medieval copies of the text, which set next to an image of the author in colloquy

---

[4] Ed. and tr. Stewart and Rand (Boethius 1918, repr. 1968), and by Watts (Boethius 1969, repr. 1976). For biographical details and further discussion, see Gibson (1982) and Minnis (1987).

[5] Unless specified otherwise, quotations from Chaucer's writings cite Benson's edition (Chaucer 1987).

with Philosophy another image of the author asleep in bed.[6] The comparative vagueness with which Boethius defined his visionary framework is shared by certain other medieval works, from Alan of Lille's twelfth-century Latin *De planctu Naturae* to Dante's influential *Commedia* and John Gower's fourteenth-century Middle English *Confessio Amantis*:[7] the visionary mode in these works allows freedom for imaginative speculation, without insisting on the necessity for provision of authenticating detail about the dream-narrator's waking existence.

LE ROMAN DE LA ROSE AND FRENCH DREAM VISIONS

Among the longest and most important of medieval vernacular dream visions is *Le Roman de la Rose* (*The Romance of the Rose*), written in French in the thirteenth century.[8] The first 4,028 lines, the work of Guillaume de Lorris, introduce a young narrator, preoccupied by thoughts of love, who recollects a dream about his pursuit of a rose in a delightful garden inhabited by personified abstractions such as Fair Welcome (*Bel Accueil*) and Standoffishness (*Daungier*). Guillaume's section of the poem broke off part of the way through the Lover's difficult pursuit of the rose; the narration was subsequently taken up and completed by Jean de Meun, who extended it by almost 18,000 lines, and expanded the central love allegory into a comprehensive exploration of knowledge. The *Roman* was a hugely popular work, surviving in over 250 manuscripts,[9] many of which contain illustrations. Chaucer translated part of it into Middle English (Fragment A of *The Romaunt of the Rose*),[10] and its influence is manifest in later medieval writing of many kinds. Features of the delicious dream garden of Guillaume's section of the poem infiltrate the gardens constructed in numerous other love

---

[6] See Courcelle (1967), plates 30, 31, 37, 40, 44, 46, 47.

[7] The *De planctu* (*The Complaint of Nature*) is translated by Sheridan (Alan of Lille 1980); the *Commedia* (*The Divine Comedy*) by Singleton (Dante Alighieri 1980–2), and the *Confessio* (*The Lover's Confession*) by Macaulay (Gower 1899–1902); these and associated works are discussed by Lynch (1988).

[8] Ed. Lecoy in *RR* (1965–70), and translated into modern English prose by Dahlberg in *RR* (1971).

[9] First surveyed by Langlois (1910), and more recently reviewed by Huot (1993), with copious discussion of the illustrations.

[10] In Chaucer (1987).

allegories, while elements and episodes of Jean's continuation (his presentation of the goddess Nature, for example), and the overall richness of detail by which the *Roman* itemizes facets of the psyche, play a formative role in later texts.

Aspects of the form and content of the *Roman* are echoed and sometimes directly alluded to in a number of other French dream poems. Those of Guillaume de Deguileville (written between about 1330 and 1358) build on the notion of the imaginative journey which is implicit in the experience of dreaming, and adapt some of the strategies of the *Roman* to the purposes of religious allegory; all three base themselves on the structure of the pilgrimage, from the *Pèlerinage de la vie humaine* (*Pilgrimage of the Life of Man*), through the *Pèlerinage de l'âme* (*Pilgrimage of the soul*) and the *Pèlerinage Jhesuchrist* (*Pilgrimage of Jesus Christ*).[11]

On secular topics, some *dits amoureux* (courtly poems on the subject of love) are framed as dreams, or make reference to scenes and land-scapes reminiscent of the garden of the *Roman* and its inhabitants: fourteenth-century examples include the *Songe Saint Valentin* (*Dream of St Valentine*) of Oton de Granson (*c*.1345–1397);[12] poems by Jean Froissart (1337–after 1404), such as the *Paradis d'amour*, the *Espinette amoureuse*, the *Joli buisson de Jonece*, and the *Temple d'honneur*;[13] the *Fonteinne Amoureuse* of Guillaume de Machaut (*c*.1300–1377).[14] These works were known to Chaucer and through his writings transmitted indirectly to English writers of the fifteenth century. While love visions of these kinds were able to exploit dreams as fantasies concerning desire and sometimes wish fulfilment, other modes of writing made use of the dream framework as a means to convey social or political commentary which might have seemed inflammatory if communicated in any more direct way: the *Songe du Vergier* (1378; extant in both Latin and French versions) was commissioned as a political statement by the French king Charles V, while the *Songe Véritable* (1406) offers, in contrast, a vision of royal corruption.[15]

---

[11] All ed. Stürzinger: Deguileville (1893, 1895, 1897).
[12] Ed. Piaget: Oton de Granson (1941).
[13] Ed. Dembowski: Froissart (1986); and Fourrier: Froissart (1972, 1975, 1979).
[14] Ed. Palmer; Guillaume de Machaut (1993).
[15] Ed. Schnerb-Lièvre: *Songe du vergier* (1982); discussed by Famiglietti (1986).

DREAM VISIONS IN MIDDLE ENGLISH

The possibilities of vision as a literary mode were evident to early
writers in English, and acknowledged in King Alfred's prose translation
of Boethius's *Consolation*,[16] and in the eighth-century poem *The Dream
of the Rood*.[17] The Latin and French visions discussed above were
accessible to English readers familiar with these languages, and writers
such as Gower, whose late fourteenth-century *Vox Clamantis* takes the
form of an apocalyptic vision,[18] continued to experiment with the Latin
tradition. The late fourteenth century was also a period of intense
interest in the potential of this form for those writing in English,
however. Chaucer's earliest surviving poem, *The Book of the Duchess*,
is a dream vision; *The House of Fame*, *The Parliament of Fowls*, and the
Prologue to *The Legend of Good Women* (all discussed below) are his
later explorations of the genre. Chaucer's friend Sir John Clanvowe also
tried his hand at a love vision on the French model, in the form of *The
Cuckoo and the Nightingale* (sometimes called *The Book of Cupid*);[19] their
London contemporary Thomas Usk chose to explore the vicissitudes of
political fortune in a Boethian prose vision called *The Testament of
Love*.[20] Poets writing in the alliterative tradition found that the dream
vision accommodated a range of purposes: in *Pearl* its framework
encloses elegy and a glimpse of the New Jerusalem;[21] in *The Parliament
of the Three Ages* a debate;[22] in *Winner and Waster*[23] and in the different
versions of *Piers Plowman* (and certain later poems in the *Piers Plowman*
tradition)[24] social and political commentary in a variety of modes. By
the start of the fifteenth century the dream vision was firmly established
in English writing.

ENGLISH POETRY IN THE FIFTEENTH CENTURY

The poems collected in this volume represent a tradition of writing
which is often called 'Chaucerian'—a term rather hard to define. The

[16] Ed. and tr. Sedgefield: Alfred the Great (1899, 1900).
[17] Ed. Swanton: *The Dream of the Rood* (1978).
[18] Ed. Macaulay (Gower 1902: iv. 3–313); tr. Stockton (Gower 1962).
[19] Ed. Scattergood (1979).   [20] Ed. Skeat (1897); and Shoaf: Usk (1998).
[21] Ed. Gordon (1953).
[22] Ed. Offord: *Parlement of the Three Ages* (1959).
[23] Ed. Trigg: *Wynnere and Wastoure* (1990).
[24] See Skeat: Langland (1886); and Barr (1993).

works of writers conceived of as 'Chaucerian' do not all share the dialectal forms of Chaucer's London English, for example, or even those of later developments of it: some (like the Scots king James I in this collection) wrote English of very different kinds. Nor is it possible to assume that writers in this tradition necessarily shared with Chaucer their range of interests or contacts: John Lydgate was a Benedictine monk; John Skelton a royal tutor and priest; Charles of Orleans a prince of the French royal blood; and the anonymous author of *The Assembly of Ladies* could have been anything. In a very general sense the term might include texts produced by authors who had read and thought about certain of Chaucer's poems; but this possibility was available to increasing numbers of would-be writers after Chaucer's death in 1400, and the spreading circulation of manuscript copies of his works, and does not add much to the specificity of our definition. References to and quotations from Chaucer appear in a number of contexts in fifteenth-century writing, and it is clear that his writings came to be well known as well as highly respected.[25] The most useful and specific way of understanding 'Chaucerian' in connection with the poems in this volume is in its suggestion that these works share a degree of self-conscious Chaucerian reference, and in certain ways explicitly announce their affiliation to (or in some instances their departures from) a particular tradition of writing which they associate with Chaucer's name.

This tradition is itself best defined by reference to Chaucer's own dream visions, which, while individual in their flavour and subject matter, share a number of common features. All, for example, address themselves at some level to aspects of secular love—whether the love and loss of *The Book of the Duchess*, or the different kinds of sexual love explored in *The Parliament of Fowls*, or the notions about love and praise in relation to poetic inspiration which inform both *The House of Fame* and the Prologue to *The Legend of Good Women*. The contexts in which love is investigated in all four of these works are, moreover, consistently 'courtly' ones, involving the concerns of people with the means to afford leisure for the cultivation and discussion of human relationships: aristocrats and the socially privileged, whose worlds would in reality have incorporated structures along the lines of the parliaments and courts and

---

[25] Spurgeon (1925) has a comprehensive collection of later references to and echoes of Chaucer. The gradual transmission of Chaucer's writings is discussed by Strohm (1982) and by Lerer (1993).

households which Chaucer depicts. Such people would have been familiar with activities like hunting (*The Book of the Duchess*), outdoor ceremony (*The Parliament of Fowls* and the Prologue to *The Legend of Good Women*), or suing for favour (*The House of Fame*); and they would have responded to the aesthetically pleasing gardens, or temples, or tapestries, or wall-paintings of Chaucer's dreams with the judgement of connoisseurs.

In keeping with this depiction of and address to a world of the cultivated and discriminating, Chaucer's dream poems make copious reference to other books and to earlier traditions of writing, both in Latin and in the vernacular languages of medieval Western Europe. Stories originating in Ovid's *Metamorphoses* and *Heroides*, or in Virgil's *Aeneid*, rub shoulders with allusions to Boethius's *Consolation*, to Macrobius's commentary on the dream of Scipio, and with echoes of the *Romance of the Rose* and of poems by Chaucer's closer contemporaries Boccaccio, Froissart, and Machaut.[26] On occasions, these books play material roles in the events recounted in Chaucer's poems: the narrator of *The Parliament of Fowls* falls asleep while reading about the dream of Scipio in an 'olde bok totorn' (line 110), and his dream begins with a recapitulation of this earlier literary vision; the narrator of *The Book of the Duchess* assuages insomnia with a 'romaunce ... fables | That clerkes had in olde tyme, | And other poetes, put in rime' (lines 48–54), and proceeds in his dream to revisit aspects of one of the stories he reads there. Chaucer seems to have been the first European writer to experiment with the possibilities of significant overlap between bedtime reading and the dreams which it can prompt.[27]

This tissue of references to other writings is clearly a purposeful intertextuality that reaches beyond compliments on the learning of prospective audiences and readers. Chaucer seems to wish in his dream poems to bring to life many of the anxieties which might preoccupy a late medieval writer—particularly one whose situation depended on the goodwill of secular patrons, and whose determination to write in an inauspicious vernacular may have invited accusations of eccentricity or wrongheadedness. Within this frame of reference, books come to figure almost frighteningly in some of the dreams. The narrator of the Prologue to *The Legend of Good Women* has to confront critics of

---

[26] See Boitani (1986).   [27] Stearns (1942).

his own poems, and is enjoined by them, as a penance for his 'missay-
ings', to produce a new work (envisaged, in concrete terms, as a
presentation manuscript destined for a specific 'real' figure: Richard
II's queen), which will give a new spin to stories from the books in his
own library. The questions which are explicitly raised in this prologue
about the creative relationship between new compositions and 'olde
appreved stories' (Prologue to *The Legend of Good Women*, line 21) are
in *The House of Fame* dramatized as something close to nightmare.

Questions of a similar kind seem to have preoccupied fifteenth-century
English writers with a new urgency, as they contemplated not just a
distant literary heritage but Chaucer's own very palpable œuvre in
relation to their own creative aspirations.[28] Skelton's characterization
of himself as 'Drede' (Fearfulness) in *The Bouge of Courte* seems in part
to reflect his trepidation before 'the great auctoryte | Of poetes olde'
(8–9); his uncertainties and humility are shared by others of the writers
whose works figure in the present anthology, and who make frequent
reference to models for their own creative practice. The author of *The
Kingis Quair* starts by relating the matter of his poem to a recollected
reading of Boethius's *De consolatione Philosophiae* (14–21), prefaces his
dream with a scene borrowed from *The Knight's Tale*, and ends by
recommending his composition to Chaucer and Gower (1374). The
dreamer of Lydgate's *Temple of Glass* sets his vision in a palace designed
to recall Chaucer's *House of Fame*, on whose walls are represented
figures from a number of other stories, several told by Chaucer
(44–142; Chaucer is mentioned by name at line 110); portions of the
discussion between the lovers in this poem are modelled on parts of *The
Book of the Duchess*.[29] Even in *Love's Renewal*, probably the work of a
native French speaker, allusions to writers of a shared European past are
woven together with Chaucerian echoes.[30] Intertextuality, contrived
with varying degrees of delicacy and humour, is significant in all the
poems collected here, and contributes to varieties of authorial position-
ing which are a part of the complexity of the 'Chaucerian' tradition of

---

[28] Such 'anxiety of influence', in relation to Chaucer, is discussed by Spearing (1985);
and Lerer (1993).

[29] See the notes to the text.

[30] Explored by Petrina (1997); Bennett (1982); and Boffey (1996).

writing in English. And many further texts, beyond those collected here, make their own distinctive commentary on this phenomenon: the Scottish dream vision by William Dunbar which has become known as *The Golden Targe*, for example, manipulates the conventionally delicious elements of the Chaucerian love vision in ways which raise questions about both love and poetic practice,[31] and which acknowledge with some comprehensiveness the 'anxiety of influence' which has been signalled as a feature of post-Chaucerian writing.[32]

COURTS AND COURTLINESS

As has been noted, Chaucer's dream poems depict a range of situations in which behaviour of a literally 'courtly' kind might be thought appropriate. Cupid and his entourage accost the narrator of the Prologue to *The Legend of Good Women*, and in the context of this court gathering he is faced with a quasi-legal judgement on the perceived bias of his writings. In *The House of Fame*, Fame holds formal court to companies of supplicants, and responds to their pleas with arbitrary justice. *The Parliament of Fowls* introduces Venus's courtly household (not unlike that of Cupid in the *Romance of the Rose*), and follows it with Nature's parliament, which debates the claims of various birds to a mate. Even in the more intimate world of *The Book of the Duchess*, the narrator exercises courtly discretion in addressing a social superior, and responding properly to his recollections of the pursuit of love. Court and household were important medieval models of social cohesiveness, and must have defined many people's experience of social processes and bonds (hence, too, their understanding of matters such as the operation of law).[33] It can hardly have seemed out of the way for a secular writer to situate discussion of important issues in the context of an imagined court or parliament, and to build creatively on some of the activities common to such bodies (hearing pleas, holding debates, inviting judgements, for example). Documentary evidence confirms that

[31] See Bawcutt: Dunbar (1996).
[32] See especially Spearing (1985); and Lerer (1993).
[33] The implications of living in court or household have been discussed by Mertes (1988); and by Starkey (1981, 1987); for more detailed discussion of the composition of English courts of the late 14th and 15th c., see Given-Wilson (1986, 1996).

most of the writers whose works feature in this collection had direct
experience of life in a court of some kind,[34] and even the anonymous
author of *The Assembly of Ladies* seems at pains to demonstrate famil-
iarity with the structures and processes of an aristocratic household.

The importance which love assumes in these court contexts (quite
apart from any connection with the anachronistic term 'courtly love'
which is often used of the body of conventions governing amorous
relationships in medieval polite society) is not especially surprising.
Courts and households were generally mixed—the all-female household
of Lady Loyalty, as depicted in *The Assembly of Ladies*, bears little
relationship to social reality—and their leisure activities and imaginative
recreation offered considerable space for semi-flirtatious conversation
and 'dalliance',[35] even for mock courts in which questions of love might
be debated and offered for judgement.[36] At a more serious level, the
representation and airing of amorous problems may have offered considerable figurative potential, whether of a specific or more generalized
kind. The sorts of 'service' which might be expected of a lover, like the
bestowing of 'grace' or 'favour' or 'mercy' which might be necessary to
any 'accord' with the object of desire, are forms of behaviour which
might be manifest in a number of secular relationships. Communications
between lord and servant, patron and would-be dependant, supplicant
and arbitrator, might in many contexts have taken the same shapes and
assumed the same vocabulary as those between lover and lady.

The appeal of certain figurative patterns which had been sanctioned
by long use in amorous contexts is cleverly exploited in some of the texts
collected here. *The Bouge of Court*, for example, repositions the fearful
lover (here in the character of 'Drede', the dream-narrator) among a
company who pursue political favour and material reward at a deter-
minedly worldly court. Rather differently, both *The Kingis Quair* and
Love's Renewal make extensive and pointed use of the figure of the
prisoner of love, a man oppressed by circumstances which keep him
from the presence of his lady, and constrained to languish in distress.[37]
Chaucer had explored this figure in *The Knight's Tale* and elsewhere,
intensifying his effects by incorporating aspects of the experiences of the
Boethian prisoner of Fortune. Since James I and Charles of Orleans

---

[34] See the biographical information cited in the headnote to each text.
[35] Effectively evoked in Stevens (1961).   [36] Green (1983).
[37] The figure is explored by Leyerle (1974); and by Boffey (1991).

were both quite literally prisoners of fortune (James captured at sea by the English, Charles taken after the battle of Agincourt), they were subsequently able to activate the figure with a range of fresh and topical implications—some quite naturally of a political kind, and highlighted by their decisions to experiment with the language and cultural capital of their captors. The autobiographical elements of the writings attributed to James and to Charles are especially pointed, indeed humorous, instances of the capacity of dream visions to explore and problematize the relationship between historical reality and imaginative construction, and their invitation to readers to 'decode' meanings is a common feature of the dream genre. A number of attempts have been made to attach the other poems collected here to particular historical circumstances,[38] and the texts' characteristic mixture of deliberate vagueness and specific detail (typified in the personal mottoes which figure in *TG* and *AL*) irresistibly provokes historicist readings.

THE WOMAN QUESTION

A different field of critical enquiry would highlight the fact that the dreams in all of the poems here are ostensibly initiated by desire, in most cases the desire of a male lover to win a lady: the narrators of *The Temple of Glass*, *Love's Renewal*, and *The Kingis Quair* all more or less identify with the central male figures of their dreams, and even *The Bouge of Court* opens with the apparatus of a dream vision on the model of *The Romance of the Rose*, as the dreamer-narrator takes advice from 'Daunger' (Standoffishness) and 'Desyre'. The focus on desire, the allegorical modes which isolate and often personify varieties of human impulse, and the construction of the poems in the form of dreams all serve to open the texts to psychoanalytical interpretations of different kinds, and like the *Roman de la Rose*, they respond fruitfully to such readings. Women play significant parts in all the texts collected here, and their voices are heard at some length, if in ventriloquized form. In *The Temple of Glass*, for example, the lady's complaints precede those of the lover and are outlined both more poignantly and with a greater specificity. In *The Assembly of Ladies*, untypically narrated by a female, much of the dream is devoted to outlining women's grievances in love. Resolution of the

---

[38] See the headnotes to individual poems, particularly to *TG*.

problems addressed in most of the dreams is left to powerful female
arbitrators (Venus in *The Temple of Glass* and *Love's Renewal*; Venus
with the help of Minerva in *The Temple of Glass*), and the male narrators
are in all cases made aware of the significance of the female Fortune to
their destinies. Aspects of this last figure are of course threatening and
likely to instil fear: 'Whome she hateth, she casteth in the dyche', as
Skelton's Drede soon learns (*The Bouge of Court*, line 115). On the
whole, though, the representation of women in these texts is unusually
positive and sympathetic.[39] The three earliest of the texts (*The Temple of
Glass, The Kingis Quair*, and *Love's Renewal*) were probably written
while the repercussions of the so-called 'querelle des femmes', a literary
dispute about women's nature and status, initiated in Paris at the very
end of the fourteenth century by Christine de Pizan, were still to be
felt,[40] and they may reflect aspects of that debate. Various of the issues
which fuelled it were addressed at intervals throughout the fifteenth
century, in works such as Alain Chartier's *La Belle Dame sans Merci*
(translated into English by Sir Richard Roos),[41] and their topicality may
have had some influence on the continuing circulation of *The Temple of
Glass* and the inspiration of *The Assembly of Ladies*.

READERS AND CIRCULATION

Apart from *The Bouge of Court*, which survives in two early printed
editions, all of the poems collected here circulated in manuscript copies
in the fifteenth and early sixteenth centuries. The authors of *Love's
Renewal* and *The Kingis Quair* do not seem to have made extensive
efforts to secure the transmission of their poems, and it may be that these
texts were available only to their close acquaintances or to some other
form of coterie readership (evidence that Charles of Orleans may have

---

[39] Chaucer's *Troilus and Criseyde*, in which Criseyde, the pattern of faithlessness, is
portrayed with interest and sympathy, may also have been significant: the poem appears
together with Chaucer's dream visions and a variety of the poems in this anthology in
Cambridge, University Library, MS Gg. 4. 27, and in Oxford, Bodleian Library, MS Arch.
Selden. B. 24 (see notes to the texts for further information on these manuscripts).

[40] See Hicks (1977); and Fenster and Erler (1990). Hoccleve's *Letter of Cupid* (ed.
Fenster and Erler) translates one of Christine de Pizan's contributions to this debate, and is
collected in various of the manuscript anthologies which contain some of the poems edited
here.

[41] Ed. Skeat (1897), pp. 299–326.

read *The Kingis Quair* does however suggest some limited circulation).[42]
Lydgate's *Temple of Glass* survives in seven complete copies, in a further
selection of fragments, and in early printed form, and was clearly quite
well known. Most of the manuscripts in which it is found are collections
of the writings of Chaucer and other contributors to the Chaucerian
tradition; some seem especially to focus on dream visions, and on poems
concerning questions of love and gender. *The Assembly of Ladies* survives in three manuscripts (in one of which, now Longleat 258, it appears
with *The Temple of Glass* and with a selection of other texts including *La
Belle Dame sans Merci*); it was printed in 1532 in William Thynne's
edition of *The Workes of Geoffrey Chaucer*, to which a number of other
non-Chaucerian texts were appended.[43] While *Love's Renewal* and *The
Kingis Quair* must have reached aristocratic readers (if only small
numbers of them), evidence gleaned from the manuscripts of the other
poems indicates a readership among gentry and cultivated urban circles.
Skelton's decision to have *The Bouge of Court* printed by Wynkyn de
Worde in 1499 may reflect some understanding on both their parts that
an established audience existed for courtly visions, and that such an
audience would be sufficiently familiar with the conventions of this
genre to comprehend the experiments which Skelton made with it.

---

[42] See Petrina (1997) and Boffey (1996).
[43] *STC* 5068, and facsimile in Brewer (1976).

John Lydgate, *The Temple of Glass*

The Temple of Glass is one of several dream visions written by the hugely prolific John Lydgate (1371–1449), a Benedictine monk of the abbey at Bury St Edmunds in Suffolk. Although much of his life must have been spent at Bury, Lydgate studied in Oxford for some years in the early fifteenth century, and lived for part of the 1420s and 1430s at Hatfield Broadoak in Essex, where he was appointed prior. As well as fulfilling commissions connected with his order and its officials (men like William Curteys, who became abbot of Bury in 1429), Lydgate produced many poems for secular patrons, and was acquainted with influential and powerful people from the ruling Lancastrian dynasty and civic government in London. Among his longer poems, the *Troy Book* (ed. Bergen (Lydgate 1906–35)) was written for Prince Henry, son of Henry IV. *The Siege of Thebes* (ed. Erdmann and Ekwall (Lydgate 1911b, 1930)) and *The Life of Our Lady* (ed. Lauritis *et al.* (Lydgate 1961)) were possibly also undertaken for this same Henry once he had become king. The massive compilation which forms *The Fall of Princes* (ed. Bergen (Lydgate 1924–27)) was supported by the patronage of Henry's brother Humphrey of Gloucester. Pageants and mummings were produced for important civic events, and a number of shorter poems served other commemorative or propagandist aims (ed. MacCracken (Lydgate 1911a); MacCracken 1908).

In the context of this huge output, it is difficult to specify a date or an occasion or a patron for *TG*, a dream vision which seems ostensibly to celebrate a prospective marriage, but incorporates a number of unusual features into its account of the proceedings of a court of love and the verdict issued by Venus in response to pleas brought by two lovers. No useful information is provided in any of the surviving manuscripts about the circumstances in which the poem was produced, and even the scribe John Shirley, who copied many of Lydgate's poems and may have had a close association with him, reveals no more than that this is 'une soynge moult plesaunt fait a la request d'un amoreux par Lidegate Le Moygne de Bury' ('a delightful dream made at the request of a lover, by Lydgate, monk of Bury'). Presumably because its subject matter seemed an improbable choice for a mature monk, *TG* has conventionally been located by Lydgate scholars as amongst Lydgate's earliest works, but there is no real support for this view, and indeed the outlines of Lydgate's career suggest that his middle years were the period of most intense activity on behalf of the secular patrons and audiences who might have found *TG* to their taste. The earliest manuscript in which the poem survives, an anthology compiled by John Shirley which is now London, British Library MS Additional 16165, has been dated to the 1420s (see Hanna 1996), and the most that can be said about the composition of *TG* is that it must have pre-dated this copy.

Scholarly efforts to read this as a *poème à clef*, and to locate in it a tissue of references to historical figures and situations, have not proved very convincing. The lovers who put their pleas to Venus have been identified variously as William Paston and Agnes Berry (MacCracken 1908), Henry V and Katherine of Valois (Moore 1912, 1913), Sir Richard Roos and Margaret Vernon (Seaton 1961), and Henry IV and Joan of Navarre (Bianco 2000), but in no case do the details offer a compelling fit. One impediment to reading the poem as a celebratory epithalamium lies in the enigma of the lady's situation, and in the hints that there are obstacles, perhaps even in the form of an existing husband, to the wished-for marriage with her fellow plaintiff (see 335–62). Further complications lie in the variant forms in which the mottoes are preserved in different manuscript copies (see 310, 550), and in the apparent impossibility of forging any consistent network of identifications between these and the fifteenth-century families with whom scholars have sought to link the circumstances which the poem presents.

Aspects of *TG*'s structure and content derive from its reference to a tradition of visions in which problems are presented, and in some cases resolved, at an allegorical 'court of love' (a 'cour d'amour' in the many French examples of the form). At such courts, amorous problems and conduct might be reviewed and assessed, with judgements offered by appropriate deities or allegorical figures. Records from France suggest that such courts had a certain life outside literary texts, and were brought into being to serve the purposes of groups of leisured aristocrats, as flirtatious debating societies for the discussion of lovers' behaviour. Poems like Guillaume de Machaut's *Jugement du Roy de Navarre* and

Jugement du Roy de Behaigne (see Palmer's translations in Guillaume de Machaut 1984, 1988*b*; Windeatt 1982) negotiate in an easy way the interpenetration of these real and fictional courts of love, offering hypothetical problems for debate which are finally resolved by the wisdom of an arbitrator who exists both within the fiction of the text and outside it, in the real world of Machaut's patrons.

Lydgate presumably knew some of these French texts, and was certainly familiar with the forms in which they were reflected in Chaucer's writings. His reading of poems like *LGWP*, whose narrator encounters the God of Love and his household and is forced to defend himself against charges of 'heresy' which the God levels at him, or of *HF*, whose narrator visits a dream temple where the Goddess Fame arbitrarily answers the requests of groups of petitioners, informs parts of *TG*. Quite apart from the court frameworks, other elements of Chaucer's dream poems (as of other works such as *TC*) seem to have provoked responses in *TG*: passages of description, and motifs such as the contrast of opposites which Lydgate develops in the lover's complaint (at 586 ff.) recall sections of *PF* and *BD*. Lydgate's wish to elaborate a response to Chaucer's writings seems to have been one significant aspect of his undertaking in *TG*, and along with his composition of *The Complaint of a Lover's Life* (also known as *The Complaint of the Black Knight*) testifies to the circulation and importance of Chaucer's minor poems in the early fifteenth century, and to a lively and continuing interest in dream visions in the French tradition.

The text of the poem used as the basis for this edition is that copied by John Shirley into BL MS Add. 16165, probably during the 1420s (see below). Shirley's decision to record the 'moult plesaunt' *TG*, together with other of Lydgate's works, in an anthology which also contains Chaucer's *Boece* and *Anelida and Arcite*, suggests some profitable contexts for reading the poem. *TG* shares with these works by Chaucer interests in the modes of complaint and consolation, and it offers in diluted form elements of Boethius's philosophical advice on the alternation of good and bad fortune and the enhancement of the one by the other (a pattern underlined by *TG*'s concern with modulations of light and darkness). Like Chaucer, Lydgate explores the female voicing of complaint; and like both Boethius and the Boethian Chaucer of *Kn T* and *TC*, he suggests the consolations of making virtue from necessity. Although the pleas are made to Venus, and the poem ostensibly concerns the resolution of difficulties in the path of a love affair, it is possible to argue that its concerns move beyond the amorous to explore more general kinds of constraint or unhappiness, and the range of virtuous ways in which these may be resisted or overcome.

Variations of form underline the patterns of appeal and response on which the poem is constructed. Within its two parts, marked by a division after line 550, are introductory sections in couplets and then a number of set-pieces, some in seven-line rhyme royal stanzas on the pattern of Chaucer's *PF* and *TC*, in which different cases are made. The lady has a 'bill' (starting at line 321) and an 'orysoun' (461); the lover a 'lamentacioun' (587), a 'supplicacioun' (721), and a further 'complaint' (990). The vision ends with a 'balade' (1361), which, following the model of *PF*, offers both a suggestion of harmonious concord and a device to waken the narrator from his dream. These experiments with form extend the possibilities of lyrico-narrative in English which had clearly interested Chaucer, and add a dimension of formal appeal to a poem which explores the genre of the love vision in an unusually earnest vein.

NOTE ON THE TEXT

Shirley's copy in BL MS Add. 16165 (S), on which this edition is based, shares many features with the text of *TG* preserved in one other manuscript, an important Chaucerian anthology, dating from the first quarter of the fifteenth century, which is now Cambridge, University Library MS Gg. 4. 27 (G) (pp. 491–510; facsimile intro. Parkes and Beadle 1979–80). Both S and G conclude with a 'complaint', addressed to a woman named Margaret. Complete copies of *TG* (with a different conclusion, and other forms of variation) survive in a number of later fifteenth-century manuscripts: Cambridge, Magdalene College, MS Pepys 2006, pp. 17–52 (P) (facsimile intro. Edwards 1985); Longleat House MS 258, fos. 1–32 (L); Oxford, Bodleian Library MS Bodley 638, fos. 16ᵛ–38 (B) (facsimile intro. Robinson 1981), MS Fairfax 16, fos. 63–82ᵛ (F) (facsimile intro. Norton-Smith 1979), and MS Tanner 346, fos. 76–97 (T) (facsimile intro. Robinson 1980). BL MS Sloane 1212 contains fragments on fos. 1, 2 and 4. *TG* was also printed by Caxton *c.*1477 (*STC* 17032), and in several other editions well into the sixteenth century. The poem's previous editors, Schick (Lydgate 1891) and

Norton-Smith (Lydgate 1966), have attempted to deduce from the surviving manuscripts that Lydgate revised the text in several stages, but the textual situation seems both more complex and more random than this. In line with their rather different arguments, Schick and Norton-Smith both chose to base their editions on the text of Tanner MS 346, supposedly representing a version 'consistent' in literary terms. The present edition, in relying on MS Add. 16165, aims to offer a state of the text as it is represented in two important early manuscripts. This is certainly different from that of Tanner 346 in some respects, but not in itself essentially inconsistent.

Shirley (on whom see Doyle 1961 and Connolly 1998; also Lerer 1993: 117–46), whose role in the transmission of the poems of both Chaucer and Lydgate was of great importance, has been criticized for rushed and slapdash copying, signs of which are evident from time to time here, and signalled in the notes. His scribal habits do however fall into some interesting categories, and the text of *TG* displays many characteristic features: confusion over names, particularly those of classical deities (see, for example, the textual notes to lines 64, 72, 119, 123, 130, 362, 808, 978); omissions and errors, some attributable to eyeskip (lines 28–9, 261–4, 345–6, 478–9, 756–62); idiosyncratic spellings (e.g. *deolful*, line 52; *harome*, line 706; past participle forms beginning with e-, such as *ehorned*, line 8). Nonetheless S has been chosen here as representing the earliest complete copy of the poem (MS G, the other early copy, has some major omissions, at e.g. 551–616, resulting from missing leaves), and because of the desirability of some extensive illustration of Shirley's scribal practice. Shirley seems, after all, to have had some special access to Lydgate's writings, and may have had some connection with him which distinguishes him from other copyists of Lydgate's works.

Emendation here is minimal and based largely on collation with MS G. Instances where these two texts differ substantively from the later copies (as at 310, 335–62, 447–53, 496–515, 550) are indicated in the textual notes. Norton-Smith's arguments for successive stages of revision in the poem, with MSS S and G representing an early draft, MSS F and B an intermediate revision, and MSS TPL a completed draft (see Norton-Smith 1958), are not entirely convincing: a number of the 'revisions' on which his argument hinges are equally explicable as the results of scribal or editorial tampering, and their confinement to particular manuscript groups is not entirely consistent.

TEXTUAL NOTES

Emendations are from G, unless indicated otherwise. Only the most striking variants between S and G are noted here.

28–9 between these two lines, S has 'And many a story mo than I reken can | Hem to rehers I trowe ther might no man', which does not appear at all in G, and would seem to make more sense later in the description (after line 96, or line 142, as the lines are numbered here, for example). The first of the lines is duplicated in 91, which suggests some confusion.

32 To] The S

47 truwe] of age S

64 sate Adon] siten doun S

72–7 G has: 'And for admete how she loste hyr lyf | And for hir trouthe ȝif I shal nat lye | How she was turnyd to a daysye'. S's version is characteristically less precise, lacking the name of Admetus.

75 Gresyldes] Crisylde G

92 ther depeynted] in the temple G

105 hurt thorowe that] hit on warly for G

110 Arrested] Acorded G etc.

112 hou] of S

119 into bole] from T etc.; in ta bole G; Triable S (presumably understood by Shirley to be the name of another of the females pursued by Jove).

123 that was] Almene G

130 Philologye] Philosophye S

142 stede] sounde S

155 here] his S

178 forse] kynde S

186 varye] vare S

199 conseylis] cofessen S

210 maryede] murdred S

229 no] omitted in S

261–4 From G. Their omission in S is perhaps the result of eyeskip, although the recurrence of the 'bright'/'sight' rhyme twice in the course of six lines may suggest some other explanation.

269 aungellyke] agreable G (S's reading may involve some reminiscence of *TC* I. 102).

271 Whos clernesse] Who clernesse S; Whos sonysch heer G

276 emeynt] so meynt G

299 in blak, in red, and white] al clad in grene and white TFB etc.

310 De mieulx en mieulx with stones and perre] TFBPL; ffresshly] in frens G

335–62 All texts other than S and G here have five different stanzas (Lydgate 1891: 13–16, and Lydgate 1966: 76–7).

345–6 Both S and G show traces of confusion in this stanza. In G, 345 and 346 read 'And euere grochynge & suspecyous | I fret with eysel that maketh hym dispytous', and 348 is omitted. In S, 346 and 348 were copied in each other's place, with the necessary transposition subsequently indicated by a scribal mark of correction.

355 waryen–wymmen ben] werreyen which wemen beyeth G

362 Adon] yowe S

373 offence] vycence S
382 olde] youre S
383 Зoure wo shal now no lengere
    ben contuned G
400 dulle] dwelle SG; dul T etc.
404 from G; Thus euery ioyes ende
    and fyne is payne S
410 governaunce] greuaunce G
434 spot of] sport or S
442 aspect] inspect S
443 t'eschewe] to shewe S
447–53 This stanza in only GSFB
470 ententyff] retentyff S
478–79 originally copied in reverse
    order, with a scribal mark
    indicating the necessary correction
496–516 These stanzas only in GSFB
499 vertuous] verenous S
513 help] mercy S
527a Supplied from G; in S this
    stanza has only six lines. The
    rhyme in 527/527a (here hede/
    goodly hede) may suggest some
    confusion here.
542 feyne] fyne S
548 restore] therfore S
549 joye] save S
550 *humblement magre*] *de mieulx en
    mieulx magre* TPL
550a rubric in G: *Yci comence la
    secunde partye de la chaunson*
551–616 omitted in G
558 And eke I want] from T etc.; And
    al thestates [*sic*] S
563 sigh] sight S
575 Ner] from T etc.; Ther S
629 Fordrevyn] Forthrowe S
630 slake lawe] to me dawe [+
    erasure] G
631 To] So S ; skyis] skye is S
638 And is nat kouthe to the harmys
    kene G

653 is kyndeld] unkyndeld S
674 I] that S
694 than] that S
695 of ony wight] to my wit S
736 spere] sight (over erasure) S
756–62 There is some confusion in
    this stanza which cannot be easily
    remedied by collation with G. In S
    the rhyme scheme goes astray; line
    756, whether intentionally or in an
    effort to make sense of confusion,
    repeats line 747.
771 kunning] benygne G
808 For deyanne felte the shotys
    kene G
829 bonde] bounde S (emended to
    preserve the rhyme with 830)
905 hir] my S
930 here] hir S
962 him] hem S; hym G
978 Thesyphone] Physyphonee S
998 inward] unware S
1008 houyn] hidde G
1057 request] byheest S
1091 t'obeye] to him S
1110 founden] fyndethe S
1141 Ye] She S
1162 Out] But S
1166 besy] lowly S
1172 'nota per Shirley' in the margin
    of S
1183 whether they] wherso thow G
1184 truwe partye] chaumpartye G
1192 to avaunte] to meche a vaunt G
1209 yyve] omitted in S; yove G;
    зyve T etc.
1214 In S, the leaf on which lines
    1214–69 were copied has been
    misbound, through a reversal of
    the central bifolium of this
    gathering, and now forms fo. 229
    of the manuscript. The misbinding

may have come about because of
Shirley's own (self-corrected)
confusion in the copying of this
gathering; see the note below for
line 1297.

1231 troubled] doubeld S; itroublid G
etc.

1256 bi] omitted in S. ferse] first S

1257 Withoute] With S

1287 paciently] placently S

1297 Against this line, at the foot of
fo. 228ʳ, Shirley has written 'passe
ouer to the nexst/leff and so
forthwith', directing the reader to
what is now fo. 230ʳ, which begins
with line 1298, 'And so forth with
in presence as they stonde'. He
must have inadvertently omitted to

copy anything on what is now fo.
228ᵛ but decided to make good his
omission. At the end of what is
now fo. 230ᵛ another note directs
the reader back to what was the
empty space, 'tourne bakwarde to
the nexst leeff Off which graunt',
where lines 1354–81, beginning 'Of
which graunt the temple evyroun'
are to be found. G preserves the
text in its correct order.

1299 Tofore] He fore S

1307 hath] omitted in S

1337 hoole of hem the lyf] ho the
loue of hem G

1365 preys] prys S

1382 melodye] maladye S

1394 avisyoun] avisyoun there S

THE ALTERNATIVE CONCLUSIONS

The texts of S and G conclude at line 1399 with the narrator's statement
that his feelings for the lady he had dreamt about were so strong that on
awakening he determined to write about her. In both manuscripts there
then follows a 'complaint' of 628 lines (edited by Schick (Lydgate 1891:
59–67)), beginning 'Ellas for thought and inward peyne', in which a
lover laments his separation from a woman named Margaret (named in
line 394) whose qualities reflect those of the daisy ('marguerite') praised
by Chaucer in *LGWP*. Towards the end of the complaint the lover
explains that 'Al be I cannot tellen al | To you I wryte in specyal | A
certaine dytee that I made | And offt sythes a balade | The whiche I
made the selff day | From you when I went away | With this compleynt
here byfore' (lines 593–99), and adds that the lady may 'reende and
brek' the 'litel booke' (lines 614, 622) if it offends her. Shirley's
colophon at the end of the complaint (MS Add. 16165, fo. 241ᵛ) reads
'Here endithe the dreme and the compleynt of the desyrous | seruant in
loue and filowyng begynnethe the compleint of Anelyda' (introducing
his copy of Chaucer's *A & A*), which seems to indicate that he thought of
TG and the complaint as an entity, understanding *TG* to be the 'certaine

dytee' mentioned in the complaint, and supposing the complaint itself to follow from the intention expressed at the end of *TG* 'to maken and to write' in praise of that poem's lady.

Although the lady of *TG* is in the texts of S and G named Margaret (line 530), the argument that the complaint was part of Lydgate's composition is not overall convincing. There are many inconsistencies between it and *TG*, not least a body of specific details about the lover's relationship to the lady and the date and circumstances of their parting. Furthermore, the conclusion of *TG* at line 1399, as reproduced here, seems in itself to offer a satisfactory degree of closure, with its neat variation on Chaucer's procedure in rounding off *BD* ('I wol, be processe of tyme, | Fonde to put this sweven in ryme | ... This was my sweven; now hit ys doon', lines 1330–4). The amalgamation of *TG* and complaint in G and S may reflect the configuration of texts in the exemplars available to *TG*'s earliest scribes. It might also illustrate the way in which a dream vision from this period, with an ending following any one of Chaucer's enigmatic models of closure, could open itself to extension of various kinds in successive copyings.

Other manuscripts of *TG* extend the conclusion of G and S with twenty-two lines made up of an intensification of the praise of the lady, and an envoy which dedicates the poem to her (Lydgate 1891: 57, Lydgate 1966: 111–12).

FURTHER READING

For a succinct account of Lydgate's life, see Pearsall (1997), and for fuller discussions of his life and works, Pearsall (1970), Schirmer (1961), and Renoir (1967), with an account of recent bibliography and studies in Edwards (1984). Editions of *TG* are those of Schick (Lydgate 1891) and Norton-Smith (Lydgate 1966). Some of the textual problems are addressed by Norton-Smith (1958). BL MS Add. 16165, used as the basis of the edition here, is discussed by Hanna (1996); Connolly (1998: 27–51); and Lyall (1989: 16–19). John Shirley's activities are reviewed here and also in Lerer (1993: 117–46); some special association with Lydgate is postulated by Edwards (1983). Attempts to associate the poem with particular individuals are presented by MacCracken (1908); Moore (1912 and 1913); Seaton (1961: 375–83); and Bianco (2000); questions of patronage are more generally discussed by Wilson (1975). Traditions of the 'court of love' are documented in Neilson (1899); Piaget (1891); and Rémy (1954–5); with more recent comment by Green (1983). The convention of the complaint is explored by Davenport (1989); Patterson (1992); and (with specific reference to the *TG*) Boffey (2000). For discussion of particular aspects of the form and themes of *TG*, see Torti (1983: 67–86) and (1986); Davidoff (1983) and (1988: 135–46); Wilson (1975); Miskimin (1977); Spearing (1976: 171–6); Fallows (1977).

Une soynge moult plesaunt fait a la request d'un amoreux par Lidegate, Le Moygne de Bury*

fo. 206ᵛ

For thought, compleynt and grievous hevynesse,
For pensyfſhed and for hye distresse,
To bed I went nou this other night,
Whan that Lucyna with hir pale light
Was joyned last with Phebus in Aquarye—   5
Amiddes Decembre, whan of Januarye
Ther be kalendes of the nwe come yere,

---

* On fo. 207 of BL MS Add. 16165 is the note 'made by daun John of þe tempull of glasse . . .'; MS G heads the text 'Here begynyth the temple of Glas' (fo. 457ᵛ).

1 *compleynt*: suffering, grief.

1–9 Like many narrators of dream visions, this dreamer goes to bed obscurely disturbed. Although the nature of his affliction is unclear, the words used in connection with it (*compleynt, hevynesse, distresse*) recall the conventional vocabulary of courtly poetry, especially courtly love poetry. The Chaucerian dreamer of *BD* (1–43) also refers in oblique terms to a malady which may be love-sickness.

2 *pensyfſhed*: thoughtfulness.   *hye*: great.

4 *Lucyna*: the moon.

4–9 Suggesting the date by the use of astronomical details (a figure of *periphrasis* well known from such instances as lines 7–8 of Chaucer's *Gen Prol* or lines 1245–55 of *Fkl T*) is here made to involve the conjunction of Lucina, the moon, with Phebus, the sun, in the zodiacal sign of Aquarius: an event located in mid-December (according to Norton-Smith (Lydgate 1966: 180), not possible; but used by Schick (Lydgate 1891: p. cxiv), actually to date the poem to 1403).

5 *Phebus in Aquarye*: the sun in (the zodiacal sign of) Aquarius.

6 *Amiddes*: in the middle of.

7 *kalendes of the nwe come yere*: the first days of the new year. According to the Roman calendar, after mid-month (the 14th, or the ides) dates were reckoned by the kalends or start of the month to follow: so dates in the latter part of December would be designated as

And derk Dyane, ehorned, nothing clere,
Had hidde hir bemys under a mysty clowde.
Withinne my bed for sor I gan me shrowde,   10
Al desolate for constreynt of my wo,
The longe nyght walowyng to and fro,
Til at the last, as I gan taken keepe,
Me did oppresse a sodeyne dedly sleep
Withinne the which me thought that I was   15
Ravyshed in spyrit into a temple of glas—
I nyst nought how fer into wildernesse—
That founded was (as by liklynesse)
Nought upon stele but upon kraggy roche
Lych yse efrore, and as I dyd aproche   20
Ageyne the sonne me thought hit shoone als clere

so many days before the kalends of January. The December setting for the dream, rather than the springtime location in the tradition of *RR*, may seem unpropitious, recalling the dream of Chaucer's *HF*, which is said to take place on 10 December; but Lydgate's reference to the 'nwe come yere' may be intended to balance this.

8 *Dyane*: Diana, the moon. *ehorned*: appearing to have horns. The moon was the planetary form of the goddess known variously as Lucina or Luna, Diana, and Proserpina (in Chaucer's *Kn T, CT* I. 2313, Emylye refers to 'tho thre formes that thou hast in thee', as she prays to Diana to preserve her chastity). Diana's horns are the twin points of the crescent moon, and may recall the horns of fashionable 15th-c. women's headdresses, castigated by Lydgate in *Horns Away* (see Lydgate 1934: 662–5); and illustrated e.g. in the famous depiction of Christine de Pizan at her desk, BL MS Harley 4431, fo. 4, reproduced on the cover of *The Treasure of the City of Ladies* (Christine de Pizan 1985), or the miniatures illustrating other of Lydgate's poems reproduced in Scott 1997, ii, plates 312 and 366.

10 *sor*: sorrow. *gan me shrowde*: covered myself.
11 *for*: on account of; *constreynt*: affliction, distress.
12 *walowyng*: turning fitfully. 13 *as I gan taken keepe*: as I was aware.
14 *sodeyne*: sudden. *dedly*: deathlike. 15 *me thought*: it seemed to me.
16 *Ravyshed in spyrit*: transported in spirit. The dream of *HF* begins in 'a temple ymad of glas' (120), dedicated to Venus, from which the dreamer is transported to Fame's house, a castle of beryl (1184) built on a rock of ice (1124–30); *PF* features 'a temple of bras' dedicated to love.
17 *I nyst nought how fer*: I did not know how far.
18 *founded was*: had its foundations. *as by liklynesse*: as it seemed.
19 *stele*: steel. *kraggy roche*: craggy rock.
20 *Lych yse efrore*: frozen like ice. *dyd aproche*: approached.
21 (silhouetted) against the sun it seemed to me that it shone as brightly.
21–32 Modulations of lightness and obscurity are characteristic of *TG* (cf. the cloudy moon, 8–9), perhaps to underline the force of Venus's concluding Boethian advice (1275–88): for discussion, see Davidoff 1983: 135–46.

As any cristal, and ever ner and ner

fo. 207ʳ
As I gan neghe this grisly dredful place

I wex astonyed—the light so in my face

Began to smyte, so persyng ever in on   25

On yche a part wher that I koude gon,

That I ne might nothing as I wolde

Abowten me considerne and byholde

The wondreful hestrys, for brightnesse of the sonne.

Til at the last certayne skyes donne,   30

With wind echaced, han hir cours went

Tofor the stremys of Tytan, and eblent,

So that I might, withinne and eke withoute,

Whereso I welk, beholde me aboute

For to report the fasoun and manyer   35

Of al that place, that was circulyer,

In compas wyse round by entayle wrought.

And whan that I had goon longe and sought

I fonde a wyket and entyrd inne als fast

Into the temple, and myn eyen cast   40

On every syde, nowe lowe and efft alofft.

And right anon as I gan walk sofft

22–3 *ever ner and ner* | *As I gan neghe*: all the time, as I came closer and closer.
24 *wex astonyed*: grew bewildered.
25 *smyte*: strike.   *persyng*: piercing. *ever in on* | *On yche a part*: continually on every side.
26 *wher that I koude gon*: wherever I went.
27–8 That I could not, as I wished, contemplate and examine.
29 *hestrys*: buildings.   *for*: because of.
30 *certayne skyes donne*: some dark parts of the sky.
31 *echaced*: driven.   *han hir cours went*: took their way.
32 *Tofor the stremys of Tytan*: before Titan's (i.e. the sun's) beams.   *eblent*: dulled (the brightness).
33 *eke*: also.   *withoute*: outside.   34 *Whereso*: wherever.   *welk*: walked.
35 *For to*: in order to.   *fasoun*: style.   *manyer*: manner, appearance.
35–40 On the significance of such dream moments of entry, see Lynch 1994, and compare e.g. *RR*, lines 497–575 (*Romaunt* 509–84), and *PF* 120–75.
37 *In compas wyse*: in a circle.   *by entayle*: in construction.   *wrought*: shaped, fashioned.
38 *goon longe*: walked for a long time.
39 *fonde*: found.   *wyket*: wicket gate.   *als fast*: immediately.
41 *efft*: next, afterwards.   42 *right anon*: immediately.   *sofft*: quietly.

(If I the sothe aright reporten shal)
I sawe depeynted upon every wal,
From eest to west, many a feyre ymage   45
Of sondry lovers, lyche as they were of age,
Sett by ordre right as they were truwe,
With lyfly colours wonder fresshe of huwe.

o. 207ᵛ   Right as me thought I sawe some sit and stande,
And some kneling with billes in hir hande,   50
And some with compleyntes woful and pytous
With deolful cher to putten to Venus,
So as she sat fleting in the see,
Upon theyre wo for to have pite.
And first of alle I sawe ther of Cartage   55
Dydo the qwene, so godely of visage,

43 *sothe*: truth. *aright*: correctly.   44 *depeynted*: painted, depicted.

44 ff. Descriptions of wall-paintings, or of murals or tapestries, are common in medieval poems of all kinds. Technically a form of *ekphrasis* (in which one medium— here, words—is used to display another), such description can highlight or intensify particular themes or topics; equally, it can contribute to a density of poetic texture, or indicate important areas of source material or influence (as the list here in part acknowledges a debt to Chaucer's poems). Lydgate's painted figures can be compared with the representations of undesirable figures on the outer wall of the garden of love in *RR* 129–463 (*Romaunt* 136–478), with the decorations inside the temple of Venus in *PF* ('peynted overal | Ful many a story' of unfortunate lovers, 284–94, some of which reappear in *TG*), with the story of Dido inside Venus's temple in *HF* (151–467); and with the figures in *AL* 456–69.

45 *feyre ymage*: pleasing image.

46 *sondry*: various. *lyche as they were of age*: just as they were alive.

47 Arranged in order according to how loyal they were.

48 *lyfly*: lively. *wonder*: wonderfully.

49 *Right as me thought*: Indeed it seemed to me.

50 *billes*: written petitions. Many of the lovers are depicted as petitioners, with formal documents, *billes* and *compleyntes*, to present to Venus as if in a court hearing of some kind.

51 *pytous*: pitiful.   52 *deolful cher*: miserable expressions. *putten*: set before.

53 *fleting in the see*: floating on the sea. This is Marine Venus, much as encountered by Charles of Orleans in *LR*, and represented in *Kn T, CT* I. 1955–63, and *HF* 130–9. The painted representation described here is distinct from the goddess whom the dreamer will later see and hear from.

54 (asking her) to have pity on their sorrow.

55 *Cartage*: Carthage. Dido, queen of Carthage, who took her own life when abandoned by Aeneas; her story is recounted in Virgil's *Aeneid* bk. IV, epistle VII in Ovid's *Heroides*, and recapitulated by Chaucer in *HF* 219–426, and *LGW* 924–1367 (see Desmond 1994).

56 Queen Dido, so pleasing of face.

That gan compleyne hir aventure and cas:
How she deceyved was of Eneas,
For alle his hestis and his othes sworne,
And seyde 'allas', that ever she was borne,   60
Whan she sawe that ded most she be.
And next I sawe the compleynt of Medee,
How that she was falsed of Jason.
And neghe by Venus sawe I sate Adon,
And al the maner howe the bore hym sloughe,   65
For wham she wept and made sorowe enoughe.
Ther saw I also howe Penolope,
For she longe hir lord might not se,
Ful offt of colour wex pale and grene.
And aldernexst was the fresshe qwene,   70
I men Alceste, the noble truwe wyff,
That for hir trouthe howe she lost hir lyff,
And transsfourmed, if I shal not lye,

57 Who complained about what had befallen her.   58 *of*: by
59 *hestis*: promises.   *othes sworne*: sworn oaths.
62 *Medee*: Medea, whose desertion by Jason is recounted in Ovid, *Metamorphoses* VII,
and *Heroides* XII; by Chaucer's contemporary Gower in *CA* V. 3227–4222, and in
Chaucer's own *LGW* 1580–679 (see Cowen 1991).
63 *falsed of*: deceived by.
64 *neghe by*: near to.   *sate*: sitting.   *Adon*: Adonis. Venus's love for Adonis, and the
episode of the boar, are told in Ovid, *Metamorphoses* X.
65 And everything concerning the way the boar killed him.
66 *wham*: whom.   *made sorowe enoughe*: grieved a great deal.
67 *Penolope*: Penelope, the wife of Ulysses, who waited loyally for him during his long
absence; the story, from Homer's *Odyssey*, was best known to the Middle Ages in Ovid's
version, *Heroides* I.
68 Because she was not able to see her husband for so long.
69 *Ful offt*: frequently.   *wex*: turned.   *grene*: sickly.
70 *aldernexst*: next of all.
70–4 These lines illustrate Lydgate's characteristically loose syntax, of which there are
other instances in *TG*; see e.g. 635–50.
71 *men*: mean.   *Alceste*: Alcestis.   *truwe*: loyal. Alcestis chose to die in place of her
husband, Admetus, but was rescued from the underworld by Hercules. The story was
available in several Latin versions, was retold by Gower (*CA* VII. 1917–43; VIII. 2640–6),
and is of central importance in *LGWP*, where Chaucer's Alceste appears, transformed into
a daisy, as the consort of Cupid, god of love.
72 *trouthe*: truth, loyalty.
73 *transsfourmed*: changed.   *if I shal not lye*: to be honest.

Into the floure cleped daysye.

Ther was also Gresyldes innocence,   75

And al hir meknesse and hir pacyence.

There was Isaude, and many another moo,

And al the turment and the cruwel wo

That she suffred for Tristram in al hir lyve.

And howe that Thesbe thorowe the hert did ryve   80

With the swerd of hir Pyramus.

And al the maner how duc Theseus

The mynatour sloughe, amidde the hous

That was so wrynkled by crafft of Dedalus,

When that he was in prysoun shitte in Crete.   85

And howe that Philles felt of lovis heete

The grete furye for Demophon, ellas,

And for his falshed and for his trespas

Upon the wal depented men might se

Howe she was honged upon a philbertis tre.   90

And mani a story mo than I rekken can

---

74 *floure*: flower.   *cleped*: called.   *daysye*: daisy.

75 *Gresyldes*: Griselda's. Griselda is the heroine of Chaucer's *Cl T*; her submission to the tests imposed by her husband, Walter, makes her an example of patient suffering.

77 *Isaude*: Isolde.   *moo*: more. The tragic story of Isolde and of her lover Tristan, the nephew of her husband, King Mark, survives in many medieval versions; see Calin 1994: 41–57.

78 *turment*: torment, agony.

80 *Thesbe*: Thisbe.   *ryve*: stab (herself). Thisbe killed herself, thinking her lover Pyramus to be dead: see Ovid, *Metamorphoses* IV. 55, and Chaucer's *LGW* 706–923.

81 *swerd*: sword.

82 *duc Theseus*: Duke Theseus. The story of Theseus and the Minotaur, a monster (half-bull, half-man), who lived in the Cretan Labyrinth constructed by Daedalus, is to be found in Ovid, *Metamorphoses* VII and VIII. Lydgate seems more interested in this aspect of the story than in Theseus's role as the lover who abandons Ariadne, the Minotaur's half-sister; her history is recounted in Ovid, *Heroides* X, and by Chaucer in *LGW* 1886–2227.

83 *sloughe*: killed.   *amidde*: in (the middle of).

84 *wrynkled*: convoluted.   *crafft*: skill.

85 *shitte*: shut.

86 *Philles*: Phyllis.   *lovis heete*: the fire of love. Abandoned by Demophon, son to Theseus, Phyllis took her own life: see Ovid, *Heroides* II, Gower, *CA* IV. 731–878, and Chaucer, *LGW* 2394–561.

87 *ellas*: alas.   90 *honged*: hanged.   *philbertis tre*: (hazel)nut tree.

91 *mo than I rekken can*: more than I can count up.

Were ther depeynted: and how that Parys wan
Feyre Eleyne, the fresshe lusty qwene,
And howe Achilles was for Polixene
Eslawe unwarly withinne Troyes toune—   95
Al this I sawe walkynge up and doune.
Ther sawe I wryten also the hole tale
Howe Phylomene into a nightyngale
Eturned was, and Progne into a swalowe;
And hou the Sabyne in a maner halowe   100
The fest of Lucresse yit in Rome toune.
Ther sawe I also the sorowe of Palamon
That he in prysoun felt, and al the smert,
And how that he thoroughe unto his hert

fo. 208ᵛ   Was hurt thorowe that casting of an eye   105
Of feyre, fresshe, the yonge Emelye;

92 *Parys*: Paris.   *wan*: won. Paris's abduction of Helen, the wife of Menelaus, led to the Trojan War: their story is recounted in Ovid, *Heroides* XVI and XVII, and is a significant part of the pre-history of Chaucer's *TC* (see I. 61–3).

93 *Feyre Eleyne*: Beautiful Helen.   *lusty*: attractive.

94 *Polixene*: Polixena. Achilles, one of the Greek heroes of the Trojan War, met his death in the temple where he expected to marry Polyxena; Chaucer knew the story and alludes to it in *BD* 1069–71.

95 *Eslawe unwarly*: murdered unawares.   *Troyes toun*: the city of Troy.

97 *hole*: whole.

98 *Phylomene*: Philomena. Tereus raped his sister-in-law Philomela and cut out her tongue, but Philomela told her sister Procne what had happened by means of embroidery, and they were revenged. Ovid tells this story, and of their changing into birds, in *Metamorphoses* VI. 424 ff., and Chaucer recounts it in *LGW* 2228–393. Cf. also *KQ* 380–5.

99 *Eturned*: turned.   *Progne*: Procne (see above).

100 *Sabyne*: Sabines.   *in a maner*: in some way.   *halowe*: celebrate, observe. The Sabines were one of the ancient Italian peoples subjugated by the Romans.

101 *fest*: feast(day).   *Lucresse*: Lucretia.   *yit*: still.   *Rome toune*: the city of Rome. Lucretia, another of the heroines of *LGW* (1680–885), was a Roman woman who took her life after being raped by Tarquin, who wished to test her fidelity to her husband; see Ovid, *Fasti* II. 685 ff., and Livy I. 57–9.

102 *Palamon*: Palamon, one of the heroes of Chaucer's *Kn T*. Lines 102–10 summarize *Kn T*, an adaptation of Boccaccio's *Teseida*.

103 *smert*: pain.   104 *thoroughe unto*: right to.   *hert*: heart.

105 *thorowe*: by, through.

106 *feyre*: beautiful.   *yonge*: young.   *Emelye*: in *Kn T*, Palamon and Arcite both fall in love with Emelye, sister to Hippolyta, the wife of Theseus, duke of Athens.

And al the stryff bytwene him and his brother,
And howe that on faught eke with that other
Withinne the grove, til they by Theseus
Arrested wer, as tellithe Chaucer to us.   110
And firthermore as I gan beholde
I sawe hou Phebus with an arowe of golde
Ewownded was thorowe owt in his syde,
Only by envye of the god Cupyde,
And howe that Dane into a laurer tre   115
Eturned was when she did fle.
And howe that Jove gan to chaunge his cope
Oonly for love of the feyre Europe,
And into bole, whenne he dide hir sewe,
List of his godhede his fourme to transmewe;   120
And that he by transmutacioun
The shappe cane take of Amphitroun
For her that was so passyng of beaute;
So was he hurte, for all his deynte,

107 *al the stryff*: the whole dispute.
108 *that on . . . that other*: the one . . . the other. *faught*: fought.
109 *Theseus*: see 106 n.   110 *Arrested*: restrained/arrested.
111 *as I gan beholde*: as I looked.
112–16 Daphne, daughter of the river-god, vowed to remain a virgin. When Phebus (Apollo) pursued her, the gods changed her into a bay tree or laurel: see Ovid, *Metamorphoses* I. 452 ff; also *TC* III. 726–7. For the nature and power of Cupid's arrows, see *RR* 907–8 (*Romaunt* 921–98), and cf. 438 and *KQ* 655–63.
113 *Ewownded*: wounded. *thorowe owt in*: right through.
115 *Dane*: Daphne (see 112 n.).
116 *Eturned was*: was transformed. *fle*: run away.
117 *gan to chaunge his cope*: changed his cloak (fig., his appearance). This refers to one of the transformations of Jove, or Jupiter, in his pursuit of women; see Ovid, *Metamorphoses* II. 833–75, and also *TC* III. 722–4.
119 *into bole*: into a bull. *sewe*: follow, pursue.
120 through his divine power, changed (lit. was pleased to change) his shape.
121 *transmutacioun*: metamorphosis. As Amphitrion, Jove fathered Hercules on Alcmena; of the many sources, see e.g. Ovid, *Amores* I. 13. 45–6, and *TC* III. 1428.
122 *The shappe cane take*: took the shape.
123 *passyng*: surpassing, supreme.
124 *for all his deynte*: in spite of all his dignity, elegance (other MSS here read *deite*, godliness).

With lovys darte, and myght hit not ascape.   125
There sawe I also howe that Mars was take
Of Vulcanus, and with Venus fownde,
And with the chenes invisible bownde.
There was also alle the poesye
Of Mercurie and Philologye,   130
And howe that sche, for his sapience,
Yweddet was to god of eloquence,
And the muses lowely dide obeye
Hegh into hevene this ladi to conveye,
And with hir songe how she was magnyfyed,   135
With Jubiter to ben stillefyed.
And uppermore depeynted men might see
Howe with hir rynge goodely Canace
Of evere foole the leden and eke the songe
Coude understonde as she welk hem amonge,   140
And howe hir brother so offten holpen was
In his meschief by the stede of bras.
And firthermore in the temple were

125 *lovys darte*: love's arrow.   *myght hit not ascape*: could not escape it.

126–8 The love of Mars and Venus was ended by Vulcan, Venus's husband, who caught them in a net; see Ovid, *Metamorphoses* IV. 171–89, and Chaucer's short poem *The Complaint of Mars* (Chaucer 1987).

127 *Of*: by.   128 *chenes*: chains.   *bownde*: bound.   129 *poesye*: poetry.

130 *Mercurie and Philologye*: Martianus Capella (fl. 5th c.) wrote the Latin *De nuptiis Philologiae et Mercurii* (The Marriage of Mercury and Philology), referred to by Chaucer in *Mer T* (*CT* IV. 1732–7) and *HF* 985 (ed. and tr. Stahl (Martianus Capella 1977)).

132 *Yweddet*: married.

133 And [how he] humbly obeyed the muses. Medieval ideas about the nine muses of poetry are discussed by Curtius 1953: 228–46.

134 *Hegh*: high.   135 *hir*: their.   *magnyfyed*: praised, exalted.

136 *ben*: be.   *stillefyed*: turned into a star.   137 *uppermore*: further up.

138 *goodely*: excellent, delightful.   *Canace*: among magic gifts distributed in Chaucer's unfinished *Sq T* are a ring, given to Canace, which permits her to comprehend the language of birds, and a miraculously swift brass horse, given to her brother. The reference to these in a catalogue of unhappy lovers relates to Canace's conversation with a female bird, which tells of its betrayal in love (*CT* V. 479–631).

139 *evere foole*: every bird.   *leden*: language.

140 *welk hem amonge*: walked among them.

141 *holpen*: helped.   142 *the stede of bras*: the brass horse (see above).

143 ff. The company of plaintiffs (similar to those in other literary courts of love, e.g. *KQ* 571–651, *AL* 540– 735, and *The Court of Love* itself, ed. Skeat 1897: 409–47, and,

Ful many an hundred thousand here and there
In sondri wyse redy to compleyne   145
Unto the goddesse of hir wo and peyne:
How they were hindred, some by envye,
And how the serpent of fals Jalousye
Ful many a lover hathe offt put abak,
And causeles on hym hathe leyde a lak.   150
And some were pleyning hyely on absence
That weren exyled and put out of presence
Thorough wikked tonges and fals suspessyone
Withouten mercy or remyssyoun.
And other eeke here servyce spent in veyne   155
Thoroughe cruell daunger and also bi disdeyne,
And some also that loved, sothe to seyne,
And of her lady were not loved ageyne.
And other eke that for povertee
Durst in no wyse hir gret adversite   160
Descover in open, lest they were refused.
Some for avaunte also weren acused,
And other eke that loved secreely
That of hir lady durst aske no mercy
Lest that of hem she wolde have despite.   165

although with different grievances, in *HF*) voice a number of sometimes very practical and doubtless quite commonly experienced hindrances: lack of means, family interference, conflicts with religious vocations.

145 *In sondri wyse*: in various ways.   146 *hir*: their.   148 *fals*: deceitful.
149 *hathe offt put abak*: has frequently turned away.
150 And unjustifiably imputed to him some deficiency.   151 *hyely*: intensely.
152 *put out of presence*: put from (their mistresses') presence.
153 *suspessyone*: suspicion.   154 *remyssyoun*: forgiveness.
155 And others also expended their service (in love) vainly.
156 *Thoroughe*: on account of.   *bi*: because of.
156 etc. Some of the abstractions which stand in the way of love recall the more detailed personifications of other love visions: e.g. here, the figure *Daungier* in *RR* 2825 ff. (*Romaunt* 3130 ff.). Lydgate's practice seems sometimes to hover just short of personification, posing some difficulties for an editor (for discussion of personification allegory, see Frank 1953).
157 *sothe to seyne*: to tell the truth.   158 *of*: by.   *her*: their.   *ageyne*: in return.
160 *Durst in no wyse*: dared not in any way.   *hir*: their.
161 *Descover in open*: openly reveal.   162 *avaunte*: boasting.
163 *secreely*: in secret.   165 Lest she would despise them.

And some also that putten ful gret wyte
On double lovers that loven thinges newe,
Thorowe whos falsnesse hindred ben the trewe.
And some ther were, as hit is offt efound,
That for hir lady haden meny a wounde   170
Endured, and in many regyoun,
Whyles that another hathe possessyoun
Al of his ladi, and berethe awey the fruyt
Of his labour and of al his suyt.
And other eke compleyned on Rychesse: 175
Howe he with tresour dothe his besynesse
To wynnen al, ageyns kynde and right,
Wher truwe lovers have no forse ne might.
And some ther were, as maydyns yonge of age,
That pleyned sore with weping and with rage   180
That thei wer compelled, ageyns al nature,
With croked eelde that mai not longe endure
For to perfourne the lust of loves pley.
For hit ne sittethe nought fresshe May
For to be coupled to olde Januare—   185
They ben so dyvers that they mot nedes varye:

166 *putten ful gret wyte*: greatly blamed.   167 *double*: deceitful.
168 *hindred ben the trewe*: true (lovers) are kept back.
169 *as hit is offt efound*: as it is often found.
170 *haden meny a wounde*: had many wounds.
171 *in many regyoun*: in many places (i.e. territories, probably).
172–4 While another has whole possession of his lady, and takes all the profit (*fruyt*) of his effort and courtship.
175 *Rychesse*: wealth.
176–7 *dothe his besynesse | To wynnen al*: expends his efforts to win everything.
177 *kynde*: the dictates of natural moral feeling.   *right*: justice.
178 *forse*: strength.   *ne*: nor.   179 *as*: such as.
179–82 The discussion of marriages of young girls to much older men leads inevitably into an allusion to Chaucer's *Mer T*, in which an old knight, Januarie, marries a much younger woman, appropriately named May. But Lydgate does not mention the climax of the tale, in which May successfully deceives Januarie about her liaison with his squire, Damyan.
180 *sore*: sorely.
181 *ageyns al nature*: completely against all natural law.
182–3 To carry out the pleasure of the game of love with bent and short-lived old age.
184 *hit ne sittethe nought*: it is not at all appropriate for.
186 *dyvers*: different.   *they mot nedes varye*: they are bound to be at odds.

For eeld es gruchyng malencolyous,
Ay ful of yre and suspessyouous,
And youthe entendethe to joye and lustynesse,
To mirthe and pley, and to gret gladnesse.   190
Ellas that ever it shoulde falle
That swete sugre coupled shoulde be with galle!
This yonge folkys cryden offt syth
And preyed Venus hir power for to kyth
Upon this meschief to shapen remedye.   195
And right anon I herd other crye
With pytous terys and with ful weping soune
Byfore the goddesse with lamentacioun,
That conseylis in hir tender youthe
And in hir chyldhode, as it is offte kouthe,   200
Entred ben in to relygyoun
Er that they had yeris of discressyoun,
That al hir lyf cannot but compleyne,
In wyde copes parfeccion to feyne,
Ful covertly to curen al hir smert   205
And shewe the contrarye outwardes of hir hert.
Thus sawe I wepen many a feyre mayde
That on hir frendes al hir wyte they leyde.
And other nexst I sawe ther in gret rage
That they were maryede in hir tendre age,   210

210^r

187 *eeld*: old age. *es*: is. *gruchyng malencolyous*: grumbling and melancholy.
188 Always angry and suspicious.
189 *entendethe*: is inclined. *lustynesse*: pleasure.
191 Alas that it should ever come about.   192 *galle:* bitterness.
193 *This*: these. *offt syth*: many times.   194 *kyth*: make known.
195 *meschief*: misfortune. *shapen*: devise.
196 *right anon*: straightaway. *other crye*: other (people) cry.
197 *pytous terys*: pitiful tears. *soune*: sound.   199 *conseylis*: lacking advice.
200 *as it is offte kouthe*: as it is often known to happen.
201–2 Were entered into religious orders before they were old enough to know anything about it.
203 And for the rest of their lives can only lament, feigning (a life of) perfection in their wide (religious) habits.
205 *curen*: hide. *smert*: pain.
206 And show outwardly the opposite of (the feelings of) their hearts.
208 *wyte*: blame. *leyde*: laid, placed.   209 *other*: other (people).

Withouten fredam of eleccyoun,
Wher love hathe seelde domynacioun:
For love at large and at libertee
Wolde frely and not with such tretee.
And other sawe I ful sere weepe and wrynge   215
That they in men founde suche varyinge:
To love a sesoun while that beaute flourethe
And by disdeyne so ungoodely lowrethe
Upon hir he clepid his lady deere,
That to him was so plesant and enter;   220
But lust with feyrnesse is so overgone
That in hir hert trouthe abydethe noon.
And some also I sawe in terys reyne
And pitously on God and Kynde they pleyne,
That ever they wolde in any creature   225
So myche beaute passing by mesure
Sette in a womman by occasyoun
A man to love to his confusyoun,

fo. 210ᵛ   And namely ther wher he shal have no grace.
For, with a looke, forby as men doon passe,   230
Wel offt fallethe, thorowe casting of an eye,
A man is wounded that he most nedis dye,
And never affter shal hir perauntre se.

211 *fredam of eleccyoun*: freedom of choice.
212 (In situations) where love seldom holds sway.
214 *Wolde frely*: would (operate) without restraint.   *tretee*: negotiation.
215 *ful sere*: in diverse ways/very sorrowfully (there may be grounds for emending *sere* to *sore* = sorrowfully).   *wrynge*: wring their hands.
216 *varyinge*: inconstancy.
217 *a sesoun*: for a short while.   *while that*: while.   *flourethe*: flourishes, blooms.
218 And then, (he) frowns with most unpleasant disdain.
219 *clepid*: called.   220 *enter*: sincere.
221 *lust*: desire.   *feyrnesse*: beauty.   *overgone*: overtaken.
222 That no truth remains in their (i.e. men's) heart(s).
223 *in terys reyne*: rain with tears (i.e. weep heavily).
224 *Kynde*: nature.   *pleyne*: complain.
226 *myche*: much.   *passing by mesure*: immeasurably surpassing.
227 *by occasyoun*: as the cause that.   230 *forby as men doon passe*: as men pass by.
231 It very often happens (that), with a glance.
232 *that he most nedis dye*: to death (lit. = so that he must die).
233 (even though) he may by chance never afterwards see her.

Why wil God doon so gret a cruwelte
To any man, or to his creature,   235
To maken him so myche wo endure
For hir, parcas, when he shal in no wyse
Rejoyse never, but so forthe as unwyse
Ledin his lyf, tyl that he be grave,
For he ne durst of hir no mercy crave?   240
(And eke, perauntre, thoughe he durst and wolde,
He cannot wit wher he hir fynde shoulde).
I saugh ther eeke, and therof had I routhe,
That some were hindred thorowe coveytyse and slouthe,
And sume also thorough hir hastynesse,   245
And other eke thoroughe hir rechlesnesse.
But alderlast as I welk and byheelde
Bysyde Pallas with hir cristal shelde
Tofore the statu of Venus sett on heght,
How that ther knelyd a lady in my sight   250
Byfore the goddesse, the whiche right as the sunne
Passethe the sterris and dothe theyre brightnesse dounne,
And Lucyfer to voyde the nightes sorowe
In clernesse passeth erly by the morowe,
And so as May hathe the soverayntee   255
Of every moneth of fayrnesse and beautee,
And as the ros in swetnesse and odour

234 *doon*: do.   235 *his creature*: something he (God) has created.
237 *parcas*: possibly.   *wyse*: way.
238 *so forthe*: ever onwards.   *as unwyse*: like a fool.
239 *Ledin*: lead.   *tyl that he be grave*: until he is buried.
240 Because he did not dare to implore mercy of her.
241–2 And also, perhaps, even though he dared to and would (do it), he does not know
where he might find her.
243 *routhe*: pity.   244 *coveytyse*: covetousness.   *slouthe*: laziness.
246 *rechlesnesse*: heedlessness, recklessness.
247 *alderlast*: last of all.   *welk*: walked.   *byheelde*: looked.
248 *Pallas*: Pallas Athene, or Minerva, goddess of wisdom; introduced here perhaps as
an indication of the nature of the Venus of *TG*; cf. *LR* 128, *KQ* 876–966.   *shelde*: shield.
249 *on heght*: on high.   251 *the whiche*: who.   *right as*: just as.
252 *Passethe*: surpasses.   *dothe theyre brightnesse dounne*: darkens their brightness.
253 *Lucyfer*: the morning star (see 1368 n.).   *voyde*: clear.
254 *clernesse*: brightness.   *passeth*: passes over.   *by the morowe*: in the morning.

Surmountethe floures, and bame of lykour

Havethe the prys, and as the rubie bright
Of alle stonys in bountee and in sight   260
[As it is knowe hath the regalye,
Ryght so this lady with hyre goodly ye,
And with stremys of hyre lok so bryght,
Surmountyth alle thourgh beaute in myn syght.]
For to telle hir gret seemlynesse,   265
Hir wommanhode, hir poort and hir fayrnesse,
Hit was a mervayle howe that ever Nature
Koude in hir werkys make a creature
So aungellyke or goodely on to se,
So femynyne or passing of beaute,   270
Whos clernesse is brighter than golde weyre
Lyche Phebus by shyning in his spere.
The goodelyhed eek of hir fresshe face,
So replenisshed of beaute and of grace,
So wel coloured by Nature and depeynt   275
As roses and lylyes togedir were emeynt
So evenly by gode proporcioun,
That, as me thought by myn inspeccioun,
I gan merveylle how God or werk of kynde
Mighten of beaute suche a tresore fynde   280

258 *Surmountethe floures*: surpasses (all other) flowers.   *bame of lykour*: (in its) moist fragrance.

259 *Havethe the prys*: most excels.

259–60 Precious stones were thought to have special powers; the 'London Lapidary' of the second quarter of the fourteenth century says of the ruby, 'the boke telleth vs the gentil rubie fyne & clene is lorde of stones . . . Hit hath the vertue of precious stones & aboue all othre' (see Evans and Serjeantson 1933: 21), and cf. *LR* 345.

260 *bountee*: power for good.   *sight*: appearance.

261 *regalye*: supremacy.   261–4 See notes on the text.   262 *ye*: eye.

262–97 The description of the lady proceeds according to a conventional rhetorical pattern, on which see Brewer 1955. The 'outdoing' topos of 251–64 is a common feature; cf. *BD* 820–32.

263 *stremys of hyre lok*: the stream of her gaze.   266 *poort*: demeanour.

267–81 On the role of Nature (or *Kynde*) in the creation of beautiful women, cf. Chaucer, *Phys T* (*CT* VI. 9–29), and *BD* 907–12.

269 *aungellyke*: angelic.   271 *weyre*: wire.

272 *Lyche*: like.   *spere*: sphere.   274 *replenisshed*: filled with.

276 *emeynt*: mingled.   278 *as me thought*: as it seemed to me.

279 *merveylle*: wonder.   *kynde*: nature.   280 *tresore*: treasury.

To gyvven hir so passing excellence:
For in gode feyth thorough hir hye presence
The temple was enlumyned envyroun.
And for to speken of condicyoun
She was the best that might been alyve,   285
For ther was noon that might with hir stryve,
To speken of bountee or of lowlynesse,
Of wommanhode or of gentylesse,
Of curteysye or of goodlyhede,
Of speche, of cher, or of semlyhed;   290

Of port benygne, and of dalyaunce
The best etaught, and therto of plesaunce;
She was the welle also of honeste,
And exemplayre and myrour was she
Of sikurnesse, of trouthe, of feythfulnesse,   295
And to alle other lady and maystresse
To shewe vertu, whoso list to lere.
And so this lady, benigne and noble of chere,
Kneling I sawe, in blak, in red, and white,
Beseching Venus, goddesse of al delyte,   300
Enbrowded al with stonys and perry
So rychely that joye it was to see,
With sondry roulles on hir garnement
For to expone the trouthe of hir entent,
And shewe fully for that hir hye noblesse,   305
Hir stedfast vertu and hir stabulnesse,

---

282 *hye*: noble.   283 *envyroun*: all around.   287 *lowlynesse*: humility.
288 *gentylesse*: nobility of character.
290 *cher*: expression.   *semlyhed*: gracefulness.
291 *Of port benygne*: of kindly bearing.   *dalyaunce*: conversation.
292 *etaught*: instructed.   *plesaunce*: pleasantness.   295 *sikurnesse*: confidence.
297 *whoso list to lere*: whoever wishes to learn.
299 For an attempt to read a distinct pattern of variation in the colours of the lady's
clothing, and her flowers, across the different MSS, see Norton-Smith 1958.
300 *delyte*: pleasure.   301 *Enbrowded*: embroidered.   *perry*: jewels.
303 *sondry roulles*: various scrolls.   *garnement*: clothing. Embroidered texts were a
relatively common feature on items of aristocratic dress (cf. the costumes described in *AL*
87–8), and it was common also to adopt mottoes in French (used elsewhere, as for
autograph purposes in manuscripts) for items of clothing; see Evans 1931: i. 94–6.
304 *expone*: relate.   305 *for that*: because of.   306 *stabulnesse*: stability.

That she was rote of womanly plesaunce.
Therfore hir word withowten varyaunce
Was up and doune, as men mighten se,
Fresshly enbrowded *humblement magree*:   310
That to seyne that she, this benigne,
Hir hert and al fully dothe resigne
Into the handes of Venus the goddesse,
Whan that hir list hir haromes to redresse.
For as me thinkethe somewhat by hir cheere   315
For to compleyne she hade gret desyre,
For in hir hande she had a lytel bille
For to declare sume part of al hir wille,
And to the goddesse hir quarell forto shewe,
Th'effect of which was this in wordes fewe: 320

[1]

fo. 212ʳ

'O lady Venus, moder to Cupyde,
That al this worlde thou hast in governaunce,
And hertis hye that hauteyn ben of pryde
Enclynest mekly to thyn obeyssaunce;
Causer of joie, relesser of penaunce,   325

307 *rote*: root.
308 *word*: motto (see 303 n.). *withowten varyaunce*: unchangingly.
310 *humblement magree*: 'humbly despite (anything)'. For details of the variations in mottoes across the different MSS, see Norton-Smith 1958.
311 *seyne*: say. *this benigne*: this gracious (person).
312 *dothe resigne*: gives up.
314 When she (i.e. Venus) wishes, to redress her (the lady's) wrongs.
315 For it seems to me rather, from her expression.
317 *bille*: written petition; *MED* gives a variety of different meanings for this word, frequently used of lovers' messages and petitions. Essentially it was a written document of some kind, ranging in formality from a personal letter to a plea or charge.
319 *quarell*: grievance.   321 *moder*: mother.
321 etc. This is the first of a number of formalized expressions of feeling from the lady and from the knight, lyric interpolations which provide variety of form and tone, and are often signalled in the various MSS by scribal notes. The lady here has a 'complaint', couched in six rhyme royal stanzas, which she puts to Venus. See the discussions of this form in Davenport 1989 and 2000.
322 *hast in governaunce*: governs.
323–4 And you who direct lofty hearts, haughty in pride, meekly to your obedience.
325 *relesser of penaunce*: you who free (people) from penance.

And with thy stremys canst every thing discerne
Thoroughe hevenly fyre of love that is eterne,

[2]

'O blisfull sterre, persant and cler of light,
Of bemys gladsome, voyder of derknesse,
Chef recomforter affter the blak night   330
To wynde woful oute of hevynesse,
Take nowe goode hede, lady and goddesse,
So that my bille your grace may atteyne
Redresse to fynde of that I nowe compleyne.

[3]

'So that you list, of youre benignyte,   335
Goodly to sen and shapen remedye
Of wikked tunges, and of the crueltee
That they may compas thorowe fals envye;
To qwenche theyre venyme and hir felonye,
Wher that they hyndre wymmen giltlesse,   340
Styntethe this werre, and lat us lyven in pees.

326 *thy stremys*: the streams of your eyes.
326 ff. Like the Venus of *LR* and *KQ*, Lydgate's goddess is associated with love in a Christian context. References to her form as the morning star enhance the possibilities of exploiting contrasts between light and darkness (cf. 1368).
327 *eterne*: everlasting.   328 *sterre*: star. *persant*: piercing.
329 *gladsome*: glad, joyful. *voyder*: banisher.
330 *Chef recomforter*: chief comfort.
331 *wynde*: lead, turn. *woful*: sorrowful people. *oute of*: from. *hevynesse*: grief.
333 *atteyne*: gain.
335–6 (And) so that it may please you, in your graciousness, to watch benevolently and direct a cure.
335–62 The essentials of the lady's complaint concern jealousy: possibly the jealousy of an old husband, but also perhaps the jealous keeping of an elderly guardian or parent, or even, by implication, the constraints exercised by over-exacting patrons. The summary of the complaints of other petitioners in the temple has opened a variety of possibilities, and it seems unnecessary to seek in the deliberate vagueness of her 'bille' reference to a specific historical occasion (details of attempts to do this are discussed in the headnote). For further discussion of the grievances raised here, see Boffey 2000.
338 *compas*: contrive.   339 *venyme*: poisonousness. *felonye*: ill-doing.
340 *Wher that*: wherever. *hyndre*: slander/grieve. *giltlesse*: innocent.
341 *Styntethe this werre*: put an end to this war.

[4]

'I pleyne also upon jalousye,
The wylde serpent, the snake tortuous,
That is so crokid and frownyng on lyve;
Efret with aysel that maketh hem suspectous—   345
By al kynde that art so envyous,
Of every thing the worst for to deme,
That ther is nothing that may his hert qweeme.

[5]

fo. 212ᵛ   'Thus is he fryed in his owen grece,
Torent and torne with his owne rage,   350
And ever froward, groynyng causelesse,
Whos raysoun fayllethe nowe in olde dotage.
This is the maner of crokid, fer in age:
Whan they ben coupled with youthe they can no more
But hem waryen—wymmen ben ful sore.   355

[6]

'Thus ever in tourment and yre furyous
We ben oppressed (allas that harde stounde!)
Right as yourself were with Vulcanus

342 *pleyne*: lament/appeal against. Cf. *TC* III. 1009–15, where jealousy is defined as a 'wikked wyvere', or snake.
344 *crokid*: twisted. *frownyng on lyve*: congenitally ill-intentioned.
345 *Efret*: consumed. *aysel*: vinegar, or a bitter drink, hence bitterness.
346 *By al kynde*: by nature.   347 (Ready) to judge the worst of everything.
348 *qweeme*: ease.   349 So he is fried in his own fat (i.e. his malice).
349–58 There has been some comment (e.g. in Norton-Smith 1958) on the 'coarseness' of this passage, which recalls the kind of female complaint satirized in *WB Prol*, or Dunbar's *Tretis of the Tua Mariit Wemen and the Wedo* (in Dunbar 1996: 33–57).
350 *Torent*: ripped apart.
351 *ever froward*: continually perverse. *groynyng*: grumbling. *causelesse*: without reason.
352 *raysoun*: (faculty of) reason. *fayllethe*: is failing.
353 This is characteristic of bent (old men), advanced in age.
354 *ben*: are. *can no more*: can (do) no more.
355 *hem waryen*: curse them (i.e. their youthful wives). *wymmen ben ful sore*: (and) women are (as a consequence) very sorely afflicted.
357 *stounde*: time, moment.   358 *Vulcanus*: Vulcan.
358–62 The allusion to Venus's adultery with Mars (see above, lines 126–8 n.) is somewhat at odds with her earlier association with the 'hevenly fyre of love that is

Ageyns youre wille and your hert bounde.
Nowe for the joye whylome that ye founde   360
With Mars your knight, upon my compleynt ruwe
For love of Adon that was so fresshe of huwe.'

[7]

And, as me thought, the Goddesse did enclyne
Mekely hir hed, and sofftly gan expresse
That in short tyme hir turment shoulde fyne;   365
And howe of hym, for whom al hir distresse
Contynued had, and al hir hevynesse,
She shoulde have joy, and of hir purgatorye
Ben holpen soone, and so forthe lyve in glorye.

[8]

And seyde, 'Doughter, for the sadde trouthe,   370
The rightful menyng and the innocence
That plannted ben withowten any slouthe
In youre persone, right voyde of al offence,
So have atteyned to oure audyence
That thoroughe oure grace ye should be wel releved,   375
I yowe byheete, of al that hathe you greved.

[9]

213^r   'And for that ye, ever of oon entent,
Withouten chaunge or mutabilite,
Have in youre peynes been so pacyent
To take lowly youre adversitee,   380
And that so longe—thoroughe the crueltee

eterne', but the lady's reference to it seems to generate the sympathetic response she
seeks.

360 *whylome*: once.   361 *ruwe*: have pity.   363 *did enclyne*: lowered.
365 *fyne*: end.   369 *Ben holpen*: be helped from.   *forthe*: from that time on.
370 *for*: because.   *sadde*: steadfast.   372 *slouthe*: neglect.
376 *byheete*: assure.
377 *for that*: because.   *ever of oon intent*: single-mindedly.
381 *thoroughe*: because of.
381–2 Saturn was traditionally known as *Infortuna Major* (cf. *KQ* 122). For
some indication of the scope of his responsibilities, see *Kn T, CT* I. 2443–69, and Lewis
1964: 105.

Of olde Satourne, my fader unfortuned—
Youres shal never more be contuned.

[10]

'And thenkith this: withinne a litell while
Hit schal aswage and overpassen sone.   385
For men be leyser passen many a myle,
And ofte also after a droppyng mone
The weder clereth: whenne the storme is done
The sonne shineth in his spere bright;
And joye awaketh whenne woo is putte to flight.   390

[11]

'Remembreth eke hou never yet no wight
Come to no worschip without some debate.
And folke also rejoyse more of light
That thei with derkenesse were wapped and mate.
No mannes chaunce is alweye fortunate,   395
Ne no wight preiseth of sugre the swetnesse
But if thai toforne have tasted bitternesse.

[12]

'Grysilde was assaied at the fulle
That turned after to her encrese of joye;

382 *unfortuned*: unfortunate.
383 *Youres*: your difficulties (understood from the *peynes* of 379).   *contuned*: continued.
385 *Hit*: it.   *aswage*: subside.   *overpassen*: pass away.   386 *be leyser*: unhurried.
387 *droppyng mone*: rainy night.   388 *weder*: weather.
390 ff. The inevitable alternation of joy and sorrow, and the enhancement of one through comparison with the other (sometimes called the doctrine of contraries), are stressed throughout *TG*. Influential formulations of the latter point are to be found in Boethius, *De cons* IV, pr. 2 (tr. in Chaucer's *Boece* as follows: 'For so as good and yvel ben two contraries, yif so be that good be stedfast, thanne scheweth the feblesse of yvel al opynly; and yif thow knowe clerly the freelnesse of yvel, the stedfastnesse of good is knowen'), in Dante, *Inferno* V. 121–3 ('Nessun maggior dolore | che ricordarsi del tempo felice nella miseria'), and in Chaucer, *TC* I. 637–48; III. 1625–8.
391 *wight*: person.   392 *worschip*: honour.   *debate*: dispute.
394 *That*: when previously.   *wapped*: covered.   *mate*: bewildered/miserable.
397 *But if*: unless.
398 *Grysilde*: see 75–6 n.   *assaied*: tested.   *at the fulle*: to the uttermost.
399 Who then turned (i.e. on Fortune's wheel) to increased happiness.

Penolope cane eke for sorowes dulle   400
For that her lord abode so longe at Troye;
Also the tourment there couth no man ackoye
Of Dorigen, floure of alle Bretayne:
Thus evere joye is ende and fyne of payne.

[13]

'And trusteth this for a conclusion: 405
Thus ende of sorowe is joye, yvoyde of drede.
For holy seyntes, thurugh her passion,
Han hevene ywonne for her soverayne mede,
And plentee gladly foloweth after nede.
And so my doughter, after youre governaunce   410
I yowe bihete ye schulle have plesaunce.

[14]

'For evere of love the manere and the gyse
Is for to hurte his servantz and to wonde,
And whanne he hath taghte hem his emprise
He can in joye make hem to habownde.   415
And sith that ye have in my lase be bownde
Withoute grucching or rebellion,
Ye most of right have consolacion.

400–1 Penelope (see 67–9 n.) also grew mournful in sorrow because her lord stayed so long at Troy (see also notes on the text).

402 *there couth no man ackoye*: no one could soothe.

403 *floure of alle Bretayne*: flower of all Brittany. In Chaucer's *Fkl T*, set in Brittany, the 'trothe' or loyalty of Dorigen to her husband Arveragus and to her would-be lover Aurelius is put to the test in an anguished conflict (see *CT* V. 1355–456 for her complaint).

404 *fyne*: conclusion. Cf. *TC* I. 952: 'And also joie is next the fyn of sorwe', and Whiting 1968: J61.

406 *yvoyde of*: free from.   407 *seyntes*: saints.   *her passion*: their martyrdom.

408 Have won heaven for their supreme reward.

410 *after youre governaunce*: following your (good) conduct.

411 *bihete*: assure.   412 *gyse*: custom, way.   413 *wonde*: wound.

414 *taghte*: taught.   *emprise*: purpose/power.

415 *habownde*: abound, overflow.

416 And since you have been bound in my lace (one of several references to the way in which Venus binds lovers: see also 1125–9, 1249–50, 1290).

417 *grucching*: grumbling.   418 *most*: must.

[15]

'This is to sayne, douteth never a dele
That ye schulle have fulle possession   420
Of hym that ye cherisshe nowe so wele,
In honest wyse, withowten offencion,
Because I knowe youre entencion
Is trewly sette, in partie and in alle,
To love hym beste and most in specialle.   425

[16]

'For he that ye have chosen yowe to serve
Shalle bene right swich as ye desire,
Withouten chaunge, fully tille he sterve,
So with my bronde I have hym sette on fyre.
And with my grace I schal hym so enspire   430
That he in hert schall be right at youre wille,
Whether so yowe list to save hym or to spille.

[17]

fo. 214ʳ

'For unto you his hert I shal so lowe,
Withowten spot of any doublenesse,
That he ne shal scapen frome the bowe—   435
Thoughe that him list, thorough unstedfastnesse—
I mene of Cupyde, that shal him so distresse
Unto youre hande with th'arow of golde,
That he ne shal scapen, thoughe he wolde.

---

419 *sayne*: say. *douteth never a dele*: never doubt a bit.   420 *schulle*: shall.
422 *offencion*: offending.   427 *swich*: such.
429 *bronde*: torch, firebrand. Venus is elsewhere represented with a torch or firebrand: see, e.g. *RR* 3424–6 (*Romaunt* 3705–10), 15778, 21251–54; *Mer T*, *CT* IV. 1727; *PF* 114.
430 *enspire*: imbue.   432 Whether it pleases you to save or to destroy him.
433 *lowe*: humble.   435 *That he ne shal scapen*: that he shall not escape.
436 Even though in his unsteadfastness he may wish to.
437 *that*: who. *distresse*: distrain.
438 Cf. 112 n; and *RR* 907 ff. (*Romaunt* 939 ff.), where Cupid's attendant carries two bows and two sets of arrows, one of gold; elaborated in *KQ* 655–63.
439 *thoughe he wolde*: though he might wish to.

[18]

'And sithe you list of pitee and of grace   440
In vertu oonly his youthe to cherys,
I shal, be aspect of my benigne face,
Make him t'eschewe every synne and vyce,
So that he shal have no maner spyce
In his corage to love thinges newe,   445
He shal to you so pleyne be founde and truwe.

[19]

'And why that I so sore to you him bynde
Is that for ye so many have forsake,
Bothe wyse, worthy and eke gentil of kynde
Pleynly refused oonly for his sake: 450
He shal to you, whether he sleepe or wake,
Be evyn suche, under hope and dred,
As you list ordeyne of your wommanhed.'

[20]

And whan this goodely, feyre and fresshe of hewe,
Humble and benigne, of trouthe crop and rote,   455
Conceyved hade how Venus gan to rewe
On hir preyers, oonly to doon boote
To chaunge hir bitternesse into swete,
She fell on knees by hye devocion
And in this wyse began hir oryson: 460

---

441 *cherys*: cherish.

442 *aspect:* look (in an astrological sense, meaning the way in which a planet looks on something; see *OED* II [4]).

444 *no maner spyce*: no taste at all.   445 *corage*: heart, disposition.

446 Cf. *AL* 137.   447 *sore*: tightly.   448 *Is that for:* is because.

449 *gentil of kynde*: noble-natured.   451 *whether he sleepe or wake*: i.e. at all times.

453 As you wish, in your womanliness, to ordain.

454 *this goodely*: this good woman (an instance of an adjectival noun).

455 *crop and rote*: blossom (top) and root (= completely). Cf. 1230, and *TC* II. 348 (other examples of Lydgate's use of this phrase are cited by Schick (Lydgate 1891), in the note to this line).

457 *doon boote*: make remedy.   460 *oryson*: prayer.

[21]

'Heyest of hye, qwene and empyresse,
Goddesse of love, of goode yit the best,
That thorowe youre bountee, withouten any vyce,
Whylome conquered the appelle at the fest
Whyche Jubiter, thorowe hys hye request,   465
To alle the goddes of love celestyal
Made in his paleys most imperyal:

[22]

'To yowe my ladi, uphalder of my lyf,
Meekly I thanke, so as I may suffys,
What ye list nowe with hert ententyff   470
So graciously for me to devyse,
That whyle I lyve, with humble sacryfyse
Upon your auters, your fest yere bi yere,
I shal ensence casten in the fyre.

[23]

'For of youre grace I am ful reconsyled   475
Frome ever trouble unto joy and ese,
That sorowes alle ben fro me exyled,
My peynes alle and fully my disese,
Sith that you list thus sodeynly to peese,

461 *Heyest of hye*: highest of high.
461–523 The lady's 'orysoun', of nine rhyme royal stanzas, constitutes another of the poem's inset lyrics.
462 *of goode yit the best*: ever the best of good (things).
464 *conquered the appelle*: won the apple.   *fest*: feast, festival.
464–67 A reference to the story of the Judgement of Paris, in which Paris (one of the sons of King Priam of Troy), invited to award a golden apple to the most beautiful of the goddesses Juno, Minerva, and Venus, favoured Venus, who then helped in his abduction of Helen of Troy. Lydgate tells the story at more length in the *Troy Book*, II. 2556 (Lydgate 1906–35: i. 218) and his account is illustrated in some MSS (for reproductions, see Ehrhart 1987: facing p. 221). The amalgamation of qualities represented by the three goddesses figures also in *KQ* and *LR*.
467 *paleys*: palace.   468 *uphalder*: maintainer.
469 *so as I may suffys*: inasmuch as I am able.   470 *ententyff*: eager.
473 *auters*: altars.   *your fest yere bi yere*: annually on your festival.
474 *ensence*: incense.   *casten*: throw.   479 *peese*: make peace.

Into gladnesse so wondurfully to tourne,   480
Having no cause frome hensforthe to mourne.

[24]

'For sithins ye so meekly list to daunte
To my servyce him that I love best,
And of youre bountee so graciously to graunt
That he ne shal varye, thoughe hym list,   485
Wherof myn hert is fully hente to rest,
For nowe and ever, lady myn benigne,
That hert and al to yowe hole I resigne.

[25]

215ʳ 'Thankyng yowe with al my ful hert
That youre grace and visytacioun   490
So humbully lyst him to converte
Fully to bene at my subjeccioun,
Withouten chaunge or transmutacioun,
Now unto his last: now joye and reverence
Be to youre name and to youre excellence!   495

'And in despyte platly of hem alle
That been to love so contraryous
I shal him cherysshe, whatsoever falle,
That is in love so pleyne and vertuous,
Maugre alle thoo that ben desyrous   500
To speken us harome, thoroughe grucching and envye
Of that ilk serpent cleped jalousye.

---

482 *sithins*: since. *daunte*: subdue.   485 *varye*: change.
486 *hente*: taken.   488 *hole*: wholly.   492 To be completely subject to me.
494 *Now unto his last*: from now until his last (day).
494–5 An echo of lines from Troilus's hymn to Love (*TC* III. 1273–4): 'laude and reverence | Be to thy bounte and thyn excellence!'
496 *platly*: clearly, openly.
496–516 These stanzas appear only in certain MSS (GSFB), and refer to the figure of 'Jealousy' previously mentioned in 342 ff.
498 *whatsoever falle*: whatever might happen.
500–1 In spite of all those who wish to speak harm of us.
502 *ilk*: same. *cleped*: called.

'And for hem, lady, if I durst preye—
Menyng no vengeaunce but correcioun—
To chastyse hem with turment or they deye   505
For hir untrewthe and fals suspessyoun
That deme the worst in hir opynyoun
Withowten desert, wherfore we wowche
To punysshe hem for theyre malebouche

'To that they may stonden in repreef   510
Unto alle lovers for hir cursednesse,
Withouten mercy, forsaken at mescheef
Whan hem list best have help of hir distresse,
And for hir falshede and for hir doublenesse;
And in despyte, right as amonge thes foules   515
Ben jayes, pyes, thees lapwynges and thes owlys.

fo. 215ᵛ   'This is al and some and chief of my request,
And hole substaunce of my ful entent,
Thanking you ever of youre graunt and hest,
Bothe nowe and ever, that ye me grace have sent   520
To conquer hym that shal never repent
Me to serve and meekly for to plese
As fynal tresor of myn hertes eese.'

503 *hem*: them. *durst*: dared to.
505 *or*: before. *deye*: die.   507 *deme*: judge. *hir*: their.
508 *withouten desert*: unjustly. *wowche*: undertake.
509 *malebouche*: slander, evil speaking. Cf. 153; a figure named *Malebouche* (*Wikkid-Tunge*) appears in *RR* 3511 ff. (*Romaunt* 3799 ff.).
510 *To that*: to (the point) that. *stonden in repreef*: stand reproved.
511 *cursednesse*: wickedness. 512 *at mescheef*: in time of need.
513 When they would most wish for mercy on their suffering.
515–16 And (to the point that they stand) despised, just as jays, magpies, lapwings and owls are (despised) among birds. These birds were traditionally associated with various undesirable qualities: see e.g. *PF*, which mentions 'the janglynge pye, | The skornynge jay' (345–6), 'The false lapwynge, ful of trecherye' (347), and 'The oule ek, that of deth the bode bryngeth' (343).
517 *al and some and chief*: the entirety. 519 *hest*: promise.
523 *fynal*: eternal.

And thanne anoon Venus cast adoune
Into hir lappe roses whyte and rede   525
And fresshe of hewe, that wenten envyroun
In compas wyse even aboute hir hede,
[And bad hyre kepe her of hir goodly hede]
Whiche shal not fade ne never waxen olde
If she hir biddyng folowe as she hathe tolde.

'And so as ye ben called Margarete,   530
Folowethe the feythe that hit dothe specifye:
This is to seyne, bethe in colde and heete
Ever of oon hert, as is the dayesye
Elyche fresshe, whiche that may not dye
Thorowe no stormes ne duresse, how it be kene,   535
Namore in wynter thanne in somer grene.

[29]

'Right so b'ensaumple, for weel or for wo,
For joye, tourment, or for adversite,
Whether that Fortune favour or be fo,

525 On the conventional iconographic association of Venus and roses see Twycross
1972: 6–14; cf. the references to her rose garland in *Kn T, CT* I. 1955–63; *HF* 135; and *KQ*
678–9.
526 *envyroun*: around.   527 *In compas wyse*: circling.
527a See notes on the text.
530 There is no single obvious explanation for the lady's identification in MSS S and G
as 'Margarete' (also the name of the lady to whom the complaint which follows *TG* in S and
G is addressed). Fr. *marguerite* is in English daisy (see here lines 533–6), and Chaucer's
LGWP, in which the virtuous and merciful Queen Alceste is represented as a daisy (cf. *TG*
74), owes something to a Fr. tradition of '*marguerite* poems' (on which see Skeat (Chaucer
1894: vol. iii, pp. xxix–xxxii); Wimsatt 1970). Wimsatt notes (p. 59) 'a feature that seems
characteristic of Marguerite poetry from its inception, which is that the name Marguerite
and the flower denoted by the name embody a transcendent ideal of which any single
woman is only a temporal embodiment'. Such embodiments appear in the alliterative poem
Pearl (ed. Gordon 1953) and in Thomas Usk's 14th-c. prose *Testament of Love* (Usk 1998;
Skeat 1897: 1–145). For attempts to identify the lady of *TG* with a real Margaret, see
MacCracken 1908 and Seaton 1961: 375–83.
531 *hit*: it (i.e. the name 'Margaret').   *specifye*: indicate.
533 *dayesye*: daisy.
534 *Elyche*: always.   535 *duresse*: hardship.   *how it be kene*: however sharp.
537 *b'ensaumple*: following this example/for example.

For povert, rychesse or prosperite,   540
That ye youre hert keepe in oon degree
To love him best, for nothing that ye feyne,
Whome I have bounde so lowe under your cheyne.'

[30]

And with that worde the Goddesse shooke hir hede
And was in pees, and spake as thoo namore.   545
And therwithal, ful femynyne of dred,
Me thought this ladi sighen gan ful sore
And sayde ageyne, 'Lady, that mayst restore
Hertes to joye frome theyre adversite—
To doon youre biddyng *humblement magre.*'   550

And thus endethe the first partye of the dreem | and
filowyng begynnethe the secound partye

Ther I was sleping and dremyng as I lay,   551
Withinne the temple me thought that I say
Gret part of folk with murmour wonderful
So heve and shove (the temple was so ful),
Everyche ful bysy in his owen cause,   555
That I ne may shortly in a clause
Descryven al the ryte and the gyse;
And eke I want the konnyng to devyse
Howe some ther were with blood, ensense and mylk,
And some with floures woot and soft as sylk,   560
And some with sparowys and dowvyes feyre and whyte,

541 *in oon degree*: exclusively.
542 *for nothing that ye feyne*: do not pretend, for anything.
546 *ful femynyne of dred*: timid in a very womanly way.
548–50 And said in answer, 'Lady, (you) who may restore hearts to joy from their
adversity: (I am ready) to do your bidding, "humbly, in spite of (anything)".'
550 See 310 n. Almost all the MSS mark the division at this point with a rubric of some
kind.
552 *say*: saw.   553 *Gret part*: a large number.   555 *Everyche*: every one.
557 *Descryven*: describe.   *ryte*: activity.   *gyse*: manner.
558 *want*: lack.   *konnyng*: skill.   560 *woot*: moist.
561 *dowvyes*: doves. Doves and sparrows are often associated with Venus; see 525 n. and
PF 351.

That for to offren gan hem to delyte
Unto the Goddesse with sigh and with preyer
Hem to releese of that they most desyre;
That for the preese, shortly to conclude,   565
I went my wey from that multytude
Me to refresshe out of the preese alloone.
And be myself as that I can gone
Withinne the estyrs, and gan a whyle tarye,
I was wel ware of a man al solitarye   570
That, as me semed, for hevynesse and doole
Hym to compleynen that he welk so soole
Withowt espying of any other wight.
And if I shal descryven hym aright,
Ner that he had been in hevynesse,   575
Me thought he was—to spek of seemlynesse,
Of shappe, of fourme, and also of stature—
The moost passing yit that Nature
Made in hir werkys, and lyke to been a man.
And therwithal, as I rehers can,   580
Of face and cheer the moost gracious
To be byloved, happy and everous,
But as it semed outwardes by his cheer
That he compleyned for lack of his desyre,
For by hymselff as he welk up and doune   585
I herde hym make a lamentacioun,
And sayde, 'Allas, what thing may this be,

216ᵛ (margin)

562 Who took pleasure in making offerings.
564 to release to them what they most desired.
565 *for the preese*: because of the crowd. The dreamer's impulse to be solitary perhaps echoes *PF* 296–7. The rites described may echo those of *Kn T, CT* I. 2425–30.
568 *as that I can gone*: as I walked.   569 *estyrs*: buildings.   *tarye*: linger.
570 The 'man al solitarye' recalls the knight encountered by *BD*'s dreamer; and hence the plaintiff of Lydgate's own *Complaint of the Black Knight* (Lydgate 1934: 382–410; and Lydgate 1966: 47–66). The overheard lament is a common feature of dream visions and courtly poems.
572 *welk*: walked.   *soole*: alone.   575 had he not been unhappy.
577 cf. *KQ* 290.   578 *passing*: surpassing.
579 *lyke to been a man*: appropriately manly.
580 *rehers*: recall.   582 *everous*: joyful.
587 This marks the start of the lover's first expanded lyric, a 'lamentacioun' (587–713), in couplets.

That nowe am bounde that somtyme was so free,
And went at large at myn eleccyoun?
Nowe I am kaught under subjeccyoun   590
For to become a verray homager
To God of Love, wher that er I cam her
Felt in myn hert right nought of loves peyne.
But nowe of newe withinne the verrey cheyne
I am enbraced—so that I may not stryve—   595
To love and serve, whyle that I am on lyve,

fo. 217ʳ   That feyre fresshe wight in the temple yondre
Right nowe I saugh, that I hade gret wonder
That ever God (as for to rekken al)
Koude make a thing so celestyal,   600
So aungellyk, in erthe to appere.
For with the perssing of hir eyen clere
I am wounded I weene so to the hert
That frome the deethe I may not astert,
And moost I merveyl that so sodeynly   605
I was yolden to be at hir mercy,
Whether hir lust to do me lyve or dye.
Withowten more I mot hir lust obeye,
And taken meekly my sodeyne aventure,
For sithe my lyff, my deethe, and eeke my cure   610
Is in hir hande, hit wolde not avayle
To gruche ageyne, for of this batayle

588 *somtyme*: once.
589 *at large*: unrestrained.   *at myn eleccyoun*: wherever I chose.
591 *verray*: true.   *homager*: one paying homage to.
594 The notion of love as imprisonment, and of a chain of love, which plays throughout this 'lamentacyon' (as also in 618 etc.) is conventional: see Leyerle 1974.
596 *on lyve*: alive.
597 The meeting in the temple perhaps recalls Troilus's first sight of Criseyde, *TC* I. 267–80; although here it is apparently (according to the lady's earlier testimony) not the first glimpse. Echoes from *TC* continue through this passage.
599 *as for to rekken al*: taking all things into account.   602 *perssing*: piercing.
603 *weene*: think.   604 *astert*: escape.   606 *yolden*: given up.
607 *hir lust*: she wishes.   *do*: make.
608 *Withowten more*: without more [discussion].   *mot*: must.   *lust*: pleasure, wish.
609 *sodeyne aventure*: unexpected fortune.
610 *sithe*: since.   *cure*: recovery.
611–12 *hit wolde not avayle* | *To gruche ageyne*: there is no point in grumbling about it.

The palme is hirs, and pleynly the victorye;
As hole subjet—for hirs is al the glorye—
I mighte it nought in no wyse acheeve.   615
Sith I am yolden, howe shulde I than preve
To gynne a werre? I wysse hit wil not ybe:
Thoughe I be loos, at large I may not fle.
O God of Love, howe sharp is nowe thyn arowe!
Howe mightest thou so pryvely and narowe,   620
Withouten cause, hurten me and wownde?
And takest noon hed my sorowes for to sounde,
But lyche a bridde that flyethe at hir desyre
Tyl sodeynly withinne the panetere
She is caught, theighe she were let a large.   625
A sodeyne tempest forcastethe nowe my barge:
Nowe up nowe doune, with wynde it is so blowe
So am I possed and almoste overthrowe—
Fordrevyn in derknesse with many sturdy wawe.
Allas, whan shal the tempest slake lawe,   630
To clere the skyis of myn adversytee,
The loode sterre whane I ne may not see—
Hit is so hydde with cloudes that been blake?
Allas, whan shal this tourment overslake?
I cannot wit, for who is hurt of newe   635
And bledethe inward tyl he be pale of hewe,
And hathe his wounde unwarly fresshe and grene,

613 *palme*: palm (leaves carried symbolically as a prize).
614 *as hole subjet*: (I, who am) wholly subject (to her).
616 *preve*: try.   617 *To gynne a werre*: in starting a war.   *I wysse*: I know.
618 *loos*: unbound.   *fle*: fly around.   620 *pryvely*: secretly.   *narowe*: strictly.
622 *sounde*: examine.   623 *lyche a bridde*: (leaves me) like a bird.
623–5 This simile seems to have an essentially Chaucerian heritage: cf. *LGWP* 130;
Romaunt 1621.
624 *panetere*: trap or snare for catching birds.
625 *theighe she were let*: though she was let out.   *a large*: at large.
626 *forcastethe*: tosses about.   *barge*: boat.
626–34 The notion of love as a tempestuous sea is ancient, but had perhaps been
reactivated for a 15th-c. audience through Chaucer's allusions in *TC* I. 415–18 and II. 1–6;
see Curtius 1953: 128–30; and Stevens 1979: 285–307.
628 *possed*: tossed.   629 *wawe*: wave.   630 *slake lawe*: become calm.
632 *loode sterre*: lode star.   634 *overslake*: abate, pass away.
635 *of newe*: newly.   637 *unwarly*: untimely.   *grene*: recent.

Ever unholpen, more kene and kene,
Of mighty Cupyde, which can so hertes daunte
That no man may in youre werre hym avaunte   640
To get hym pryse but oonly by meeknesse,
For ther ne vayllethe stryff ne sturdynesse—
So may I say that with a looke am yolde,
And have no power to stryve, thoughe I wolde.
Thus stande I even betwene lyf and deethe,   645
To love and serve, whyle me lastethe breethe,
In swyche a place where I dar not pleyne
Lyche him that is in turment and in peyne
And knowethe nought to whome for to discure.
For ther that I have hyely sette my cure   650
I dar not weel, for dreed of foule daunger
And for unknowe, tellen yow the fere
Of lovys bronde is kyndeld in my brest.
Thus am I murdred and sleyne at the leest

fo. 218ʳ Thus pryvely with myn owen thought.   655
O Venus, lady, whom that I have saught,
So wisshe me now what is best to do
That am destraught with myself so
That I ne wot what wey to tourne,
Save by myself soleyne for to mourne,   660
Hangyng in balaunce bitwene hope and dred,

638 *unholpen*: unhealed.   639 *daunte*: subdue, overcome.
640–1 (To the extent) that no man may claim to win honour in your (i.e. Cupid's/the lady's) battle except through meekness.
642 For neither conflict nor strength are worth anything there.
643 *am yolde*: have yielded.   646 *whyle me lastethe breethe*: while I am alive.
647 *swyche*: such.   649 *to whome for to discure*: to whom to tell his troubles.
650 *ther that*: there, where.   *hyely sette my cure*: directed my strenuous effort.
651 *weel*: well, indeed.   *daunger*: scorn.
652 *unknowe*: unknown (risks).   *fere*: fire.
657 *wisshe*: direct.   660 *soleyne*: alone.
661 ff. This allegorical battle between the personifications of hope and 'drede' and 'daunger' owes something to the tradition of *RR*, and more generally to the notion of *Psychomachia*, a battle between virtues and vices, formalized in the 4th-c. Latin poem text of this title by Prudentius. Norton-Smith's rhetorical term for this is *thymomachia*; he compares Lydgate's *Complaint of the Black Knight*, 491–515 (Lydgate 1934, 1966); Schick adduces *TC* V. 1207 (Lydgate 1891).

Withouten comfort, remedy, or red.
For Hope me bidethe poursuwe and assaye,
And Drede ageynward answerethe and seythe "nay";
And nowe with Hope I am sette alofft,   665
But Dred and Daunger, hard and nothing soffte,
Have overthrowe my trust and put adoune.
Nowe at my large, nowe fetterd in prysoune,
Nowe in tourment, and nowe soone in glorye,
Nowe in paradyss, and nowe in purgatorye,   670
As man dispeyred in a double werre;
Born up with Hope and thanne anoon Daungerre
Me drawethe aback and seythe "hit shal not be".
For wher as I, of myn adversite,
Am bolde some tyme mercye to requere,   675
Thanne komethe Despeyre and gynneth me to lere
A newe lesson, to Hope al contrarye—
They ben so dyvers they wolde do me varre.
And thus I stande dismayed in a traunce,
For whanne that Hope wer lykly me t'avaunce   680
For Drede I trowe I dare not oon worde speke.
And if hit be so that I not outbreke

218ᵛ   To telle the haromes that greven me so sore
But in my self encresce hem more and more,
And to be slayne fully me delyte,   685
Thanne of my deethe she is nothing to wyte,
For but if she my constreynt pleynli knewe
Houwe shoulde she ever upon my peynes rewe?

662 *red*: advice.   663 *bidethe*: commands. *poursuwe*: give chase.
664 *ageynward answerethe*: answers back.   665 *sette alofft*: set up.
668 *at my large*: unconstrained.
668–70 An example of the rhetorical figure *anaphora*.
671 *werre*: conflict, war.   674 *wher as I*: when.   675 *requere*: ask for.
676 *gynneth me to lere*: teaches me.   678 *do me varre*: make me change.
680 For when Hope might be on the point of advancing me.
682 *outbreke*: break out, burst out.   683 *haromes*: wrongs.
684 *encresce hem*: make them grow.
685 And take the utmost pleasure in being slain.
686 *nothing to wyte*: not at all to blame.
687–8 For unless she plainly knew of my distress how should she ever pity my
grievances?

Thus offt tymes with Hope I am meved
To telle hir al of that I am agreved   690
And to be hardy on me for to take
To aske mercy; but Dred thanne dothe awake
And thorowe wanhope aunswerethe me ageyne
That better were, than she hade desteyne,
To dye anoon, unknowe of ony wight,   695
And therwithal Hope anoon yit
Me gan beholde to preyen hir of grace,
For sith al vertues ben pourtreyid in hir face
Hit were not sitting that mercy were bihynde.
And right anoon withinne myself I fynde   700
A newe plee, brought on me with Dreed,
That me so masethe that I see no speede,
Bycause he seethe astonyed al my blood—
I am to symple and she is knowe so goode.
Thus Hope and Dred in me wil not sesse   705
To plede and stryve myn haromes to peese.
But yit doutelesse, or that I be ded,
Of my distresse sithe I can no red
But stonde doumbe, stille as any stoone,
Before the goddesse I wil me hast anoon   710

fo. 219ʳ   And me compleyne with more pleyne sermon;

689 *meved*: moved.
690–2 To reveal to her all (the ways) in which I am wronged, and to be sufficiently bold to ask for mercy.
693 *wanhope*: despair.   *aunswerethe*: answers.   694 *hade desteyne*: scorned (me).
696 *anoon yit*: still.   697 *Me gan beholde*: looked at me.   *preyen*: ask.
698 *ben pourtreyid*: are depicted, registered.
699 It would not be appropriate that mercy were (left) behind.
700 *right anoon*: straight away.   701 *plee*: plea.   *on me with*: against me by.
701 ff. In keeping with the court ambiance of the poem, the altercation between Hope and Drede uses some significantly legalistic words: *plee* (701), *plede* and *stryve* (706), *to peese* (706), *compleyne* (711).
702 *masethe*: stuns.   *speede*: advancement.
703 Because he perceives that I am surprised through and through.
704 *to*: too.   *knowe*: renowned.   705 *sesse*: cease.
706 *myn haromes to peese*: to assuage my wrongs.   707 *or*: before.
708 *I can no red*: I am at a loss.
709 *But stonde*: except to remain. 'doumbe, stille as any stoone' is proverbial (Whiting 1968: S762), but cf. also the long list of citations from Chaucer and other of Lydgate's works in Schick's note to this line (Lydgate 1891; line 689 in his edition).
711 *more pleyne sermon*: clearer words.

Thoughe dethe be fyne and ful conclusioun
Of my request, yit wol I hym assaye.'
And right anoon me thoughte that I sey
This deolfull man (as that I have memorye)   715
Ful lowly entren into the oratorye,
And kneling doune with al humble wyse
Before the goddesse, and gan anoon devyse
His pytous querell with a deolful chere,
Seying right thus, anoon as ye shal here: 720

the supplicacion of | the Louer

[1]

'Redresser of soroful, O Citheria,
That with the stremys of thi plesaunt heet
Gladest the cuntreys of al Cirea,
Wher thou hast chosen thy paleys and thy sete,
Whos brightful beemys been wasshen and offt wete   725
Withinne the ryver of Elycon the welle:
Have now pitee of that I shal the telle,

[2]

'And nought desdeynethe, of your benignitee,
My mortal woo, lady and goddesse,

712–13 Even though death is the end and ultimate conclusion of my request, I shall still pit myself against him.

714 *sey*: saw.   715 *deolfull*: miserable.

716 The *oratorye* seems to be a small room, leading off the main hall, reserved for private prayer. In *Kn T*, Chaucer describes similar small rooms above the gates to the 'theatre' where the lists are to be constructed (*CT* I. 1885–917), and cf. the oratory used for prayer in Henryson's *Testament of Cresseid* (Bawcutt and Riddy 1987: 170–93), 120.

718 *devyse*: relate.   719 *querell*: complaint, accusation.

721 *Citheris*: an alternative name for Venus, derived from her association with the island of Cythera; cf. Chaucer's uses of this form in *Kn T* (*CT* I. 2215), *PF* 113, *TC* III. 1255.

721–867 The interiorized 'lamentacioun' is turned into a 'supplicacion', of twenty-two rhyme royal stanzas, addressed to Venus.

723–26 'the cuntreys of al Cirea' are rather vaguely conceived. By 'Cirea' Lydgate may mean Syria; or he may follow Chaucer, in *A & A* 17 and *HF* 521–2, who locates a town of Cirra (actually at the mouth of the river Pleistus, which flows from Mount Parnassus) near Mount Parnassus, and follows contemporary precedent in understanding Helicon to be a well (rather than the mountain it actually is) somewhere near there.

Of grace and bountee and mercyful pitee   730
Benignely to helpen and to redresse.
And thoughe so be I cannot wel expresse
The grevous haromes that I feele in myn hert,
Hathe neverthelasse mercy of my smert.

[3]

'This is to seyne, O clere hevyns light,   735
That nexst the sunne sercled have your spere,
Sithe ye me hurten with your dredful might
By influence of beemys that ben cleer,
And that I bye youre servyce nowe so deer:
As ye me brought in to this maladye,   740
Beothe gracious and shapen remedye.

[4]

fo. 219ᵛ   'For in you hoolly lyethe help of al this cas,
And knowen best my sore and al my peyne—
For dred of deethe howe I ne dar, allas,
To asken mercy onys ne to compleyne.   745
Now with youre fere hir hert so restreyne—
Withouten more or I dye at the leest—
That she may wit what is my request:

[5]

'Howe I nothing in al this worlde desyre
But to serve holly and truwely to myne ende   750
That goodely fresshe, so wommanly of chere,
Withouten chaunge, whyle I have lyff and mynde;

734 *smert*: pain.   735 *seyne*: say.

736 who have set your sphere, in the form of a circle, next to that of the sun; *sercled* here seems to mean 'set in the form of a circle' (as Norton-Smith (Lydgate 1966), line 716 n.): Venus's sphere is next to that of the sun in the arrangement of concentric planetary spheres envisaged by ptolemaic cosmology.

739 *bye youre servyce*: pay the penalty for serving you.   *deer*: dearly.

741 *Beothe*: be.   742 *hoolly*: entirely.   *cas*: event.

743 *knowen*: (you) know.   745 *onys*: once.

746 *fere*: fire.   *restreyne*: restrain.   748 *wit*: know.

750 In his note on the imperfect rhyme in 750–2 (line 732 n. in Lydgate 1966), Norton-Smith suggests that *mynde* 'probably represents an original *mende*, evidenced in South-Eastern texts'.

And that ye wolde me suche a grace nowe seende
Of my servyce that she nought disdeyne,
Sith hir to serve may I me nought restreyne,   755

[6]

'Withoute more er I dye at the leest
Sith Hope hathe gif me al this hardynesse
To love hir best, and me never restreyne
Whyles that I lyve, with al my bisynesse
To drede and serve, thoughe Daunger never assent.   760
And here upon ye knowen myn entent,
So let me never with Daunger more be shent.

[7]

'For in myn hert emprynted is so sore
Hir shappe, hir fourme, and al hir seemlynesse;
Hir poort, hir cheere, hir goodenesse more and more;   765
Hir wommanhode and eeke hir gentylesse,
Hir trouthe, hir feyth, and eke hir kyndenesse;
With alle vertues, yche sette in his degre:
Ther is no lacke but oonly of pitee.

[8]

220ᵣ   'Hir sad demyng, of wille nought varyable;   770
Of looke kunnyng, and roote of al plesaunce,
And exemplayre of alle that ben stable;
Discrete, prudent, of wysdam sufficeaunce;

754 That she should not be disdainful of my service.   757 *hardynesse*: boldness.
760 *thoughe Daunger never assent*: though Standoffishness never agree (to my succeed-
ing in love).
762 *shent*: harmed.
763 Cf. Chaucer, *Mer T* (*CT* IV. 2178): 'Ye bene so depe enprented in my thoght'.
764 The description of the lady stresses the virtues central to the medieval ideal of
womanhood: truth, stability, discretion, 'governaunce', along with the lack of the virtue of
pity or mercy so necessary to the lover's well-being.
765 *poort*: demeanour.   *cheere*: expression, mood.
768 *yche sette*: each one placed.
770 *sad demyng*: sober judgement (see textual note).
771 *Of looke kunnyng*: knowledgeable-seeming/competent-seeming.
772 And exemplar of all steadfast people.
773 *of wysdam sufficeaunce*: (with) an abundance of wisdom, amply wise.

Mirrour of wit, ground of governaunce:
A world of beaute compassed in hir face,   775
Whos persaunt looke dothe thorowe myn herte race.

[9]

'And ever ful secree and wondurfully truwe,
A welle of fredam and right bountevous,
Alwey encressing in vertu newe and newe;
Of speche goodely, and wondur gracious;   780
Al voyde of pryde, to pore folkes pitous:
So that—if I shortly shal not feyne—
Save upon mercy I can nothing compleyne.

[10]

'What wonder that thoughe I be with dred
Inly oppressed for to asken grace   785
Of hir that is a qwene of wommanhed?
For wel I wot that in so heghe a place
It wil not ben; therfore I over pace,
And take lowly what woo I endure
Til ye of pitee me take into youre cure.   790

[11]

'But oon avowe pleynly I here make:
That whether she do me lyve or ellys dye
I wil not grucchen, but humbelly hit take
And thank God and humbelly obeye.
For by my trouthe myn hert shal not reneye,   795
For lyff ne dethe, mercy nor daunger,
Of wille ne trouthe, but ben at hir desyre.

774 *ground of governaunce*: foundation of (self-)control.
776 *persaunt*: piercing.   777 *secree*: discreet.   778 *fredam*: generosity.
779 *newe and newe*: more and more.   780 *wondur*: wonderfully.
781 *Al voyde*: completely devoid.   782 *if I shortly shal not feyne*: briefly, in truth.
784 *What wonder that thoughe I be*: Little wonder that I should be.
788 *over pace*: pass over.   790 *cure*: care, keeping.   792 *do me*: make me.
795 *reneye*: resist.

[12]

To ben as trewe as was Antoneus
To Cleopatre whyle him lasted brethe,
Or to Thesbe younge Pyramus   800
Was feythful founde til him departed dethe.
Right so shal I, til Antrapos me sleeth,
For wele or woo hir feythful man be founde
Unto my last, lyche as myn hert is bounde,

[13]

'And love als weel as dyd Achillees   805
Unto his laste the feyre Polixene,
Er as the gret famous Ercules
Whiche felt of love the shottes sharp and kene.
Right so shall I sey as that I mene
Whyle that I lyve hir drede most and serve,   810
For lak of mercy theighe she do me sterve.

[14]

'Nowe ladi Venus, to whome nothing unknowe
Is in the worlde ehid ne nought may be—

798 *Antoneus*: Antony. The story of Cleopatra and Antony constitutes the first of Chaucer's *LGW*; for the sources of the story which were available to medieval writers (it was also known to Gower, although perhaps through Chaucer's account), see Chaucer 1987: 846.

800 *Thesbe*: Thisbe (see 80 n.).

801 *him departed dethe*: death separated him (from her).

802 *Antrapos*: a common form of the name of Atropos, who of the three classical Fates was held to be responsible for cutting the thread of existence; cf. *TC* IV. 1546–7, 'Attropos my thred of lif tobreste | If I be fals!'

804 Until my last (moment), so my heart is bound (to her).

805 *Achillees*: see 94 n.

807 *Er*: or. *Ercules*: the story of Hercules and Deianira is recounted in Ovid, *Heroides* IX and Gower, *CA* VIII. 2559–62. Hercules in fact deserted Deianira for Iole.

808 Cf. *TC* II. 57–8: 'Pandarus . . . | Felt ek his part of loves shotes keene'.

811–12 While I live I will fear and serve her most of all, even though, with her lack of mercy, she should make me die.

812 Venus is here credited with an omniscience which supports arguments that the poem's concerns reach beyond those simply of lovers.

813 *ehid*: hidden from.

For ther is nothing so heghe ne so lowe
May be conseyled frome youre pryvetee—   815
Fro whome my mening is nowe not secree,
But wyten fully that myn entent is truwe
And lyche my trouthe: nowe on my peynes ruwe.

[15]

'For more of grace than presumpcioun
I ask mercy, and not of duetee;   820
Of lowe humblesse, withouten offencyoun,
That ye enclyne, of youre benignytee,
Youre audyence to myn humylitee
To graunt hit me, that to you clepe and calle,
Yit ye releese some day my peynes alle.   825

[16]

fo. 221ʳ   'And sithe ye have the guerdon and the meede
Of alle lovers pleynly in youre hand,
Nowe of youre grace and pitee takethe heede
Of my distresse, that am under youre bonde
So lowly bounden, as ye wil understonde.   830
Now in that place wher I tooke first my wownde
Of pitee suffrethe myn help may be founde,

[17]

'That as she hurt me first with a sight
Right so with help late hir me susteene;
And as the streemys of hir eyen bright   835
Whilome myn hert with wowndes sharp and keene
Thorowe perced have, that yit been fresshe and grene,

---

815 *conseyled*: concealed. *pryvetee*: secret knowledge.   817 *wyten*: know.
818 *lyche my trouthe*: like (i.e. as true as) my faithfulness.
819–20 For I ask mercy from your compassion rather than from (any sense of) your
obligation.
822 *enclyne*: lower, turn.   823 *audyence*: hearing.
824 *that to you clepe*: who cries to you.
825 *Yit*: yet   826 *guerdon*: reward.   *meede*: recompense.
829 *bonde*: bond.   832 though your pity, allow that my help may be found.
834 *late*: let. *susteene*: sustain.

So as she hurt, so late hir me socure,
Or ellys certayne I may no whyle endure.

[18]

'For lacke of speche I cane sey nowe no more: 840
I have gret mater but I can not pleyne;
Mi witt is dulle to tellen al my sore.
A mowthe I have, and yit for al my peyne
For want of wordes I may not nowe atteyne
To tellen half that dothe myn hert greeve,   845
Mercy abidyng til yow me list releeve.

[19]

This is th'effect of my preyer fynalle:
With deethe of mercy, releesse for to fynde.
For hert, body, thought, lyff, lust, and al,
With al my resoun, and my ful mynde,   850
And my fyve wittes, of oon assent I bynde
To hir servyce, withowten any stryff,
To make hir pryncesse of my dethe and lyff.

[20]

'Beseche I yowe, of ruthe and of pitee,
Goodely planete, O ladi Venus bright,   855
That ye youre sone, of his deytee—
Cupyde I mene—that with his dredful might,
And with his bronde that is so clere of light,
Hir hert so to fyren and to marke
As whylome ye me henten with a spark;   860

[21]

'That even lyche, and with the same fyre,
She may be hette as I nowe brenne and melt,
So that hir hert be flaumed by desyre

---

838 *socure*: succour.   844 *atteyne*: be able.
846 Waiting for mercy until it pleases you to relieve me.
849 Cf. *TC* V. 1319: 'With herte, body, lif, lust, thought, and al'.
856 *deytee*: godliness.   860 *whylome*: earlier, before.   *henten*: took.
862 *hette*: heated.   *brenne*: burn.   863 *flaumed*: inflamed.

That she may knowe with fervence howe I swelt.
For of pitee pleynly if she felt   865
The selff heete that dothe myn hert enbrace
I hope of ruthe she wolde do me grace.'

[22]

And therwithal, right as that me thought,
Towardes this man ful benignely
Gan cast hir eye liche as that she rought   870
Of his disese, and seyde ful in goodely:
'Sith hit is so that thowe so humbely
Withouten grucching oure hestes list obeye,
Towardes youre help anoon I wil purveye.

[23]

'And eke my sone Cupyde that is so blynde   875
He shal ben helping, fully to perfourne
Youre hole desyre, that nothing be behynde,
Ne shal be kept: so we shal refourme
The pitous compleynt that makethe the to mourne,
That she for whome thou sorowe most in hert   880
Shal thoroughe hir mercy releesse al thy smert.

[24]

fo. 222ʳ   'Whane she seethe tyme, thorowe your purveyaunce
Bethe nought to hasti, but suffre the alwey wele:
For in abyding thoroughe lowly obeyssaunce
Lythe redresse of al that ye nowe feele;   885
And she shal be als truwe as eny steele

---

864 *fervence*: fervour.   *swelt*: swelter.   866 *selff*: same.
867 *hope*: think.
868 *right as that me thought*: just as it seemed to me.
870 *Gan cast*: (Venus) cast.   *rought*: cared.
871 *ful in goodely*: (= *in ful goodely wyse*) with great benevolence.
872 *hestes*: commandments.   *list*: are pleased to.   874 *purveye*: provide.
877 *behynde*: neglected, wanting.   882 *purveyaunce*: providence.
883 Do not be overhasty, but continue to be patient.   885 *Lythe*: lies.
886 *als truwe as eny steele*: proverbial (Whiting 1968: S709), and cf. also Epilogue to *Mer T, CT* IV. 2426.

To you alloone, thoroughe youre might and grace,
If humbully ye byde a lytel space.

[25]

'But understondethe that al hir cherisshing
Shal be so grounded upon al honestee   890
That no wight shal, thorowe yvell compassing,
Demyn amysse of hir in no degree.
But neyther mercy, routhe, ne pitee
She shal not have, ne take of you noon hede
Firther than longethe unto hir wommanhede.   895

[26]

'Be not astonyed of no wilfulnesse,
Ne not dispeyred of the dilacioun;
Lat resoun brydell lust by buxumnesse
Withowte grucching or ellys rebellyoun,
For joye shall filowe al this passyoun.   900
For who cane suffre turment and endure
Ne may not faylen that filowe shal his cure.

[27]

'Toforne alle other she shal you love best,
So shal I hir, withowten offencyoun,
By influence enspyren in hir brest,   905
In honest wyse, with ful entencioun
For to enclyne by clene affeccioun
Hir hert fully on you to have ruthe,
Bycause I knowe that ye mene but truthe.

[28]

'Go nowe to hir, as she stant asyde,   910
With humble chere, and putt the in hir grace,

222^v

889–95 For the tenor of the advice here, cf. *KQ* 897–903.
891 *yvell compassing*: evil scheming.   892 *Demyn amysse*: think badly.
895 More than is appropriate to her status as a woman.
896 *wilfulnesse*: obstinacy.   897 *dilacioun*: delay.
898 *buxumnesse*: obedience.   900 *filowe*: follow.
902 It cannot fail that his remedy will come next.
903 *Toforne*: before.   904 *offencyoun*: cause for offence.
906 *wyse*: manner.   910 *stant*: stands.

And al byforne late hope be thy guyde:
For thaughe that dred wolde with the pace
Hit sitt wele, but looke that thou arace
Out of thyn hert wanhope and despeyre   915
To hir presence or thou have repeyre.

[29]

'And mercy first thy wey shal redy make,
And honest menyng afore do thy message
To make mercy in her hert awake;
And sikurnesse, to firther thy vysage,   920
With humble porte to hir that is so sage
Shal meenys ben, and I myself also
Shal the fortunen or al thy tale be do.

[30]

'Go forthe anoon and be right of goode chere,
For specheless for nothing maystowe spede.   925
Be goode of trust and be nothing in were,
Sith I myselff shal helpen in this nede.
For at the leest, of hir goodelyheede,
She shal to the hir audyence enclyne
And lowly here til thou thy tale fyne.   930

[31]

'For wel thu wost (yif I shal not feyne)
Withouten speeche thou mayst no mercy have:

---

912 *al byforne*: before all other things. *late*: let. A similar emphasis on hope is
expressed in *KQ* 736–42, and also in some of the English poems of Charles of Orleans
(B23, B29, B37, and B41 in Charles of Orleans 1994, ed. Arn).
913 *with the pace*: walk with you, keep you company.
914 *Hit sitte wele*: it is very fitting. *arace*: tear from, eradicate.
916 Before you return to her presence.
918 *menyng*: intention. *afore*: in advance.
920 *sikurnesse*: safety, security. *firther*: further, recommend.
922 *meenys*: mediators.
923 Shall (bring you good) fortune before your story is over.
925 For you will make no headway speechless.   926 *were*: doubt.
931 *wost*: know. *yif*: if.

For who that wil of his pryvee peyne
Fully be cured, his lyff to help and save,
He most meekly oute of his hertes grave   935
Deskover his wownde and shewe it to his leeche,
Or ellys dye for defaute of speeche.

[32]

'For he that is in meschief reklesse
To sechen help, I holde him but a wrecche;
And she ne may thyne hert bring in pees   940
But thy compleynt to hir erys strecche.
Woldest not be cured, and list no salve seche?
Hit wol not be: for no wight may atteyne
To come to blisse if him list lyve in peyne.

[33]

'Therfore at oonys go in humble wyse   945
Byfore thy lady and lowely knele adoune,
And in al trouthe thy wordes so devyse
That she of the may have compassyoun.
For she that is so hye of renoun
In alle vertues, as qwene and sovereyne   950
Of wommanhod, shal ruwe upon thy peyne.'

And whanne the goddesse this lesson hade tolde,
Abouten me so as I cane beholde
Right sore astonyed I stode, as in a traunce,
To seen the maner and the countenaunce   955
And al the chere of this woful man,
That was of hewe pale and dedly wan,

---

933 *pryvee*: secret.
933 ff. Cf. Boethius, *De cons* I, pr. 4 (in Chaucer's translation, 'Yif thou abidest after helpe of thi leche, the byhoveth discoure thy wownde'), and *TC* I. 857–8: 'For whoso list have helyng of his leche, | To hym byhoveth first unwre his wownde'.
935 *most*: must.   *his hertes grave*: the depths of his heart.
936 *Deskover*: reveal.   *leeche*: doctor, physician.
937 *defaute*: lack.   938 *reklesse*: heedless.
941 Unless your complaint reaches her ears.
942 Would you be cured without wishing to seek a healing ointment?
953 As I looked around me.

With dreed oppressid oonly in his thought,
Makyng his cher as that him recched nought
Of lyf ne dethe, ne what so him betyde,   960
So myche feer he hade on every syde
To put him forthe forto telle his peyne
Unto his ladi, othir to compleyne

fo. 223ᵛ   What woo he felt, tourment, or diseese,
What deedly sorowe his hert did seese;   965
For rowth of whiche of his wo to endyte
My penne I feele qwakyng as I wryte.
Of him I had so gret compassyoun
That to rehers his weymentacyoun
That wel I wot thoughe with myself I stryve   970
I want konnyng his peynes to descryve.
Ellas, to whome shal I for help calle?
Nought to the Muses, for cause that they al
Helpen of right in joye and not in woo,
And in maters that delyten also—   975
Wherfor they nyl not nowe dyrette my style,
Nor me enspyren, allas the harde whyle.
And I can no firther but to Thesyphone
And to hir sustren for to helpen me,
That bene goddesses of turment and of peyne: 980

958–60 His thoughts utterly weighed down with fear, with an expression as if he cared
nothing for life or death, or whatever might happen to him.

963 *othir*: or.   965 *did seese*: seized.

965–6 Cf. *TC* IV. 13–14: 'And now my penne, allas, with which I write, | Quaketh for
drede of that I moste endite'. Schick cites many further instances of Lydgate's use of this
figure (Lydgate 1891); see also Hammond 1927: 437 n.

966 *rowth*: pity.   *endyte*: relate, write about.   969 *weymentacyoun*: lamentation.

970–1 I know well that though I struggle (with it), I lack the skill to describe his hurt.

973 *the Muses*: the nine Muses of poetry.   *for cause*: because.

974 *of right*: properly.   975 *delyten*: give happiness.   976 *dyrette*: guide.

977 *whyle*: time.

978 *Thesyphone*: Thesiphone (emended here following G; Shirley's copy in S has
'Physyphonnee') was one of the classical Furies. She is invoked in *TC* I. 6 ('Thesiphon,
thow help me for t'endite | Thise woful vers, that wepen as I write'), and with the other
Furies, or Erinyes, again at IV. 22–6 ('O ye Herynes, Nyghtes doughtren thre ... Megera,
Alete, and ek Thesiphone ... This ilke ferthe book me helpeth fyne').

979 *sustren*: sisters.

Nowe let youre terys into myn ynke reyne,
With peynful wordes my papir for to blotte,
This wofull mater not peynt but to spotte,
To telle the maner of this dredful man
Upon his compleynt whane he first bigan   985
To telle his lady, whan he gan declare
His hidde sorowes and his yvell fare
Whiche at his hert constreyned him so sore,
Th'effect of whiche was this withouten more:

Balade of the lover

[1]

224ʳ 'Pryncesse of youthe and floure of gentylesse,   990
Ensample of vertu, grounde of courteysye,
Of bounte roote, qween and ek maystresse
To alle wymmen howe they shal hem guye,
The sothefast myrour goode t'exemplyfye
The right wey to the porte of wommanhed: 995
What I shale say? of mercy takethe heed—

[2]

'Beseching first unto youre hye noblesse,
With qwakyng hert of myn inward drede,
Of grace and pitee—and not of rightwysnesse—
Of verray routhe, to helpen in this neede.   1000
This is to seye, O welle of goodelyheed,

---

981 *terys*: tears.   *reyne*: rain.

981 ff. The narrator asks that the Furies' tears may mix with his ink and so inform the 'peynful' words of the complaint on which he is to embark; but adds modestly that he will be unable adequately to portray ('peynt') the emotion therein, only to 'spotte', or hint patchily, at it.

987 *yvell fare*: wretched state.

990–1059 This 'ballade' or complaint, of ten rhyme royal stanzas, forms another of the inset lyrics. Skelton mentions in *BC* 253 a song with the title 'Princes of youghte'. This may possibly have been an extract from *TG* which gained currency in a musical setting; conversely, Lydgate may have taken his opening line from an existing song. See Fallows 1977.

993 *guye*: conduct.   995 *porte*: bearing, demeanour.

999 *rightwysnesse*: justice.

That I ne rechche thoughe ye do me dye
So you list first to here what I seye.

[3]

'The dreedful strooke, the gret force and might
Of god Cupyde, that no man may rebelle,   1005
So inwardly thoroughe out my hert right
Eperced hathe that I ne may concele
My houyn wound, or I ne may appelle
Unto no gretter, his mightyhed so fast
You for to serve hathe bounde unto my last,   1010

[4]

'That hert and body hole is to you yeolde,
For lyff or dethe, to youre servyse allooone,
Right as the mighty goddesse Venus wolde.
Tofore hir meekly whan I made my moone
She me constreynid withouten chaunge in oone   1015
To your service, and never for to feyne,
Whether you list to do me eese or peyne.

[5]

fo. 224ᵛ

'So that I can nothing but mercy crye
Of you my lady, and—chaunging for no newe—
That you list goodely byseen, or that I dye;   1020
Of verrey routh upon my peynes ruwe,
For by my trouthe, and ye the sothe knewe
What is the cause of myn adversitee,
Of my disese ye wolden have pite.

1002 *rechche*: care.   1003 *So*: so (long as).   1004 *dreedful*: fearful.
1005 *rebelle*: disobey.   1007 *Eperced*: pierced.
1008 *houyn*: own.   *appelle*: appeal.
1009–10 to no higher power, since his powerfulness has bound (me) so tightly to serve you until I die.
1011 *yeolde*: yielded.   1013 *wolde*: wants.
1015 *chaunge in oone*: any change.   1016 *feyne*: dissemble/hesitate.
1019 *chaunging for no newe*: not changing for any new (lady).
1020 *byseen*: contemplate, take notice of.   *or that*: before.
1022 *and*: if.

[6]

'For unto yowe trewe and eke secree   1025
I wil be bounde, to serve as I best can,
And therwithal als lowe in eche degree
To you aloone as ever yit was man
Unto his ladi, frome tyme that I began,
And so shal forthe withowten any slouthe   1030
Whyles that I lyve, by god and by my trouthe.

[7]

'For levir I had to dyen sodaynly
Than you offenden in any maner wyse,
And suffre peynes inwardes pryvely
Than my servyce ye shulden nowe despise.   1035
For I right nought wil axen in no wyse
But for youre servant ye wold me accepte,
And whan I trespas me goodely to correct,

[8]

'And for to graunt of mercy this preyer—
Oonly of grace and wommanly pitee—   1040
Frome day to dai that I might beter lere
Yow for to plese, and therwithal that ye
Whan I do mysse list to techen me
In youre servyce how that I may amende
Frome hensfforthe, and never yoo offende.   1045

[9]

'For unto me hit dothe enoughe suffyse
That for youre man ye wolde me receyve,
Fully to been as you list to devyse
Right as ferforthe my wittes may conceyve;
And therwithal, lyche as ye perceyve   1050

1028 *in eche degree*: in every respect.   1030 *slouthe*: laziness, slacking.
1031 *Whyles that*: as long as.   1032 *levir I had*: I would prefer.
1036–7 For I will not ask for anything at all, in any way, except that you would take me
as your servant.
1041 *lere*: learn.   1043 *do mysse*: do wrong.
1049 *Right as ferforthe*: just as far as.   1050 *lyche as*: just as, to the extent that.

That I be truwe, to guerdoun of your grace
Or ellys me punysshe affter my trespace.

[10]

'And if so be that I may not atteyne
Unto your mercy, yit graunteth at the leest
In youre service, for al my wo and peyne,   1055
That I may dye affter my beheest.
This is al and some, fyne of my request:
Oonly with mercy your servant forto save,
Or mercylesse that he may be grave.'

[11]

Whanne this benyngne, of hir entent so truwe,   1060
Conceyved hathe the compleynt of this man,
Right as the fresshe, rody roos newe
Of hir colour to wexen she began.
Hir blood astonyed so frome hir hert ran
Into hir face, of femynyntee,   1065
Thoroughe honest dreed abaysshed so was she,

[12]

And humbelly she gan hir eyen cast
Towardes him, right of hir benyngnytee,
So that no word bi hir lippes past
For hast ne dreed, mercy ne pitee.   1070
For so demened she was in honestee
That unavysed nothing hir astert,
So myche of resoun was compast in hir hert.

1057 *al and some*: everything. *fyne*: purpose.   1059 *grave*: buried.
1060 *this benyngne*: this gracious (lady).
1061 *Conceyved hathe*: took in, comprehended.
1062 *rody*: reddish. *roos*: rose. Cf. *PF* 442–5: 'Ryght as the freshe, rede rose newe |
Ayeyn the somer sonne coloured is, | Ryght so, for shame al wexen gan the hewe | Of this
formel [female eagle] . . . '.
1063 *wexen*: change.   1066 *abaysshed*: bewildered.
1071–3 For she conducted herself with such honesty that nothing escaped her thought-
lessly, such reasonableness was enclosed in her heart.

[13]

Til at the last of routhe she did abreyde
Whan she his trouthe and menyng did feele,   1075
And to him ful godely spake and seyde:
'Of youre behestes and youre menyng wele,
And your servyce, so feythful every dele,
Whiche unto me so lowly nowe ye offre,
With al myn hert I thank you of your profre.   1080

[14]

'For als myche as youre entent is sette
Oonly in vertue, brydeld under dred,
Ye most of right needis fare the bette
Of youre request, and the better spede.
But as for me, I may of wommanhede   1085
No firthir graunt you in myn entent
Than as my lady Venus wol ful assent,

[15]

'For she wele knowethe I nam not at my large
To done right nought but by hir ordenaunce,
So am I bounde under hir dredful charge   1090
Hir list t'obeye withouten varyaunce.
But for my part, so hit be plesaunce
Unto the goddes, for trouthe in your empryse
I you accepte fully to my servyce.

1074 *she did abreyde*: she burst out.
1077–122 The lady's acceptance of the lover might be considered as a formal response
to the supplication of 990–1059.
1078 *every dele*: in every part.   1080 *profre*: proffer.
1081 *For als myche*: forasmuch.   1081–4 Cf. *KQ* 1002–8.
1082 *brydeld*: restrained.
1083 You must inevitably, and rightly, do better with your request, and be more
successful.
1086 *firthir*: further.   1088 *I nam not at my large*: I am not at liberty.
1089 *but by hir ordenaunce*: unless by her commandment.
1091 *Hir list t'obeye*: to obey her wish.
1092 *so hit be plesaunce*: as long as it pleases.
1093 *empryse*: undertaking.

[16]

'For she myn hert hathe in subjeccion   1095
Whiche hole is youres and never shal repent,
In thought, n'en dede, in myn eleccyoun.
Witnesse on Venus that knowethe myn entent
Fully to byde hir doome and jugement,
So as hir list disposen and ordeyne   1100
Lyche as she knowethe the trouthe of bothe us tweyne.

[17]

'For unto the tyme that Venus list provyde
To shape a wey for oure hertes ese,
Bothe ye and I most nedes the tyme abyde
To take in gree and not for oure disese   1105
To gruchche ageyne, til she list to appese
Oure hidde woo, so inly that constreynethe
Frome day to day so oure hertes pleynethe.

[18]

'For in abyding of woo and al affraye
Who that can suffre is founden remedye,   1110
And for the best ful offt is made delaye
Or men ben helid of hir maladye.
Wherfore, as Venus list this mater guye,
Lat us agreen and take al thing for the best
Til she list sette oure hertis bothe at rest.   1115

[19]

'For she hit is that byndeth and can destreyne
Hertis in oon, this fortunate planeete,

1097 *n'en dede*: nor in deed.   *eleccyoun*: choice.
1099 *byde*: wait for.   *doome*: decision.   1103 *shape*: contrive.
1105 *To take in gree*: to take in good part.   *for our disese*: on account of our difficulty.
1106–8 To grumble in return, until it pleases her to soothe our secret sorrow, which so
pressingly forces our hearts to complain from day to day.
1109–10 For whoever knows how to endure protracted sorrow and affliction finds a
remedy.
1111 And very often delay occurs for the best of reasons.
1112 *Or*: before.   1113 *guye*: direct.
1116 *destreyne*: hold fast. The allusions to Venus's role in binding lovers together, a
reflection of her wider powers of holding elements in harmony, recalls the 'canticus Troili',

And can relesse lovers of her peyne
To tourne fully hir bitter into sweete.
Now blissfull goddesse, doun streght from thi sete 1120
Us to fortune caste youre streemys sheene
Lyche as ye knowen that we trouthe meene.'

[20]

And therwithal, as I myn eyen caste
To parceyve the maner of thees tweyne
Before the goddesse meekly as they paste, 1125
Me thought I sey with of golde a cheyne
Venus anoon enbracen and constreyne
Theyre bother hertis in oon for to persever
Whyles that they lyve, and never for to dissever.

[21]

226ᵛ Seying right thus with a benyngne cheere: 1130
'Sith hit is so they been under my might
Mi wille is this: that ye, my doughter dere,
Fully accepte this man, as hit is right,
Unto youre grace anoon here in my sight
That ever hathe been so lowly you to serve; 1135
Hit is good skylle youre thank that he deserve.

[22]

'Youre honour sauf and eeke youre wommanhed,
Hym to cherisshe hit sittithe you right wele
Sithe he is bounde under hope and dred,

TC III. 1744–71, and, more obliquely, III. 1–49. Both of these passages are closely related to Boethius, *De cons* II, m. 8 ('al this accordaunce [and] ordenaunce of thynges is bounde with love, that governeth erthe and see, and hath also comandement to the hevene . . . This love halt togidres peples joyned with an holy boond', in Chaucer's translation); cf. also IV, m. 8.

1117 *in oon*: in one.
1120 *doun streght from thi sete*: straight down from your seat.
1121 *Us to fortune*: to bring us good luck.   1123 *caste*: turned.
1124 *parceyve*: observe. *tweyne*: two.   1125 *paste*: passed.
1126 *sey*: saw. 1128 *Theyre bother hertis*: both their hearts.   1129 *dissever*: part.
1136 *Hit is good skylle*: it is fitting.
1137 With your honour and femininity protected.
1138 *hit sittethe you right wele*: it is very fitting for you.

And with my cheyne that is golde yche dele.   1140
Ye most of mercy shapen that he feele
In youwe some grace for his long servyse,
And that in haste, lyche as I shal devyse.

[23]

'This is to seyne that ye taken heed
Howe he to yowe moost feythful is and trewe   1145
Of alle youre servauntiz, and nothing for his meede
Of yowe ne axethe, but that ye on him ruwe;
For he hathe vowed to chaaungen for no nuwe,
For lyfe nor dethe, for joye ne for peyne,
Ay to be youres so as yowe list ordeyne.   1150

[24]

'Wherfore yowe moste, or ellys it were wronge,
Unto youre grace him fully to resceyve
In my presence; bycause he hathe so longe
Hoolly ben youres—as ye may conceyve—
That frome youre mercy nowe if I him weyve   1155
I wil my self recorde crueltee
In youre persone, and gret lack of pitee.

[25]

fo. 227ʳ   'Lat him so trouthe fynde truwe ageyne;
For longe servyce guerdoun him with grace,
And late pitee awey doon his peyne.   1160
For tyme is nowe daunger to race
Out of youre hert, and mercy in to pace,
And love for love hit wolde wele seeme
To gyve ageyne, and thus I pleynly deeme.

1140 *yche dele*: every bit.
1150 To be yours always, as long as you wish to command (it).
1152 *resceyve*: receive.   1155 *weyve*: turn away.   1161 *race*: tear.
1162 *to pace*: to go in.
1163–4 Cf. *TC* II. 390–2: '... Certein, best is | That ye hym love ayeyn for his lovynge | As love for love is skilful guerdonynge'.

[26]

'And as for him I wille been his borowe   1165
Of lowlyhed and besy attendaunce:
How hit shal be bothe at even and morowe
Ful diligent to doon his observaunce,
And ever awayting for to doon plesaunce.
Wherfore, my sone, list and take hede: 1170
Fully obeye as I shal the reede.

[27]

'And first of alle my wille is that ye be
Feythful in hert and constant as a wal;
Truwe, humble and meeke, and therwithal secree,
Withoute chaunge in partye or in al.   1175
And for no turment that the fallen shal
Tempest the not, but ever in stedfastnes
Roote thyne hert, and voyde doublenesse.

[28]

'And firthermore have in reverence
These wymmen alle for thy ladyes saake,   1180
And suffre never that men do hem offence
For love of oon; but everwher undertake
Hem to defende, whether they sleepe or wake.
But ay be redy to holden truwe partye
With al thoo that to hem have envye.   1185

1165 *borowe*: surety.   1166 *lowlyhed*: humility.   *besy*: assiduous.
1171 *reede*: advise.

1172 Listed commandments of love are common in courtly poems of this kind: cf. *RR* 2229 (*Romaunt* 2175).

1173 'constant as a wal' is proverbial (Whiting 1968: W11–18), but see also Schick's list of Chaucerian examples (Lydgate 1891: 1153 n.).

1176–8 Do not be disturbed by any torment that may befall you, but root your heart always in steadfastness, and cast out deceit.

1177 Cf. Chaucer's *Truth*, line 8 (Chaucer 1987): 'Tempest thee noght al croked to redresse'.

1182 *everwher*: everywhere.

1184 *holden truwe partye*: behave as a loyal supporter.

[29]

'Be curteys ay and lowly of thy speche,
To ryche and pore fresshe and wel beseyne,
And ever besy weyes for to seche
Alle truwe lovers to releesse of hir peyne;
Sith thou art oon, of no wight have desdeyne,   1190
For love hathe power hertis for to daunte
For no cherisshing never to avaunte.

[30]

'Be lusty eek, al voyde of tristesse,
And take no thought but ever be jocound;
Ne be not pensyf for noon hevynesse,   1195
And with thy gladnesse let sadnesse ay be found.
Whane wo approchethe let mirthe moost habonde
As manhode axeth, and thoughe thou fele smert
Late not to fele knowen of thyn hert.

[31]

'And al vertues bisy be to suwe;   1200
Vyces eschuwe ay for the love of oon,
Ne for no talys thyn hert ne remuwe—
Worde is but wynde: hit shal soone overgoon.
What ever thou here, be doumbe as any ston,
And soone to aunswere that thou the not delite   1205
For here she stant that al this shal the qwyte.

1188 *seche*: seek.   1191 *daunte*: overcome.
1193 *lusty*: cheerful.
1194 *take no thought*: don't be pensive.   1196 *sadnesse*: steadfastness, gravity.
1197 *moost habonde*: be plentifully present.
1198 *As manhode axeth*: as manliness requires.
1199 *Late*: let.   *to fele*: too many.   1200 *suwe*: pursue, observe.
1201 *eschuwe*: put from you.   *oon*: one (lady).
1202 (Don't let) your heart be moved by any rumours.
1203 *overgoon*: pass over.   *Worde is but wynde*: proverbial (Whiting 1968: W643).
1204 *doumbe as any ston*: see 709 n.
1205–6 Don't take pleasure in being quick to answer, for she who will pay you back for
all this (i.e. reward you according to your behaviour) is standing here.

[32]

'And whether thou be absent or in presence
Noone others beawtee lat in thyn hert myne
Sith I have yyve her of bountee excellence
Above alle other in vertue for to shyne;   1210
And thenk in fyre howe men ben wont to fyne
This pured golde to put hit at assaye:
So the to preve thou art put in delaye.

[33]

. 229ʳ

'But tyme shal come thou shalt for thi suffraunce
Be wel apayed and thanked for thy meede,   1215
Thy lyves joye and al thy sufficeaunce,
So shal goode hope ay thy brydell lede.
Lat no dispeyre hinder the with drede
But ay thy trust upon hir merci grounde
Sith noon but she may thy soores sounde.   1220

[34]

'Eche houre and tyme, and every day and yere
Be lyche feythful, and varye not for lyte.
Abyde awhyle, and then of thy desyre
The tyme neghethe thow shalt the moost delyte.
And lat no sorowe in thyn hert byte   1225
For desyring, sithe thou shalt for thy mede
Rejoys in pees the floure of wommanhede.

[35]

'Thenk howe she is the worldes sunne and light,
The sterre of beutee, floure eke of fayrnesse—

1208 *myne*: penetrate.   1209 *yyve*: given.
1211 *ben wont*: are in the habit of, usually.   *fyne*: refine.
1212 *pured*: molten.   *put hit at assaye*: test it.
1213 In the same way you are subjected to delay in order to prove yourself.
1214 (and 1224) The significance of time to the resolution of difficulties informs also *KQ*
925–31 and the action of *LR*.
1215 *apayed*: rewarded.   *meede*: recompense.
1217 *thy brydell lede*: lead your bridle.   1220 *sounde*: heal.
1222 *lyche*: alike, consistently.   *lyte*: trivial things.   1224 *neghethe*: approaches.
1227 *Rejoys*: Enjoy (the company of).

Bothe crop and roote, and eke the ruby bright,   1230
Hertis to glade troubled with derknesse,
And howe I made hir thyn hertis emparesse.
Be glad therfore to been under hir bonde.
Now come nerre, doughter, and take him by the honde,

[36]

'Unto this fyne, that affter alle thy shoures   1235
Of his turment he may be glad and light
Whan thoroughe our grace ye taken him to youres
For evermore anone here in my sight.
And firthermore I wil, as hit is right,
Withoute more his langour for to lisse   1240
In my presence anoon that ye him kisse.

[37]

'That ther may be of alle youre olde smertis
A ful releesse, under joye assured,
And that oon lok be on youre bother hertis
Shutt with my key of golde so wel depured,   1245
Oonly in signe that ye ben rekured
Youre hole desyre, here in this holy place
Withinne my temple nowe, this yere of grace.

[38]

'Eternally be bounde of assuraunce
The knott is knitte which may not been unbounde,   1250
That alle the goddis of this allyaunce—

1230 *crop*: top, blossom.   1232 *emparesse*: empress.

1234 *honde*: hand. Cf. *Kn T* (*CT* I. 3093–5): ' "Com neer, and taak youre lady by the hond." | Bitwixen hem was maad anon the bond | That highte matrimoigne or mariage'.

1235 *Unto this fyne*: to this purpose.   *shoures*: showers, fits.

1239 *wil*: desire, order.

1240 Without more (delay), to ease his pining.

1244 *oon lok*: one lock (on the locking of hearts with a key, cf. *RR* 1999–2004 (*Romaunt* 2087 ff.)).   *youre bother*: both of your.

1246 *in signe*: to signify.   *ye ben rekured*: you have obtained (among the usages cited in *MED* are several legal ones).

1249 *be*: by.   *bounde*: bond.

1251 This 'allyaunce' is partly a network of family relationships (apart from Mars, Venus's lover), partly a grouping sanctioned by *Kn T*, in which all somehow figure.

Satourne and Jove and Mars as hit is founde—
And thowe Cupyde that first did him wownde
Shul ber recorde and evermore be wreke
Of which of yow theyre trouthe first dothe breke,   1255

[39]

'So that bi th'aspectes of hir ferse lookis
Withoute mercy shal falle the foule vengeaunce
For to be raced cleene out of my bookis
In wheche of you be founden varyaunce.
Therfore at onys settithe your plesaunce   1260
Fully to been, whyle ye have lyf and mynde,
Of oon acorde unto youre lyves ende;

[40]

'That if the spirit of reproved jalousnesse
In any wyse wolde youre hertes assayle,
To meeve or stir to bring in doublenesse   1265
Upon your trouthe to gyven a batayle,
Late not youre corage ne your force fayle,
Ne noon assautes you flitten or remewe,
For unassayde men may no trouthe preve.

[41]

28ʳ 'For whyte is whitter if hit be sette by blacke,   1270
And swoot is swetter affter bitternesse,
And falsnesse is dryve and put abacke
Wher trouthe is rooted withouten doblenesse.
Withowte preef may not be sikurnesse
Of love nor hate, and therfore of you two   1275
Shal love be more sith hit is bought with wo,

1254 *wreke*: avenged.   1258 *raced cleene*: cleanly erased.
1266 *gyven a batayle*: make conflict.   1268 *flitten*: alter.   *remewe*: change.
1269 *unassayde*: untried.
1270 *sette by*: placed next to; a further reference to the doctrine of contraries (see lines
391–416 n. and *TC* I. 642).
1271 *swoot*: sweetness.   1272 *dryve*: driven.   1274 *sikurnesse*: confidence.
1276 *bought with wo*: purchased with sorrow.

[42]

'As every thing is hade more in deyntee
And more of pryce whanne hit is dere abought,
And eek that love stant more in surtee
That longe toforne with peyne, woo and thought   1280
Conquerid is whan hit is first sought.
For every conqueste hathe his excellence
In his poursuyt as he fyndeth resistence.

[43]

'Right so to you more swoote and agreable
Shal love be founde, I do you pleynly sure,   1285
Withoute gruchching that ye wer sufferable
So lowe, so meeke paciently t'endure,
That al at onyes I shal nowe do my cure
For nowe and ever youre hertis so to fynde
That nought but dethe the knott shal unbynde.   1290

[44]

'Nowe in this mater what shoulde I lenger dwelle?
Komethe off at onys and dothe as I have sayde.
And first, my doughtir that is of bountee welle,
In hert and thought be gladde and wel apayed
To doon him grace that hathe so longe obeyed   1295
Youre lustis ever, and I wol for his sake
Of trouthe to yowe by bounde, I undertake.'

[45]

fo. 230ʳ   And so forthwith in presence as they stonde
Tofore the goddis, this lady feyre and weel

1277 *hade more in deyntee*: held more precious.
1279 *stant more in surtee*: stands more confidently.
1283 As he encounters resistance in the pursuit. A marginal note here in the MS, perhaps intended to preface what follows, reads 'et ideo . . . ; per Shirley' ('and there-fore . . . ; by Shirley').
1285 *sure*: assure.   1286 *sufferable*: patient, long-suffering.
1288 *al at onyes*: at once.   *do my cure*: take care.   1289 *fynde*: endow.
1292 *Komethe off*: come on.   1294 *apayed*: satisfied.
1297 *by*: be.

Hir humble servant tooke goodely by the hande   1300
As he tofore hir meekly did ther kneele,
And kist him affter fulfillyng every deele,
Frome poynt to poynt, in ful thriffty wyse,
As ye tofore Venus have herde devyse.

[46]

Thus is this man to joye and al plesaunce   1305
From hevynesse and his peynes olde
Ful reconsyled, and hath ful sufficeaunce
Of hir that ever mant weel and wolde;
That in goode feyth, and if I telle shoulde
The inwarde joye that did hir hertis brace,   1310
For al my lyff hit were to lyte a space.

[47]

For he hathe wonne hir that he lovethe best,
And she to grace hathe take him of pitee,
And thus hir hertis been bothe sette at rest
Withowten chaunge or mutabilitee,   1315
And Venus hathe of hir benignytee
Confermed all (what shoulde I lenger tarye)
Thees tweyne in oon, and never forto varye,

[48]

That for the joye in the temple aboute
Of this acorde bi gret solempnytee   1320
Was laude and preysing, withinne and withoute,
Joye unto Venus and to the deytee
Of god Cupide, so that Calyope

1302 *every deele*: in every way.
1303 *in ful thriffty wyse*: in a very becoming way.
1308 *ever*: always.   *mant weel and wolde*: meant well and desired (the best).
1309 *and if I telle shoulde*: if I should tell.   1310 *brace*: clasp.
1311 My whole lifetime would be too short a space.
1317 *what shoulde I lenger tarye*: why should I delay.
1323 *Calyope*: Calliope is the Muse of epic poetry; cf. *HF* 1399–1401: 'So song the myghty Muse, she | That cleped ys Caliope, | And hir eighte sustren eke'.

And alle hir sustren in hir armonye
Can with hir songe the goddes to magnyfye.   1325

[49]

And alle at onys with notys lowde and sharp
They did honnour and hir reverence,
And Orpheus amonges hem with his harp
Gan stringis touche with bisy dilygence,
And Amphyoun, that hathe suche excellence   1330
In musik, ay did his bisynesse
To plese and qweme Venus the goddesse,

[50]

Oonly for cause of this affinytee
Bytwixe thees tweyne not likly to dessever,
And every lover of lowe and hye degrce   1335
Gan Venus prey, frome thens forthe and ever,
That hoole of hem the lyf may parsevere,
Withouten eende, in suche plyte as they gunne—
In more encrees that hit of harde was wonne.

[51]

And thus the goddes, heryng this request,   1340
As she knewe the cleene entencyoun
Of bothe hem tweyne, hathe made a ful beheest,
Parpetuelly, by confirmacyoun,
Whyles that they lif of oon affeccyoun

1324 *sustren*: sisters. *armonye*: harmony.

1325 Praised the gods with their song.

1328 *Orpheus*: for the story of Orpheus, poet and harper, see Ovid, *Met.* X. 1–63, and Boethius, *De cons* III, m. 12.

1330 *Amphyoun*: Amphioun was king of Thebes and another famous harper; cf. Chaucer, *Mer T* (*CT* IV. 1715–17): 'Biforn hem stoode instrumentz of swich soun | That Orpheus, ne of Thebes Amphioun, | Ne maden nevere swich a melodye'.

1332 *qweme*: give pleasure to.

1333 *affinytee*: relationship, alliance; according to *MED*, a word which can be used in the context of relationships of many kinds: those of patronage and social grouping, for example, as well as the sexual or familial.

1337–9 That their life (together) may continue entirely, without end, in the manner in which they began—more so, since it was won with hardship.

1343 *Parpetuelly*: perpetually, eternally. *by confirmacyoun*: ratified.

They shul endure (ther is no more to seyne)   1345
That neyther shal have mater to compleyne.

[52]

So ferforthe ever in oon eternale see
The goddes have, in hir heghe prescyence,
Fully devysed thoroughe hir deyte,
And hoole concludid, bi final influence,   1350
That thoroughe theyre witt and just provydence
The love of hem, by rayce and by fortune,
Withowten chaunge shal ever more contune.

[53]

228ᵛ   Of which graunt the temple envyroun
Thoroughe hye comfort of hem that were present   1355
Anoon was goonne with a melodyous soun—
Namely of thoo that trouthe in love ment—
A balade newe with good avysement
Before the goddis, of notys lowde and cleer,
Singing right thus as ye shul affter heer: 1360

Balade

[54]

'Feyrest of sterris that with your persaunt light
And with the feyrnesse of your stremys cleer
Causin in love hertis to be light
Oonly thorough shyning of your glade speere,

1347 *So ferforthe*: Thus far.   *see*: jurisdiction, seat of authority.
1348 *prescyence*: foreknowledge.   1352 *rayce*: forward progress.
1354 *envyroun*: all around.   1356 *was goonne with*: rang with.
1357 *thoo*: those.   1358 *with good avysement*: well contrived.
1361–81 This 'balade newe', sung by all members of the assembled company 'that trouthe in love ment', is the last of the inset lyrics in *TG*. It is set apart from its surroundings not by means of a change of rhyme scheme or stanza form (it continues in rhyme royal) but by a distinctive refrain, repeated at the end of each of its three stanzas, which gives it virtually the shape of a lyric *ballade* on the model of the French *forme fixe* (see Wimsatt 1991: 44–5). Concluding song or melody is a familiar device in dream poems (cf. e.g. *PF*, Clanvowe's *Boke of Cupide* (Scattergood 1979; line 289)), serving the needs of both formal closure and verisimilitude; its strains can serve to wake the dreamer back to 'real life'.

Nowe laude and preys, O lady Venus dere,   1365
For to youre name, that have withouten sinne
This man fortuned his lady for to wynne.

[55]

'Willi planete, O Esperus, lady bright,
That woful hertis kan appeese and steere,
And ever be redy, thoroughe youre grace and might,   1370
To help alle thoo that biggen love so dere,
And have pore hertis so offt sette afyre,
Honnour to yowe alle that been herinne
That this man have fortuned his ladi wynne.

[56]

'And, mighty goddesse, day sterre affter night,   1375
Glading the morowe whanne the sune apperethe
To voyde derknesse thoroughe fresshnesse of your light
Oonly with twinkeling as that hit clerethe,
Nowe we you thanken, that yow seethe or herethe,
That ye this man—and never for to twynne—   1380
Fortuned have his lady for to wynne.'

fo. 231ʳ   Right with the noys and hevenly melodye
Which that they made in her armonye
Thorowe owt the temple for this mannys sake
Owt of my sleepe anoon I did awake,   1385
And sere astonyed knewe as tho no red
For sodeyne chaunge oppressed soor with dred.

1368 *Willi*: propitious.   *Esperus*: Venus is addressed first as Hesperus, the evening star, and then in the following stanza as the morning star, Lucifer. See North 1988: 242, for reference to the Ciceronian and Boethian formulations of this duality; North quotes from Cicero's *De natura rerum*, 'The star of Venus . . . is called Lucifer in Latin when it precedes the sun, but Hesperos when it follows' (cf. Boethius, *De cons* III, m. 1; IV, m. 6). This point in *TG* marks a return to the concern with modulations of light and darkness made prominent in the opening section.

1371 *biggen*: buy.   1380 *twynne*: part.

1386–7 And painfully stunned, knew then no advice, sorely oppressed with fear in the sudden change; Cf. *Romaunt* 3859: 'I was astoned, and knew no red'.

Me thought I was ay ligging in a traunce,
So clene awey was thoo my remembraunce
Of al my dreme; wherof gret thought and wo   1390
I hade in hert, and nist what to do
For hevynesse I hade elost the sight
Of hir that I, al the longe night
Hade dremed of in myn avisyoun;
Wherof I made gret lamentacioun,   1395
Bycause I hade never in my lyff aforne
Seyne noon so feyre, sith tyme that I was borne,
For love of whame, so as I kan endyte,
I pourpost here to maken and to wryte.   1399

1388 *ligging*: lying. The narrator is obscurely affected by the dream, and seems suddenly to propose himself as the lady's lover—not illogical, if the dream itself is considered as an objectification of love problems which caused the 'grevous hevynesse' he experienced before sleep. Equally, though, the ending leaves open other possibilities: e.g. that he is simply affected by the great goodness of the lady of whom he has dreamed, or that the object of his newly forged admiration is Venus. Vagueness of this kind is peculiarly apt in the context of a dream vision, and a favourite ploy; cf. e.g. *BD*.

1389 *awey*: gone.   *thoo*: then.   1391 *nist*: did not know.

1394 *avisyoun*: dream.

1398 *so as I kan endyte*: insofar as I am able to write.   1399 *pourpost*: intended.

1399 Shirley's copy, and that of MS G, continue with a complaint of 628 lines, in octosyllabic couplets, addressed to one Margaret (Lydgate 1891: 59–67). For discussion of this, and of the version of the conclusion found in other copies, see the note on the text above.

James I of Scotland, *The Kingis Quair*

The Kingis Quair, or 'King's Book', receives its title from a note in the single manuscript in which the text survives: 'Herefter followis the quair maid be King James of Scotland the first callit the kingis quair and maid quhen his majeste wes in Ingland' (Bodleian Library, MS Arch. Selden. B. 24, fo. 191ᵛ; the spelling in this transcription has been slightly modernized). A note in Latin in the scribe's hand at the end of the text, 'Quod Jacobus primus scotorum rex illustrissimus' (fo. 211ʳ), corroborates some of these details. Although the manuscript was compiled very late in the fifteenth century, possibly even at the start of the sixteenth, the king named in these notes was James I of Scotland (1394–1437), the son of King Robert III. Political turmoil in Scotland during his father's reign necessitated James's removal from his country, but on his journey of escape to France in 1406 the young boy was captured by the English and imprisoned in the Tower of London. Although he succeeded to his father's title in 1407, he was to remain a captive until 1423/4, moving between the Tower and other strongholds—Nottingham Castle, Windsor, Westminster—and at times accompanying his captor, Henry V, on military campaigns in France. After the successful conclusion of negotiations for his release, James married Joan Beaufort (a granddaughter of John of Gaunt and Katherine Swynford, and hence of English royal blood), and returned with her to take the throne in Scotland. He was murdered in 1437.

The contents of the 'Quair' associated with James match the circumstances of his life in significant ways. Its linguistic forms have been characterized as 'Anglo-Scottish', and support the probability that it was composed by a Scot who had resided in England for some time. The poem is constructed in the form of a recollection, in which the narrator looks back over the concluding stages of a period of imprisonment he once suffered. He relates a glimpse of a beautiful woman from his prison window, which led subsequently to a dream revelation in which he visited Venus's court and learned in turn from her, and from

Minerva and Fortune, about the nature and role of virtuously directed earthly love. On waking, he recalls, he was offered miraculous hope, in the form of a message carried by a bird to his prison window, and was then soon released into a period of happiness and prosperity. The end of the poem comments positively on the role of Fortune in the pattern of events which have been recollected, and offers thanks and prayers.

The framework of the poem clearly owes much to Chaucer's *PF* and *BD* in its incorporation of bedtime reading which is to relate to the dream: the poem begins with the narrator's recollection of reading in bed. Here, though, the chronology is altered, for the reading prompts not a fresh dream but the memory of one already experienced, and the vision turns out not to be inspired by the reading but rather clarified by the interpretation of it which the reading later makes possible. The book which preoccupies the narrator at the start of the poem is Boethius's *De consolatione Philosophiae* (*The Consolation of Philosophy*; ed. and tr. Stewart and Rand (Boethius 1918), tr. Watts (Boethius 1969)), and he is able to draw a pointed analogy between his own incarceration and Boethius's captivity. This is intensified by a further tissue of references to Chaucer's *Kn T*, another story of imprisonment, imbued by Chaucer himself with Boethian resonances.

While the *Quair* is clearly concerned to expound Boethian philosophy, and to explore the advice of the *Consolation* that concentration on absolute virtue offers a means of resisting the sorrows brought by changes of fortune, its narrative upends the pattern of Boethius's own history, and demonstrates the virtuous possibilities of earthly happiness which can follow from an upward passage on Fortune's wheel. For this narrator, too, a human relationship holds liberating and fortunate potential, rather than consigning him (as it mostly does the lovers of *Kn T*, or Chaucer's Troilus) to a metaphorical prison of love. The positive presentation of the goddesses Venus and Fortune in this poem (underlined by their association with Minerva, goddess of wisdom), suggests a number of interesting parallels: with Lydgate's Venus in *TG*, for example, who is concerned to bind lovers virtuously in her golden chain; and with the goddesses in Charles of Orleans's *LR*, whose role is similarly worked optimistically into what is effectively a covert autobiography.

Recent studies have highlighted the status of *KQ* as 'life writing' of an unusual kind, and have investigated its comments on the processes of memory, and on the capacity of the creative imagination to reformulate and redirect images absorbed from other texts. The special interest which prompted its copying in Scotland at a date very much later than its probable composition (which is generally assumed to have followed fairly quickly after James's release from captivity) suggests also that it may have demonstrated for Scots readers a vigorous and pleasing range of cultural appropriations.

NOTE ON THE TEXT

The text here is edited from the single surviving copy, on fos. 192–211 of Oxford, Bodleian Library MS Arch. Selden. B. 24 (facsimile in Boffey and Edwards 1997). This is an anthology of poetry in the Chaucerian tradition, containing *TC*, several dream visions (*BD*, *PF*, *LGWP*, Lydgate's *Complaint of the Black Knight*, Clanvowe's *Boke of Cupid*), and some Scottish poems. It seems to have been owned by Henry Sinclair, earl of Orkney (a descendant of James I), and may also have been made for him, possibly in several distinct periods of compilation. *KQ* is copied by two scribes, the first of whom finished his stint at line 1239. There are textual obscurities at several points in the stints of both scribes, probably reflecting transmissional complexities of various kinds: this copy was made many years after the composition of the poem, by scribes who did not share (and at times may not have understood) the dialect of its author. There are some emendations in the present edition (all indicated in the textual and explanatory notes), but on the whole I have attempted to make sense of the text as it is copied. Expansion of contracted forms in the manuscript has posed some difficulty, particularly in respect of words like 'my^t' and 'tho^t' which the scribes write variously in uncontracted form as both 'mycht'/'myght' and 'thocht'/'thoght'. I have in general opted for the -gh expansion.

TEXTUAL NOTES

27 poleyt] poetly	91 maid a cros] maid a +
29 thogh] tho^t	108 lakkit] lak
40 thir] their	130 nine] ix
51 eyen] eyne	142 brode] brede

192	he me more] he more	978	Nald] Wald
230–31	Transposed	1034	that] it
341	lo] to	1053	I] he
392	twenti] xx^{ti}	1117	remewis] supplied
402	he] sche	1154	thoght] supplied
421	sche] he	1210	waking] walking
531	am caryit] ane cryit	1212	Towert] Couert
745	aspectis] effectis	1279	thus] this
746	effectis] aspectis	1307	flour] flouris
747	othes byndand] otheres bynd &	1318	glitteren] glateren
751	by] supplied	1322	exilte] exilkee
770	prese] peres	1323	quhele] quhile
775	that] than	1324	in lufe] and lufe
813	stynt in] stynten	1366	fatall] fotall
836	or] supplied	1370	thank] think; lif] supplied
940/942	Transposed		

FURTHER READING

Skeat (James I 1911), Mackay Mackenzie (James I 1939), Norton-Smith (James I 1971, repr. 1981), McDiarmid (James I 1973), and Jack and Rozendaal (1997: 17–56) offer annotated editions of the whole text. Bawcutt and Riddy (1987: 25–42) include extracts with valuable notes. The manuscript is available in a facsimile (Boffey and Edwards 1997), and the language of *KQ* is discussed by Jeffery (1978) and by Boffey and Edwards (1999). Biographies of James I include Balfour-Melville (1936) and Brown (1994). Petrina (1997) is a recent book-length study; Scheps and Looney (1986) list bibliography up to 1976.

Aspects of the poem are explored in many articles: Ebin (1974) (and more briefly in 1988: 50–5), Scheps (1971), and Carretta (1981) discuss its use of other texts; Preston (1956) and Quinn (1980–1) comment on the unity of the poem in relation to Fortune and processes of memory; Boffey (1991) and Spearing (2000) explore the image of the poet as prisoner and *KQ*'s relationship to *LR*; Miskimin (1977) and MacQueen (1988) discuss patterning in *KQ*; Mapstone (1997) suggests possible political readings.

Herefter followis the quair maid be King James
of Scotland the first callit the kingis quair and
maid quhen his majeste wes in Ingland

fo. 192^r

Heigh in the hevynnis figure circulere
The rody sterres twynklyng as the fyre;
And in Aquary, Citherea the clere
Rynsid hir tressis like the goldin wyre,
That late tofore in faire and fresche atyre   5
Through Capricorn heved hir hornis bright
North northward; approchit the mydnyght,

Quhen as I lay in bed allone waking,
New partit out of slepe a lyte tofore,
Fell me to mynd of mony diverse thing,   10
Off this and that—can I noght say quharfore—
Bot slepe for craft in erth myght I no more,

---

1 *hevynnis*: heavens. *figure circulere*: dome. This line is repeated at 1372.

2 *rody*: reddish. This line is a present participle clause, characteristic of the style of the poem, in which *twynklyng* can be understood as 'were twinkling'.

3 Aquarius: between 11 January and 10 February, acc. to McDiarmid (James I 1973); 21 January–18 February acc. to Norton-Smith (James I 1981). Cf. *PF* 113–19, where Venus is invoked as the inspiration of a philosophical dream about love. Some editors, following Skeat (James I 1911), would here emend *Citherea* to *Cinthia*, the moon, conventionally referred to as horned, but the horns of line 6 may, as Norton-Smith (James I 1981) suggests, be imagined as the 'horns' of a headdress. Cf. *TG* 8 n.

4 *Rynsid*: washed, rinsed. *wyre*: wire. The *goldin wyre* is a conventional image; cf. *TG* 271, and, for a long list of examples, the note to this line in Schick's edition (Lydgate 1891).

5 *late tofore*: a little before. *atyre*: clothing, headdress.

6 *Capricorn*: the zodiacal sign of Capricorn. *heved*: heaved, carried.

7 *North northward*: moving northward. *Approchit*: close to; cf. *PF* 117. Venus has changed from an evening to a morning star in her passage through Capricorn and Aquarius (the water-carrier) in January and February. These details correspond to the planetary conjunctions early in 1424, the year of James's marriage and release.

8 *Quhen*: when.   9 *New partit*: recently awakened.   *a lyte tofore*: a little before.

10 *Fell me to mynd*: there came to my mind (thoughts).   *mony*: many.

11 *can I noght say quharfore*: I can't say why.

12 *for craft in erth*: by any means on earth.

For quhiche as tho coude I no better wyle
Bot toke a boke to rede apon a quhile;

Off quhiche the name is clepit properly   15
Boece, efter him that was the compiloure,
Schewing counsele of Philosophye,
Compilit by that noble senatoure
Off Rome, quhilom that was the warldis floure,
And from estate by fortune a quhile   20
Forjugit was to povert in exile.

And thereto, here, this worthy lord and clerk,
His metir swete full of moralitee,
His flourit pen so fair he set awerk,
Descryving first of his prosperitee,   25
And out of that his infelicitee,
And than how he, in his poleyt report,
In philosophy can him to confort.

13 *For quhiche*: therefore.   *as tho*: then, on that occasion.   *coude*: knew.   *wyle*: strata-
gem. The reading of a book as a prelude to a dream follows Chaucerian precedents in *BD*
44–9 and *PF* 17–21.
14 *quhile*: while.   15 *clepit*: called.
16 *Boece*: Boethius (*c.*480–*c.*525), a Roman public servant and consul whose philosophical treatise on fortune, *De consolatione Philosophiae* (see Stewart and Rand (Boethius 1918,
repr. 1968); Watts (Boethius 1969, repr. 1976)), was widely known in the Middle Ages. It
was translated into English prose by Chaucer as *Boece*, and into English verse in 1410 by
John Walton (1925). For further discussion, see Intro., pp. 2–3. *efter*: after.   *compiloure*:
author.
17 *counsele*: advice.   *Philosophye*: the personified 'Philosophy', who advises Boethius
in his misfortune.
19 *quhilom*: once.   *the warldis floure*: flower, ornament of the world.
20 *estate*: prosperity, high rank.   *a quhile*: for a time.
21 *Forjugit*: condemned; charged with opposing the Roman ruler Theodoric, Boethius
was imprisoned and put to death in Pavia in Lombardy.
22 *thereto*: with that.   *here*: here (in this book).
23 *metir swete*: delightful poetical lines.
24 Set his rhetorically eloquent pen so beautifully to work (Boethius's *De cons* is,
strictly, a prosimetry, in which verse and prose are mixed).
25 *Descryving*: describing.   26 *out of*: after.   *infelicitee*: misfortune.
27 *poleyt*: polished, elegant.   28 *can him to confort*: took comfort.

For quhich, thogh I in purpose at my boke
To borowe a slepe at thilke tyme began,   30
Or ever I stent, my best was more to loke
Upon the writing of this noble man,
That in himself the full recover wan
Off his infortune, povert and distresse,
And in tham set his verray sekernesse.   35

fo. 192ᵛ   And so the vertew of his youth before
Was in his age the ground of his delytis.
Fortune the bak him turnyt, and therfore
He makith joye and confort that he quit is
Off thir unsekir warldis appetitis.   40
And so aworth he takith his penance,
And of his vertew maid it suffisance,

With mony a noble resoun, as him likit,
Enditing in his faire Latyne tong,
So full of fruyte and rethorikly pykit,   45
Quhich to declare my scole is over yong;
Therfore I lat him pas, and in my tong
Procede I will agayn to my sentence
Of my mater, and leve all incidence.

The long nyght beholding, as I saide,   50
Myn eyen gan to smert for studying.
My buke I schet and at my hede it laide,

29–30 Although I intended at that time to obtain sleep from my book (i.e. to use it to get to sleep).
   31 Before I stopped, (I thought) my best (course) was to look further.
   33 *recover*: recovery. *wan*: won.   35 *verray sekernesse*: true security.
   39 *quit*: freed.   40 *thir*: those. *unsekir*: unstable. *warldis*: world's.
   41 *aworth he takith*: he patiently bears.   42 *suffisance*: wealth, satisfaction.
   43 *as him likit*: as it pleased him.   44 *Enditing*: composing.
   45 *rethorikly pykit*: rhetorically adorned.
   46 *my scole is over yong*: my learning is too immature.
   47 *pas*: go. *tong*: (own) language. The matter of *De cons* is summarized as far as Boethius's discussion of virtuous stoicism. The author of *KQ* uses Boethius's circumstances and philosophy as a point of departure, but proceeds to narrate a history with a different shape and a different resolution.
   48 *sentence*: subject.   49 *incidence*: incidental matter.
   50 *beholding*: gazing (at my book)/reading.   52 *schet*: shut.

And doun I lay but ony tarying,
This mater new in my mynd rolling:
This is to seyne, how that eche estate   55
As Fortune lykith thame will translate.

For sothe it is, that on hir tolter quhele
Every wight cleverith in his stage,
And failyng foting oft, quhen hir lest rele—
Sum up, sum doun—is none estate nor age   60
Ensured, more the prynce than the page;
So uncouthly hir werdes sche devidith,
Namly in youth, that seildin ought providith.

Among thir thoughtis rolling to and fro
Fell me to mynd of my fortune and ure: 65
In tender youth how sche was first my fo
And eft my frende, and how I gat recure
Off my distresse; and all myn aventure
I gan ourhayle, that langer slepe ne rest
Ne myght I nat, so were my wittis wrest.   70

193^r   Forwakit and forwalowit, thus musing,
Wery forlyin, I lestnyt sodaynlye,

---

53 *but ony tarying*: without any delay.
54 *new*: afresh. *rolling*: turning over.   55 *seyne*: say. *estate*: rank.
56 *thame will translate*: will change them.
57 *sothe it is*: truly. *hir tolter quhele*: her unsteady wheel. For other depictions of Fortune's wheel, cf. *De cons* II, pr. 2; *LR* 403 ff.; and for the iconography see Patch 1927 and Courcelle 1967, plates 65 ff.
58 *wight*: person. *cleverith*: clambers. *stage*: apportioned place.
59 *failyng foting*: losing (their) footing. *quhen hir lest rele*: when she is pleased to turn.
61 *Ensured*: secure. This line echoes parts of *Kn T, CT* I. 922–6, 3030.
62 *uncouthly*: strangely. *hir werdes sche devidith*: she shares out her lots.
63 *seildin*: seldom. *ought providith*: foresees anything.
65 *ure*: luck. The narrator reviews the shape of his own past life, in which—unlike Boethius—he has been 'translated' from misfortune to prosperity.
67 *gat recure*: recovered.   68 *aventure*: fortune.
69 *gan ourhayle*: reconsidered. *langer*: longer.   70 *wrest*: troubled.
71 *Forwakit and forwalowit*: tired out with wakefulness, and exhausted from tossing and turning (this and the following line perhaps echo of *The Man of Law's Tale, CT* II. 596–7).
72 *Wery forlyin*: weary from lying in bed. *lestnyt*: listened. *sodaynlye*: suddenly.

And sone I herd the bell to matyns ryng,
And up I rase, no langer wald I lye.
Bot now, how trowe ye? swich a fantasye   75
Fell me to mynd that ay me thoght the bell
Said to me: 'Tell on, man, quhat the befell.'

Thoght I tho to my self: 'Quhat may this be?
This is myn awin ymagynacioun;
It is no lyf that spekis unto me.   80
It is a bell, or that impressioun
Off my thoght causith this illusioun
That dooth me think so nycely in this wise.'
And so befell as I schall you devise.

Determyt furth therewith in myn entent,   85
Sen I thus have ymagynit of this soun,
And in my tyme more ink and paper spent
To lyte effect, I tuke conclusioun
Sum newe thing to write. I set me doun,
And furthwithall my pen in hand I tuke   90
And maid a cros, and thus begouth my buke.

---

73 *sone*: soon. *matyns*: midnight matins. The first verse of midnight matins is *Domine labia mea aperies et os meum annunciabit laudem tuum*: 'Lord thou will open my lips and my mouth will publish thy praise', Psalm 50: 15, which seems to anticipate the command at line 77; see McDiarmid (James I 1973: 119). The striking bell in *BD* 1322–3, which serves to wake the dreamer, also prompts him to write.

74 *rase*: rose. *langer*: longer. *wald*: would.

75 *how trowe ye*: can you believe it? *swich a fantasye*: such an imagining.

76 *Fell me to mynd*: came to my mind. *ay me thoght*: it seemed to me continuously.

77 *quhat the befell*: what happened to you.   78 *tho*: then.

79 *awin*: own.   80 *lyf*: (living) person.

81–2 *impressioun* | *Off my thoght*: the working of my imagination.

83 *dooth me think*: causes me to think. *nycely*: foolishly. *in this wise*: in this way.

84 *devise*: relate.

85 At that, settled straightway in my intention   86 *Sen*: since. *soun*: sound.

88 *lyte*: little. *tuke conclusioun*: decided.

90 *furthwithall*: forthwith. *tuke*: took.

91 *maid a cros*: drew (the sign of) a cross (or possibly 'crossed myself': scribes often began their copy of a text with a cross, and teaching alphabets opened with the sign of a cross before the letter 'a'; see further the notes to this line in Norton-Smith (James I 1981), and Skeat (James I 1911)). What begins here is effectively a book within a book: the narrator of the poem retells within it his composition of a 'book' recounting his prison-dream. *begouth*: began. *buke*: book.

Thou youth, of nature indegest,
Unrypit fruyte with windis variable;
Like to the bird that fed is on the nest
And can noght flee, of wit wayke and unstable;   95
To fortune both and to infortune hable,
Wist thou thy payne to cum and thy travaille,
For sorow and drede wele myght thou wepe and waille.

Thus stant thy confort in unsekirnesse,
And wantis it that suld the reule and gye: 100
Ryght as the schip that sailith stereles
Upon the rok most to harmes hye,
For lak of it that suld bene hir supplye,
So standis thou here in this warldis rage,
And wantis that suld gyde all thy viage.   105

193ᵛ   I mene this by my self as in partye:
Though Nature gave me suffisance in youth,

---

92 *indegest*: confused, unready.

92–105 The address to 'youth' (beginning with an unmetrical line which some editors have been tempted to emend) confirms the poem's focus on past experience, and its concern with the acquisition of philosophical wisdom, through time and through the workings of reason and imagination.

93 (at the mercy of) variable winds, (like) unripened fruit.

95 *flee*: fly.   *wayke*: weak.   96 *fortune*: (good) fortune.   *hable*: liable.

97 *Wist thou*: if you knew.   *travaille*: labour.

98 For Chaucerian precedents to the conjunction of weeping and wailing, see *Cl T*, *CT* IV. 1212, and *Mer T*, *CT* IV. 1213.

99 *stant*: stands.   *unsekirnesse*: instability.

100 And you lack whatever should rule and guide you.

101 *Ryght as*: just like.   *stereles*: rudderless. This line introduces the ancient topos of the ship, to be used from 101–68 (and implicitly elsewhere in the poem) with flexible and telling effect. For a general survey of its history, see Curtius 1953: 128–30, and for specific comparisons, Boethius, *De cons* I, m. 5, and *TC* II. 1–7.

102 *most to harmes hye*: must hasten to dangers.

103 For the lack of what should help her.

104 *this warldis rage*: the storm of worldly life.

105 And lack what should guide all your journey.

106 *by my self*: with reference to myself.   *in partye*: in part.

107 *suffisance*: wealth, sufficiency. In line with the various medieval schemes for dividing the human life-span into different ages (on which see Burrow 1988a), the narrator here seems to be distinguishing between innocent and unguided 'youth' (which could comprehend infancy, childhood, adolescence, and young manhood) and a time of life governed by

The rypenesse of resoun lakkit I
To governe with my will, so lyte I couth
Quhen stereles to travaile I begouth,   110
Amang the wawis of this warld to drive,
And how the case anon I will discrive.

With doutfull hert, amang the rokkis blake
My feble bote full fast to stere and rowe,
Helples, allone, the wynter nyght I wake,   115
To wayte the wynd that furthward suld me throwe.
O empti saile, quhare is the wynd suld blowe
Me to the port, quhare gynneth all my game?
Help, Calyope, and wynd, in Marye name!

The rokkis clepe I the prolixitee   120
Off doubilnesse that doith my wittis pall.
The lak of wynd is the deficultee,
In enditing of this lytill trety small.
The bote I clepe the mater hole of all;
My wit, unto the saile that now I wynd   125
To seke connyng, though I bot lytill fynd.

At my begynnyng first I clepe and call
To yow, Cleo, and to yow, Polymye,

reason. Some schemes located the start of this period at the age of 30, the approximate age
of James I at his release and marriage.

109 *To governe with*: with which to govern.   *so lyte I couth*: so little I knew.
110 *to travaile I begouth*: I began to travel.   111 *Amang*: among. *wawis*: waves.
112 *how the case*: how events turned out. *anon*: immediately. *discrive*: describe.
113 *doutfull*: fearfull.   114 *full*: very.   115 *wake*: remain awake.
116 *wayte*: await. *furthward*: forward. *throwe*: drive.   117 *quhare*: where.
118 *gynneth*: begins. *game*: joy.
119 *Calyope*: Calliope, muse of epic poetry. *in Marye name*: in the name of Mary (cf.
HF 1400). The boat on which James I was travelling to France was named the *Maryen-knyght* (Brown 1994: 17).
120 *clepe*: call.   120–1 *prolixitee | Off doubilnesse*: deceitful prolixity.
121 *doith my wittis pall*: makes dull my wits.   122 *deficultee*: difficulty.
123 *enditing*: composing. *trety*: treatise, poem.   124 *mater hole*: whole subject.
125 *wynd*: turn.   126 *seke*: seek. *connyng*: skill.   127 *clepe*: cry out.
128 Clio, muse of history, is invoked by Chaucer in *TC* II. 8–9, and Polyhymnia, muse
of sacred song, in Chaucer's *A & A*, 15.

With Thesiphone, goddis and sistris all,
In nowmer nine, as bokis specifye; 130
In this processe my wilsum wittis gye,
And with your bryght lanternis wele convoye
My pen, to write my turment and my joye!

194ʳ In ver, that full of vertu is and gude,
Quhen Nature first begynneth hir enprise, 135
That quhilum was be cruell frost and flude
And schouris scharp opprest in mony wyse,
And Synthius gynneth to aryse
Heigh in the est amorow, soft and swete,
Upward his course to drive in Ariete— 140

Passit, bot mydday, foure greis evin,
Off lenth—and brode his angel wingis bryght
He spred upon the ground doun fro the hevin,
That for gladnesse and confort of the sight,
And with the tiklyng of his hete and light, 145
The tender flouris opnyt thame and sprad
And in thair nature thankit him for glad.

129–30 *goddis*: gods. *nowmer*: number. Tisiphone is one of the Furies (invoked in *TC* I. 6–11), although here she is apparently assumed to be one of the nine muses, or a relation.

131 *processe*: account. *wilsum*: wandering. *gye*: guide. 132 *convoye*: direct.

134 *ver*: spring. *vertu*: power (of growth). James's sea-journey and capture took place in March, but spring is also the season commonly linked with youth; cf. MacCracken's edition of Lydgate's *Testament*, 278–394 (Lydgate 1911: 329–62).

135 *enprise*: undertaking. 136 *quhilum*: formerly. *be*: by.

137 *mony wyse*: many ways. 138 *Synthius*: Cynthius, the sun. *gynneth*: begins.

139 *amorow*: in the morning.

140 *Upward*: northward. *in Ariete*: in the zodiacal sign of Aries.

141–2 *Passit*: past. *bot*: only by. *foure greis evin*: | *Off lenth*: exactly four degrees of longitude. For the most convincing explanation of this difficult passage, see Bawcutt and Riddy 1987: 317. Lines 141–2 are here taken to identify the date—16 March 1406, the day on which the sun reached four degrees of Aries in longitude by midday. *brode*: wide.

143 *fro*: from. 144 *That*: so that. 145 *tiklyng*: light touch.

146 *opnyt thame*: opened themselves. *sprad*: spread.

147 *for glad*: for joy.

Noght ferre passit the state of innocence,
Bot nere about the nowmer of yeris thre—
Were it causit throu hevinly influence   150
Off goddys will, or othir casualtee,
Can I noght say—bot out of my contree,
By thair avise that had of me the cure,
Be see to pas tuke I myn aventure.

Purvait of all that was us necessarye,   155
With wind at will, up airly by the morowe,
Streight unto schip, no longer wald we tarye,
The way we tuke—the tyme I tald toforowe—
With mony 'fare wele' and 'sanct Johne to borowe'
Off falowe and frende, and thus with one assent 160
We pullit up saile and furth oure wayis went.

Upon the wavis weltering to and fro,
So infortunate was us that fremyt day
That, maugre playnly quhethir we wold or no,
With strong hand, by fors, schortly to say,   165
Off inymyis takin and led away
We weren all, and broght in thair contree:
Fortune it schupe non othir wayis to be.

---

148 *Noght ferre passit*: not far past.
149 *nere about*: around. The first seven years of life constituted the age of innocence (see Burrow 1988*a*). James locates his journey and capture 'about three years' beyond this state; in March 1406 he was 11.
151 *casualtee*: contingency.   153 *avise*: advice.   *cure*: charge.
154 *Be see*: by sea.   *aventure*: chance.   155 *Purvait of*: provided with.
156 *at will*: as desired.   *airly by the morowe*: early in the morning.
157 *wald we tarye*: would we delay.   158 *the tyme . . . toforowe*: as I said before.
159 *sanct Johne to borowe*: St John be your protection (a phrase of leave-taking; cf. *LR* 698).
160 *falowe*: companion.   *with one assent*: united.   161 *furth*: forth.
162 *weltering*: rolling.
163–4 That unfriendly day was so unfortunate for us that, utterly regardless of whether or not we wished it.
165 *schortly to say*: to put it briefly.   166 *inymyis*: enemies.
168 *schupe*: contrived.

Quhare as in strayte ward and in strong prisoun,
So ferforth of my lyf the hevy lyne—   170
Without confort, in sorowe abandoun—
The secund sistir lukit hath to twyne
Nere by the space of yeris twise nyne,
Till Jupiter his merci list advert
And send confort in relesche of my smert.   175

194^v

Quhare as in ward full oft I wold bewaille
My dedely lyf, full of peyne and penance,
Saing ryght thus: 'Quhat have I gilt, to faille
My fredome in this warld and my plesance?
Sen every wight has thereof suffisance   180
That I behold, and I, a creature,
Put from all this, hard is myn aventure!

'The bird, the beste, the fisch eke in the see,
They lyve in fredome, everich in his kynd,
And I a man, and lakkith libertee!   185
Quhat schall I seyne? Quhat resoun may I fynd
That fortune suld do so?' Thus in my mynd

169 *Quhare as*: where.   *in strayte ward*: under strict guard.
170 *So ferforth*: henceforward.   *hevy lyne*: sad thread.
171 *abandoun*: wholly given over to.
172 *The secund sistir*: Lachesis, second of the three Fates, charged with spinning the thread of life.   *lukit hath to twyne*: has taken care to spin.
173 Around the length of twice nine years (James was captured in 1406, and married and released in February 1424, after a captivity of eighteen years).
174 *Jupiter*: Traditionally held to be benevolent as a planetary deity, Jupiter was known as 'Fortuna major'.   *list advert*: was pleased to direct.
175 *relesche*: release.   *smert*: suffering.   177 *dedely*: deathly.
178 *gilt*: done wrong.   *faille*: lose.   179 *plesance*: happiness.
179–87 Together with 190–6, these lines effectively constitute a condensed prisoner's lament, putting questions familiar from Boethius, *De cons*, and other Boethian texts; see Boffey 1991.
180 *Sen*: since.   182 *aventure*: chance.
184 *everich in his kynd*: each according to its nature.
185 *lakkith libertee*: liberty is wanting.
186 *seyne*: say.

My folk I wold argewe, bot all for noght:
Was non that myght that on my peynes rought.

Than wold I say: 'Gif God me had devisit   190
To lyve my lyf in thraldome thus and pyne,
Quhat was the cause that he me more comprisit
Than othir folk to lyve in swich ruyne?
I suffere allone amang the figuris nyne,
Ane wofull wrecche that to no wight may spede,   195
And yit of eviry lyvis help hath nede!'

The long dayes and the nyghtis eke
I wold bewaille my fortune in this wise,
For quhich, agane distresse confort to seke,
My custum was on mornis for to ryse   200
Airly as day—O happy exercise,
By the come I to joye out of turment!—
Bot now to purpose of my first entent:

Bewailing in my chamber thus allone,
Despeired of all joye and remedye,   205
Fortirit of my thought and wobegone,
And to the wyndow gan I walk in hye
To se the warld and folk that went forby;
As for the tyme, though I of mirthis fude
Myght have no more, to luke it did me gude.   210

188 *argewe*: question. The 'folk' were James's attendants during his imprisonment, for details of whom see Brown 1994: 17–19.
189 *that myght*: who could do anything about it.   *rought*: had pity.
190 *Gif*: granted that.   *devisit*: designed.
191 *thraldome*: imprisonment.   *pyne*: suffering.
192 *comprisit*: destined.   193 *ruyne*: misery.
194 *figuris nyne*: nine numerals (the comparison is with a zero or cipher, which lacks all value except when associated with other numerals).
195 *spede*: be of use.   196 *eviry lyvis*: everyone's.   197 *eke*: also.
198 *in this wise*: in this way.   199 *agane*: against.
201 *Airly*: early.   *exercise*: habit.
202 *By the*: through you.   *come I*: I came.   203 *entent*: design.
204 Cf. *TC* I. 547, 'Bywayling in his chambre thus allone'.
206 *Fortirit of*: exhausted by.   207 *gan I walk*: I walked.   *in hye*: in haste.
208 *forby*: past.
209 *As for the tyme*: for the moment.   *mirthis fude*: food of happiness.

o. 195^r

Now was there maid fast by the touris wall
A gardyn faire, and in the corneris set
Ane herbere grene, with wandis long and small
Railit about; and so with treis set
Was all the place, and hawthorn hegis knet,   215
That lyf was none walking there forby
That myght within scarse ony wight aspye.

So thik the bewis and the leves grene
Beschadit all the aleyes that there were;
And myddis every herbere myght be sene   220
The scharp grene swete jenepere,
Growing so faire with branchis here and there
That, as it semyt to a lyf without,
The bewis spred the herber all about.

And on the small grene twistis sat   225
The lytill swete nyghtingale, and song
So loud and clere the ympnis consecrat
Off lufis use, now soft, now lowd among,

211 *maid*: constructed. *fast by*: close to. *touris wall*: wall of the tower. The prisoner's
first sight of his lady in a May-time garden, in which she appears as a 'floure' (277), recalls
Kn T, *CT* I. 1033–79. The garden itself is imagined as divided by means of intersecting
paths into four arbours, one in each corner. Juniper trees grow up from the centre of
each arbour, and their overspreading branches meet across the paths. Cf. the garden
described in *AL* 1–70, and (in terms of the shady privacy described in 214–19), *Romaunt* B.
1391–400.

212 *in the corneris set*: in (each of) the corners was made.

213 *herbere*: arbour. *wandis*: palings. *small*: delicate.

215 *hegis*: hedges. *knet*: joined together.   218 *bewis*: boughs.

219 *Beschadit*: shaded.   220 *myddis*: in the middle of.

221 *jenepere*: juniper.   223 *without*: outside.   225 *twistis*: branches.

225–38 Harmonious birdsong is a common feature of dream gardens; cf. *RR* 494–508;
PF 190–2; Clanvowe, *The Boke of Cupide* (Scattergood 1975), 69–75; Dunbar, *The Golden
Targe* (Bawcutt and Riddy 1987: 205–14), 19–21. The birds are often envisaged as choirs of
clerks, singing love's 'service' or 'liturgy', as in the influential French poem by Baudouin
de Condé, *La messe des oiseaux* (ed. Schèler 1866–7).

226 *nyghtingale*: nightingales. *song*: sang.

227–8 *ympnis consecrat | Off lufis use*: the sacred hymns of love's service. *among*: at
times.

That all the gardyng and the wallis rong
Off thaire swete armony; and lo the text   230
Ryght of their song, and on the copill next:

'Worschippe, ye that loveris bene, this May,
For of your blisse the kalendis ar begonne,
And sing with us, "Away, winter, away!
Cum, somer, cum, the swete sesoun and sonne!"   235
Awake, for schame, that have your hevynnis wonne,
And amorously lift up your hedis all!
Thank Lufe that list yow to his merci call.'

Quhen thai this song had song a lytill thrawe
Thai stent a quhile, and therewith, unaffraid,   240
As I beheld and kest myn eyne alawe,
From beugh to beugh thay hippit and thai plaid,
And freschly in thair birdis kynd arraid
Thair fetheris new, and fret thame in the sonne,
And thankit Lufe that had thair makis wonne.   245

230 *armony*: harmony.

230–1 In the MS, these lines are transposed; the emendation adopted here is that proposed by Bawcutt 1987.

231 *Ryght*: precisely. *copill*: stanza.

232 *ye that loveris bene*: you who are lovers.

232–8 Interpolated songs are common in 14th- and 15th-c. courtly narratives, in English and in other European vernaculars. The special status of the song here is signalled by a scribal note of 'cantus' next to line 232. A song welcoming summer occurs in *PF* 680–92 (and cf. the brief quotation in *LGWP* F170).

233 Cf. *TC* II. 7, 'But now of hope the kalendes bygynne'.

233 *kalendis*: first days.

236 *that have*: (you) who have. *hevynnis*: heavens (i.e. blissful mates).

238 *that list*: whom it pleases.   239 *a lytill thrawe*: for a short time.

239–52 The birds' behaviour seems designed to throw into relief the imprisoned spectator's solitude and inactivity. The stanzas which follow develop the network of images concerning imprisonment and liberation which tie together the literal events of the narrative and its philosophical themes. The ideas and their presentation draw on Boethian traditions and on an ancient topos of love as imprisonment; see Ebin 1974, Leyerle 1974, and Boffey 1991.

240 *stent*: stopped.   241 *kest myn eyne alawe*: looked downwards.

242 *beugh*: bough. *hippit*: hopped.

243 *in thair birdis kynd*: in their birds' way. *arraid*: arranged.

244 *fret thame*: preened themselves.   245 *makis*: mates.

195^v

This was the plane ditee of thair note,
And therwithall unto my self I thought,
'Quhat lyf is this, that makis birdis dote?
Quhat may this be? How cummyth it of ought?
Quhat nedith it to be so dere ybought?   250
It is nothing, trowe I, bot feynit chere,
And that men list to counterfeten chere.'

Eft wald I think: 'O Lord, quhat may this be,
That Lufe is of so noble myght and kynde,
Lufing his folk? And swich prosperitee   255
Is it of him as we in bukis fynd?
May he oure hertes setten and unbynd?
Hath he upon oure hertis swich maistrye,
Or all this is bot feynyt fantasye?

For gif he be of so grete excellence   260
That he of every wight hath cure and charge,
Quhat have I gilt to him or doon offense,
That I am thrall and birdis gone at large,
Sen him to serve he myght set my corage?
And gif he be noght so, than may I seyne,   265
Quhat makis folk to jangill of him in veyne?

Can I nought elles fynd bot gif that he
Be lord, and as a god may lyve and regne,
To bynd and louse and maken thrallis free,
Than wold I pray his blisfull grace benigne '   270
To hable me unto his service digne,

246 *plane*: clear.   *ditee*: text.   *note*: music.
248 *lyf*: manner of life.   *dote*: act foolishly.   249 *of ought*: from anything.
250 Why must it be so dearly bought?
251 *feynit chere*: deceitfulness. The identical rhymes in 251–2 suggest some scribal corruption; *chere* in 252 could reasonably be emended to *here*.
252 And (caused by the fact) that it pleases people to dissemble their feelings.
253 *Eft*: then.   *wald*: would.   254 *kynde*: nature.   255 *swich*: such.
256 *of him*: from him.   257 *setten*: fix.   258 *maistrye*: mastery.
259 *feynyt fantasye*: false imagining.   261 *cure*: care.
262 *gilt*: done wrong.   263 *thrall*: prisoner.   *gone*: go.
264 *Sen*: since.   *set my corage*: direct my heart.
266 *jangill*: talk idly.   267 I cannot conclude otherwise than that if.
269 *louse*: unloose.   271 *hable me unto*: fit me for.   *digne*: worthy.

And evermore for to be one of tho
Him trewly for to serve in wele and wo.'

And therwith kest I doun myn eye ageyne,
Quhare as I saw walking under the toure,   275
Full secretly new cummyn hir to pleyne,
The fairest or the freschest yong floure
That ever I sawe, me thoght, before that houre;
For quhich sodayne abate anone astert
The blude of all my body to my hert.   280

fo. 196ʳ   And though I stude abaisit tho a lyte,
No wonder was, forquhy my wittis all
Were so overcom with plesance and delyte,
Onely throu latting of myn eyen fall,
That sudaynly my hert become hir thrall   285
For ever, of free wyll, for of manace
There was no takyn in hir swete face.

And in my hede I drewe ryght hastily,
And eftsones I lent it forth ageyne
And sawe hir walk, that verray womanly,   290
With no wight mo bot onely women tweyne.
Than gan I studye in my self and seyne:
'A, swete, ar ye a warldly creature,
Or hevinly thing in liknesse of nature?

276 *new cummyn*: newly arrived.   *hir to pleyne*: to amuse herself.
279 *abate*: casting down (*abate*, from ME *abaten*, can be variously glossed as 'faintness', 'shock', or (as here) 'casting down' (of the eyes)).   *astert*: escaped.
281 *abaisit*: abashed.   *tho*: then.   *a lyte*: a little.
282 *No wonder was*: it was not surprising.   *forquhy*: because.
284 *latting*: letting.   *eyen*: eyes.   286 *manace*: threat.   287 *takyn*: token.
289 *eftsones*: immediately.   *lent*: leaned.
290 *verray womanly*: truly feminine being; *womanly* here is an adjective used as a substantive; cf. 458, *that fair*, and instances in *TG* 577, and *TC* I. 458.
291 *mo*: more.   *tweyne*: two.   292 *studye*: deliberate.
293 *warldly*: earthly.
293–4 Cf. Palamon's words about Emelye in *Kn T, CT* I. 1101: 'I noot wher she be womman or goddesse', and Troilus's uncertainty about Criseyde: 'But wheither goddesse or womman, iwis, | She be, I not' (*TC* I. 425–6, and cf. I. 105). The topos has a long classical history, briefly sketched by Norton-Smith (James I 1981: 64).
294 *in liknesse of*: simulating.

'Or ar ye god Cupidis owin princesse,   295
And cummyn ar to louse me out of band?
Or ar ye verray Nature the goddesse,
That have depaynted with your hevinly hand
This gardyn full of flouris as they stand?
Quhat sall I think, allace, quhat reverence   300
Sall I minster to your excellence?

'Gif ye a goddesse be, and that ye like
To do me payne, I may it nought astert.
Gif ye be warldly wight that dooth me sike,
Quhy lest God mak you so, my derrest hert,   305
To do a sely presoner thus smert
That lufis yow all, and wote of noght bot wo?
And therfore, merci, swete, sen it is so.'

Quhen I a lytill thrawe had maid my moon,
Bewailling myn infortune and my chance,   310
Unknawin how or quhat was best to doon,
So ferre I fallyng into lufis dance
That sodeynly my wit, my contenance,
My hert, my will, my nature and my mynd,
Was changit clene ryght in anothir kynd.   315

196ᵛ   Off hir array the forme gif I sall write,
                Toward hir goldin hair and rich atyre,

---

295 Probably Venus, although in *LGWP* F.212–13, 'Cupidis owin princesse' is Alceste.

296 *cummyn ar*: have come.   *louse*: loosen.   *band*: bondage.

297 *verray*: truly. Nature appears also in *PF* 302 ff. See Economou 1972 for general discussion.

298 *depaynted*: painted.   301 *minster*: perform.   303 *astert*: escape.

304 *dooth me sike*: makes me sigh.

305 *Quhy lest God*: why does it please God.   *derrest*: dearest.

306 *To do smert*: to cause pain (to).   *sely*: miserable.

307 *all*: wholeheartedly.   *wote*: knows.   308 *sen*: since.

309 *thrawe*: while.   *moon*: complaint.   310 *infortune*: misfortune.

311 *Unknawin*: not knowing.   *doon*: do.

312 *lufis dance*: a term familar from *RR* (3936), and made current in ME by Chaucer: *Romaunt*, 4300; *TC* II. 553 and 1106; IV. 1431; *CT* I. 476.

313 *contenance*: demeanour.   316 *array*: clothing.   *forme*: style, fashion.

317 *Toward*: with regard to.   *atyre*: headdress.

In fret-wise couchit with perllis quhite
And grete balas lemyng as the fyre,
With mony ane emeraut and fair saphire,   320
And on hir hede a chaplet fresche of hewe,
Off plumys partit rede and quhite and blewe;

Full of quaking spangis bryght as gold,
Forgit of schap like to the amorettis,
So new, so fresch, so plesant to behold;   325
The plumys eke like to the flour jonettis
And othir of schap like to the flour jonettis,
And above all this there was, wele I wote,
Beautee eneuch to mak a world to dote.

About hir nek, quhite as the fyre amaille,   330
A gudely cheyne of smale orfeverye,
Quhareby there hang a ruby, without faille,
Lyke to ane hert schapin verily,
That as a sperk of lowe so wantounly
Semyt birnyng upon hir quhyte throte.   335
Now gif there was gud partye, God it wote!

318 Set with a fretwork of white pearls.

319 *balas*: spinel-rubies; on the associations of these jewels, see the notes to *LR* 345, 378, and *TG* 259–60; for the details of dress cf. also *AL* 528–36. *lemyng*: gleaming.

322 *plumys*: feathers. *partit*: divided. *quhite*: white.

323 *quaking spangis*: quivering spangles.

324 *Forgit of schap*: fashioned in shape. *amorettis*: loveknots.

326 *flour jonettis*: *jonettis*, from OF *jaunette*, 'yellow' (hence 'yellow flowers', pehaps St John's wort or water-lilies), may have been chosen for its punning allusion to the name of Joan Beaufort.

327 The repetition of *flour jonettis* is probably a scribal error (unless for special emphasis): editors have emended variously to *flour burnettis* (Norton-Smith in James I 1981); *round crokettis* (Skeat in James I 1911); *margarettis* (McDiarmid in James I 1973).

328 *wote*: know.   329 *eneuch*: sufficient. *dote*: act foolishly.

330 *quhite*: white. *fyre amaille*: gleaming enamel.

331 *gudely*: lovely. *smale*: delicate. *orfeverye*: goldsmith's work.

332 *Quhareby*: from which. *hang*: hung. *without faille*: truly.

333 *schapin*: shaped.   334 *lowe*: fire. *wantounly*: lightly.

335 *Semyt*: seemed (to be).

336 *partye*: perhaps 'match' (between the whiteness of the throat and the necklace), or (less plausibly) 'potential marriage partner'.

And for to walk that fresche Mayes morowe
An huke sche had upon hir tissew quhite,
That gudeliar had noght bene sene toforowe
As I suppose, and girt sche was a lyte,   340
Thus halflyng louse for haste; lo, swich delyte
It was to see hir youth in gudelihed,
That for rudenes to speke thereof I drede.

In hir was youth, beautee with humble aport,
Bountee, richesse and wommanly facture—   345
God better wote than my pen can report—
Wisdome, largesse, estate and connyng sure.
In every poynt so guydit hir mesure,
In word, in dede, in schap, in contenance,
That Nature myght no more hir childe avance.   350

197ʳ   Throw quhich anon I knew and understude
Wele that sche was a warldly creature,
On quhom to rest myn eye, so mich gude
It did my wofull hert, I yow assure,
That it was to me joye without mesure.   355
And at the last, my luke unto the hevin
I threwe furthwith, and said thir versis sevin:

'O Venus clere, of goddis stellifyit,
To quhom I yelde homage and sacrifise,
Fro this day forth your grace be magnifyit,   360

338 *huke*: cloak.   *tissew*: rich fabric.
339 *gudeliar*: better.   *toforowe*: before.   340 *girt*: girdled.   *a lyte*: lightly.
341 *halflyng louse*: half untied.   *swich delyte*: so delightful.
342 *gudelihed*: beauty.   343 *rudenes*: discourtesy.   344 *aport*: bearing.
345 *Bountee*: goodness   *facture*: form.
347 *largesse*: generosity.   *estate*: dignity.   *connyng sure*: sound understanding.
348 *so guydit hir mesure*: moderation so guided her.
350 *avance*: advance, perfect. Cf. *Phys T*, *CT* VI. 9–13.
352 *warldly*: earthly.   353 *mich*: much.   355 *without mesure*: immeasurable.
356 *at the last*: finally.   *luke*: gaze, eyes.   357 *versis*: (verse) lines.
358 *stellifyit*: made into stars. This statement of loyalty and prayer to Venus recalls
Palamon's dedication of his service to the goddess in *Kn T*, *CT* I. 1101–11.
359 *yelde*: give.

That me ressavit have in swich wise,
To lyve under your law and do servise.
Now help me furth, and for your merci lede
My hert to rest, that deis nere for drede.'

Quhen I with gude entent this orisoun   365
Thus endit had, I stynt a lytill stound,
And eft myn eye full pitously adoun
I kest, behalding unto hir lytill hound
That with his bellis playit on the ground.
Than wold I say, and sighe therewith a lyte: 370
'A, wele were him that now were in thy plyte!'

Anothir quhile the lytill nyghtingale
That sat apon the twiggis wold I chide,
And say ryght thus: 'Quhare ar thy notis smale
That thou of love has song this morowe tyde?   375
Seis thou nought hir that sittis the besyde?
For Venus sake, the blisfull goddesse clere,
Sing on agane and mak my lady chere.

And eke I pray, for all the paynes grete,
That for the love of Proigne, thy sistir dere,   380
Thou sufferit quhilom, quhen thy brestis wete
Were with the teres of thyne eyen clere
All bludy ronne—that pitee was to here

361 *ressavit*: received. *in swich wise*: in such a way.
363 *furth*: forward. *for*: because of.   364 *deis*: dies. *nere*: nearly.
365 *entent*: intentions. *orisoun*: prayer.   366 *stynt*: stopped. *stound*: while.
367 *eft*: then.   368 *behalding unto*: looking at.
371 It would be well with whoever were now in your situation.
372 *quhile*: time.   374 *smale*: thin, piping.   375 *morowe tyde*: morning.
376 *the besyde*: beside you.   378 *mak my lady chere*: welcome my lady.
380 *Proigne*: the story of Procne and Philomela is told by Ovid, *Metamorphoses* VI.
424 ff. Tereus raped Philomela, sister of his wife, Procne, and cut out her tongue to render
her silent, but she sewed the story into an embroidery which Procne understood.
Eventually all three were turned into birds: Procne into a swallow, Philomela into a
nightingale, and Tereus into a lapwing. Chaucer tells the story in *LGW* 2228–393, and cf.
Gower, *CA* V. 5551 ff., and *TG* 98.
381 *quhilom*: formerly.   383 *bludy ronne*: bloodshot.

The crueltee of that unknyghtly dede,
Quhare was fro the bereft thy maidenhede—   385

197^v

Lift up thyne hert and sing with gude entent,
And in thy notis swete the tresoun telle
That to thy sistir, trewe and innocent,
Was kythit by hir husband false and fell;
For quhois gilt, as it is worthy wel,   390
Chide thir husbandis that are false, I say,
And bid thame mend, in the twenti devil way!

O lytill wrecche, allace, maist thou nought se
Quho commyth yond? Is it now tyme to wring?
Quhat sory thought is fallin upon the?   395
Opyn thy throte! Hastow no lest to sing?
Allace, sen thou of resoun had felyng,
Now, swete bird, say ones to me "pepe".
I dee for wo, me think thou gynnis slepe!

Hastow no mynde of lufe? Quhare is thy make?   400
Or artow seke, or smyt with jelousye?
Or is he dede, or hath he the forsake?
Quhat is the cause of thy malancolye,
That thou no more list maken melodye?
Sluggart, for schame! Lo, here thy goldin hour   405
That worth were hale all thy lyvis laboure!

---

385 *fro the bereft*: stolen from you.   389 *kythit*: shown.   *fell*: violent.
390 *quhois*: whose.   *worthy wel*: very proper.   391 *thir*: these.
392 *mend*: amend.   *in the twenti devil way*: a common expression of impatience (lit. 'in the way of twenty devils') to be translated approximately as 'by all possible means'.
394 *yond*: yonder.   *wring*: lament.   396 *lest*: desire.
397 *of resoun*: rightfully.   *felyng*: the capacity to feel.
399 *dee*: die.   *thou gynnis slepe*: you are falling asleep.
400 *mynde*: thought.   *make*: mate.   401 *seke*: sick.   *smyt*: smitten.
402 *the forsake*: forsaken you.   *he*: the MS here reads 'sche', but since the nightingale has been addressed as Philomela it would appear to be female, and so to have a male lover.
404 *That thou no more list*: that it doesn't please you any more.
405 *Lo, here*: here is.   406 *worth were*: would be worth.   *hale*: completely.

Gyf thou suld sing wele ever in thy lyve,
Here is in fay the tyme and eke the space.
Quhat, wostow than sum bird may cum and stryve
In song with the, the maistry to purchace?   410
Suld thou then cesse? It were grete schame, allace.
And here, to wyn gree happily for ever,
Here is the tyme to syng, or ellis never.'

I thought eke thus: gif I my handis clap,
Or gif I cast, than will sche flee away;   415
And gif I hald me pes, than will sche nap;
And gif I crye, sche wate noght quhat I say.
Thus quhat is best wate I noght, be this day,
Bot blawe wynd, blawe, and do the levis schake,
That sum twig may wag and mak hir to wake!   420

fo. 198ʳ   With that anon ryght sche toke up a sang,
Quhare com anon mo birdis and alight.
Bot than to here the mirth was tham amang!
Over that to, to see the swete sicht
Off hyr ymage, my spirit was so light   425
Me thought I flawe for joy without arest,
So were my wittis boundin all to fest.

408 *in fay*: truly.   *space*: opportunity.
409 *wostow*: do you think.   *stryve*: contend.
409–10 There may be an echo here of the traditional strife between the nightingale and
the cuckoo, alluded to in Clanvowe's *Boke of Cupide* (Scattergood 1975), which is copied in
MS Arch. Selden. B. 24 with *KQ*.
410 *the maistry to purchace*: to win the upper hand.   411 *cesse*: stop.
412 *gree*: victory.
415 *cast*: throw a stone. In Clanvowe's *Boke of Cupide*, the narrator throws a stone at the
birds.
416 *hald me pes*: perhaps to be emended to *my pes*, although *pes* here may be an
adjectival form ('quiet').   *nap*: sleep.   417 *wate*: knows.   418 *be*: by.
419 *blawe*: blow.   *do*: make. These words are possibly the refrain or first line of a well-
known song.
420 *wag*: move.
421 *anon ryght*: immediately.   *sche*: see 402 n. and textual note.
422 *Quhare*: at which.   *com*: came.   *mo*: more.
423 (What a pleasure) to hear the joy they made!
424 *Over that to*: and beyond that.   426 *flawe*: flew.   *arest*: stop.
427 *boundin all to fest*: wholly captivated.

And to the notis of the Philomene
Quhilkis sche sang, the ditee there I maid,
Direct to hir that was my hertis quene,   430
Withoutin quhom no songis may me glade;
And to that sanct, walking in the schade,
My bedis thus with humble hert entere
Devotly I said on this manere:

'Quhen sall your merci rew upon your man,   435
Quhois service is yit uncouth unto yow,
Sen quhen ye go, there is noght ellis than?
Bot hert, quhere as the body may noght throu,
Folow thy hevin: quho suld be glad bot thou,
That swich a gyde to folow has undertake?   440
Were it throu hell, the way thou noght forsake!'

And efter this the birdis everichone
Tuke up anothir sang full loud and clere,
And with a voce said: 'Wele is us begone,
That with oure makis ar togider here.   445
We proyne and play without dout and dangere,
All clothit in a soyte full fresch and newe,
In lufis service besy, glad and trewe.

And ye, fresche May, ay mercifull to bridis,
Now welcum be ye, floure of monethis all.   450

428 *Philomene*: Philomela, the nightingale.
429 *Quhilkis*: which. *ditee*: song.   430 *Direct*: directed to.
431 *glade*: cheer. There is a discreet connection made here between fulfilment in love and literary creativity; cf. the composition of songs initiated at the end of *LR* (which like *KQ* may draw on the precedent of *BD*).
432 *sanct*: saint.   433 *bedis*: prayers.
434 The lady is made the object of quasi-religious devotion, conventional in love poetry.
435 *rew*: take pity.   436 *yit*: still. *uncouth*: unknown.
438-9 But heart, follow your heaven where the body may not pass.
441 *thou noght forsake*: do not give up.
444 *a voce*: one voice. *Wele is us begone*: things have happened well for us. The birds' several songs here recall the songs alluded to in *LGWP* F138-9, F145-7, F170.
446 *proyne*: preen. *dout*: fear.   447 *soyte*: livery, oufit.
449 *bridis*: birds.

For noght onely your grace upon us bydis,
Bot all the warld to witnes this we call,
That strowit hath so playnly over all
With new, fresche, swete and tender grene:
Oure lyf, oure lust, oure governoure, oure quene.'   455

This was thair song, as semyt me, full heye,
With full mony uncouth swete note and schill,
And therewithall that fair upward hir eye
Wold cast amang, as it was Goddis will,
Quhare I myght se, standing allone full still,   460
The fair facture that nature for maistrye
In hir visage wrought had full lufingly.

And quhen sche walkit had a lytill thrawe
Under the swete grene bewis bent,
Hir fair fresche face, as quhite as ony snawe,   465
Scho turnyt has and furth hir wayis went.
Bot tho began myn axis and turment:
To sene hir part and folowe I na myght,
Me thoght the day was turnyt into nyght.

Than said I thus: 'Quhareto lyve I langer,   470
Wofullest wicht and subject unto peyne?
Of peyne? No—God wote, ya! for thay no stranger
May wirken ony wight, I dare wele seyne.
How may this be, that deth and lyf, bothe tweyne,
Sall bothe atonis in a creature   475
Togidder dwell, and turment thus nature?

451 *upon us bydis*: remains with us.
453 *That strowit hath*: (you who) have strewn.
454 *grene*: greenery.   456 *full heye*: very loud.
457 *uncouth*: marvellous.   *schill*: shrill.   458 *fair*: fair (one).
459 *amang*: at times.   461 *facture*: features.   *for maistrye*: as a masterpiece.
466 *furth hir wayis went*: went on her way.   467 *axis*: fever.
468 To have seen her part (when) I could not follow.
469 A succinct example (cf. 479, 492–6) of the figure used in *BD* 599–615.
470 *Quhareto*: for what purpose.
472 *ya*: yes.   *stranger*: more strongly.   *thay* may be an unexpressed plural, *peynes* (see
the note to this line by Skeat in James I 1911).
473 *wirken*: afflict.   475 *atonis*: at once.

'I may noght ellis done bot wepe and waile,
Within thir cald wallis thus ilokin.
From hennsfurth my rest is my travaile;
My drye thrist with teris sall I slokin,   480
And on my self bene all my harmys wrokin.
Thus bute is none, bot Venus of hir grace
Will schape remede, or do my spirit pace.

As Tantalus I travaile ay butles
That ever ylike hailith at the well   485
Water to draw with buket botemles
And may noght spede, quhois penance is an hell.
So by my self this tale I may wele telle,
For unto hir that herith noght I pleyne,
Thus, like to him, my travaile is in veyne.'   490

99ʳ   So sore thus sighit I with my self allone
That turnyt is my strenth in febilnesse,
My wele in wo, my frendis all in fone,
My lyf in deth, my lyght into dirknesse,
My hope in feere, in dout my sekirnesse,   495
Sen sche is gone; and God mote hir convoye
That me may gyde to turment and to joye.

The long day thus gan I prye and pour,
Till Phebus endit had his bemes bryght

---

478 *cald*: cold.   *ilokin*: locked up.   479 *travaile*: labour, suffering.
480 *thrist*: thirst.   *slokin*: slake.   481 *harmys*: wrongs.   *wrokin*: avenged.
482 *bute*: remedy.   *bot*: unless.   483 *do . . . pace*: make . . . go.
484 *travaile*: toil.   *butles*: in vain. Tantalus was doomed to stand in a well from which
he could never drink (cf. *BD* 704–9).
487–8 suggest some confusion with the punishment given to the daughters of Danaus
(the Belides; see Ovid, *Metamorphoses* IV. 464–5), whose punishment was to try to fill with
water a jar with holes in it.
485 *ever ylike*: constantly.   *hailith*: draws.   487 *spede*: progress.
488 *by my self*: in relation to myself.   493 *fone*: enemies.
495 *dout*: uncertainty.   *sekirnesse*: security.
496 *God mote hir convoye*: may God go with her.   498 *prye*: peer.   *pour*: stare.
498–501 A similar transitional stanza in *PF* 99–105 marks the division between the
reading of Macrobius's *Commentary on the Dream of Scipio* and the dream which it inspires.
499 *Phebus*: the sun.

And bad go farewele every lef and flour;   500
This is to say, approch gan the nyght,
And Esperus his lampis gan to light,
Quhen in the wyndow, still as any stone,
I bade at lenth and kneling maid my mone.

So lang till evin, for lak of myght and mynd   505
Forwepit and forpleynit pitously,
Ourset so sorow had bothe hert and mynd,
That to the cold stone my hede on wrye
I laid, and lent amaisit verily,
Half sleping and half swoun, in swich a wise,   510
And quhat I met I will yow now devise:

Me thoght that thus all sodeynly a lyght
In at the wyndow come quhare that I lent,
Off quhich the chamber wyndow schone full bryght,
And all my body so it hath overwent,   515
That of my sicht the vertew hale iblent,
And that withall a voce unto me saide:
'I bring the confort and hele, be nought affrayde.'

And furth anon it passit sodeynly
Quhere it come in, the ryght way ageyne;   520

500 *bad go farewele*: sent on its way.
502 *Esperus*: Hesperus, the evening star (cf. *TG* 1348); an astrological periphrasis, perhaps modelled on *Fkl T*, *CT* V. 1016–18.
504 *bade*: remained.   *mone*: complaint (perhaps conceived as another formal lament).
505 *evin*: evening.   *myght*: strength.   *mynd*: reason.
506 *Forwepit and forpleynit*: wearied with weeping and complaining.
507 *Ourset so sorow had*: sorrow had overcome.
508 *on wrye*: sideways.   509 *amaisit*: dazed.
510 *swoun*: swooning.   *wise*: way.   511 *met*: dreamed.   *devise*: relate.
512 The dreamer is somehow taken up in the beam of light. For the general situation and the comforting voice, cf. Acts 12: 7, and also the angel's reassurance to the shepherds at the Nativity, as recounted in Luke 2.
513 *come*: came.   515 *overwent*: covered.
516 *the vertew hale iblent*: the power (was) completely blinded.
517 *withall*: moreover.   *voce*: voice.   518 *hele*: healing, salvation.
519 *it*: probably the beam of light.
520 *ryght*: exact.

And sone, me thought, furth at the dure in hye
I went my weye, nas nothing me ageyne,
And hastily, by bothe the armes tweyne,
I was araisit up into the air,
Clippit in a cloude of cristall clere and fair;   525

199^v   Ascending upward ay fro spere to spere
Through air and water and the hote fyre,
Till that I come unto the circle clere
Off Signifer, quhare fair, bryght and schire,
The signis schone, and in the glade empire   530
Off blisfull Venus am caryit now
So sudaynly, almost I wist noght how.

Off quhich the place, quhen I come there nye
Was all, me thought, of cristall stonis wroght.
And to the port I liftit was in hye,   535
Quhare sodaynly—as quho sais 'at a thoght'—
It opnyt, and I was anon in broght

521 *sone*: soon.   *dure*: door.   *in hye*: at speed. The ease which which he leaves the room is of particular significance for this narrator, who has been a prisoner.

522 *nas nothing me ageyne*: nothing prevented me.

524 *araisit*: raised. Cf. *HF* 541–8 and 972–8, where the dreamer is carried up in the claws of an eagle, and speculates on Boethius's assertion (*De cons* I, m. 1) that the soul can mount on wings of Philosophy beyond the earth to its proper home.

525 *Clippit*: embraced.

525–31 In the Ptolemaic universe of medieval cosmology the earth was situated at the centre of multiple concentric spheres. The closest of these were those of the other four elements—air, water, and fire. Next came *Signifer*, the zodiac, with its twelve signs. Beyond this were the spheres of the different planets (Moon, Mercury, Venus, Sun, Mars, Jupiter, Saturn in order, moving outward from the earth), and finally the *primum mobile*, the sphere of the fixed stars. For a summary, see Lewis 1964: 92–121.

526 *spere*: sphere.   528 *clere*: bright.

529 *Signifer*: the zodiac.   *schire*: clear.

530 *signis*: signs (of the zodiac).   *empire*: realm.

531 The MS reading of *ane cryit* does not make good sense, although editors have interpreted the line as 'where now someone cried out (to announce the arrival of the dreamer)'. An emendation has been adopted here.

532 *almost I wist noght how*: I scarcely knew how.

533 *place*: palace.   *nye*: near.

534 *wroght*: made.   535 *port*: gate.

536 as (if) one should say 'in a trice'. *as quho sais* is an expression used by Chaucer; cf. *TC* III. 267, and *BD* 559; *thoght* was proverbially swift.

Within a chamber large, rowm and faire,
And there I fand of peple grete repaire.

This is to seyne, that present in that place   540
Me thought I sawe of every nacioun
Loveris that endit thair lyfis space
In lovis service, mony a mylioun;
Off quhois chancis maid is mencioun
In diverse bukis, quho thame list to se,   545
And therefore here thair namys lat I be.

The quhois aventure and grete labour
Above thair hedis writin there I fand:
This is to seyne, martris and confessour
Eche in his stage, and his make in his hand;   550
And therwithall thir peple sawe I stand
With mony a solempt contenance,
After as lufe thame lykit to avance.

Off gude folkis that fair in lufe befill
There saw I sitt in order, by thame one,   555
With hedis hore, and with thame stude Gude Will

538 *rowm*: spacious.

539 *fand*: found. *repaire*: assembly. For similar congregations of lovers, see *TG* 144–246 and *AL* 540–735.

543 *mony a mylioun*: many million.   544 *chancis*: adventures.

545 *quho thame list to se*: whoever might wish to see them. *in diverse bukis*: narratives of love by, for instance, Chaucer ('he hath toold of loveris up and doun | Mo than Ovide made of mencioun | In his Episteles, that been ful olde'; *Introduction to the Man of Law's Tale, CT* II. 53–5); Gower (see *CA* VIII. 250 ff.), and Lydgate (*TG* 55–110).

546 *lat be*: pass over.

547 *The quhois*: whose. *adventure*: fortunes.

549 *martris and confessour*: martyrs for love, and those who confessed (before the point of martyrdom) their allegiance to it. *LGW* is conceived as 'a glorious legende | Of goode wymmen' (F483–4), a collection of the lives of love's saints.

550 *stage*: assigned place. *make*: companion, partner.   552 *solempt*: solemn.

553 Accordingly as it pleased love to advance (or possibly order) them.

554 *that fair in lufe befill*: for whom it turned out happily in love.

554–654 Cf. *TG* 143–246. Four different categories of lovers (old, young, hooded, and discontented) are first introduced (554–74) and then described in more detail to the dreamer by an anonymous voice (576–644).

555 *by thame one*: by themselves.   556 *hore*: grey. *stude*: stood.

To talk and play; and after that anon
Besyde thame and next there saw I gone
Curage amang the fresche folkis yong,
And with thame playit full merily and song.   560

And in ane other stage endlong the wall
There saw I stand in capis wyde and lang
A full grete nowmer; bot thair hudis all,
Wist I nought quhy, atour thair eyen hang,
And ay to thame come Repentance amang   565
And maid thame chere, degysit in his wede;
And dounward efter that yit I tuke hede.

Ryght overthwert the chamber was there drawe
A trevesse thin and quhite, all of plesance,
The quhich behynd standing there I sawe   570
A warld of folk, and by thair contenance
Thair hertis semyt full of displesance,
With billis in thaire handis, of one assent
Unto the juge thair playntis to present.

And therwithall apperit unto me   575
A voce, and said: 'Tak hede, man, and behold:
Yonder there thou seis the hiest stage and gree
Off agit folk with hedis hore and olde;
Yone were the folk that never change wold
In lufe, bot trewly servit him alway,   580
In every age, unto thair ending day.

559 *Curage*: a personification of strength, or possibly desire.   561 *endlong*: along.
562 *capis*: copes.   563 *hudis*: hoods.   564 *atour*: over.
565 *amang*: continuously.
566 *maid thame chere*: welcomed them.   *degysit*: dressed.   *wede*: outfit.
567 *dounward*: further down (the groups).   568 *overthwert*: across.
569 *trevesse*: dividing curtain.   *plesance*: fine cloth from Piacenza (and cf. 625). The hall is divided by a curtain, made of the same fine light fabric as the clothing of Venus and Fortune in *LR* 127 and 353.
572 *displesance*: displeasure.
573 *billis*: petitions.   *of one assent*: all in agreement/all on one theme.
574 *playntis*: complaints.   576 *voce*: voice.
577 *seis*: see.   *hiest*: highest.   *stage*: rank.   *gree*: degree.   578 *agit*: aged.

'For fro the tyme that thai coud understand
The exercise of lufis craft the cure,
Was none on lyve that toke so moch on hand
For lufis sake, nor langer did endure   585
In lufis service; for, man, I the assure,
Quhen thay of youth ressavit had the fill
Yit in thair age tham lakkit no gude will.

'Here bene also of swich as in counsailis
And all thare dedis were to Venus trewe.   590
Here bene the princis faucht the grete batailis,
In mynd of quhom ar maid the bukis newe.
Here ben the poetis that the sciences knewe,
Throwout the warld, of lufe in thair swete layes,
Swich as Ovide and Omere in thair dayes.   595

fo. 200ᵛ

'And efter thame, down in the next stage,
There as thou seis the yong folkis pleye,
Lo, thise were thay that in thair myddill age
Servandis were to lufe in mony weye,
And diversely happinit for to deye: 600
Sum sorowfully for wanting of thare makis,
And sum in armes for thaire ladyes sakis;

'And othir eke by othir diverse chance,
As happin folk all day as ye may se:
Sum for dispair without recoverance,   605

583 The practice of the business of the art of love.   584 *on lyve*: living.
587 *ressavit had the fill*: had enjoyed their fullness of youth.
589–90 Here are also such (people) as were true to Venus in all their thoughts and deeds.
591 *faucht*: who faught.
592 *mynd*: memory. *the bukis newe*: recent narratives of the lives of famous lovers (possibly a reference to texts such as *TC*, or to 15th-c. versions of similar stories).
593 *sciences*: doctrines. *knewe*: made known.   594 *layes*: poems, songs.
595 *Omere*: Homer. Ovid's poems were widely known in the Middle Ages, both in Latin and in vernacular adaptations. The association of Homer with love poetry is probably due to the wide circulation of romanticized versions of the story of Troy, such as Guido delle Collone's 13th-c. Latin *Historia Destructionis Troiae*: see Benson 1980.
596 *stage*: level.   600 *happinit*: chanced.   601 *wanting*: lack.
605 *recoverance*: recovery.

Sum for desyre surmounting thair degree,
Sum for dispite and othir inmytee,
Sum for unkyndenes without a quhy,
Sum for to moch, and sum for jelousye.

'And efter this, upon yone stage doun,   610
Tho that thou seis stond in capis wyde,
Yone were quhilum folk of religioun
That from the warld thair governance did hide
And frely servit lufe on every syde
In secrete, with thair bodyis and thair gudis.   615
And lo, quhy so thai hingen doun thaire hudis:

'For though that thai were hardy at assay
And did him service quhilum prively,
Yit to the warldis eye it semyt nay—
So was thair service half cowardy;   620
And for thay first forsuke him opynly
And efter that therof had repenting,
For schame thair hudis our thair eyne thay hyng.

'And seis thou now yone multitude on rawe
Standing behynd yone traverse of delyte?   625
Sum bene of tham that haldin were full lawe,
And take by frendis, nothing thay to wyte,
In youth from lufe into the cloister quite;

---

606 *surmounting thair degree*: aspiring above their rank.
607 *dispite*: malice. *inmytee*: enmity.   608 *without a quhy*: unjustified.
609 *to moch*: excess (in love).
612 *quhilum*: formerly. *folk of religioun*: religious.
612–44 Cf. *TG* 196–214. Difficulties such as these, for those under obligation to religious vows, or forced into unhappy marriages, seem to have been generally and seriously acknowledged.
613 *governance*: conduct.   615 *gudis*: goods.   616 *quhy so*: the reason.
617 *hardy at assay*: bold in the struggle.   618 *prively*: in secret.
619 *it semyt nay*: it did not seem (to be so).
620 *half cowardy*: cowardice, in part.
621 *for*: because. *him*: i.e. Love. *opynly*: in public.   623 *our*: over.
624 *on rawe*: in a line.   626 *haldin were full lawe*: were abased.
627 *frendis*: relatives. *nothing thay to wyte*: they being in no way to blame.

And for that cause are cummyn recounsilit
On thame to pleyne that so tham had begilit.   630

'And othir bene amongis thame also
That cummyn are to court on lufe to pleyne
For he thair bodyes had bestowit so
Quhare bothe thair hertes gruch there-ageyne,
For quhich in all thair dayes, soth to seyne,   635
Quhen othir lyvit in joye and plesance,
Thair lyf was noght bot care and repentance,

'And quhare thair hertis gevin were and set,
Were coplit with othir that coud noght accord.
Thus were thai wrangit that did no forfet,   640
Departing thame that never wold discord.'
Off yong ladies fair and mony lord,
That thus by maistry were fro thair chose dryve,
Full redy were their playntis there to gyve.

And othir also I sawe compleynyng there   645
Upon Fortune and hir grete variance
That, quhere in love so wele they coplit were,
With thair swete makis coplit in plesance,
So sodeynly maid thair disseverance,
And tuke thame of this warldis companye   650
Withoutin cause—there was non othir quhy.

629 *recounsilit*: newly advised.
630 *pleyne*: complain.   *begilit*: tricked, beguiled.
632 For the notion of a court of love, where petitions might be presented and wrongs
redressed, cf. *TG*, and see Neilson 1899, Piaget 1891, Rémy 1954–5, Green 1983, Boffey
2000.
634 *gruch*: protest.   *there-ageyne*: in opposition.   638 *gevin*: given.
639 *accord*: live harmoniously.   640 *wrangit*: wronged.   *forfet*: misdeed.
641 Separating those who would never have disagreed.
643 Who thus had been driven by force from their choice.
645–51 This is essentially the situation of the dreamer in *LR*.
647 *That*: Who (i.e. Fortune).   *coplit*: joined.
649 *maid thair disseverance*: separated them.   650 *of*: from.
651 *quhy*: reason.

And in a chier of estate besyde,
With wingis bright, all plumyt bot his face,
There sawe I sitt the blynd god Cupide,
With bow in hand that bent full redy was.   655
And by him hang thre arowis in a cas,
Off quhich the hedis grundyn were full ryght,
Off diverse metals forgit fair and bryght.

And with the first that hedit is of gold
He smytis soft, and that has esy cure.   660
The secund was of silver, mony fold
Wers than the first and harder aventure.
The thrid of stele is schot without recure.
And on his long yalow lokkis schene
A chaplet had he all of levis grene.   665

_{201ᵛ}   And in a retrete lytill of compas,
Depeyntit all with sighis wonder sad—
Noght swich sighis as hertis doith manace
Bot swich as dooth lufaris to be glad—
Fond I Venus upon hir bed, that had   670
A mantill cast over hir schuldris quhite:
Thus clothit was the goddesse of delyte.

---

652 *chier of estate*: throne of state.   *besyde*: close by.
652–65 The description of Cupid seems inspired by *Kn T*, *CT* I. 1963–6, where he is
similarly winged, blind, and bearing a bow with arrows.
653 *plumyt*: covered with feathers.   *bot*: except for.   656 *hang*: hung.
656–63 The potential of Cupid's arrows to inflict wounds of both a harmful and a
fortunate kind derives from Ovid, *Metamorphoses* I. 468–71, and is developed in e.g. *RR*
924 ff. (*Romaunt* 939–91) and *PF* 211–17; cf. also *TG* 112.
657 *grundyn*: sharpened.   *full ryght*: expertly.   658 *forgit*: fashioned.
660 *smytis*: strikes.   *soft*: gently.   661 *fold*: times.   662 *aventure*: fortune.
663 *thrid*: third.   *recure*: (possibility of) recovery.   664 *yalow*: yellow.
665 In *RR* 895–6 (*Romaunt*, 907– 8), the God of Love wears a chaplet of red roses.
666 *retrete*: private chamber.   *compas*: space.
666–72 The depiction of Venus is modelled on *PF* 260–6 (and cf. *LR* 123–8), but is
pointedly less threatening.
667 *Depeyntit*: painted.   *wonder*: extremely.   *sad*: intense.
668 *doith manace*: threaten.   670 *Fond*: found.   671 *quhite*: white.
672 *delyte*: pleasure.

Stude at the dure Fair Calling, hir uschere,
That coude his office doon in connyng wise,
And Secretee, hir thrifty chamberere,   675
That besy was in tyme to do servise,
And othir mo that I can noght on avise.
And on hir hede of rede rosis full swete
A chapellet sche had, faire, fresch and mete.

With quaking hert, astonate of that sight,   680
Unnethis wist I quhat that I suld seyne,
Bot at the last, febily as I myght,
With my handis, on bothe my kneis tweyne,
There I begouth my caris to compleyne.
With ane humble and lamentable chere   685
Thus salute I that goddesse bryght and clere:

'Hye quene of lufe, sterre of benevolence,
Pitouse princes and planet merciable,
Appesar of malice and violence
By vertew pure of your aspectis hable,   690
Unto your grace lat now bene acceptable
My pure request, that can no forthir gone
To seken help bot unto yow allone.

673 *Fair Calling*: Fair Welcome; cf. Belacoil, or Fair Welcome, *RR* 2787 ff. (*Romaunt* 2979 ff.) who greets the Lover by the rose-bush.   *uschere*: door-keeper.

674 Who knew how to execute his duties skilfully.

675 *Secretee*: Secrecy; for Secrecy as the handmaiden of Love, cf. Gower, *CA* III. 825–7.   *thrifty*: fine.   *chamberere*: handmaid.

676 *in tyme*: at the appropriate time.   677 *on avise*: tell of.

678–9 Venus wears a garland of red roses in *Kn T*, *CT* I. 1960–1, and in *TG* 525–7, wears red and white roses (this detail is not present in all texts of *TG*; see Norton-Smith 1958).

679 *mete*: fitting.   680 *astonate of*: astonished by.   681 *Unnethis*: scarcely.

683 *With my handis*: with my hands (outstretched).   684 *begouth*: began.

685 *chere*: countenance.   686 *salute*: greeted.

686–721 The dreamer addresses Venus as a planetary power, not simply as a goddess. The petition for mercy is commonplace in medieval love poems, addressed sometimes to Venus and sometimes to the object of love (cf. *LR* 715–42).

687 *Hye*: exalted.   *sterre*: star.

688 *Pitouse*: compassionate.   *princes*: princess.

689 *Appesar*: pacifier.   690 *pure*: unadulterated.   *hable*: powerful.

692 *pure*: poor.   *gone*: go.

'As ye that bene the socour and swete well
Off remedye, of carefull hertes cure,   695
And in the huge weltering wavis fell
Of lufis rage, blisfull havin and sure,
O anker and keye of oure gude aventure,
Ye have your man with his gude will conquest:
Merci, therefore, and bring his hert to rest.   700

202ʳ   'Ye knaw the cause of all my peynes smert
Bet than my self, and all myn aventure
Ye may convoye, and as yow list convert
The hardest hert that formyt hath Nature.
Sen in your handis all hale lyith my cure,   705
Have pitee now, O bryght blissfull goddesse,
Off your pure man, and rew on his distresse.

'And though I was unto your lawis strange
By ignorance and noght by felonye,
And that your grace now likit hath to change   710
My hert to serven yow perpetualye,
Forgeve all this, and schapith remedye
To saven me, of your benigne grace,
Or do me sterven furthwith in this place.

'And with the stremes of your percyng lyght   715
Convoy my hert that is so wobegone

694 *socour*: relief.
695 *carefull*: sorrowfull.   *cure*: healer.   696 *weltering*: rolling.   *fell*: cruel.
696–7 These lines evoke an image of love as a perilous sea, in keeping with the images
of the sea of life and the sea of fortune which inform earlier parts of the poem (see above,
101 ff.).
697 *havin*: haven.   698 *anker*: anchor.   *keye*: harbour.
699 *with his gude will*: with his voluntary agreement.   *conquest*: conquered.
701 *my peynes smert*: the pain of my wounds.   702 *Bet*: better.
703 *convoye*: guide.   704 *formyt*: formed.
705 *Sen*: since.   *all hale*: wholly.
708 *unto . . . strange*: not conversant with.   709 *felonye*: wrongdoing.
710 *your grace now likit hath*: it has now pleased your grace.
712 *schapith*: fashion.   714 *do me sterven*: put me to death.
715 This reference to Venus's streams of light may be intended as a retrospective
explanation of the beam of light which announced the dreamer's journey to her sphere
(512–25).

Ageyne unto that swete hevinly sight
That I, within the wallis cald as stone,
So swetly saw on morow walk and gone,
Law in the gardyn ryght tofore myn eye: 720
Now, merci, quene, and do me noght to deye.'

Thir wordis said, my spirit in dispair,
A quhile I stynt, abiding efter grace.
And therwithall hir cristall eyen fair
Me kest asyde, and efter that a space   725
Benignely sche turnyt has hir face,
Towardis me full plesantly conveide,
And unto me ryght in this wise sche seide:

fo. 202ᵛ   'Yong man, the cause of all thyne inward sorowe
Is noght unknawin to my deite,   730
And thy request, bothe now and eke toforowe,
Quhen thou first maid professioun to me.
Sen of my grace I have inspirit the
To knawe my lawe, contynew furth, for oft
There as I mynt full sore, I smyte bot soft.   735

'Paciently thou tak thyne aventure:
This will my son Cupide, and so will I.
He can the stroke, to me langis the cure
Quhen I se tyme; and therefore humily
Abyde and serve and lat Gude Hope the gye.   740
Bot for I have thy forehede here present
I will the schewe the more of myn entent.

---

718 *cald*: cold.   719 *on morow*: in the morning.   720 *Law*: below.
721 *do me noght to deye*: do not make me die. Cf. *TC* V. 83–4: 'And he ful softe and sleighly gan hire seye, | "Now holde your day, and do me nat to deye" '.
723 *stynt*: ceased.   *abiding efter*: waiting for.
725 *Me kest asyde*: looked away from me.   *space*: while.
727 *conveide*: moved.   730 *unknawin*: unknown.   *deite*: godly person.
731 *toforowe*: earlier.   732 *maid professioun*: declared (your) faith.
735 *mynt*: aim.   *sore*: hurtfully.   736 *thou tak*: accept.
737 *will*: wishes.   738 *He can the stroke*: He struck you.   *langis*: belongs.
739 *humily*: humbly.   740 *the gye*: guide you.
741 *forehede*: reason (thought to be located in the forehead).

'This is to say, though it to me pertene
In lufis lawe the septre to governe,
That the aspectis of my bemes schene   745
Has thair effectis, by ordynance eterne,
With othes byndand; mynes to discerne
Quhilum in thingis bothe to cum and gone—
That langis noght to me to writh allone.

'As in thyne awin case now may thou se,   750
Forquhy, lo, that by otheris influence,
Thy persone standis noght in libertee;
Quharefore, though I geve the benevolence,
It standis noght yit in myn advertence
Till certeyne coursis endit be and ronne,   755
Quhill of trew servis thow have hir graice iwone.

'And yit, considering the nakitnesse
Bothe of thy wit, thy persone and thy myght,
It is no mach of thyne unworthyness
To hir hie birth, estate and beautee bryght.   760
Als like ye bene as day is to the nyght,
Or sek-cloth is unto fyne cremesye,
Or doken foule onto the fresche dayesye.

743 *pertene*: pertains to/belongs to. This is a difficult stanza, as all editors agree. It seems likely that the scribe mistakenly transposed *effectis* and *aspectis* in lines 745–6. I have followed Skeat and Norton-Smith in taking the ampersand in the MS in line 47 to be a scribal error for the participial suffix *-and*, and in understanding *mynes* in 747 as *menys*, 'means', although in other respects my interpretation of the stanza is not the same as theirs.
744 *septre*: sceptre, supreme power.   746 *ordynance eterne*: eternal decree.
747 *byndand*: binding.   *mynes*: powers.   *discerne*: see.   748 *Quhilum*: at times.
749 *langis noght to me*: is not my responsibility.   *writh*: direct.
751 *Forquhy*: since.   *that by otheris influence*: the influence both of other planets (mentioned in 747), and perhaps of other people.
753 *geve*: give.   754 *advertence*: control.
755 *coursis*: (planetary) movements.   *endit be and ronne*: have finished and run (their course).
756 *Quhill*: until.   *iwone*: won.   757 *nakitnesse*: bareness.
758 *myght*: power.   759 *mach of*: match between.
761 *Als like ye bene*: you (two) are as alike.
762 *sek-cloth*: sack-cloth.   *cremesye*: crimson cloth.
763 *doken*: docks.   *dayesye*: daisy.

'Unlike the mone is to the sonne schene,
Eke Januarye is like unto May,   765
Unlike the cukkow to the phylomene—
Thair tabartis ar noght bothe maid of array;
Unlike the crow is to the papejay,
Unlike in goldsmythis werk a fischis eye
To prese with perll or maked be so heye.   770

fo. 203ʳ   'As I have said, unto me belangith
Specialy the cure of thy seknesse.
Bot now thy matere so in balance hangith
That it requerith to thy sekirnesse,
The help of othir mo that bene goddes,   775
And have in thame the menes and the lore
In this matere to schorten with thy sore.

'And for thou sall se wele that I entend
Unto thy help, thy welefare to preserve,
The streight weye thy spirit will I send   780
To the goddesse that clepit is Mynerve.
And se that thou hir hestis wele conserve,
For in this case sche may be thy supplye
And put thy hert in rest als wele as I.

---

765 A contrast probably suggested by *Mer T, CT* IV. 1245–2418, in which an old knight, January, marries a young girl named May.

766 *phylomene*: nightingale. Possibly an allusion to Clanvowe's *Boke of Cupide* (Scattergood 1975).

767 *tabartis*: coats, hence 'plumage'.   *maid of array*: made to match (*array* = arrangement).

768 *papejay*: parrot.   769 *fischis eye*: fish-eye stone (ichthyophthalmite).

770 *prese*: appraise, value.   *with*: alongside.   *maked be so heye*: be considered so valuable.

773 *matere*: business.   774 *to thy sekirnesse*: for your security.

775 *othir mo*: more others.   776 *menes*: means.   *lore*: learning.

777 *to schorten with*: with which to cut short.   *sore*: grief.   778 *sall*: shall.

778–9 *I entend | Unto thy help*: I am disposed to help you.

780 *streight*: direct.

781 *clepit*: called.   *Mynerve*: Minerva was the Roman goddess of wisdom, and so traditionally associated with reason and virtue.

782 *hestis*: commandments.   *conserve*: keep.   783 *supplye*: help.

'Bot, for the way is uncouth unto the   785
There as hir dwelling is and hir sojurne,
I will that Gud Hope servand to the be;
Youre alleris frend, to let the to murn,
Be thy condyt and gyde till thou returne,
And hir besech that sche will in thy nede   790
Hir counsele geve to thy welefare and spede;

'And that sche will, as langith hir office,
Be thy gude lady, help and counseilour,
And to the schewe hir rype and gude avise,
Throw quhich thou may, be processe and labour,   795
Atteyne unto that glad and goldyn floure
That thou wald have so fayn with all thy hart.
And forthirmore, sen thou hir servand art,

'Quhen thou descendis doun to ground ageyne,
Say to the men that there bene resident,   800
How long think thay to stand in my disdeyne,
That in my lawis bene so negligent
From day to day, and list tham noght repent,
Bot breken louse and walken at thair large?
Is now left none that thereof gevis charge?   805

'And for,' quod sche, 'the angir and the smert
Off thair unkyndenesse dooth me constreyne

785 *uncouth*: unknown.   786 *There as*: where.   *sojurne*: residence.
787 Good Hope appears also in *TG* 892, 1197.
788 The friend of you all, to prevent you from grieving; *alleris* is a fossilized form of the genitive plural of the adjective *aller*, to accord with a plural possessive pronoun (Good Hope is the friend of *all* mortals).
789 *condyt*: conductor.   791 *spede*: success.
792 *langith*: is appropriate to.   794 *rype*: mature.
795 *processe*: course of time.   796 *Atteyne unto*: win.
797 *wald have*: desire.   *fayn*: gladly.
801 *stand in my disdeyne*: remain disdainful of me.
802 *in my lawis*: in (observing) my laws.
803 *list tham noght repent*: are not pleased to repent.
804 *louse*: loose.   *at thair large*: at large.
805 *gevis charge*: assumes responsibility for.   806 *for*: because.
807 *dooth me constreyne*: causes distress (to).

My femynyne and wofull tender hert,
That than I wepe, and to a token pleyne,
As of my teris cummyth all this reyne   810
That ye se on the ground so fast ybete
Fro day to day, my turment is so grete.

'And quhen I wepe and stynt in othir quhile—
For pacience that is in womanhede,
Than all my wrath and rancoure I exile—   815
And of my cristall teris that bene schede
The hony flouris growen up and sprede
That preyen men, ryght in thaire flouris wise,
Be trewe of lufe and worschip my servise.

And eke in takin of this pitouse tale,   820
Quhen so my teris dropen on the ground,
In thair nature the lytill birdis smale
Styntith thair song and murnyth for that stound;
And all the lightis in the hevin round
Off my grevance have swich compacience,   825
That from the ground they hiden thair presence.

'And yit in tokenyng forthir of this thing,
Quhen flouris springis and freschest bene of hewe,
And that the birdis on the twistis sing,
At thilke tyme ay gynnen folk to renewe   830
That servis unto love, as ay is dewe,
Most commonly has ay his observance,
And of thair sleuth tofore have repentance.

809 *to a token pleyne*: as a clear token of this.
810 *As of my teris*: from my tears.
810–33 In the traditional medieval categories, Venus was considered a 'hot and moist' planet, associated with rain; see Lewis 1964: 92–121; and Chaucer, *Lenvoy de Chaucer a Scogan* 11 n.; *Kn T, CT* I. 2664–6; and *The Complaint of Mars* 89 n.
811 *ybete*: beat.   813 *stynt*: stop.   *in othir quhile*: at other times.
817 *hony*: sweet.   *sprede*: flourish.
818 *in thaire flouris wise*: in their flower-like way.   819 *worschip*: honour.
820 *takin*: token.   823 *stound*: time.   825 *compacience*: compassion.
828 *springis*: spring up.   831 *ay*: always.   *dewe*: due.
832 (and which) generally always has its (due) observance.
833 *sleuth tofore*: earlier negligence.

'Thus maist thou seyne that myn effectis grete,
Unto the quhiche ye aught and maist weye,   835
No lyte offense to sleuth is or forget.
And therfore in this wise to tham seye
As I the here have bid, and conveye
The mater all the better tofore said.
Thus sall on the my charge bene ilaid.   840

204ʳ   'Say on than, quhare is becummyn, for schame,
The songis new, the fresch carolis and dance,
The lusty lyf, the mony change of game,
The fresche array, the lusty contenance,
The besy awayte, the hertly observance   845
That quhilum was amongis thame so ryf?
Bid tham repent in tyme and mend thair lyf.

'Or I sall, with my fader old Saturne,
And with al hale oure hevinly alliance,
Oure glad aspectis from thame writh and turne   850
That all the warld sall waile thair governance.
Bid thame by tyme that thai have repentance,

834–6 Thus you may see that it is no small offence to neglect or forget my powerful influences, to which you ought and must pay heed.

837 *wise*: way.   838 *bid*: commanded.

840 *charge*: injunction.   *bene ilaid*: be laid.

841 *quhare is becummyn*: what is become of.

841–6 This lament for things past works a variation on the so-called *ubi sunt* formula or topos (on which see Woolf 1968: 96); for a later Scottish parallel, see *The Testament of Cresseid* (Bawcutt and Riddy 1987), 416–33.

842 *carolis*: carols, but also possibly ring-dances.

843 *lusty*: pleasant (the repetition in the following line may indicate some scribal corruption).   *mony change of game*: many varieties of pastime.

844 *array*: clothing.   *contenance*: behaviour.

845 *besy awayte*: busy attendance.   *hertly observance*: devoted service (of love).

846 *ryf*: widespread.

847 *in tyme*: quickly.   *mend thair lyf*: amend their way of living.

848 Venus's father is Jupiter; Saturn, the oldest of the planetary gods, is her grandfather. She uses *fader* as a general term for an older person, as Saturn similarly, in *Kn T* (*CT* I. 2453), addresses Venus as 'My deere doghter Venus'.

849 *al hale*: the whole of.   850 *writh*: remove.   851 *waile*: lament.

852 *by tyme*: in good time.   *have repentance*: repent.

And thair hertis hale renew my lawe,
And I my hand fro beting sall withdrawe.

'This is to say, contynew in my servise,   855
Worschip my law, and my name magnifye
That am your hevin and your paradise,
And I your confort here sall multiplye,
And for your meryt here perpetualye
Ressave I sall your saulis, of my grace,   860
To lyve with me as goddis in this place.'

With humble thank and all the reverence
That feble wit and connyng may atteyne,
I tuke my leve; and from hir presence
Gude Hope and I togider bothe tweyne   865
Departit ar, and schortly for to seyne,
He hath me led by redy wayis ryght
Unto Minervis palace, fair and bryght.

Quhare as I fand full redy at the yate
The maister portar callit Pacience   870
That frely lete us in unquestionate.
And there we sawe the perfyte excellence,
The said renewe, the state, the reverence,
The strenth, the beautee and the ordour digne
Off hir court riall, noble and benigne.   875

fo. 204ᵛ   And straught unto the presence sodeynly
Off Dame Minerve, the pacient goddesse,
Gude Hope my gyde led me redily;

853 *hale*: wholly.   854 *beting*: correction.
860 *Ressave*: receive.   *saulis*: souls.   863 *connyng*: skill.
866 *Departit ar*: left.   867 *redy*: accessible.   *ryght*: direct.
869 *yate*: gate.
870 In *PF* 239–43, Patience sits with Peace outside the temple of Venus.
871 *frely*: generously.   *unquestionate*: without question.   872 *perfyte*: perfect.
873 *said renewe*: Skeat's suggested translation of 'orderly renewal' (= routine) has not
satisfied some editors (McDiarmid (James I 1973); Norton-Smith (James I 1981)), who
have emended to *sad renowne*, 'sober glory'.   *state*: stateliness.
874 *ordour digne*: worthy order.   875 *riall*: royal.
876 *straught*: straight.   *sodeynly*: suddenly.

To quhom anon with dredefull humylnesse
Off my cummyng the cause I gan expresse,   880
And all the processe hale unto the end
Off Venus charge, as likit hir to send.

Off quhich ryght thus hir answer was in bref:
'My son, I have wele herd and understond
Be thy reherse the mater of thy gref,   885
And thy request to procure and to fond
Off thy pennance sum confort at my hond,
Be counsele of thy lady Venus clere,
To be with hir thyne help in this matere.

'Bot in this case thou sall wele knawe and witt   890
Thou may thy hert ground on swich a wise
That thy labour will be bot lytill quit.
And thou may set it in othir wise,
That wil be to the grete worschip and prise;
And gif thou durst unto that way enclyne,   895
I wil the geve my lore and disciplyne.

'Lo, my gude sone, this is als mich to seyne
As, gif thy lufe be sett all uterly
On nyce lust, thy travail is in veyne,
And so the end sall turne of thy folye   900
To payne, and repentance—lo, wate thou quhy?
Gif the ne list on lufe thy vertew set,
Vertu sal be the cause of thy forfet.

879 *dredefull humylnesse*: fearful humility.
882 *as likit hir to send*: as it pleased her to send (it).
884 Cf. *TG* 869–75.   885 *Be thy reherse*: from your account.
886 *fond*: obtain.   887 *Off*: for.   *at my hond*: from my hand.
890 *witt*: understand.   891 *ground*: rest, found.   892 *quit*: repaid.
894 *worschip*: honour.   *prise*: praise.   895 *enclyne*: tend.
897 *mich*: much.   899 *nyce*: foolish.   901 *wate*: do you know.
902 If it does not please you to attach virtue to your love.
902–10 The Christian significance of Minerva's advice becomes clear in these lines (908 *corner-stone*: cf. Psalm 118: 22; Eph. 2: 20; I Peter 2: 6, etc.), and in the following stanza Virtue seems to be equated with God.
903 *forfet*: wrongdoing.

'Tak Him before in all thy governance,
That in His hand the stere has of you all,   905
And pray unto His hye purveyance
Thy lufe to gye, and on Him traist and call
That corner-stone and ground is of the wall
That failis noght; and trust, withoutin drede,
Unto thy purpose sone He sall the lede.   910

fo. 205ʳ

'For lo, the werk that first is foundit sure
May better bere a pace and hyare be
Than othirwise, and langer sall endure
Be monyfald, this may thy resoun see,
And stronger to defend adversitee.   915
Ground thy werk therfore upon the stone,
And thy desire sall forthward with the gone.

'Be trewe and meke and stedfast in thy thoght,
And diligent hir merci to procure,
Noght onely in thy word—for word is noght   920
Bot gif thy werk and all thy besy cure
Accord therto (and utrid be mesure)
The place, the hour, the maner and the wise,
Gif mercy sall admitten thy servise.

' "All thing has tyme", thus sais Ecclesiaste,   925
And "wele is him that his tyme wel abit".
Abyde thy tyme, for he that can bot haste

905 *stere*: guidance.
906 *purveyance*: providence.   907 *gye*: guide.   *traist*: trust.
908 *ground*: foundation.   909 *failis noght*: does not fail.
911 *foundit sure*: securely founded.   912 *pace*: layer, storey.   *hyare*: higher.
914 *monyfald*: many times.   915 And (will be) a stronger defence in adversity.
917 *forthward*: forward.   *gone*: go.
921 *Bot gif*: unless.   *besy cure*: active thoughts.
922 Agree (and unless they are spoken with moderation).
923 (And unless) the place . . . (agree).
925 *Ecclesiaste*: Ecclesiastes 3: 1. Cf. Chaucer, *Mer T, CT* IV. 1972: 'For alle thyng hath tyme, as seyn thise clerkes'.
926 *wele is him*: happy is the man.   *abit*: waits for.
927 *can bot haste*: knows only how to hurry.

Can noght of hap, the wise man it writ,
And oft gud fortune flourith with gude wit.
Quharefore, gif thou will be wele fortunyt,   930
Lat wisedome ay to thy will be junyt.

Bot there be mony of so brukill sort
That feynis treuth in lufe for a quhile,
And setten all thaire wittis and disport
The sely innocent woman to begyle,   935
And so to wynne thair lustis with a wile.
Swich feynit treuth is all bot trechorye,
Under the umbre of heid ypocrisye.

For as the fouler quhislith in his throte,
That in the busk for his desate is hid,   940
And feynis mony a swete and strange note
Diversely, to counterfete the brid,
Till sche be fast lokin his net amyd:
Ryght so the fatour, the false theif I say,
With swete tresoune oft wynnith thus his pray.   945

05ᵛ   'Fy on all swich! Fy on thair doubilnesse,
Fy on thair lust and bestly appetite,
Thair wolfis hertis in lambis liknesse,
Thair thoughtis blak hid under wordis quhite.

---

928 *hap*: good fortune. *the wise man*: the words of wisdom of Ecclesiastes, now thought to be the work of an unknown author, were formerly attributed to Solomon, son of David. *writ*: writes.

931 *junyt*: joined.   932 *mony*: many. *brukill*: brittle, frail.

932–8 Cf. *TG* 215–22.   933 *feynis*: feign.   934 *disport*: diversion.

935 *sely*: hapless.   936 *wile*: trick.

937 *all bot trechorye*: nothing but treachery.

938 *umbre*: shadow. *heid ypocrisye*: hidden hypocrisy.

939 *fouler*: bird-catcher (an expanded proverb: Whiting 1968: F582) *quhislith*: whistles.

940 *busk*: bush. *desate*: deception. 940 and 942 are transposed in the MS, but seem to offer better sense in the order adopted here.

942 *Diversely*: in different ways.

943 *fast*: firmly. *lokin his net amyd*: imprisoned right in his net.

944 *fatour*: deceiver.   945 *pray*: prey.   948 *wolfis*: wolves'.

Fy on thair labour, fy on thair delyte,   950
That feynen outward all to hir honour
And in thair hert hir worschip wold devoure.

'So hard it is to trusten now on dayes
The warld—it is so double and inconstant—
Off quhich the suth is kid be mony assayes,   955
More pitee is; for quhich the remanant
That menen wele and ar noght variant,
For otheris gilt ar suspect of untreuth
And hyndrit oft, and treuely that is reuth.

'Bot gif the hert be groundit ferm and stable   960
In Goddis law thy purpose to atteyne,
Thy labour is to me agreable,
And my full help, with counsele trew and pleyne,
I will the schewe, and this is the certeyne.
Opyn thy hert therfore and lat me se   965
Gif thy remede be pertynent to me.'

'Madame,' quod I, 'sen it is your plesance
That I declare the kynd of my loving,
Treuely and gude, withoutin variance,
I lufe that flour abufe all othir thing;   970
And wold bene he that to hir worschipping
Myght ought availe, be him that starf on rude,
And nouthir spare for travaile, lyf nor gude!

'And forthirmore, as touching the nature
Off my lufing, to worschip or to blame,   975

---

950 *labour*: efforts.   952 *worschip*: reputation, honour.
953 *now on dayes*: nowadays.
955 *suth*: truth.   *kid*: (made) known.   *assayes*: proofs.
956 *remanant*: remainder.   957: *variant*: fickle.
959 *hyndrit*: hindered.   *reuth*: pity.   960 *ferm*: firmly.   964 *the*: (for) you.
966 *pertynent to me*: my responsibility.   968 *kynd*: nature.
969 *gude*: virtuously.   970 *abufe*: above.   971 *bene*: be.
972 Might avail something, by Him that died on the cross.
973 *nouthir spare*: not refrain.
975 *to worschip or to blame*: whether (it is to her) honour or blame.

I darr wele say and therein me assure,
For ony gold that ony wight can name,
Nald I be he that suld of hir gude fame
Be blamischere in ony point or wyse,
For wele nor wo, quhill my lyf may suffise.   980

206ʳ   'This is th'effect trewly of myn intent
Touching the swete that smertis me so sore.
Giff this be faynte, I can it noght repent
Allthough my lyf suld forfaut be therefore.
Blisfull princes, I can seye yow no more,   985
Bot so desire my wittis dooth compace
More joy in erth kepe I noght bot your grace.'

'Desire,' quod sche, 'I nyl it nought deny,
So thou it ground and set in Cristin wise.
And therfor, sone, opyn thy hert playnly.'   990
'Madame,' quod I, 'trew withoutin fantise,
That day sall I never uprise
For my delyte to covate the plesance
That may hir worschip putten in balance.

'For oure all thing, lo, this were my gladnesse: 995
To sene the fresche beautee of hir face,
And gif it might deserve, be processe,
For my grete lufe and treuth to stond in grace,
Hir worschip sauf. Lo, here the blisfull cace

976 *me assure*: pledge myself.
978 I would not be the man who should in any point or respect blemish her good reputation.
980 *quhill my lyf may suffise*: as long as my life may last.
982 *swete*: sweet (one).   983 *faynte*: untrue.   984 *forfaut*: lost.
986 But desire so circumscribes my senses that . . .
987 I take account of no joy on earth except your favour.
989 *Christin*: Christian.   990 *opyn*: open, unclose.
991 *fantise*: dissembling.
992–3 The day will never come (*lit.* I shall never rise up on that day) when my pleasure craves the enjoyment . . .
994 *in balance*: in jeopardy.   995 *oure*: above.   *were*: would be.
997 *deserve*: merit.   *processe*: course of time.
999 *Hir worschip sauf*: her honour (being kept) safe.

That I wold ask, and thereto attend   1000
For my most joye unto my lyfis end.'

'Now wele,' quod sche, 'and sen that it is so,
That in vertew thy lufe is set with treuth,
To helpen the I will be one of tho
From hensforth; and hertly, without sleuth,   1005
Off thy distresse and excesse to have reuth
That has thy hert, I will pray full fair
That Fortune be no more thereto contrair.

'For suthe it is, that all ye creaturis
Quhich under us beneth have your dwellyng   1010
Ressaven diversely your aventuris.
Off quhich the cure and principall melling
Apperit is, withoutin repellyng,
Onely to hir that has the cuttis two
In hand, bothe of your wele and of your wo.   1015

fo. 206ᵛ   'And how so be that sum clerkis trete
That all your chance causit is tofore
Heigh in the hevin, by quhois effectis grete
Ye movit ar to wrething, lesse or more,
Quhare in the warld, thus calling that therefore   1020
"Fortune", and so that the diversitee
Off thair wirking suld cause necessitee;

1000 *attend*: hope for.   1004 *tho*: those.
1005 *hertly*: wholeheartedly.   *sleuth*: neglect.
1006–7 *Off thy . . . | That has thy hert*: of the . . . in your heart.   *excesse*: attack (of suffering).
1008 *contrair*: opposed.   1011 *Ressaven*: receive.
1012 *cure*: responsibility.   *melling*: interference.
1013 *Apperit*: clear.   *repellyng*: contradiction.   1014 *cuttis*: lots.
1014–15 These lines refer to the goddess Fortune, whose nature is discussed in the following four stanzas, and whom the dreamer will encounter at 1110.
1016 *how so be*: although.   *trete*: write, consider.
1016–43 The discussion of predestination draws on Boethius, *De cons* V, pr. 2 and pr. 3, a passage whose arguments also inform *TC* IV. 960–1078.
1018 *effectis grete*: powerful influences.   1019 *wrething*: changes of fortune.
1020 *Quhare*: wherever.   1022 *wirking*: operations.

Bot othir clerkis halden that the man
Has in him self the chose and libertee
To cause his awin fortune, how or quhan   1025
That him best lest, and no necessitee
Was in the hevin at his nativitee,
Bot yit the thingis happin in commune
Efter purpose, so cleping thame "Fortune".

'And quhare a persone has tofore knawing   1030
Off it that is to fall purposely,
Lo, Fortune is bot wayke in swich a thing,
Thou may wele wit, and here ensample quhy:
To God, that is the firste cause onely
Off every thing, there may no fortune fall.   1035
And quhy? for He foreknawin is of all.

'And therfor thus I say to this sentence:
Fortune is most and strangest evermore
Quhare leste foreknawing or intelligence
Is in the man; and, sone, of wit or lore   1040
Sen thou art wayke and feble, lo, therfore
The more thou art in dangere and commune
With hir that clerkis clepen so "Fortune".

'Bot for the sake and at the reverence
Off Venus clere, as I the said tofore,   1045
I have of thy distresse compacience,
And in confort and relesche of thy sore
The schewit here myn avise therfore.

1024 *chose*: choice.   1026 *him best lest*: best pleases him.
1027 *nativitee*: birth.
1028 *in commune*: in common.   1029 *Efter purpose*: according to a purpose.
1030 *tofore knawing*: prior knowledge.   1031 *purposely*: providentially.
1032 *wayke*: weak.   1033 *ensample*: reason.   1036 *foreknawin*: prescient.
1037 *to this sentence*: on this subject.
1038 *most*: most influential.   *strangest*: strongest.
1039 *leste*: least.   1042 *in . . . commune*: involved with.
1043 *clepen*: call.   1047 *relesche*: relief.
1048 *schewit*: showed.

Pray Fortune help, for mich unlikly thing
Full oft about sche sodeynly dooth bring.   1050

fo. 207ʳ   'Now go thy way, and have gude mynd upone
Quhat I have said in way of thy doctryne.'
'I sall, madame,' quod I, and ryght anon
I tuke my leve. Als straught as ony lyne,
Within a beme that fro the contree dyvine   1055
Sche percyng throw the firmament extendit,
To ground ageyne my spirit is descendit.

Quhare in a lusty plane tuke I my way,
Endlang a ryver plesant to behold,
Enbroudin all with fresche flouris gay,   1060
Quhare throu the gravel, bryght as ony gold,
The cristall water ran so clere and cold
That in myn ere maid contynualy
A maner soun, mellit with armony,

That full of lytill fischis by the brym,   1065
Now here, now there, with bakkis blewe as lede
Lap and playit, and in a rout can swym
So prattily, and dressit thame to sprede
Thair curall fynnis as the ruby rede,
That in the sonne on thair scalis bryght   1070
As gesserant ay glitterit in my sight.

1049 *mich unlikly thing*: many improbable things.
1052 *doctryne*: instruction.
1055 *beme*: beam (of light).   *contree*: country, region.
1058 *lusty*: delightful.   *plane*: plain.
1058–78 These stanzas introduce a *locus amoenus* ('beautiful place' or earthly paradise) common in dream visions. See Curtius 1953: 183–202; and cf. the opening sections of *RR* (*Romaunt*, 645–700, 1349–438); *BD* 397–442; *PF* 172–210. Favoured ingredients are fresh water, temperate air, lush plants and trees, and plentiful fish and animals.
1059 *Endlang*: along.   1060 *Enbroudin*: embroidered.
1063 *ere*: ear.
1064 A sort of sound that was harmoniously mingled.   1065 *brym*: edge.
1066 *blewe*: blue.   *lede*: lead.
1067 *Lap*: leaped.   *rout*: shoal.   *can swym*: swam.
1068 *prattily*: prettily.   *dressit thame*: prepared.   *sprede*: spread.
1069 *curall*: coral.   *fynnis*: fins.   1071 *gesserant*: armour-plating.

And by this ilke ryver syde alawe
Ane hye-way fand I like to bene,
On quhich on every syde a long rawe
Off treis saw I, full of levis grene,   1075
That full of fruyte delitable were to sene.
And also, as it come unto my mynd,
Off bestis sawe I mony diverse kynd:

The lyoun king and his fere lyonesse,
The pantere, like unto the smaragdyne,   1080
The lytill squerell full of besynesse,
The slawe ase, the druggar, beste of pyne;
The nyce ape, the werely porpapyne,
The percyng lynx, the lufare unicorne
That voidis venym with his evour horne.   1085

07ʳ   There sawe I dresse him new out of hant
The fery tiger, full of felonye;

1072 *ilke*: same. *alawe*: lower down.
1073 *hye-way*: highway. *like to bene*: as it were.
1076 *delitable*: delectable. *to sene*: to see.   1077 *come*: came.
1078–1101 The catalogue of animals, introduced in 1078 with a formula which perhaps echoes *PF* 196 ('Squyrels, and bestes smale of gentil kynde') and promises an elaboration of it, is modelled on an ancient poetic form (see Curtius 1953: 195). *PF* has its own catalogues of trees (176–82) and birds (330–64); later Scottish catalogues of birds and animals can be found in *The Buke of the Howlat* (Bawcutt and Riddy 1987: 46–84, lines 14–39) and in *The Trial of the Fox*, one of Henryson's *Fables* (ed. Fox (Henryson 1981: 34–47, lines 887–921)). The list in *KQ* seems designed to highlight the dreamer's return to the realm of earthly creatures, and the benevolently created fullness and order of the world into which he is shortly to be liberated.
1079 *fere*: companion.
1080 *pantere*: panther. *smaragdyne*: emerald. The similarity of the panther to an emerald is not obvious, but the panther's features as highlighted in medieval bestiaries—its beauty, its multi-coloured markings, and its likeness to Christ—duplicate the qualities held to belong to the *smaragdyne*. For illustration and discussion of the information customarily included in bestiaries, see White 1954 and George and Yapp 1991.
1082 *slawe*: slow. *ase*: ass. *druggar*: drudge. *pyne*: toil.
1083 *nyce*: foolish. *werely*: warlike. *porpapyne*: porcupine.
1084 *percyng*: sharp-sighted. *lufare*: lover. The lynx was renowned for its keen sight. The unicorn, traditionally attracted to virgins, was caught by placing a virgin in its path and waiting for it to jump into the virgin's lap. Its horn was said to clear poison from water.
1085 *voidis*: dispels. *venym*: poison. *evour*: ivory.
1086 *dresse him*: get up. *hant*: lair.   1087 *fery*: restless.

The dromydare, the standar oliphant,
The wyly fox, the wedowis inemye;
The clymbare gayte, the elk for alblastrye,   1090
The herknere bore, the holsum grey for hortis,
The hair also that oft gooth to the wortis;

The bugill drawar by his hornis grete,
The martrik sable, the foynyee, and mony mo;
The chalk-quhite ermyn tippit as the jete,   1095
The riall hert, the conyng and the ro,
The wolf that of the murthir nought say "ho",
The lesty bever and the ravin bare,
For chamelot the camel full of hare,

With mony an othir beste diverse and strange   1100
That cummyth nought as now unto my mynd.
Bot now to purpose: straucht furth the range
I held a way, ourhailing in my mynd
From quhens I come, and quhare that I suld fynd

1088 *dromydare*: dromedary.   *standar*: standing.   *oliphant*: elephant. It was believed that the elephant had no knee-joints, and so slept in a standing position.

1089 *wedowis*: widow's.   *inemye*: enemy. The fox was the widow's enemy because it stole hens (cf. Chaucer, *NPT*, *CT* VII. 2821–3446, and Henryson's fable of *The Cock and the Fox* (ed. Fox, Henryson 1981: 19–27, lines 411–24)).

1090 *clymbare gayte*: goat that climbs.   *alblastrye*: crossbowmanship. The elk's skin was used to cover shields (elkhorn may also have been used, as oxhorn was, in the making of crossbows).

1091 The boar for listening, the healing badger for injuries. Badger grease was used in medicinal plasters.

1092 *hair*: hare.   *wortis*: vegetable patch. Probably a reference to the hare's tendency to nibble cultivated *wortis* ('greens').

1093 *bugill*: wild ox.   *drawar*: for drawing.

1094 *martrik*: marten.   *foynyee*: beech marten.

1095 *tippit as the jete*: tipped (black) like jet. The ermine's tail is tipped with black.

1096 *riall*: royal.   *conyng*: coney.

1097 The wolf that never says 'stop!' to murder.

1098 *lesty*: skilful.   *ravin*: ravenous.   *bare*: bear. The beaver was reputedly skilful both in building and in escaping from hunters by biting off its genitals, which contained a desirable medicinal substance.

1099 The hairy camel for making camlet (a costly fabric).

1102 *straucht furth the range*: straight along the row.

1103 *ourhailing*: re-examining.   1104 *quhens*: whence.   *come*: came.

Fortune the goddesse, unto quhom in hye   1105
Gude Hope my gyde has led me sodeynly.

And at the last, behalding thus asyde,
A round place wallit have I found,
In myddis quhare eftsone I have spide
Fortune the goddesse, hufing on the ground,   1110
And ryght before hir fete, of compace round,
A quhele, on quhich clevering I sye
A multitude of folk before myn eye.

And ane surcote sche werit long that tyde,
That semyt to me of diverse hewis.   1115
Quhilum thus, quhen sche wald turne asyde,
Stude this goddesse of fortune and remewis.
A chapellet with mony fresche anewis
Sche had upon hir hed, and with this hong
A mantill on hir schuldris, large and long,   1120

208^r That furrit was with cremyn full quhite,
Degoutit with the self in spottis blake.
And quhilum in hir chier thus a lyte
Louring sche was, and thus sone it wold slake
And sodeynly a maner smylyng make,   1125
And sche were glad; at one contenance
Sche held noght, bot ay in variance.

1105 *in hye*: quickly.   1107 *behalding*: looking.   1108 *wallit*: walled.
1109 *In myddis quhare*: in the middle of which.   *eftsone*: very soon.   *spide*: saw.
1110 *hufing*: stationary. For the depiction of Fortune, cf. *LR* 336–418, and see Patch
1927. Here (as indicated at 1129) she has a pit beneath her wheel.
1111 *compace*: shape.   1112 *clevering*: clambering.   *sye*: saw.
1114 *surcote*: overgarment.   *werit*: wore.   *that tyde*: at that time.
1114–17 *LR* (339–57) also presents Fortune in a coat of changeable colours; like the
mantill of *KQ*, it is decorated with ermine (351–2).
1115 *hewis*: colours.   1116 *Quhilum*: at times.
1117 *Stude*: stood.   *remewis*: changes.
1118 *anewis*: ringlets.   1120 *large*: wide.   1121 *eremyn*: ermine.
1122 Spotted with the same in the black tips (of ermines' tails).
1123 *chier*: behaviour.   *lyte*: little.
1123–7 In *LR* (400–2) Fortune's expression is similarly changeable.
1124 *Louring*: frowning.   *slake*: cease (frowning).
1126 *And*: as if.   *contenance*: demeanour.   1127 *ay in variance*: forever changing.

And underneth the quhele sawe I there
An ugly pit, depe as ony helle,
That to behald thereon I quoke for fere.   1130
Bot o thing herd I, that quho therein fell
Com no more up agane tidingis to telle.
Off quhich, astonait of that ferefull syght,
I ne wist quhat to done, so was I fricht.

Bot for to se the sudayn weltering   1135
Off that ilk quhele that sloppar was to hold,
It semyt unto my wit a strong thing,
So mony I saw that than clymben wold,
And failit foting, and to ground were rold;
And othir eke that sat above on hye   1140
Were overthrawe in twinklyng of an eye.

And on the quhele was lytill void space,
Wele nere oure-straught fro lawe to hye,
And they were war that long sat in place,
So tolter quhilum did sche it to-wrye.   1145
There was bot 'clymbe', and right dounward 'hye',
And sum were eke that fallyng had sore,
Therefor to clymbe thair corage was no more.

I sawe also that quhare sum were slungin
Be quhirlyng of the quhele unto the ground,   1150

1129 *ony*: any.   1130 *quoke*: quaked.   1131 *o*: one. *quho*: whoever.
1132 *Com*: came. *tidingis to telle*: to tell news (of it).   1133 *astonait*: astonished.
1134 *ne wist*: did not know. *done*: do. *fricht*: frightened.
1135 *weltering*: rolling. The *weltering* of Fortune's wheel draws together a number of earlier references to precarious movement: the uncertainty of youth; tossing at sea.
1136 *ilk*: same. *sloppar*: slippery.   1137 *strong*: strange.
1138 *than*: then. *clymben wold*: wanted to climb.
1139 *failit foting*: lost (their) footing. *rold*: rolled.
1141 *overthrawe*: overthrown.
1143 Almost over-stretched (= full to capacity) from the bottom to the top.
1144 *war*: wary.
1145 *tolter*: unsteadily. *quhilum*: at times. *to-wrye*: turn about.
1146 *There was bot*: there was (nothing) but. *hye*: hurry.
1147 *sum were eke*: there were also some. *had sore*: were hurt.
1148 *corage*: desire, strength.   1149 *slungin*: tossed. 1150 *quhirlyng*: whirling.

Full sudaynly sche hath up ythrungin,
And set thame on agane full sauf and sound.
And ever I sawe a new swarme abound,
That thoght to clymbe upward upon the quhele
In stede of thame that myght no langer rele.   1155

And at the last, in presence of tham all
That stude about, sche clepit me be name,
And therewith apon kneis gan I fall,
Full sodaynly hailsing, abaist for schame;
And smylyng thus sche said to me in game: 1160
'Quhat dois thou here? quho has the hider sent?
Say on anon and tell me thyn entent.

'I se wele by thy chere and contenance
There is sum thing that lyis the on hert.
It stant noght with the as thou wald, perchance?'   1165
'Madame,' quod I, 'for lufe is all the smert
That ever I fele, endlang and overthwert.
Help of your grace me, wofull wrechit wight,
Sen me to cure ye powere have and myght.'

'Quhat help,' quod sche, 'wold thou that I ordeyne,   1170
To bring the unto thy hertis desire?'
'Madame,' quod I, 'bot that your grace dedeyne,
Off your grete myght, my wittis to enspire
To win the well that slokin may the fyre

1151 *up ythrungin*: thrust (them) up.   1152 *sauf*: safe.
1153 *ever*: continually.   1155 In the place of those who could turn no longer.
1157 *clepit*: called.   1158 *gan I fall*: I fell.
1159 *hailsing*: greeting.   *abaist*: humbled.   1160 *in game*: jestingly.
1161 *dois thou*: are you doing.   *the hider sent*: sent you here.
1164 *lyis the on hert*: oppresses your spirit.
1165 Things don't stand for you as you would wish, perhaps?
1166 *for*: on account of.
1167 *endlang and overthwert*: in length and breadth (i.e. all over).
1172 *bot that your grace dedeyne*: only that your grace would deign.
1174 *well*: good fortune / source of water.   *slokin*: quench.

In quhiche I birn. A, goddesse fortunate,   1175
Help now my game that is in poynt to mate!'

'Off mate?' quod sche. 'O verray sely wreche!
I se wele by thy dedely colour pale
Thou art to feble of thy self to streche
Upon my quhele, to clymbe or to hale   1180
Withoutin help; for thou has fundin stale
This mony day withoutin werdis wele,
And wantis now thy veray hertis hele.

'Wele maistow be a wrechit man callit
That wantis the confort that suld thy hert glade,   1185
And has all thing within thy hert stallit
That may thy youth oppressen or defade.
Though thy begynnyng hath bene retrograde,
Be froward opposyt quhare till aspert,
Now sall thai turne and luke upon the dert.'   1190

fo. 209ʳ   And therwithall unto the quhele in hye
Sche hath me led, and bad me lere to clymbe,
Upon the quhich I steppit sudaynly.
'Now hald thy grippis,' quod sche, 'for thy tyme,
An hour and more it rynnis over prime: 1195

1175 *birn*: burn.

1176 *game*: chess-game.   *in poynt to mate*: on the point of being mated. Possibly an allusion to *BD* 618–84, where the man in black encountered by the dreamer tells of his chess-game with Fortune.

1177 *verray*: truly.   *sely*: simple.   1178 *dedely*: deathly.

1179 *of thy self*: in yourself.   *streche*: stretch up.   1180 *hale*: pull.

1181 *fundin stale*: found tiresome.

1182 *This mony day*: these many days.   *werdis wele*: good fortune.

1183 *wantis*: lack.   *hertis hele*: heart's welfare.

1186 *stallit*: shut up.   1187 *defade*: dispirit.   1188 *retrograde*: backward.

1189 This line is particularly hard to comprehend. The best sense of the passage from 1188–90 seems to be: 'Although your beginnings have been backward (in terms of the movement of Fortune's wheel), opposed by ordinance until *aspert* (severe); now *they* (i.e. those previously moving upward on Fortune's wheel) will turn and look at the earth'.

1190 *dert*: earth, ground.   1191 *in hye*: quickly.

1192 *bad*: ordered.   *lere*: learn.   1194 *grippis*: grasp.

1195 *rynnis over prime*: runs past prime (the first part of the day, 6–9 a.m.). The dreamer's life is imagined as the course of one day (see Burrow 1988a: 55–66). Prime,

To count the hole, the half is nere away—
Spend wele therfore the remanant of the day.

'Ensample,' quod sche, 'tak of this tofore,
That fro my quhele be rollit as a ball;
For the nature of it is evermore   1200
After ane hicht to vale and geve a fall—
Thus, quhen me likith, up or doune to fall.
Fare wele,' quod sche, and by the ere me toke
So ernestly that therwithall I woke.

O besy goste ay flikering to and fro,   1205
That never art in quiet nor in rest
Til thou cum to that place that thou cam fro,
Quhich is thy first and verray proper nest:
From day to day so sore here artow drest,
That with thy flesche ay waking art in trouble,   1210
And sleping eke, of pyne so has thou double.

Towert my self all this mene I to loke:
Though that my spirit vexit was tofore
In swevyng, als sone as ever I woke
By twenti fold it was in trouble more;   1215
Bethinking me with sighing hert and sore,

---

although variable, often signified 9 a.m., so to be an hour or so past prime would be to have almost reached the halfway point in life. In 1423/4 James was 29.

1196 *hole*: whole (the whole of a man's life: 70 years).   *nere away*: nearly gone.
1197 *remanant*: remainder.   1198 *this*: these.   *tofore*: before.
1201 *hicht*: height.   *vale*: fall.   1202 *quhen me likith*: whenever it pleases me.
1203 *ere*: ear. Fortune's tweaking of the dreamer's ear as a device to conclude the dream is an original touch, but may be compared to the waking prompts in *LR* 550–1.
1204 *ernestly*: severely.   1205 *goste*: spirit.   *ay*: always.   *flikering*: fluttering.
1207 *fro*: from.   1209 *artow drest*: are you afflicted.
1210 *flesche*: bodily form.   1211 *pyne*: pain.
1212 I mean all this to refer to myself (cf. 106). The MS reading *Couert* might be understood to mean 'hidden' (as Norton-Smith (James I 1981), who translates the line as 'Myself being hidden [i.e.concealed in prison], this outburst I mean to contain'), but scribal confusion between the letters T and C could easily explain a misreading of *Touert* (towards, concerning).
1213 *vexit*: troubled.   1214 *swevyng*: dreaming.
1216 *Bethinking me*: reflecting.

That nan othir thingis bot dremes had,
Nor sekirnes, my spirit with to glad.

And therwith sone I dressit me to ryse,
Fulfild of thought, pyne and adversitee,   1220
And to my self I said in this wise:
'A merci, Lord, quhat will ye do with me?
Quhat lyf is this? Quhare hath my spirit be?
Is this of my forethoght impressioun,
Or is it from the hevin a visioun?   1225

fo. 209ᵛ 'And gif ye goddis, of youre purviance,
Have schewit this for my reconforting,
In relesche of my furiouse pennance,
I yow beseke full humily of this thing,
That of your grace I myght have more takenyng,   1230
Gif it sal be as in my slepe before
Ye schewit have.' And forth withoutin more

In hye unto the wyndow gan I walk,
Moving within my spirit of this sight,
Quhare, sodeynly, a turture quhite as calk   1235
So evinly upon my hand gan lyght,
And unto me sche turnyt hir full ryght,

1217–18 That I had nothing but dreams, and no security, to gladden my spirit.

1219 *dressit me*: prepared.

1220 *Fufild*: preoccupied. Cf. *PF* 89: 'Fulfyld of thought and busy hevynesse'.

1223 *hath . . . be*: has . . . been.

1224 *forethoght*: what I was thinking about before I went to sleep. The narrator questions the nature of his dream, in line with conventional medieval categories (see Kruger 1992, and *HF* 1–54); it may be a genuine *somnium*, or simply the result of the meaningless thoughts which precede sleep (described in *PF* 99–105).

1226 *purviance*: providence.   1227 *reconforting*: comfort.

1228 *relesche*: relief.   *furiouse*: severe.   1229 *beseke*: beseech.   *humily*: humbly.

1230 *more takenyng*: further token.   1234 *Moving . . . of*: considering.

1235 *turture*: turtle-dove.   *quhite as calk*: white as chalk. The dove could symbolize faithful love (see *PF* 582–88) and also God's grace in the form of the Holy Spirit (Genesis 8; Acts 2). In *Le Pèlerinage de l'Ame* (*The Pilgrimage of the Soul*), the white dove of *Grace Dieu* brings a text to advise the Pilgrim when he is thrown from Fortune's wheel; see McDiarmid (James I 1973: 72).

1236 *evinly*: precisely.   *gan lyght*: alighted.   1237 *full ryght*: directly.

Off quham the chere in hir birdis aport
Gave me in hert kalendis of confort.

This fair bird ryght in hir bill gan hold   1240
Of red jorofflis with thair stalkis grene
A fair branche, quhare written was with gold
On every list, with branchis bryght and schene,
In compas fair, full plesandly to sene,
A plane sentence; quhich as I can devise   1245
And have in mynd, said ryght on this wise:

'Awak, awak! I bring, lufar, I bring
The newis glad that blisfull ben and sure
Of thy confort. Now lauch and play and syng,
That art besid so glad an aventure: 1250
For in the hevyn decretid is the cure.'
And unto me the flouris fair present,
With wyngis spred hir wayis furth sche went.

Quhilk up anon I tuke and, as I gesse,
Ane hundreth tymes or I forthir went   1255
I have it red, with hert full of glaidnese;

1238 *chere*: demeanour.   *aport*: bearing.   1239 *kalendis*: first signs, beginning.
   1240 *bill*: beak.   *gan hold*: held. The stint of the second scribe begins at this point. It is
difficult to picture quite what is described here. Skeat explains it as one spray of flowers 'on
every edge . . . of which a sentence was written in gold letters, ornamented with bright
flourishes'; McDiarmid, on the other hand, understands the bird to carry a scroll illuminated with gillyflowers. As the words stand, they seem to indicate writing *on* the spray of
flowers; the *branchis bryght and schene* may be flourishes of some kind. Representations of
the gillyflower or pink in 15th-c. art suggest that 'it stood for virtuous love and marriage';
see Sutton and Visser-Fuchs 1997.
   1241 *jorofflis*: gillyflowers, pinks.   1242 *branche*: spray.
   1243 *list*: edge.   *branchis*: flourishes.   1244 *compas*: shape.   *to sene*: to look at.
   1245 *plane*: clear.   *sentence*: inscription, text.   *devise*: relate.
   1246 *on this wise*: as follows, in this way.
   1247 *lufar*: lover. *Awak! awak!* signals more than the simple waking from the dream: it
marks the point of the narrator's entry into what is virtually a new life.
   1248 *The*: you.   *newis*: news.   *ben*: are.   1249 *lauch*: laugh.
   1250 *besid*: close to.   1251 *decretid*: decreed.
   1252 *present*: having presented.
   1253 *hir wayis furth sche went*: she went on her way.
   1254 *Quhilk*: which (flowers).   *tuke*: took.   1255 *or*: before.   *forthir*: further.
   1256 *glaidnese*: gladness.

And half with hope and half with dred it hent,
And at my beddis hed with gud entent
I have it fair pynnit up: and this
First takyn was of all my help and blisse.   1260

The quhich treuly efter, day by day,
That all my wittis maistrit had tofore,
From hensferth the paynis did away;
And schortly, so wele Fortune has hir bore
To quikin treuly day by day my lore,   1265
To my larges that I am cumyn agayn
To blisse with hir that is my sovirane.

Bot for als moche as sum micht think or seyne,
fo. 210ʳ   Quhat nedis me apoun so littil evyn
To writt all this? I answere thus ageyne: 1270
Quho that from hell war croppin onys in hevin
Wald efter o thank for joy mak sex or sevin!
And every wicht his awin swete or sore
Has maist in mynde, I can say you no more.

Eke quho may in this lyfe have more plesance   1275
Than cum to largesse from thraldom and peyne—
And by the mene of luffis ordinance,
That has so mony in his goldin cheyne?
Quhich thus to wyn his hertis sovereyne

1257 *hent*: took up.   1258 *beddis hed*: bed-head.
1259 *fair*: well. *pynnit*: pinned.   1260 *takyn*: token.
1261 *The quhich* seems to refer back to the *help and blisse* of the preceding line, and obliquely to indicate the *sovirane* of 1267.
1262 *maistrit*: overpowered.   1264 *has hir bore*: conducted herself.
1265 *quikin*: stimulate. *lore*: learning.   1266 *larges*: liberty.
1267 *sovirane*: sovereign.
1268 *for als moche*: for as much. *micht*: might. *seyne*: say.
1269–70 Why do I need, even upon so little, to write all this?
1271 *Quho*: whoever. *war croppin*: had crept. *onys*: once.
1272 *o*: one.   1274 *maist*: most.
1276 *cum*: he who comes. *thraldom*: captivity.
1277 *mene*: means. *luffis ordinance*: love's command.
1278 *mony*: many. *cheyne*: chain.
1279 *Quhich thus*: and so in this way. For love's golden chain, see Boethius, *De cons* II, m. 8, echoed in *TC* III. 1744–64 and *Kn T, CT* I. 2991, and *TG* 1106.

Quho suld me wite to write tharof, lat se! 1280
Now sufficiante is my felicitee.

Beseching unto fair Venus abufe
For all my brethir that ben in this place,
This is to seyne, that servandis ar to lufe
And of his lady can no thank purchase, 1285
His pane relesch, and sone to stand in grace,
Both to his worschip and to his first ese,
So that it hir and resoun noght displese.

And eke for thame that ar noght entrit inne
The dance of lufe bot thidderwart on way, 1290
In gude tym and sely to begynne
Thair prentissehed; and forthirmore I pray
For thame that passit bene the mony affray
In lufe and cummyng ar to full plesance,
To graunt tham all, lo, gude perseverance. 1295

And eke I pray for all the hertis dull
That lyven here in sleuth and ignorance,
And has no curage at the rose to pull,
Thair lif to mend and thair saulis avance
With thair swete lore, and bring thame to gude chance. 1300

1280 *wite*: blame.   *lat se*: let us see.   1281 *sufficiante*: sufficient.
1282 *abufe*: above.
1282–1302 This comprehensive prayer responds to the request made to lovers in the opening stanzas of *TC* (I. 22–46): 'preieth for hem ... And biddeth ek for hem ...' etc.
1283 *brethir*: brethren.   1285 *purchase*: obtain.
1286 *relesch*: relieve.   *sone to stand in grace*: (may he) soon stand in (her) grace.
1287 *worschip*: honour.   *first ese*: his supreme comfort.
1288 So long as it displeases neither her nor reason.
1289 *thame*: them.   *entrit inne*: entered into.
1290 *The dance of lufe*: cf. 1278, where Love's golden chain holds lovers in harmony. *thidderwart on way*: on their way there.
1291 *sely*: happy.   *to begynne*: (may they) begin.
1292 *prentissehed*: apprenticeship.
1293 *that passit bene*: who have passed.   *the mony affray*: the many struggles.
1298 *at the rose to pull*: to pluck the rose, an expression which derives from *RR* 21775–8.
1299 *mend*: improve.   *thair saulis avance*: advance their souls.
1300 *lore*: learning.

And quho that will noght for this prayer turn,
Quhen thai wald faynest speid that thai may spurn!

To rekyn of every thing the circumstance
As hapnit me quhen lessen gan the sore
Of my rancoure and wofull chance   1305
It war to long. I lat it be tharefor.

fo. 210ᵛ   And thus this flour—I can seye no more—
So hertly has unto my help attendit
That from the deth hir man sche has defendit.

And eke the goddis mercifull wirking,   1310
For my long pane and trewe service in lufe,
That has me gevin halely myn asking,
Quhich has my hert for evir sett abufe
In perfyte joy (that nevir may remufe
Bot onely deth), of quhom, in laud and prise,   1315
With thankfull hert I say richt in this wise:

Blissit mot be the goddis all
So fair that glitteren in the firmament;
And blissit be thare mycht celestiall,
That have convoyit hale with one assent   1320
My lufe, and to so glade a consequent.
And thankit be fortunys exilte
And quhele, that thus so wele has quhirlit me.

1301 *turn*: turn (to listen).
1302 That they may stumble when they would most like to succeed!
1303 *rekyn*: record.   1304 *hapnit me*: happened to me.
1306 *war*: would be.
1307 *this flour*: this flower: another discreet reference to the lady.
1308 *hertly*: completely.   1310 *wirking*: effects.
1312 *gevin*: granted.   *halely*: wholly.   *asking*: request.
1314–15 that nothing but death may ever take away.
1315 *prise*: praise.   1317 *Blissit mot be*: blessed be.   1319 *mycht*: power.
1320 *convoyit*: guided.   *hale*: completely.   1321 *consequent*: result.
1322 *fortunys exilte*: the exile imposed by Fortune. Some editors have read this as
fortunys exiltree, glossed as 'Fortune's axle-tree'.
1323 *quhele*: wheel.   *quhirlit*: whirled.

Thankit mot be and fair in lufe befall
The nychtingale, that with so gud entent   1325
Sang thare of lufe the notis swete and small,
Quhair my fair hertis lady was present,
Hir with to glad or that sche forthir went.
And thou, gerafloure, mot ithankit be
All othir flouris for the lufe of the.   1330

And thankit be the fair castell wall,
Quhare as I quhilom lukit furth and lent.
Thankit mot be the Sanctis Marciall
That me first causit hath this accident.
Thankit mot be the grene bewis bent,   1335
Throu quhom and under first fortunyt me
My hertis hele and my confort to be.

For to the presence swete and delitable
Rycht of this floure that full is of plesance,
By processe and by menys favorable,   1340
First of the blisfull goddis purveyance,
And syne throu long and trew contynuance
Of veray faith, in lufe and trew service,
I cum am. And forthir in this wise:

Unworthy, lo, bot onely of hir grace,   1345
In lufis yok that esy is and sure,

11^r

1324: *fair in lufe befall*: may good luck in love come to.
1328 To gladden her before she went on.
1329 And as for you, gillyflower—all other flowers must be thanked for the love of you!
1332 *quhilom*: formerly.   *lent*: leaned.
1333 *Sanctis Marciall*: saints of the month of March, when the narrator embarked on his sea-voyage (140).
1334 *accident*: turn of events.   1335 *bewis*: branches.
1336–7 Through and under which it was first my good fortune that my heart's cure and my comfort (was) to be (found).
1338 *delitable*: delectable.
1340 *processe*: course of time.   *menys favorable*: propitious workings.
1341 *purveyance*: providence.   1342 *syne*: then.
1346 *lufis yok*: love's yoke; a familiar phrase, also found in Clanvowe, *The Boke of Cupide* (Scattergood 1979), 140, and in *Cl T, CT* IV. 113 ('that blisful yok'), and *Mer T, CT*

In guerdoun of all my lufis space
Sche hath me tak hir humble creature.
And thus befell my blisfull aventure
In youth, of lufe that now from day to day   1350
Flourith ay newe. And yit forthir I say:

Go, litill tretisse, nakit of eloquence,
Causing simplesse and povertee to wit,
And pray the reder to have pacience
Of thy defaute and to supporten it;   1355
Of his gudnesse thy brukilnesse to knytt,
And his tong for to reule and to stere
That thy defautis helit may ben here.

Allace, and gif thou cummyst in the presence
Quhare as of blame faynest thou wald be quite,   1360
To here thy rude and crukit eloquens,
Quho sal be thare to pray for thy remyt?
No wicht, bot geve hir merci will admytt
The for gud will, that is thy gyd and stere,
To quhame for me thou pitously requere.   1365

IV. 1285 ('this yok of mariage') and 1837 ('blessed be the yok that we been inne').   *esy*: comfortable.

   1347 *guerdoun*: reward.   *space*: extent, duration.

   1351 *Flourith*: flourishes.   *ay*: continually.   *newe*: afresh.

   1352 *tretisse*: treatise.   *nakit*: bare.

   1352–79 The last four stanzas form an *envoy*, similar to the conclusions of *TC* and of *TG*. On the history of this device, see Norton-Smith 1974: 175–6. An appeal for the reader's indulgence or assistance is often made (as here, 1352–8), and an exclamation of unworthiness (1361).

   1353 Causing (readers) to know your simpleness and poverty.

   1355 *defaute*: lack.   *supporten it*: make it good.

   1356 *brukilnesse*: weakness.   *knytt*: mend.

   1357 *tong*: language.   *reule*: govern.   *stere*: direct.

   1358 *helit*: remedied.   1359 *cummyst*: come.

   1360–1 Where you would most gladly be free of blame for making heard your unpolished and crooked eloquence.

   1362 *remyt*: forgiveness.

   1363–4 No one, unless their mercy will admit you for good will, which is your guide and rudder.

And thus endith the fatall influence
Causit from hevyn quhare powar is commytt
Of govirnance, by the magnificence
Of him that hiest in the hevin sitt;
To quhame we thank, that all oure lif hath writt   1370
(Quho coutht it red) agone syne mony a yere
Hich in the hevynnis figure circulere.

Unto inpnis of my maisteris dere,
Gowere and Chaucere, that on the steppis satt
Of rethorike quhill thai were lyvand here,   1375
Superlative as poetis laureate,
In moralitee and eloquence ornate,
I recommend my buk in lynis sevin,
And eke thair saulis unto the blisse of hevin.

1367–8 *powar is commytt* | *Of govirnance*: power of governance is committed.
1369 *hiest*: highest.
1370 *To quhame*: whom.   *writt*: written. This is a problematic line (see textual note).
The emendations here are those proposed by Skeat.
1371 *Quho coutht it red*: whoever knows how to read it.   *agone syne*: past.
1372 A repetition of the first line of the poem.
1373 *inpnis*: poems.   *maisteris*: masters.
1374 *steppis*: steps. Lydgate is conventionally included alongside Chaucer and Gower in many 15th-c. invocations and dedications of this sort. His absence here may be explained by the fact that he was still alive when the poem was composed.
1375 *lyvand*: living.   1377 *ornate*: flourished.
1378 *lynis sevin*: seven-line stanzas (*or* in these seven lines). The form used is the rhyme royal stanza of *Troilus* and *PF*. For the possible significance of seven and multiples of seven in the poem, see MacQueen 1988: 59–60.
1379 *saulis*: souls.

Charles of Orleans, *Love's Renewal*

Charles of Orleans (1394–1465), well known since the fifteenth century as the author of many poems in French, was also probably responsible for an English sequence of lyrics and short narrative poems, corresponding in part to the French texts. Son of Louis of Orleans, who was brother to Charles VI of France, and of Valentina Visconti, daughter of the duke of Milan, Charles was given the upbringing and education appropriate to a future magnate, and was at 12 married to Isabelle, widow of the English king Richard II. He represented a valuable hostage when captured by the English after the battle of Agincourt in 1415, and was detained in England for twenty-five years as a privileged prisoner of war, maintaining a household and sending servants on commissions to France and within England, where his brother John of Angoulême was held separately in captivity. In 1440 the duke of Burgundy succeeded in negotiating Charles's freedom, and he returned to France to base his court at Blois. His second wife, Bonne d'Armagnac (whom he married in 1411 after Isabelle's death in 1410), died in France in 1435, and on his release from captivity Charles married the duke of Burgundy's niece, Marie de Clèves. Most of the French and English poems attributed to him take the form of love lyrics, and many can be linked to a putative sequence which documents a relationship with a distant lady, her death, and the courtship of a successor.

Charles's French poems (edited by Champion (Charles of Orleans 1923–7)) survive in several substantial manuscript collections, including a personal autograph anthology (Paris, Bibliothèque Nationale, fonds français 25458; see Champion 1907) and a sumptuously illustrated volume prepared in England for Edward IV and later Henry VII's son Prince Arthur (London, British Library, Royal 16. F. ii; edited by Fox (Charles of Orleans 1973)). The English poems are mainly confined to British Library MS Harley 682 (edited by Arn (Charles of Orleans 1994); Steele and Day (Charles of Orleans 1970)), and appear to have circulated less widely. It is still unclear whether the composition of the French poems preceded that of the English ones, or indeed whether Charles was responsible for both versions: the duke of Suffolk, one of his English guardians, and the husband of Chaucer's granddaughter Alice, has been proposed as a likely translator (see Jansen 1989). On the other hand, features of language and style in the English poems support the case for their composition by a non-native speaker (see Arn 1993); Charles is known to have become proficient in English, and to have had access to English books as well as to his large library of Latin and French material.

Like the sequence of French poems which were copied first in Charles's personal manuscript, the English poems of British Library MS Harley 682 have been copied in a sequence, organized to document the relationships of a 'prisoner' with two women, and are framed and punctuated by narrative sections such as the one below, for which no French equivalent, if it ever existed, has survived. The sequence of English poems begins as an allegory in which the narrator, who names himself as Charles of Orleans, pledges his service to the God of Love and begins the courtship of lady 'Bewte' (Beauty) by means of poems which he sends to her. He describes himself as a prisoner, both literally and in terms of his enthralment to love. The following eighty-four ballades (generally of three eight- or ten-line stanzas, with a shorter envoy) chart his progress, first addressing and celebrating the lady, and then lamenting her sudden death. A short dream sequence intervenes, in which the poet is commanded to change his allegiance from Youth to 'Elde', and at the end of which he retires from the service of Love to a place called 'No Care', to compose a 'feast' of what survive as seventy-eight roundels on the subject of love. In the ensuing narrative section, which constitutes the extract below (starting at line 4638 in Arn's edition (Charles of Orleans 1994) and Steele's edition (Charles of Orleans 1970)), the poet is asked by an acquaintance to write a complaint against Fortune. As he sits by the sea, having completed his commission, he dreams of both Fortune and Venus, who bring him a new lady, present in bodily form among the company of courtly people he joins when he wakes. The sequence ends with further ballades concerning the new courtship, and songs on the subject of love.

In its conception and in the questions it raises about the inspiration and appropriate matter of poetry, the sequence has much in common with other medieval lyrico-narratives concerned with love (Dante's *Vita nuova*, or Machaut's *Voir Dit*, for example), presenting courtly versifying in conjunction with an unfolding individual history to effect a commentary on the nature of poetic endeavour. In the extract here, the poet's vision of Venus and Fortune affords suggestive comparison with the investigations of love in *TG* and *KQ*, while the descriptive details, the handling of dialogue, and the form (the seven-line rhyme royal stanzas used in Chaucer's *PF*), draw interestingly on an amalgam of French and English traditions of courtly writing. The visual details are unusually full, and the dreamer's reactions both to his dream and to the waking encounter which follows it are suggested with humour and delicacy.

NOTE ON THE TEXT

The text here is edited from fos. 111^r–125^r of London, British Library MS Harley 682, the single surviving copy of the sequence of English poems associated with Charles (fragments of another copy made from this exemplar also survive: see Charles of Orleans 1994: 122–3). This is a careful and workmanlike manuscript, with evidence of revision and correction. The notes below record emendations, some based on marginal corrections.

TEXTUAL NOTES

34 so smothe] added in margin; MS
   so moche
87 an hir] am hir
106 thus] this
151 deyvere] deyuure
152 ere] are
345 balyse] balayse
347 aryse] arayse
370 weche that wroft wer yn a range]
   added in margin to replace
   cancelled: some at ful right vary
   straunge

394 ston] son
440 whylle] added in margin; MS
   bille
443 sekith] seith
459 Owttesepte] Owlle septe
530 yon] any
583 y ne wiste not] y not how
622 sit] set
655 yn] ny
656 cawse] sawse

Many of the English poems of BL MS Harley 682 (Charles of Orleans 1970; 1994) can be compared with parallel French versions (Charles of Orleans 1923–7). Purcell (1973) contains selections of lyrics in both English and French, and Pearsall (1999) a selection of lyrics and extracts from the narrative sections. Biography, and interesting detail about Charles's reading, is covered in Champion (1911) and McLeod (1969). Fox (1969) offers critical appreciation of the French poems. Arn (1990) and (1993), and Spearing (1991), concentrate on the English ones, and the essays collected in Arn (2000) cover both English and French. For discussion of lyrico-narratives in a wider European context, see Poirion (1965) and Burrow (1988a).

Love's Renewal

11ʳ   Now felle me, when this jubile thus was made,   [4638]
           Not kowde y ellis but wandir up and downe,
           Musyng in my wakyng dremys sad.
           Myn ydille thought so besy gan me rowne
           That alle the hertis dwellyng in a towne   5
           Ne nad, no no, so smalle to doon as y,
           For in No Care thus lyvid y, wot ye whi?

---

1 *felle*: befell. *jubile*: feast of rejoicing, or celebration, sometimes with religious significance; here, the 'banquet' of poems which have been offered after the death of the first lady, to celebrate retirement from the service of Love (Charles of Orleans 1970: 103–55; Charles of Orleans 1994: 247–312).

2 *Not kowde y ellis but*: I could do nothing except.

3 *wakyng dremys sad*: miserable daydreams.

4 *ydille*: unoccupied. *besy*: busily. *gan me rowne*: whispered to me.

5 *hertis*: hearts, beings. 6 *Ne nad*: had not. *so smalle*: so little.

7 *No Care*: an allegorical location, signifying indifference; in the 'Vision in Complaint', after the death of the first lady, the narrator is claimed from Youth by Age, is released by Cupid and Venus from his service to Love, and settles in 'the castelle of no care' (Charles of Orleans 1970: 86–102; Charles of Orleans 1994: 207–47). *wot ye whi*: do you know why.

Seyng y nadde as lady nor maystres,
As laboure noon me left nas, soth to say,
Without it were to here evensong and masse,   10
And for the sowle of my swet hert to pray;
Which esy liif y ledde this many day
Without it were that sum oon, he or she,
Wolde me complayne of ther adversite,

fo. 111ᵛ   And pray me that y wolde suche labour take   15
Of ther complayntis, as they to me tolde,
In a roundelle or balade them to make.
This, for y was so moche to love biholde
In my fer afore past dayes olde,
Ther nas to Love so sympille servyng wight   20
But that y fayne wolde plese hem, if y might.

As now but lat that on me ded requere
Forto biwayle fortunes stabilnes,
And tolde me alle the case of his matere.
And y that fayne wolde doon hem alle gladnes   25
Had tane on me right so the bisynes,
And took me so myn enke and papir to.
And for bicause me thought it best to do,

8 *nadde*: had not.   9 No work (in the service of love) was left me, truly.
10 *Without it were*: were it not.   13 *Without it were*: apart from when.
  15 The commissioning of 'complaints' by friends, in drawing attention to the narrator's
reputation as a poet and his temporary exclusion from the service of love, underlines a
concern with creativity and its inspiration which is investigated in many courtly visions and
lyrico-narratives: some of these are discussed by Poirion 1965.
  18–21 Thus, because I was so much beholden to love in my former, past days, long
since, there was no such artless a servant of love that I would not gladly please them, if I
might.
  22 *As now but lat*: As, recently.   *on*: someone.   *me ded requere*: requested me.
  23 The subject of the poem requested by the friend serves to objectify the narrator's
own preoccupations and, like the bedtime reading of *PF*, *BD*, and *KQ*, acts as a clarifying
preface to the dream. The labour of writing also plausibly leads to sleep.
  24 *the case of his matere*: the details of his story.   26 *tane*: taken.
  27 *took me . . . to*: equipped myself with.   *enke*: ink.
  28 *for bicause*: since.

Forth bi my silf thus went y me alone
Toward the see where nygh my bidyng was,   30
To y come to an high, huge rokke of stone
That to biholde hit glemshid bright as glas;
Where as y fonde a benche of mosse and gras
So smothe ygrowe and eek so verry soft
That it was liik a carpet as me thought.   35

Where as anoon that downe my silf y sat
And gan me muse to maken this complaynt
Syn it must nede be doon, as wot yow what,
And that y kan not make it ovyr quaynt;
But nevyrtheles these were my wordis faynt   40
I for him seide, and gan my papir sprede
112ʳ   And wrote right thus, if so ye list to rede:

'O thou Fortune, that causist pepille playne   [4680]
Upon thi chaunge and mutabilite,
Did y thee so y blamyd wrong, certayne,   45
For stabille yet herto as fynde y the,
Withouten chaunge forto prevaylen me;
But where as first thou fond me in symplesse,
Thou holdist me in myn adversite
So that y may biwayle thi stabilnes.   50

<hr>

30 *bidyng*: residence. The sequence as a whole contains several references to glimpses of the sea. During his imprisonment, Charles was kept, among other places, at Dover and Calais (MacLeod 1969: 189–94).

31 *To*: until.   32 *glemshid*: gleamed.

33 Naturally mossy, or artificially turfed, benches of this sort appear in *LGWP* F204 and *The Floure and the Leaf* (Pearsall 1962, 1990), lines 50–3.

35 *as me thought*: it seemed to me.   36 *anoon*: immediately.

38 *as wot yow what*: you know the way.

39 And since I can't write elaborately (a modesty topos)

40 *faynt*: poor, feeble.

43 The form changes for this inset complaint, composed of seven eight-line ballade or 'Monk's Tale' stanzas (see *CT* VII. 1991–2766), with refrain (technically, on the model of the French *formes fixes*, it is a double *balade*, with envoy).

45 If I were to do so (i.e. complain) I would blame you wrongly, certainly.

46 *yet herto*: always up to now.   47 *prevaylen*: advance, benefit.

48 *symplesse*: lowliness.

'And yet fulle many holde opynyoun
As that thou shulde now hurt and now amende,
And gladly als of thi condicioun
A sympille wight in honure to ascende,
And most in weele as don him downe descende.   55
But y may welle contrary lo witnes,
For of my wrecchid liif y fynde noon ende
So that y may biwayle thi stabilnes.

'For welle y se how ricches ascendith
And alle folke bisy him to plese and yeve,   60
Where as the sympille wight descendith
Of alle lothid, and noon him lust releve;
Among whiche on am y, in suche myschef:
Ordaynyd love, but to moche bisynes
Thou hast me geve my ladi to acheve,   65
So that y may biwayle thi stabilnes.

'Thorugh which y wynne more maugre oft then love
fo. 112ᵛ   By my to bisy demenyng.
And yet, God wot that sitt above,
I most desire of any erthely thing   70
To doon alle that as were to hir plesyng.
But of rewdenes thou gevist me such larges

---

51 There are echoes here of *TC* IV. 958–1078, where Troilus considers the workings of destiny and fortune, and of Chaucer's short poem *Fortune* (in Chaucer 1987). The paradox that an evidently 'changeable' fortune is in fact supremely stable is at the heart of Boethius's *De cons*, central also to *KQ* and *TG*, but the writer here perceives only steadfast malevolence rather than a benevolent capacity for change. On the general medieval background, see Lewis 1964 and Patch 1927.

53 *gladly*: habitually.   *als*: also.   *of thi condicioun*: characteristically.

54 *to ascende*: (cause) to ascend.

55 And cause to fall down (the person) most in prosperity.

56 *contrary*: to the contrary.   59 *ricches*: riches; hence 'a wealthy person'.

60 *yeve*: give to.   62 *noon him lust releve*: it pleases no one to provide for him.

63 *myschef*: distress.   64 *ordaynyd love*: commanded to love.   *bisynes*: difficulty.

67 *maugre*: hostility.   68 *to bisy demenyng*: over-anxious behaviour.

71 *alle that as were*: all that would be.

72 *rewdenes*: boorishness.   *larges*: abundance.

That thank to pike me wantith the konnyng,
So that y may biwayle thi stabilnes.

'Alas Fortune, now were me wondir wise;   75
Sett me in wey my lady forto plese.
And if that y have tane to high emprise
I pardoun axe, and that thou not displese,
But turne thi whele my langour to apese,
And of my smert to shape me sum redresse;   80
For yet thou baytist me in noyous lesse
So that y may biwayle thi stabilnes.

For my dulle rewdenes hath no governaunce,
Thorugh my demenyng, hir to doon plesere;
And yet, God wot, as that y have pusshaunce,   85
I sett myn hert, my wille and my desere
Hir forto serve, but alle to gret an hir
I willid have, thorugh fonnyd wilfulnes.
But me prevaylith werryng nor prayere—
So that y may biwayle thi stabilnes.   90

'Now farewelle Fortune with thi stedfast face,
For as y fynde right so y write of thee.
And yn my refrait though y thee manace
Thou oughtist not me thenke displesid be,
Though y say trouthe as that thou dost to me,   95
But evir truse and rewe on my distres

113ʳ

73 That I lack the skill to curry favour.
75 *were me wondir wise*: defend me very carefully.
77 *to high emprise*: to exalted an enterprise.
78 *axe*: ask. *that thou not displese*: and (ask) that you be not displeased.
79 *langour*: misery.   80 *smert*: pain. *shape*: contrive.
81 *baytist*: feed. *noyous lesse*: evil pasture (possibly to be emended to *noiousnesse*: antipathy, dislike).
83 *governaunce*: influence.   84 *hir to doon plesere*: to please her.
85 *as that*: as far as. *pusshaunce*: power.   87 *hir*: payment.
88 *willid*: wanted to. *fonnyd*: foolish.
89 *prevaylith*: profits. *werryng*: hostility.
93 *refrait*: refrain. *manace*: threaten.
95 *as that thou dost*: about what you do.   96 *truse*: make peace.

That y endure in suche adversite,
So that y may biwayle thi stedfastnes.'

And when that y had made this poor bille
So hevy gan myn eyeliddis way   100
That even therwith into a slepe y fille.
And alle be hit that sum folkis say
To trust on dremys nys but trifille play,
Yet oon may mete the dreme wel yn his sevyn
As aftirward that shalle bifalle him evyn.   105

Unto record y take myn autour thus
Of him that wrote the straunge avisioun,
(Which callid was the prewdent Macrobius)
How it bifille unto kyng Scipioun.
So nys hit no to myn opynyoun   110
Fully noon to take onto thym hid,
Forwhi y thinke it thus, so God me spede,

That hit doth to the body signyfy
What aftirward as shulde unto him falle—
Alle othir trust y holde it fantesy—   115
If so that oon koude welle remembre alle.
But to my tale as this retourne y shalle,

99 *bille*: document.   100 *way*: weigh.   101 *fille*: fell.
102–16 Allusions to contemporary opinions about the significance of dreams are
common in dream vision poems such as *RR* 1–20 and *HF* 1–65, and also in other contexts:
see, for example *TC* V. 358–85, and *NPT*, *CT* VII. 3077–156. Classical and medieval
theories are summarized by Kruger 1992, and by Spearing 1976: 1–47.
103 *nys but trifille play*: is simply idle foolishness.
104 *mete*: dream.   *sevyn*: sleep.   105 *evyn*: exactly.
106 *Unto record*: as witness   107 *avisioun*: dream, vision.
110–11 It is not at all my inclination to disregard them.
112 *Forwhi*: since.   *so God me spede*: may God help me.   113 *body*: person.
114 *falle*: happen.   115 *trust*: belief.
116 Dreams were categorized according to different systems in the Middle Ages. The
influential discussion of Macrobius distinguished between dreams caused by mundane
preoccupations or physiological disturbances and the more significant categories of revelation and enigmatic vision. In terms of these categories, the dream described here contains
elements of the *oraculum* (revelation by an authoritative figure) and the *somnium* (a vision
requiring interpretation). Other systems of categorization are discussed by Kruger 1992.
117 *as this*: thus.

That as y lay and slepte thus on the rokke
That on the cleef upon the banke out stokke,

Ovir the see, where that the roryng waves   120
Did overcast the gravelle here and there,
As that y slepe, in sweven y saw this:
A lady, nakid alle thing save hir here,
And on hir hed liik as a crowne she were
Of dowfis white, and many a thousand payre   125
Hie over hir gan fletter in the ayre.

About hir wast a kercher of plesaunce,
And on hir hond an owle y sigh sittyng.
Upon the waves, owt more suffisaunce,
Me thought afer she came to me fletyng,   130
And verily, it semyd me wakyng

---

119 *cleef*: cliff. *out stokke*: projected.

121 *overcast*: throw about.   122 *As that*: while.

123–8 The lady's emergence from the sea, with her headdress and convoy of doves, would to medieval readers familiar with mythography have immediately identified her as Venus (see Twycross 1972). The miniature which illustrates Chaucer's *Complaint of Mars* in Oxford, Bodleian Library MS Fairfax 16 (Norton-Smith 1979, frontispiece) gives a good idea of the traditional iconography (although here Venus carries, as more usually, a shell). For other descriptions of Venus in dream visions, cf. *HF* 133; *PF* 237–8, 261–73; *KQ* 666–72; *TG* 53.

123 *alle thing*: completely. *here*: hair.   125 *dowfis*: doves. *payre*: pairs.

126 *gan fletter*: fluttered.

127 *wast*: waist. *a kercher of plesaunce*: a scarf made from fine fabric from Piacenza (cf. *PF* 272; *KQ* 569), with a pun on the sense of *plesaunce* as 'delight'.

128 *sigh*: saw. Venus's birds were doves (less often, sparrows), and she was usually represented carrying a conch or sea-shell (although Chaucer gives her variously a comb, *HF* 136, and a citole or kind of zither, *Kn T*, *CT* I. 1955; see Twycross 1972). As noted in Steele (Charles of Orleans 1970), the owl is usually associated with Pallas, goddess of wisdom, who appears together with Venus and her doves in scenes which depict the Judgement of Paris (as in Lydgate's *Troy Book* II. 2556; cf. also Minerva in *KQ* 876–966 and Pallas in *TG* 248). In the dream context here, the confusion of attributes perhaps underlines the mysteriousness and ultimately the wisdom of the advice Venus is to offer. The owl was traditionally also the bird of sleep and of death.

129 *owt more suffisaunce*: without further support.

130 *afer*: from afar. *fletyng*: floating (cf. the descriptions in *HF* and *Kn T* mentioned above in 128 n.).

131 *me wakyng*: I was awake.

And went me downe unto the bank apace
To undirstonde of hir what that she was.

When she came nere than gan y to hir say:
'Good thrift, madame, to yowre streight sidis tayne.   135
But whidir wandre ye this wersome way?
Have y no service myght be to yow fayne?
Me thynke this watir is unto yow payne,
Ne nys hit?' 'No, no, noon nys hit, ywis,'
Coth she, and as y shope me hir to kis   140

She wayfid me and lokid passyng straunge.
'What, nys?' quod she, 'as purse is of an ay?'
And even forbasshid hir coloure gan to chaunge.
'Knowe ye not me?' 'No.' 'Yes.' 'Nay, certes, nay.'
'No, ye wil not se poore folk nowaday.   145
Who is hit, who that oft hath bete your hound?'

fo. 114ʳ   For which y stood so masid in that stound

That y not koude oon sely word abreide,
For sene y had hir, how y nyste not where;
To that, eft sone she this unto me seide: 150
'Charlis,' quod she, 'y thanke yowre deyvere

132 *apace*: quickly.   133 *what that she was*: who she was.
135 *good thrift*: good luck (cf. *TC* III. 1247–50).   *streight sidis tayne*: two slim flanks (an overly familiar greeting).
136 *whidir*: where.   *wersome*: wearisome.   137 *fayne*: pleasing.
138 *is unto yow payne*: is troublesome to you.   139 *Ne nys hit*: isn't it.
140 *Coth*: said.   *shope me*: prepared.
141 *wayfid*: disregarded.   *lokid passyng straunge*: looked very distant.
142 *nys*: affected.   *as purse is of an ay*: smooth like an eggshell.
143 *even*: quite.   *forbasshid*: embarrassed, outraged.
145 *ye wil not se*: you won't acknowledge.
146 Who is it, that has often beaten your dog? (perhaps a vanished idiom), or (if *hound* and *stound* are taken as variant forms of *hond* and *stond*), Who is it, that has often pressed your hand (as a pledge)?
147 *masid*: confused.   *stound*: time, moment.   148 *sely*: simple.   *abreide*: utter.
149 *how y nyste not where*: I knew not how or where.
150 *To that*: until.   *eft sone*: in a moment.
151–4 I thank you for the duty you will do to me, such as my followers previously (did), and were it not that you would be acquitted (i.e. make it up to me), I might well indeed say that you were to blame (for not recognizing me and duly greeting me). The narrator refers

That ye shal make, suche as my folkis ere,
And but so were that ye shulde ben aquyt,
Iwis, y myght wel say ye were to wite.'

When that y herde hir calle me bi my name,   155
And that y wel had lokid on hir face,
Myn hert in me hit quoke for verry shame,
For wel y wiste that Venus then hit was,
And seide: 'Madame, y putt me to yowre gras,
And pardone me, as of yowre gret nobles,   160
That y forgat yow of my symplesse.'

'Yow pardone what? what nedith this?' quod she,
'Yowre mendis is as passyng light to make.'
But how lede ye yowre liif, good, lete us se?'
'As an ancre, madame, in clothis blake.'   165
'So thynkith me ye have professioun take,
Or ellis ye cast to fonde sum ordir newe,
For strike ye are from rosett out and blewe.'

'A trouthe ye say me soth, so sett me well:
For as for blew y clothe therin myn hert,   170
And alle the rosett is y-entirmelle;
I kepe therin my pover thought covert:

to himself as Charles of Orleans several times in the sequence: see Steele in Charles of
Orleans 1970; Arn in Charles of Orleans 1994, lines 6, 2720, 3044.

157 *quoke*: trembled.   159 *putt me to yowre gras*: put myself at your mercy.

163 *mendis*: reparation. *passyng light*: very easy.

164 *good*: worthy man, excellent person (cf. e.g. *TC* I. 1017; IV. 1660).

165 *ancre*: anchorite. For the solitude and black clothing of the bereaved lover, cf. *BD*
445–513.

166 *professioun take*: taken vows (as on entering a religious order).

167 *cast*: plan. *fonde*: found. *ordir*: religious order.

168 *strike ... out*: struck out. *rosett*: rose-colour. Blue was conventionally the colour
of faithfulness in love (cf. Steele in Charles of Orleans 1970; Arn in Charles of Orleans
1994, lines 1153–4, 'the coloure blew | Which hewe in loue is callid stedfastnes', and the
poem *Against Women Unconstant*, ascribed to Chaucer, and in Chaucer 1987, in which the
unfaithful lady is told 'In stede of blew, thus may ye were al grene'); *rosett* perhaps recalls
the lovers in the garden of *RR*.

169 *trouthe*: truth. *soth*: indeed. *so sett me well*: I'm pleased to say.

171 *y-entirmelle*: intermingled.   172 *pover*: poor.

fo. 114^v   Alle suche as esy arne, not suche as smert,
                       For in tawny y leie alle them aside
                       And to my deth in blak my silf y bide.'   175

                       'Whi so?' quod she, 'Dwelle ye not in No Care?'
                       'Soth dwelle y so, liik as a masid man
                       That hath a bidyng, and wot not where.
                       For though y whilom fer from sorow ran,
                       Yet wol he, lo, for ought that evyr y kan,   180
                       Be with me to and to, wil y or no,
                       And as my frend thus cherisshe y my fo.'

                       'But how is it? how cometh he to yow so?
                       Ye dwelle asondir fer.' 'Nay, sothely, nere.
                       'For when me happith here or there to go,   185
                       And thenke that yondir, lo, my lady dere
                       Gaf me this word, or made me suche a chere,
                       And aundir herede y hir so swetely syng,
                       And in this chambre led y hir daunsyng;

                       'In yondir bayne so se y hir alle nakid,   190
                       And this and that y sawe hir yondir worche;

173 *esy*: pleasant.   *smert*: sting.

174 *tawny*: browny-yellow, has no particular symbolic associations, but is presumably appropriate for painful thoughts.

175 *to my deth*: until my death.

177 *masid*: bewildered. The narrator's characterization of himself recalls elements of both the dreamer and the Man in Black in *BD* (see *BD* 7–15, 583–97, etc.).

178 *bidyng*: residence.   179 *whilom*: formerly.

181 *to and to*: side by side.   *wil y or no*: whether or not I wish it. For parallels in ideas and phrasing, cf. *BD* 581–97.

184–206 Cf. *TC* V. 561–81. Processes of memory, and their capacity to inhibit or inspire poetic creativity, are similarly important in *BD*, *KQ*, and other dream visions.

184 *asondir fer*: far apart.   185 *me happith . . . to go*: it happens that I go.

187 *made me suche a chere*: looked at me in such a way.

188 *aundir*: yonder, over there.   *herede*: heard.

190 *bayne*: bath. Bathing was sometimes a communal activity in the Middle Ages, as described by Wood 1981: 371–4, and illustrated in Uitz 1988: plate 57.

191 *worche*: do.

Here y fond hir slepe, and yondir wakid,
And in this wyndow pleide we at the lorche,
And from this stayre y lad hir to the chirche,
And bi the way this tale y to hir tolde, 195
And here she gaf me, lo, this ryng of gold;

'And there at post and piler did she play,
And so y first my love unto hir tolde;
. 115^r And there aferd she start fro me away,
And with this word she made myn hert to bold, 200
And with this word, allas, she made me cold;
And yondir sigh y hir this resoun write,
And here y baste hir fayre round pappis white;

'In such a towre also y sigh hir last—
And yet wel more a thousand thoughtis moo, 205
How in that bed the liif eek from hir past.
Thus ay newly aquaynt y me with woo,
To that to chirche he doth me forto goo
And for hir sowle upon my knees pray.
Lo, thus my lyvis tyme y dryve away. 210

'For charge nave y of thing to me bileft
Of good nor harme more then y telle yow this.
And as foryet y care nothing of theft,
For thorugh the deth my thoughtis riche y mys,
That stede of hit the wallis bare y kis, 215

---

193 *lorche*: a game similar to backgammon (further described by Arn in Charles of Orleans 1994: 57–60).
194 *stayre*: staircase. *lad*: led.
197 *post and piler*: a game, similar to prisoner's base (see Steele in Charles of Orleans 1970: pp. xxxvii–xxxviii, and Arn in Charles of Orleans 1994: 60–2).
199 *aferd*: frightened.
200 Cf. *PF* 144–5. *to bold*: grow bold. 202 *resoun*: text. *sigh*: saw.
203 *baste*: kissed. *pappis*: breasts. 205 *moo*: more.
207 *ay newly*: ever afresh. 208 *To that*: until. *he doth me*: he makes me.
211 *charge nave y of*: I care not for. *bileft*: left.
213 *as foryet*: like a forgotten thing.
214 *thoughtis riche*: precious thoughts. *y mys*: I lack.
215 *stede of hit*: instead of her.

Or ellis a glove or smokke y from hir stale
Which was the shitht of hir y lovyd and shalle.

'Unto this paynfulle ded professioun
Mi hert and y are swore unto my last,
Withouten chaunge or newe opynyoun,   220
But this service to kepe to me stedfast,
Ay to remembre on my joyes past;
And y that so must doon, that wold y lere,
Where that y dwelle from woo then fer or nere.

fo. 115ᵛ   'Thus have y told yow my poore ancre liif,   225
And what professioun that y am to bounde.
How thenke ye, lo, nys hit contemplatiif?'
'No, certis.' 'Whi?' 'Ye do yowre silf confound.'
'Whi, wherof serve y now but bete the ground
As that y goo? Ellis helpe y unto nought.'   230
'Ye, fy!' quod she, 'Nay, chaunge ye muste that thought.

'Remembre must ye that ye ar a man,
And have of nature als yowre lymys goode.
So ought ye kyndely thenk me spend it than,
Or ellis ye were to moche to blame, bi the roode,   235

---

216 *smokke*: chemise. *stale*: stole.

217 *shitht*: shift.   218 cf. 166, 226.   219 *my last*: my death.

221 *service*: duty, office.

223–4 And I who must do this would learn (from you) whether (you think) I dwell far from misery or close to it (a rhetorical question designed to answer the concern which Venus expressed for his welfare at 164 ff.).

224 *Where*: whether.   225 *ancre*: anchoritic.   226 *to bounde*: bound to.

227 *contemplatiiff*: contemplative, as opposed to the active life of the world.

228 *confound*: destroy, condemn.

229–30 Why, what use am I now beyond treading the ground as I walk? I serve no other purpose.

232 Venus reminds the dreamer that he must not simply give in to the sin of despair. In prompting him to re-enter the service of Love she represents not simply sexual desire but also the regenerative potential of love as a force for cosmic order and harmony. See Bennett 1957: 93–9 for discussion of the 'wanton' and the 'lawful' Venuses.

233 *lymys*: limbs.

234 *kyndely*: according to nature. *thenk me*: it seems to me. *spend it*: put it (your life) to use.

235 *bi the roode*: by the cross.

Though that yowre hert so trewly stonde or stode
Yowre ladi to. O what, now she is goo,
What vaylith here to stroy yowre silf in woo?

'Ye may as wel chese yow a lady newe
And for hir sowle as dayly forto pray,   240
And ben in hert to hir as verry trewe,
As wilfully to doon yowre silf to day,
And forto spende in vayne yowre tyme away.
For though ye take a lady in yowre arme,
God wot, as now hit doth hir litille harm.'   245

'Alas, madame,' seide y, 'that ye shulde say!
Durst y yet speke so fowl a word as this?
For ben she ded myn hert must serve hir ay
As y have swore, and so shalle doon ywis,
For in good trouthe ellis did y fer amys.   250
Allas, madame, speke me therof no more;
The more ye speke the more me grevith sore.

'And where ye say that y shulde ben a man,
A wrecche am y, an ofcast creature.
For who is she that joy of me wolde han,   255
That am forfadid so in my figure?
Certis, to wrappe me in a sepulture
Me sittith bet, as wisly God me save,
Then in myn armes a newe ladi have.'

236–7 Even though your heart stands or stood faithfully by your lady.
237 *goo*: gone.   238 *vaylith*: avails. *stroy*: destroy.   239 *chese*: choose.
240 And pray for her soul as many times a day (as for your former lady).
242 *day*: die.   245 *hir*: i.e. the previous lady.   246 *say*: say this.
247 *Durst*: would I dare.
248 *ben she ded*: even though she is dead.   *ay*: always.   249 *ywis*: indeed.
250 *fer amys*: very wrongly. The dreamer takes it as a rule of love's service that
dedication to a lady must be total and permanent. Courtly poems often debate such issues:
Le Jugement du Roi de Behaigne, by Guillaume de Machaut (tr. and ed. Palmer (Guillaume
de Machaut 1984); Windeatt 1982), presents for judgement the question of whether it is
better to lose a loved one through death or through faithlessness.
254 *ofcast*: outcast.   255 *han*: have.   256 *forfadid*: faded.
257 *sepulture*: grave.
258 *Me sittith bet*: better befits me.   *as wisly God me save*: as surely as God may save me.
259 *Then*: than.

16ʳ

'Now bi my soth, that were a worthi toy!   260
So preve ye welle ye are not worth at alle.
What nede y, lo, to paynt or make it koy?
And in this case yowre silf so shame ye shalle,
And me and alle my folke in generalle,
For alle may say my service is to badde   265
That ye nave lust to serve me as ye had.

'And more, therin ye do yowre lady shame,
For alle the world wol thynke hit, verily,
And sche had ben as folk hath gen hir name
Ye wolde have tane an othir hastily.   270
But they wil say ye doon it for a sy,
And clakke of hir a fulle ungoodly clawse:
Thus shalle ye doon hir shame without a cause.'

'Allas, madame, as wisly fynde y blis
As me were loth to shame it yow or yowris,   275
And most of alle my lady dere, ywis.
But y se deth so crewelly devowris
fo. 116ᵛ   Suche folkis fayre, and in cheef of ther flowris,
That as me thynk hit is a choys in vayne
To chesen that on shalle not long attayne.   280

'For chase y me a lady, lo, this day—
As welle y wot that shal me not bitide—
Yet shulde y drede the deth of hir alway,

260 *toy*: jest.   261 *preve*: prove.   *at alle*: (anything) at all.
262 *paynt*: conceal, embellish.   *make it koy*: speak with reserve.
265 *my service*: the service done to me. Venus is comically concerned that the dreamer's
refusal to re-enter the service of love may reflect badly on her reputation.
266 *that ye nave lust*: that you have no wish.
269 *And*: if.   *gen hir name*: spoken of her.   270 *tane*: taken.
271 *sy*: aspersion (or perhaps *fy*: reproach).
272 say unflattering things about her.
274–5 As surely as I may come to heaven, I would be unwilling to shame you or your
followers.
278 *in cheef of ther flowris*: in the prime of their lives.
279 It seems to me a futile choice.
280 *attayne*: keep possession of.   281 *chase y me*: were I to choose for myself.
282 As much as I know that it will not happen to me.

To thynke how yong and fayre my lady dide.
Thus gif y shulde my service newe provide,   285
Then brought y me in sorow dubbil fold:
As first to thynke upon my dayes old,

'And then agayne upon my service dewe—
How were me best to sett my governaunce
To get the favour of my lady newe,   290
So hard it is in takyng acqueyntaunce:
For that which is unto sum oon plesaunce,
An othir wille parcas ben with hit wroth.
The craft of love is straunge, who to hit goth.

'For some they joy hem in a port al straunge,   295
And othir some in gladsom demenyng,
And some wil thynke "he usith fillith of chaunge!",
And some wil deme this word is flateryng,
Thus newe to lere were y in my gidyng.
For alle knew y my lady verry wel,   300
Anothir newe, y knowe hir nevyr a del.'

'O, what!' quod she, 'ye make a gret perail
To love, me thynke; ye nede not don hit so.
For if ye cast in love prevayle,

---

284 *To thynke*: thinking. *dide*: died.   285 *gif*: if.
286 The double sorrow here is firstly recollecting the dead lady, and secondly setting about winning the new one. Cf. the 'double sorwe' of Troilus (*TC* I. 1), first in declaring his love to Criseyde, and then losing her to another lover.
288 *dewe*: current, due.   289 *sett my governaunce*: conduct myself.
292 *sum oon*: some people.   293 *parcas*: perhaps.
294 *who to hit goth*: (for) whoever practises it. Love is frequently referred to as a 'craft' or a 'skill', with appropriate rules and forms of behaviour; cf. 'the craft of fyn lovynge', *LGWP* F544.
295 *joy hem*: take delight in.   *port*: conduct.   *straunge*: distant.
296 *gladsom demenyng*: cheerful bearing.
297 *fillith of chaunge*: abundance of fickleness/bad behaviour characterized by its changeableness.
299 if I were to be so uncouth in my conduct.   300 *my lady*: my former lady.
301 *Anothir newe*: a new lady.   *nevyr a del*: not a bit.   302 *perail*: fuss, trouble.
304–14 The metre changes here, for no apparent reason, from lines of five to lines of four stresses.
304 *cast . . . prevayle*: plan to win.

Spare not to speke, spede ye so or no.   305
Parde, noon wol bicome yowre foo
For yowre good wille, this ben ye sewre;
Hit were to moche agayne nature.

'And where ye care for yowre havour—
Where ye shulde ben mery or sad—   310
Loke wher ye cast stonde in favour,
And who that most in prays is had
With hir, where he loke glom or glad,
Folow the same, if that ye kan,
And hard is but ye plese hir than.   315

'And where ye wolde as have mor dred of deth,
Had ye a lady, for hir then your silf,
Parde, deth in yowthe not alle a sleth:
Some may ye se that lyve four score and twelfe,
And bi that howre were tyme for the to delve!   320
So fy! for shame, ye ought to trust the best
Of every dowt to sett yowre hert at rest.

'And where ye cast alway from love withdrawe,
A, feith! y trowe yowre labour vaylith not;
For when ye se that that ye nevir saw   325
It may wel happe yow thynke ye never thought.'
And as y threw myn eye therwith aloft

305 *Spare not*: do not omit.   *spede ye so or no*: whether or not you're successful.
306 *Parde*: by God.   307 *For*: on account of.   *sewre*: certain.
309 *care*: are anxious about.   *havour*: conduct.   310 *Where*: whether.
311 study the place (i.e. the woman with whom) you plan to have favour.
312–13 *most in prays is had* | *With hir*: is most esteemed by her.
313 *glom*: miserable.   315 It will be difficult then for you not to please her.
316 And where you (were saying that) you would be more worried about death.
317 *then your silf*: than for yourself.
318 By God, death does not destroy everyone in youth.
319 *four score and twelfe*: until they are 92.
320 And then it would be time for you to dig (a grave).
321 *the best*: the best (advice).   323 *cast*: intend.
324 *vaylith not*: is worthless.
325–6 When you see what you've never seen before, then you may well think what
you've never thought. An impossibility topos: Venus's words mark the transition to the
next stage of the vision. For the phrasing, cf. *TC* V. 992–3.

Me thought y saw descendyng in the ayre
A chare of gold, so verry riche and fayre,

That forto se hit nas no wondir lite   330
The ricches of the stones therupon,
Whiche drawen was with two large stedis white,
And as me thought on whelis foure it ran.
Abowt it als y sigh fulle many on
That did hir payne to put it forth and shove,   335
And in this chayre ther sat a quene above

That forto say yow how she ware hir gere,
Hit was ydoon hardly at poynt devise;
And if that y shalle say yow what sche were,
But verry god, me thought it passyng nyse—   340
Alle though it riche were of a wondir prise—
For evyrmore the coloure gan to chaunge,
So semyd me hir surcot verry straunge.

For the body was kowchid, thorugh and thorugh,
As evyrmore a saphir and a balyse,   345
That to biholde it, as y tolde yow now,
So as the playtis up and downe aryse,
So did dyverse the hewe in sondry wise;

329 *chare*: chariot.   330 *no wondir lite*: no small wonder.
335 *did hir payn*: exerted themselves.   *put it forth and shove*: push and move it on. Those anxious for good fortune and prosperity cluster around the chariot, similar to the throng who seek good fortune in *BC*.
336 Details of the dress and appearance of this new figure identify her as Fortune long before her name is announced at 463. On the association of love with Fortune, see Patch 1927: 90–8 (in *HF* 1547–48, Chaucer associates Fortune with the goddess Fame).
337 *forto say yow*: in order to tell you.   *gere*: apparel.
338 It was managed confidently, to perfection.   340 *nyse*: extraordinary.
342 For these details of Fortune's dress, cf. Patch 1927: 46–8.
343 *surcot*: outer garment.   344 *kowchid*: embroidered.
345 *As evyrmore*: all over.   *balyse*: spinel ruby. The associations of these jewels include prosperity and success in love: see Evans and Serjeantson 1933: 21, and cf. *TG* 259–60.
347 *playtis*: pleats.   *arayse*: moved.
348 *dyverse*: change.

For though on wey the safir shewid blew,
This way the balise geveth a purpil hew.   350

And as the surcot forgoth in substaunce
Of ermyn, and is powdrid round abowt,
So was it wrought with fyn pynche and plesaunce,
And in the stede of powdryng alle without,
As y biheld, right wel persayve y mought   355
How it was sett ful thikke with laughyng eyene,
But many moo that wepte y myght aspien.

fo. 118ʳ

Upon the whiche she ware a mantelle large
That many fold was festid with a lace,
Bicause only hit bare so gret a charge,   360
Of which the coloure blak nor grene it nas,
But most liik to a raynbow hewe it was,
Forwhi the silkis were so verry straunge
That ay from blew to reed or grene thei chaunge,

Of which the tissew ran in clowde werk;   365
And as thei brak now there and here,
Some with rayne and tempest lokid derk,
And out of othir smote sonne-bemys clere,
And othir some were worst in a manere

---

349 *on wey*: one way.

351 *forgoth*: is outstanding (Arn (in *Charles of Orleans* 1994), in a note to this line, suggests an emendation to *forgeth*: counterfeits).   *in substaunce*: exceedingly. Cf. the ermine trimmed mantle worn by Fortune in *KQ* 1120–2.

352 *powdrid*: spotted.   353 *pynche*: possibly a pleated fabric.

354 And in the place of the spotting on the outside.

355 *ryght wel persayve y mought*: I could well see. The image of Fortune's 'double visage' (cf. 401–2) is common. See Chaucer, *Boece* II, pr. 1, line 58; Patch 1927: 43–4.

359 *many fold*: in many folds.   *festid*: fastened.   *lace*: cord.

360 *charge*: load.   362 For the phrasing, cf. *BD* 855–7.

363 *Forwhi*: since.

365 *tissew*: fabric (specifically a rich fabric, often interwoven with silver and gold). *clowde*: cloud-like.

366 *brak*: parted.

369 *worst*: woven (or possibly a scribal error for *wroft*, wrought).

Of moonys, weche that wroft wer yn a range,   370
Some at a wane, some cresyng after chaunge.

A bordir had this mantelle eek theron
That praty was and riche in verry dede,
For made it was a brere of gold that ron
Now here and there, with rosis whit and reede   375
Upon the which, and levis as thei sprede;
Some loose, some fast, thei sett were ful of ston,
And that of perlis passyng many oon.

The lynyng of hit was with nedille wrought
So playn, so thikke, so smothe, so pratily   380
With litille litille flowris soft:
The soven and the daisy,
But most of pancy myght y spy.
Abowt hir nek also she ware
A serpe, the fasson to declare: 385

Hit wrought was fulle of broken balis
Of dise, and as they fillen out,
Bi lynkis and so downe avalis,

18ʳ

370 *weche that wroft wer yn a range*: which were fashioned in a row. Fortune was often associated wth the moon, a symbol of mutability; see Patch 1927: 50.
371 *at a wane*: waning.   *cresyng*: waxing, increasing.
372 *eek*: also.   373 *praty*: pretty.
374 *made it was*: it was made as.   *brere*: dog-rose.
377 They were set full of gems, some loose, some fixed.
378 *passyng*: very. Because of their appearance, pearls were associated with the moon— a connection explored in *Pearl* (see Gordon 1953).
380 *playn*: smooth.   *pratily*: sweetly.
380–406 The metre changes again from five-stress to four-stress lines; cf. 304–14.
381 Like jewels, many flowers carried symbolic associations; see Evans 1931: i. 61–4.
382 *soven*: germander speedwell, or possibly forget-me-not, Fr. *soveneȝ*, whose name means 'remember'. The daisy's significance is explored in *LGWP* F40–57, where it is described as 'fulfilled of al vertu and honour' (F54). Cf. also the symbolism in *AL* 535.
383 *pancy*: pansy, Fr. *pensée*, 'thought'. Alternative English names for this flower include heart's-ease and love-in-idleness.
385 *serpe*: collar, necklace.   *the fasson to declare*: its features as follows.
386–7 *balis* | *Of dise*: sets of dice. Fortune is commonly depicted playing games of chance such as dice and chess: see Patch 1927: 81, and cf. *BD* 618–84.
387 *fillen out*: fell.   388 *Bi lynkis*: in strings.   *avalis*: descend.

    To se them how they werle abowt
    Hit wondir was, withouten dowt: 390
    Whi they turnyd so many chaunsis,
    And that so ful of verryaunces.

    Hir crowne was made with wavis nyse,
    And sett ful of karbonkil ston,
    The reysyng up with flowre delise.   395
    Her heer also so bright it shon
    That it was hard to loke it on,
    Which spredde hir shuldris alle abrod
    And alle the chayre in which she rood.

    Hir visage was eek wel ymade,   400
    But then sumwhile she lowrid sore,
    And even as soune she lokid glad;
    And in hir hond a wheel she bore,
    And gan to turne it evyrmore,
    That berel was, me thought, or glas,   405
    And this was wreten in compas:

    'I shal rayne, y rayne, y have raynyd',
    And 'y owt-rayne' was wreten last of al,
fo. 119ʳ   On which that many folkis hem constraynyd

391 *chaunsis*: chances.   392 *verryaunces*: changes.
393 *wavis nyce*: skilful waves (i.e. a scalloped edge).
394 *karbonkil*: carbuncle.
395 *reysyng up*: point of each wave.   *flowre delise*: fleur-de-lys, lily.
398 *alle abrod*: all around.   399 *rood*: rode.
400 *wel ymade*: well fashioned.   401 *lowrid*: frowned. Cf. *KQ* 1124–5.
402 *even as soune*: just as quickly.
403 Fortune is sometimes represented on or near a large wheel (Patch 1927: 147–80, with illustrations); here she holds it.
405 *berel*: beryl, a transparent green/blue stone, and a term also used of crystal (cf. *AL* 455). It was generally associated with good fortune in love; see Evans and Serjeantson 1933, and cf. *HF* 1184.
406 *in compas*: round about it. Representations of Fortune's wheel often show four figures at different points around the rim, each associated with one of the four Latin tags which in this text are translated into ME: *Regnabo, Regno, Regnavi, Sum sine Regno*; see Patch 1927: 164–6; and Pickering 1970: plates 1b, 2a, 2b, 3a.
408 *owt-rayne*: reign longer than others.
409 *hem constraynyd*: pushed themselves. The depiction in *KQ* 1138–55 is very similar.

To gete aloft, that sone downe from hit falle,   410
And wolde clyme, that myght no thing at alle.
And othir some they sat up passyng hy,
Among the which that on y myght aspy

So inly fayre, so fulle of goodlynes,
So wel ensewrid bothe of port and chere,   415
That this bithought me, lo, dowtles,
How that it was myn owen self lady dere,
And ay the more, the more she came me nere.
'Allas,' quod y, 'but lyvith my lady yet?
Nys she not she, that y se yondir sitt?'   420

So that y stood so masid and formad
That y not kowd but stele to gase hir on,
To Venus saw how sore y was bistad,
And to me seide 'Where loke ye, doty fon?'
But my heryng so fer was fro me gon   425
That y not herde nor wiste what that y seide
To me she shook, so that y with abrayde,

And with a sigh y seide hir thus: 'Allas!
O fayre madame, now be myn helpe or never.
For Jhesu wot, y stond now in the cas   430
That certis, swete, the deth were to me lever
Then that y shulde from hir as now dissever,
Which is my lady, hie on yondir whel.'
'Ye, wo is me,' quod she, 'for yowre seek heel!

411 And who wished to climb (onto it), who could not at all.
414 *inly*: extremely.
415 *ensewrid*: assured. *port*: bearing. *chere*: expression.
421 *masid*: astonished. *formad*: distracted.
422 That I could only go on gazing at her, motionless.
423 (and 427). *To*: until. *how sore y was bistad*: how miserably I was placed.
424 *doty fon*: simple-minded fool. The conversation between Venus and the dreamer is comically peppered with colloquialisms such as this; cf. 460, 597.
426 *not herde*: did not hear. *wiste*: knew.   427 *abrayde*: started.
431 *lever*: preferable.   432 *dissever*: part.   434 *sick heel*: sickness.

'I trowe that ye have spide a mase,   435
Or ye have tane sum sodeyne swevene;
For wheron ist, good, that ye gase?'
'A, Quene,' quod y, 'I kan not nemene
Hir name that cometh downe from hevene;
And in hir hond she hath a whylle   440
Wheron y see my lady welle.

'I pray yow turne abowt not hastily,
But as it were who sekith for othir thing,
And loke where so that ye kan ought aspy
What that she is, or gesse to yowre semyng.'   445
'No more,' quod she, and lete downe falle a ryng
To pyke a countenaunce, so wot ye what,
And turnyd as it had ben bowt for that,

And so bigan to cast hir eye aside
Of which look for shame therwith she blosht.   450
'A, seynt Antone! but turne yow, hide, hide, hide!
Allas, that ther nar ny of hir sum boch.'
'But wherof, la! this fer, madame? O towch!
Bi verry god, ye are to ferfulle oon.'
'Ye, ye, my sone, y wolde some were agoon,   455

---

435 *spide a mase*: seen a vision; comically, Venus offers the suggestion that the incredu-
lous dreamer must be dreaming.

436 *tane*: taken, been overcome by.

438 *nemene*: name. The dreamer is still ignorant of the identity of Fortune, even though
he clearly sees her wheel, and he suggests an elaborate ruse which will allow Venus a closer
inspection.

440 *whylle*: wheel.   443 But as if you were someone looking for something.

444–5 And look if you can see at all who she is, or guess, as it seems to you.

447–8 To make a pretext of some kind, you know, and turned round, as if for that.

450–62 Venus seems alarmed that Fortune may catch her in an apparently compromis-
ing situation with the dreamer.

450 *blosht*: blushed.

451 *seynt Antone*: possibly St Anthony of Padua, popularly invoked to help in finding
lost objects; the associations of St Anthony of Egypt (with monks, healing, and pigs,
among other things) seem less appropriate in this context.

452 Alas, that there is not some bush near her (to hide).

453 *fer*: fear. *towch*: tush.   454 *to ferfulle oon*: you are too frightened.

455 *y wolde some were agoon*: I wish some (of these people) were gone.

'For trowe ye that they wol not thynke amys
That fynde as this—no more but ye and y?'
'Whi gef thei doo? What kan thei thynk on this?
Owttesepte—my lady, clene y them defy!'
'Ye, baw! my sheele straw in yowre ey!　　　　460
For though ye men in such case litille care,
It sittith welle we wymmen to ben ware.

'Yond same is Fortune. How, knowe ye hir not?'
'O no, Madame—whi, yes! Bi god, now, now,
Y am, y am right wel on hir bithought!　　　　465
She stale with deth my lady—wot ye how?—
Which yondir sitt. Bi god, y make a vow,
Might y hir reche anoon y shulde hir sle!'
'Yee, nar ye holde? ye are to perlous be!

'Now good, graunt us letter of yowre pese.　　　　470
But is hitt aynd yowre lady that ther sit?'
'O yee!—O nay, no, nyst—O, yes, dowtles!'
'O trouthe! me thynke ye ought wel borow wit,
For out of drede wot ye hit is not hit,
Alle be she fayre and wel vnto hir liik.　　　　475
A, ye, my frend, kan ye suche motis piik?

456 *trowe*: believe.　*thynke amys*: take wrongly.
457 Who find only you and me here.　　　458 *Whi gef*: what if.
459 *Owttesepte*: except (an effective use of the rhetorical figure of *aposiopesis*: a sudden breaking-off).　*clene*: completely.
460 Bah! shell-straw (i.e. a piece of husk, a mote) in your eye (the sense here is not clear, and there has possibly been some scribal corruption).
462 We women need to be very careful.
468 *reche*: reach, get near to.　*sle*: kill. The dreamer assumes that Fortune, whom he blames for the death of the first lady, is consistently malevolent. One function of the dream is to reveal to him that Fortune's 'stabilnes' (referred to in the refrain of the ballade which he composes before falling asleep) is a providential capacity for constant change.
469 Is there no holding you? You are too dangerous!
470 Now, good sir, give us written testimony that you'll keep the peace.
471 *aynd*: formerly.　　　472 *nyst*: is not.
474 *out of drede*: without doubt.　*hit is not hit*: it is not she.
475 *Alle be*: even though she is.
476 *suche motis piik*: take note of such small points (in order to make the distinction). Since the dreamer has in fact mistaken the new lady for the old one, there is some comic sarcasm here.

'I have aspide ye, marchaunt, at the fayre:
Ye lust not on a sympil market see
That cast yow to engros up such a payre,
As that your ladi was, this semith me,   480
And now this same, which lakkith no bewte.
Ye wold ben ditid sothely, were this knowe,
As for a regrater of the fayre, y trowe.

'I wend that ye wold nevyr bie nor selle
Suche litille ware, but ye it had forswore,   485
But nowe ye nave not so, me thynkith welle,
Of which Fortune thank y, not yow, therfore.

fo. 120ᵛ   And if your hert be sett on hir so sore
Spede if ye kan; y cast yow not prevayle,
Forwhi ye have eschewid my counsayle.   490

'And nevyrtheles y seide it for the best,
As have y joy, more for yowre ese then myn;
For as me thought, hit more were for your rest
A lady chese then thus your silf forpyne.
As that y tolde yow now right wel a fyn   495
When ye had sene parcas ye nevyr saw
It myght wel happe yow fynde a bon to gnaw.

'And how is now? What, cast yow love or no?
It is not she, y put yow out of drede,

477 *marchaunt*: merchant.
478–81 As it seems to me, it doesn't please you to see a simple bargain, you (who) set about to buy up a pair like this—your previous lady, and now this one here, who doesn't lack any beauty herself.
482 *ditid*: indicted.   *were this knowe*: if this were known.
483 *regrater*: monopolist.   *fayre*: market/fair ladies.   484 *wend*: thought.
485 *litille ware*: small goods.   *ye it had forswore*: you had given it up.
486 But now it seems to me clearly that you have not.   487 *Of which*: for which.
489–90 Be successful if you can; I predict that you will not profit, since you have refused my advice.
492 *As have y joy*: as I have pleasure (an asseveration).   *ese*: pleasure, relief.
494 *chese*: choose.   *your silf forpyne*: torment yourself.
495 *wel a fyn*: thoroughly.   496 *parcas*: perhaps.
498 *cast yow*: do you intend.   499 *out of drede*: out of doubt.

So whethir, wil ye love or lete hir go?'   500
'Allas, lady, what is me best do rede.
I am so smyten with hir goodlihede
That next my lady but y love hir best
I am not liik to sett myn hert at rest.

'And ner it no that she is hir so liik   505
Not shulde y love hir, nor noon lyvyng,
The which sight doth my dedly hert aqueke
That syn that deth made karfulle departyng
Bitwene me and my lady, saw y thyng
Thorugh which y felt on only joy at al   510
Nor yet, owt this, y wot y nevyr shal.

'For levyr were me serve hir, lo, for nought,
Then to ben kyng of al this world so round.
If so were onys that she myght knowe my thought
Y nolde no more desire upon the ground;   515
And without yow that may it not be found.
Thus redles in my wery gost y stond:
Save liif and deth y put it in yowre hond.

'Have y doon messe, then ax y yow pardoun;
Have y my deth desert, then let me dy.   520
Beth not my foo, o welaway, so soun!
If y offendid have, y mercy cry,
And as ye lust me now this mater gy

---

500 *whethir*: which.   501 *me best*: best for me. *do rede*: advise.
502 *goodlihede*: goodness.   503 Unless I love her best, after my (former) lady.
504 *liik*: likely.   505 If it were not that she is so like her.
507 *doth my dedly hert aqueke*: makes my lifeless heart tremble.
508 *karfulle departyng*: sorrowful division.
509 *saw y thyng . . .*: I never saw anything . . .
511 *owt this*: apart from this.   512 *levyr were me*: I would rather.
515 I would wish for nothing further on earth.
516 *without yow*: without your help.
517 *redles*: lacking advice. *wery gost*: tired spirit. *stond*: remain.
518 Between life and death, I put it (the matter) in your hands.
519 *doon messe*: done amiss. *ax*: ask.   520 *desert*: deserved.
521 *welaway*: alas.   523 And as it pleases you now to direct this matter for me.

I me content in alle thing moche or lesse.
What may y more then axe yow foryefnesse?'   525

'Then alle forgeve—y am not so crewelle
To yow, as ye to serve me were alle straunge—
So that hensforth yowre hert in every delle
Ye geve it hir, and never forto chaunge.
And for yon wheel renyth so gret a raunge   530
That it is hard for yow to come hir to,
Then shall y telle yow how that ye shal do:

'Hange hir, upon my kercher of plesaunce,
And y shal brynge thee up to hir aloft.'
'Madame, y shalle obey your ordinaunce.'   535
'Nay, yet abide, my frend, y am bithought—
As for Fortune, y wille ye sle hir nought:
That shal ye promys me yet or ye go.'
'Madame, alle this it nedith not, no, no,

fo. 121ᵛ

'For alle the world y graunt unto hem pese,   540
Save only deth that slew my lady dere—
Therof ye must me pardone, lo, dowtlese,
For him to love y kan in no manere,
Though that y lyvid here a thousand yere.'
'Nay, sothely, lo, ye resoun have in that.   545
But honge now on my kercher, wot ye what!'

And so dredles hir kercher thus y took,
And as me thought she bare me up so hie
That even for fere to falle therwith y quok,

525 *foryefnesse*: forgiveness.
527 *as ye . . . straunge*: as you were odd about serving me.
528 *so that*: on condition that.   *delle*: part
530 *for*: because.   *renyth so gret a raunge*: turns in so great a circuit.
533 *hir*: here.   *kercher of plesaunce*: cf. 127.   535 *ordinaunce*: order, decree.
536 *y am bithought*: it occurs to me.   537 *sle*: kill.
538 *or ye go*: before you go.   540 I make my peace with all the world.
545 *ye resoun have in that*: you are right about that. Venus, responsible for procreation, is
like the dreamer an enemy of death.
546 *wot ye what*: you know.   547 *dredles*: without fear.
549 *quok*: quaked. Cf. the dreamer's flight with the eagle in *HF* 541–1050.

And gan 'O lady Venus, mercy!' cry   550
So lowde that it awook me verily,
And fond my silf wher as y was downe layd.
And in myn hond as y from slepe abreid

Yet se y wel a gret pese of plesaunce
The which y took and in my bosum put   555
So forto kepe it in remembraunce.
And for bi cause that y nedis mut
Muse on my dreem, y sett me up afoot,
And so gan wandre in my thoughtis sade
To that y come undir a grene wood shade,   560

Upon a launde, the gras soft, smothe and fayre
That likyng gret hit was me to bihold.
And homward thus as y gan me repayre
I fond a company, some yong some olde,
That gan eche othir fast in armys hold,   565
For at the post and piler did thei play,
And alle were gentil folkis, dar y say,

As ladies and ther wymmen many oon,
With many a squyer and many a knyght,
Among the whiche myn eyen spide anoon   570
The selfe lady, bi verry god of myght,

551 *awook me*: woke me up. *verily*: indeed. The frightened cry which makes the dreamer start from his sleep can be compared to the sudden movements which end the dreams in *KQ* and *BC*.

552 *as y was downe layd*: where I lay down.   553 *abreid*: started.

554 *pese of plesaunce*: portion of fabric. The fragment of Venus's scarf retained by the dreamer effectively blurs the distinction between his waking and dream experiences. Cf. *KQ* 1235–60, where a turtle-dove brings to the narrator a message which corroborates the promise given to him in his earlier dream of the goddess Fortune.

557 *y nedis mut*: I had to.   558 *sett me up afoot*: stood up.

561 *launde*: plain.   562 It was a great pleasure for me to look at it.

565 *fast*: firmly.   566 *the post and piler*: cf. 197.   567 *gentil*: well born.

568 The 'wymmen', although 'gentil folkis', serve the ladies in the same way that the squires serve the knights (cf. the distinction made in *AL* 5–8).

571 *selfe*: same. *bi verry god of myght*: by all-powerful God. The narrator's waking encounter with the lady of his dream justifies the belief expressed at 102–16 in the prophetic nature of visions.

That y se Fortune bere so high on hight.
But how me than? had y more joy or woo?
Now certis wel y kan not telle yow, noo,

For joyful was y on hir to biholde,   575
Bicause she was so liik my lady swete,
But me to queynt not durst y be so bold
Nad be the dreem that y did of hir mete,
That Venus had hir helpe to me bihight
As y have to yow told what that she said,   580
For which that I tho the lesse me dismayd.

Now was ther on had knowen me tofore
That me aspide, and y ne wiste not how
And in his corse he fel, and had fortore
His hose, at which fulle many of hem lough.   585
'Now laughe,' seide he, 'for some han pleid ynough!'
Which to me spake 'Y thank yow, frend, my fal,
For nad ye be y had hit not at all!

'But nevyrtheles ye ar welcome, parde,
So now gef rome! take here a pleyer in   590
For he shal pley his pagaunt now for me,
Though that his chekis be but passyng thyn.

fo. 122ᵛ   Set forth, let se how fayre ye kan bigynne.'
'Nay, good cosyne,' seide y, 'therof no more.'
'Seynt Yve, ye shalle! see, that myn hose is tore!'   595

573 *how me than*: how was I then?
577 *me to queynt*: to acquaint myself.   *not durst y*: I did not dare.
578 *Nad be*: had it not been for.   *mete*: dream.   579 *bihight*: promised.
581 *tho*: then.   582 *tofore*: previously.   583 *ne wiste not*: did not know.
584 *corse*: turn in the game.   *fortore*: torn.
585 *fulle many*: very many.   *lough*: laughed.   586 *han pleid*: have played.
587–8 Who spoke to me, 'I thank you, friend, for my fall, for I wouldn't have had it if
you had not been there!'
590 *gef rome*: make some space.   591 *play his pagaunt*: act his part (in the game).
592 His thin cheeks are a symptom of the melancholy described in 1–11.
595 *Seynt Yve*: possibly St Ivo of Brittany, the patron saint of judges, since the narrator
is invited to offer a judgement on the torn hose (or as suggested in the note by Arn to this
line in Charles of Orleans 1994, a reference to St Ives near Huntingdon, a town 'famous for
its cloth dealers and so appropriately invoked when one has torn one's clothes').

Bi hond he hent me so, and to the place
He drew me in. 'Is ther noon othir bote?'
Seide y, 'Noo, no, ye get no bettir grace.'
Quod y, 'Then must y to, that nedis mote.'
And so to renne y gan to make a foot,   600
And wel y wot y ran not long abowt
Or that y on had towchid of the rowt,

And as the corse thus drove me here and there
Unto my lady newe so streight y went,
With gastful hert that quoke for verry fere   605
How me were best to uttir myn entent.
Yet at the last on this pooreposse ybent
When that ther stood no mo but she and y,
'A questioun wold y axe of yow lady.'

'Of me?' quod she, 'Now, good, what thing is that?'   610
'It is not smalle, madame, y yow ensewre:
I put a case if so myn hert it sat
To yow in love above eche creature,
Told y it yow, wold ye it so diskever
And make of it a skoffe or yet a play,   615
In which percas my liif so myght it way?'

'God helpe me, nay. Why, wat erthely wight
That lovyd me unto myn honour evyr,
Sothely me thynke y did him gret unright
Without the more he were unto me lever.   620
Eek who wil skorne, skoffe on, for y will never,

596 *hent*: took.   597 *Is ther noon othir bote*: is there no other remedy.
599 Said I, 'Then I'd better do what I have to do.'   600 And so I hastened to run.
602 *Or that*: before. *towchid*: touched. *rowt*: crowd.   603 *corse*: game, course.
605 *gastful*: timid.
606 (about) how it would be best for me to speak my intentions.
607 *pooreposse*: purpose. *ybent*: determined.   608 *no mo*: no more.
612–14 Just suppose that if my heart were affected by love for you beyond every other
being, I were to tell you of it, would you reveal it.
615 *skoffe*: joke.
616 *way*: weigh down with anxiety/weigh in the balance (cf. 625).
618 *unto myn honour*: respectfully.   619 *unright*: wrong.
620 Unless he were to be more dear to me (on that account)

For bett y wot in suche case how me sit
To doon, and ellis y had but litille witt.'

'Mercy, madame, for y stond in the case
That bothe my liif and deth doth on yow hong.   625
For certis, swete, but ye have on me grace
As for my deth y must it nedis fong.
I kan not say that y have lovyd yow long,
But welle y wott y love yow so, my dere,
That bothe ye are my joy and payne in fere.   630

'My payne are ye only for fere and drede
The which y have to playne yow of my greef;
And then my joy—that is yowre goodlihede
Forto bihold, and shalle while that y lyve.
Ther nys no more, but from this tyme do preve   635
In any thing where that y be yowre man,
And if ye othir fynde, so sle me than.

'This is hit alle that y of yow desere:
That as yowre gostly child ye wold me take,
And ye to ben my fayre shrift-fadir dere,   640
To here the poore confessioun that y make;
And that ye not my simpilnes forsake,
For half so moche y dar not to yow say
As that y wolde and these folk were away.

fo. 123ᵛ   'Eek not y eft from this tyme how aquaynt   645
Without the helpe of yow, myn owne swet hert—

---

622 *bett*: better. *how me sit*: how it is fitting for me.   624 *case*: situation.
625 *hong*: depend.   627 Then I must receive my death.
628–30 Cf. the third tersel eagle's declaration of love in *PF* 470–3.
630 *in fere*: together.   632 Which I have when I complain to you of my sorrow.
635 *do preve*: put to the test.   636 *where that*: whether or not.
637 *othir*: otherwise.
639 *gostly child*: penitent. Cf. the penitent/confessor relationship suggested elsewhere
in the sequence of poems, in roundel 57 (Charles of Orleans 1970, 1994, lines 3969–80).
640 *shrift-fadir*: father confessor.   642 *forsake*: disregard.
644 *and these folk were away*: if these people were gone.
645 *not y*: I do not know. *eft*: henceforward. *how aquaynt*: how to become (better)
acquainted.

Allas! bewar, yowre coloure gynnys faynt;
Pynne up yowre kercher, kepe yowre face covert.
Ye mow say how the sonne hit doth yow smert.'
'Bi my good soth, y holde yow nyse,' quod she,   650
And did right so, and syns seide to me,

'I trowe wel ye have my rewde haver sene,
The which ye prayse so cleyn out mesure.
Gramercy yow therof, and not yowre eyene
For which yn me thei fynde no such figure   655
To cawse yow of so gret a payne endure.
But many suche as ye in wordis dy
That passyng hard ther graffis ar to spy.'

'Also to lett yow speke that may y not,
And when ye lust so say me what ye wol.   660
But forto love it cometh not in my thought,
Save only on which plesith me at fulle,
Nor y cast not to me noon othir pulle;
But in alle that ye love in good entent
I thank yow; but wist y ye othir ment,   665

'God helpe me so, y shulde yow then eschew—
But then y gesse ye wolde myn honour more?'
'Now dredles, lo, madame, that is yet trew,
For lever nad y ben to liif ybore
Then that y shulde for any gref or soore   670

647 *gynnys faynt*: grows pale.
649 *the sonne hit doth yow smert*: the sun burns you.
650 *nyse*: delicate, discreet.   652 *rewde haver*: unsophisticated behaviour.
653 *so cleyn out mesure*: so immoderately.
654–6 Thank you very much (for your praise)—and not your eyes, which can find no
such figure in me to cause you to endure so much pain.
657 *in wordis dy*: utter dying words.   658 Yet it's very hard to see their graves.
659 And I cannot prevent you from speaking.
662 Except someone who pleases me in every way.
663 Nor do I intend to attract anyone else to me.
665 *wist y ye othir ment*: if I knew you meant otherwise.   666 *eschew*: avoid you.
667 *ye wolde myn honour more*: you are more concerned for my honour.
668 *dredles*: without doubt.
669 For I should rather not have been born.

Wil you more fer then ye may goodly graunt

fo. 124ʳ   Unto me, wrecche—durste y say yowre servaunt?

'But wold God ye knew myn hert eche deel!
Kan ye not rede?' 'Yes, so, so,' quod she.
'O what, dere hert, though fer from yow y dwel   675
Yet wil ye graunt me writ to yow, parde,
And not disdayne yow on hit forto see,
And send me so of hit sum word agayne
If that y shulde desire yow such a payne?'

'The raket cometh—y graunt hit yow; writ on,'   680
And so an othir came and afore hir stood
For which that y must nedis ben agoon.
Yet nevyrtheles me thought it did me good
That she so moche knew of myn hert, by the rood,
And so we ran a corse or two, no more,   685
Or that we must depart, unto my sore,

For Crepusculus that revith day his light
Gan in the west his clowdy mantel shake,
And for bicause y fastid lo that nyght
From oon to oon of them my leve y take;   690
But lord, so that myn hert bigan to quake
When that y take shulde of my lady leve
And for no thing it wold me not bileve.

---

671 *Wil you more fer*: wish from you more.   672 *durste*: dare.
673 *ye knew myn hert eche deel*: you knew every bit of my heart.
674 *so so*: moderately well/yes, yes. Skills of literacy were not always necessary (especially for women) in court and household contexts where others could be called upon to read aloud or act as amanuenses. The narrator does suggest at 202, however, that the first lady could write.
676 The initiation of a new courtship marks the point at which the narrator can return to the composition of lyrics which record his own desires and emotions—a contrast to the situation immediately before the dream, where he wrote simply on the instruction of those who commissioned poems from him.
678 And send me some reply to it.   679 *desire yow*: ask of you.   *payne*: labour.
680 *raket*: noisy crowd.   684 *by the rood*: by the cross.
686 *Or that*: until.   *unto my sore*: to my sorrow.
687 *Crepusculus*: twilight (cf. *Fkl T, CT* V. 1015).   *revith*: takes from.
689 *for bicause*: since.   *fastid*: fasted.   690 *take*: took.
693 *bileve*: cease.

She blusshid reed to see how that y ferde
For as y kist y seide 'Now welcome, sorow.'   695
'Ye made me gast,' quod she, 'yshrympe your berd!
But may ye not abide here to tomorow?'
'A madame, no. Farewel, seynt Johne to borow.'
'Bi holy God, y trow bet that ye may,
Ellis come and se us, lo, sum othir day.'   700

'Madame, a trouthe, y thanke yowre ladiship.
It may me happe to se yow here this weke.'
Thus did y so depart the feleship
And gan me forth to my poor loggyng peke,
But alle that nyght myn hert did rore and seke,   705
For nought me nyst as what was best to do
To speke or writ, when next y came hir to.

But nevyrtheles to this purpos y felle,
That when y myght, for fere of forgetyng,
Bi mouth y wolde my mater to hir telle,   710
And, lak of space, to take it bi writyng;
For which that thus bigan my new servyng
When that y fond my tymys of laysere,
As sewith next if it lust yow to here.

Of fayre most fayre, as verry sorse and welle,   [5352]
From yow me cometh, as brefly to expres,   716

694 *ferde*: did.
696 *gast*: terrified.   *yshrympe your berde*: may your beard shrivel (presumably a playful rejoinder).
697 *to*: until.
698 *seynt Johne to borow*: St John be your safeguard; St John the Baptist was the patron saint of the Knights Hospitallers (Knights of St John) who guarded pilgrims to the Holy Land. Cf. *KQ* 159.
699 *y trow bet that ye may*: I think you had better (remain).
701 *a trouthe*: truly.   704 *loggyng*: residence.   *peke*: slink.
705 *rore*: wail.   *seke*: sigh.   706 *For nought me nyst*: I didn't know for anything.
709 *for fere of forgetyng*: for fear that she might forget me.
710 *Bi mouth*: perhaps a pun, suggesting both 'by (word of) mouth' and 'with a kiss'.
711 *lak of space*: if the opportunity was lacking.
713 *tymys of laysere*: periods of free time.   714 *sewith*: follows.
715–42 A *ballade*, with refrain, of three eight-line stanzas and a four-line envoy; it marks the start of the group of lyrics with which the sequence concludes.
715 Fairest of fair, the source and spring (of beauty).

Such love that y ne may it from yow helle.
Alle shulde y die, God take y to witnes,
Desire me takith with such a ferventnes
That y must nedis put me at your wille,   720
Wherso ye lust of rigoure or kyndenes
Me forto save or do me payne or spille.

I wot my gilt it hath deservid deth
That y was bold to sett so high myn hert,

But in good feith, while that me lastith breth,   725
For payne or woo y may it not astert,
As forto take yow nere me then my shert.
To bridille love y kan no bett skile,
But bynde me hool to yow, for payne or smert,
Me forto save or do me payne or spille   730

What ye me geve y may it not denye
But hit agre as for myn aventure.
But by my trouth unto the howre y dye
I shalle be to yow trewe, y yow ensewre,
As hert kan thynke, and not forto discure   735
What ye me say, and wille y kepe it stille,
So am y yowre, tofore eche creature,
Me forto save or do me payne or spille

O mercy, swete, allas, y kan no more,
But what yow list my lust hit must fulfille.   740
But for my love sumwhat y wold therfore
Me forto save or do me payne or spille.

---

717 *helle*: conceal.

721–2 Whether it should please you, in severity or kindness, to save me or to hurt and destroy me.

724 *That*: in that.   726 *astert*: escape (the desire).

727 *nere me then my shert*: closer to me than my shirt.

728 I know no better art to restrain love.   729 *hool*: entirely.

731 *denye*: refuse to accept.   732 But accept it as my chance.

735 As (any) heart can conceive, and will not reveal.

737 *tofore eche creature*: before anyone else.

740 It will be my pleasure to do everything you wish.

741 *for*: (in return) for.   *sumwhat y wold*: I should like something.

The Assembly of Ladies

The Assembly of Ladies, the single anonymous poem in this anthology, is a woman's dream, recounted retrospectively by a lady to a man with whom she falls into conversation. Like the dream of *TG*, it concerns the offering of pleas at a court, but here the plaintiffs are all women, and the figure from whom they seek redress is not Venus but Lady Loyalty. Unlike *TG*, no answer to the complaints is given in the dream, and the women who make them are simply promised fuller hearing by Lady Loyalty at a future parliament. There is an enigmatic quality to this vision, whose narrator is tantalizingly unforthcoming about her own circumstances (lines 15–21, 75–6), to the extent of withholding her own plea when asked to present it (410–13), and the poem seems deliberately to hold back from the castigation of men which its concentration on women and their view of love would seem to promise (see, for example, lines 145–54). The locating of the encounter between the narrator and her male interlocutor in a maze is perhaps designed to call to mind the inherently puzzling nature of love and its problems.

The 'assembly' or gathering of women which the poem depicts is in itself a matter of some interest. No real household or court of this period could have excluded men to the extent that this vision does—even a female religious house would have included male priests and lower functionaries—and Lady Loyalty's court is a fantasy possible only in a dream. Its closest analogues in late medieval literature are the female assemblies presented in religious allegories such as *The Abbey of the Holy Ghost* (see Blake 1972: 88–102) or in polemical writings such as Christine de Pizan's *Book of the City of Ladies* (Christine de Pizan 1983, tr. Richards). Parallels could also be drawn with the company of women who follow Cupid and Alceste in Chaucer's *LGWP* (another dream, of course), with *The Isle of Ladies* (Pearsall 1990: 63–140), and, more remotely, perhaps, with the bevy of female personifications who lay siege to Dunbar's dreamer-narrator in *The Golden Targe* (Dunbar 1996: 231–45). The five ladies and four gentlewomen described at the start of

AL produce a significant total of nine, possibly meant to prompt associations with the nine muses of poetry or with the group of nine famous women of antiquity who were in the later Middle Ages cited in association with the celebrated Nine (male) Worthies. The Worthies featured prominently in art and pageantry—they appear, for example, in *The Flower and the Leaf* (Pearsall 1962, 1990), a courtly poem roughly contemporary with *AL*—and they may have served to underline iconographically the potential of groups of women for the purposes of socially enlivening courtly debate.

Certain aspects of *AL* seem calculated to appeal to a taste for details of fashionable contemporary style, whether in the recollection of such groups of women, or in French phrases, or in matters of clothing, architecture, or garden design: much attention is paid to descriptions of dress, to the maze in which the narrator walks with her companions and the garden in which she had her dream (17–70), and to Lady Loyalty's castle, 'Plesaunt Regard' (158–72). Emphasis is also laid on the observance of proper social distinctions and etiquette, especially among the members of Lady Loyalty's female household; the handling of the bills containing the complaints (540–81) is described in detail which would not be out of place in a manual of instruction for would-be courtiers. Questions of social organization seem to be a major interest in this poem, whose focus on women may in some ways extend the *querelle des femmes* so important in Middle English poems of the Chaucerian tradition, but which stops short of committing itself to a pro- or anti-feminist view, and seems in fact less interested in this issue than in more general aspects of the way communities work.

The poem survives in three manuscripts which all include other texts in the tradition of Chaucerian love vision and debate: MS Longleat 258, for example, contains Chaucer's *A & A*, *PF*, and the complaints of *Pity* and of *Mars* (all in Chaucer 1987), along with *TG* and some translations of debate poems from French: *La Belle Dame sans Merci* (Skeat 1897: 299–326), *The Eye and the Heart* (Hammond 1911), and Lydgate's *Churl and Bird* (Lydgate 1934: 468–85, ed. MacCracken). The poem's association with Chaucer was confirmed by its inclusion in William Thynne's collected *Workes*, printed in 1532 (*STC* 5068; facsimile intro. Brewer 1976), and it remained a part of the Chaucerian apocrypha until weeded out by nineteenth-century editors. Scholars interested in its female narrator have traditionally linked it with *The Flower and the Leaf*, another poem long associated with Chaucer's works, which is narrated in a woman's voice (Longleat 258 once contained this poem, although it has been lost from the manuscript). Dating and authorship remain matters for speculation. All three of the surviving manuscripts date from the third quarter of the fifteenth century, at the earliest (see 'Note on the text'). Pearsall 1962 has argued that features of style and of the fashions described suggest a date of composition during the reign of Edward IV (1471–83), and makes the case that the author of *AL* may also have written the romance *Generydes* (Pearsall 1961). Discussions of the evidence for female authorship reflect in interesting ways the changing critical climate: Skeat (1900 *a*) argued for female authorship of both *FL* and *AL*, and even suggested a specific candidate; Pearsall (1961, 1962, and 1990) has been more cautious, and the modifications to Skeat's case have been reviewed by Barratt (1987 and 1992).

NOTE ON THE TEXT

AL survives in three fifteenth-century manuscripts: British Library, Additional 34360 (A), fos. 37^r–49^r; Cambridge, Trinity College, R. 3. 19 (Tr), fos. 55^r–65^v; and MS 258 at Longleat House (L; the property of the Marquis of Bath), fos. 58–75^v. The first of these, copied in London, probably before 1485, by a prolific scribe who had access to manuscripts copied by John Shirley (see *TG*, 'Note on the text'), probably preserves the earliest surviving text of *AL* and is used as the basis of this edition. The Trinity and Longleat copies share a number of variants, and Longleat was used by William Thynne in 1532 for the printed edition of *AL* which he included in his collection of poems by and associated with Chaucer (Th; see Fletcher 1979). The textual notes below follow Pearsall 1962 in referring to Tr, L, and Th collectively as T.

TEXTUAL NOTES

29 an] T; om. A

33 missing in A; supplied from Tr

50 me] from T; my A

53 masonry] T; mesure A

57 With] T; Was A

124–5 Transposed in A

153 be to] T; be A
162 and] T; om. A
163 wyndowes] A; bay wyndowes T
167 every] T; ever A
182 yeve] T; yove A
241 with] T; on A
260 at] T; om. A
281 Than opened she] T; Than she opened she A
293 for] T; om. A
303 hir] T; theyr A
308 *A moy*] T; O moy A
310 worde] T; om. A
311 Forsoth] T; Ferforth A.
345 se] T; she A
377 yow] T; om. A
398 or] or theyre T; al A
418 we] T; ye A

430 There] T; They A
461 how] T; om. A
463 how Melusene] how Enclusene A; Hawes the shene T
479 foure] T; A iiij
491 as] T; al A
519–32 omitted from A; supplied from Tr
534 In] T; Of A
571 it] T; om. A
580–81 transposed in A
598 *lever*] T; leur A
617 made] T; om. A
637 used it] T; it used A
694 as] T; om. A
697 knewe] L, Th; knowe A, Tr
720 court] T; comfort A
747 grete] T; om. A
748 now] T; how A

311 se] T; she A

FURTHER READING

Editions of *AL* are in Skeat (1897: 380–404), and Pearsall (1962) and (1990); Fletcher (1987) provides a facsimile of one of the surviving MSS (Trinity College, Cambridge R. 3. 19), and Brewer (1976) of Thynne's printed edition. Questions of authorship are addressed by Skeat (1900*a* and 1900*b*: 110–11, 139–41); by Pearsall (1961 and 1990); by Barratt (1987 and 1992); and by Boffey (1993*b*). General critical appreciation of the poem is to be found in Stephens (1973); McMillan (1982) (which also discusses *FL*); and Evans and Johnson (1991). Davidoff (1988: 146–59) discusses the framework (as does also, more generally, Phillips 1997); Doob (1990: 171–5) the notion of the maze; and Boffey (2000) the nature of the complaints. The constitution of medieval households is described in Mertes (1988). Boffey (2001) explores references to the Female Worthies in post-Chaucerian writing.

The Assembly of Ladies

In Septembre, at fallyng of the leef—
The fressh season was altogydre done
And of the corn was gadred in the sheef—
In a gardyn, abowte tweyne after none,
There were ladyes walkyng, as was ther wone: 5
Foure in nombre, as to my mynde doth falle,
And I the fift, symplest of alle.

Of gentilwymmen foure ther were also,
Disportyng hem everiche after theyr guyse,
In crosse aleys walkyng be two and two,   10
And som alone, after theyr fantasyes.
Thus occupied we were in dyvers wise,
And yit in trowth we were nat alone:
Theyr were knyghtis and squyers many one.

1–3 The autumn opening, unusual in a love vision of this sort, is perhaps intended to
signal that this is to be a dream about problems: cf. the openings of *BC*, *TG*, and of
Chaucer's *HF*.

2 *altogydre*: altogether.   *done*: finished.   3 *gadred*: gathered.

4 *tweyne after none*: two (o'clock) in the afternoon. Indulgence in courtly outdoor
activities of various kinds features often in dream visions, from *RR* onwards: cf. *KQ* 275–6,
LR 561 ff. A garden similar to this one, also the preserve of ladies, is described by Chaucer
in *TC* II. 813–26. The 'aleys' are probably sanded paths, which were often bordered with a
rail (see line 42). The characteristic features of late medieval gardens are discussed and
illustrated in Harvey 1990: on beds of this sort see figures 13A and 13B, from a manuscript
of René d'Anjou's *Livre du Cueur d'Amours Espris*, c.1465 (Österreichische National-
bibliothek, MS 2617).

5 *ther wone*: their custom, habit.   6 *as to my mynde doth falle*: as I remember.
7 *fift*: fifth.

8 A distinction is here made between higher-ranking 'ladyes' (5) and 'the gentil
wymmen', who although accompanying them in their activities are in some sense in
their service (the distinction might also apply to the knights and squires). Some of the
boundaries between gentry and aristocracy are discussed by Morgan 1986.

9 Each taking amusement in their own way.   10 *crosse aleys*: intersecting paths.
11 *after theyr fantasyes*: according to their whims.   12 *dyvers wise*: different ways.
13 *yit*: yet.

Whereof I serve? on of hem asked me.　　　　　　　15
I seyde ageyne, as it fil in my thought:
'To walke aboute the mase, in certeynte,
As a womman that nothyng rought.'

He asked me ageyn whom I sought,
And of my coloure why I was so pale.　　　　　　　20
'Forsoth,' quod I, 'and therby lith a tale.'

'That must me wite,' quod he, 'and that anon.
Telle on, late se, and make no taryeng.'
'Abide,' quod I, 'ye be an hasti one.
I let yow wite it is no litle thyng:　　　　　　　　25
But for because ye have a grete longyng
In yowre desire this procese for to here,
I shal yow telle the playne of this matiere.

It happed thus that in an afternone
My felawship and I, by one assent,　　　　　　　　30
Whan al oure other busynesse was done,
To passe oure tyme into this mase we went
And toke oure weyes yche aftyr other entent.

---

15 *whereof I serve*: what was I doing here. Direct and indirect (reported) speech are merged here: the question may also have the sense 'What is your office?'

16 *ageyne*: in reply.　*fil*: came.

17 *mase*: maze. Mazes with low walls or hedges became a feature of gardens in the later Middle Ages and beyond: see Harvey 1990: 112; Doob 1990: 103–12; and (specifically on *AL*), Doob 1990: 171–5; and Evans and Johnson 1991.

18 Like a woman with no cares.

21 *Forsoth*: in truth.　*quod*: said.　*therby lith a tale*: there lies a story.

22 *That must me wite*: I must know that.　*anon*: immediately. Pearsall 1990 notes that the impersonal use of *must* with a personal object, as here 'it is necessary (for me) to', is a favourite usage of the author of *AL*.

23 *late se*: let [me] see.　*taryeng*: delay.　26 *for because*: since.

27 *procese*: story.　28 *playne*: plain truth.

28 ff. The complex chronology of the opening, which involves the narrator's recollection of an occasion when she talked to a knight and told him of a former occasion in the garden when she fell asleep, seems characteristic of the structure of late medieval vision poems: cf. *KQ*.

29 *happed*: happened.　30 *felawship*: companions.

33 And chose our paths each with a different plan.

Som went inward and went they had gon oute,
Som stode amyddis and loked al aboute,   35

And soth to sey som were ful fer behynde
And right anon as ferforth as the best;
Other there were, so mased in theyr mynde,
Al weys were goode for hem, both est and west.
Thus went they furth and had but litel rest,   40
And some theyr corage dide theym so assaile
For verray wrath they stept over the rayle.

And as they sought hem self thus to and fro
I gate my self a litel avauntage:
Al for-weryed, I myght no further go,   45
Though I had wonne right grete for my viage,
So come I forth into a streyte passage
Whiche brought me to an herber feyre and grene
Made with benchis, ful craftily and clene,

That, as me thought, myght no creature   50
Devise a bettir by proporcioun.
Save it was closed wele, I yow ensure,
With masonry of compas environ

». 38ʳ

34 *went . . . went*: went . . . thought.   35 *amyddis*: in the middle.
36 *soth to sey*: to tell the truth.   *ful fer*: very far.
37 And then immediately as far forward as the best.   38 *mased*: confused.
39 *Al weys*: all paths.   *hem*: them.   40 *went they furth*: they went forward.
41 And for some, their determination so overcame them.
42 *For verray wrath*: in pure anger.   *rayle*: low fence.
43 *sought hem self*: looked for each other/looked out for their own advantage.
44 *gate*: got.
45–6 Completely exhausted, I could go no further, though I had greatly profited from my route.
47 *come I forth*: I came out.   *streyte*: narrow. The 'streyte passage' may be a tunnelled or trellissed alley; cf. Harvey 1990, plate IVB.
48 *herber*: arbour.   *feyre*: beautiful. An arbour, sometimes with benches covered in turf, was a common feature of medieval gardens; this one recalls the 'litel herber' in which the dreamer of Chaucer's *LGWP* falls asleep (F203–9, G97–101) and the arbour in which the lady of *KQ* is first spotted (212–17).
49 *craftily*: skilfully.   *clene*: neatly.   50 *as me thought*: it seemed to me.
51 *a bettir by proporcioun*: one better proportioned.
52–3 It was very safely enclosed, I assure you, encircled with stonework all round (T's reading of 'masonry' seems preferable to A's 'mesure').

Ful secretly, with steyres goyng down;
In myddes the place a tornyng whele, sertayne,   55
And upon that a pot of margoleyne,

With margarites growyng in ordynaunce
To shewe hemself as folk went to and fro,
That to behold it was a grete plesaunce;
And how they were accompanyed with mo—   60
Ne m'oublie-mies and sovenez also;
The poore penses ne were nat disloged there:
No, no, God wote, theyr place was every where.

The floore beneth was paved faire and smoth
With stones square of many dyvers hewe,   65
So wele joyned that, for to sey the soth,
Al semed on, who that non other knewe.
And underneth the streames, newe and newe,
As silver newe bright spryngyng in such wise
That whens it com ye cowde it nat devise.   70

A litel while thus was I alone
Beholdyng wele this delectable place.

54 *steyres*: steps.

55 *In myddes*: in the middle of.   *tornyng*: revolving. The wheel has been taken to be a
turnstile of some kind, a spiral staircase, or (perhaps most likely) a stone wheel, laid flat
rather like a sundial, and capable of revolving. This would most easily accommodate the
pot of marjoram.

56 *margoleyne*: marjoram.

56–62 All the flowers mentioned here are emblematic of aspects of loyal and virtuous
love: see Evans 1931: i. 61–4. The attributes of the daisy are important in Chaucer's *LGWP*,
whose narrator worships the flower and encounters a representation of it in the form of
Alceste, consort of the god of love; some of the flowers are depicted on Venus's mantle in
LR 381–3.

57 *margarites*: daisies.   *in ordynaunce*: in ordered arrangement.

59 *plesaunce*: pleasure.   60 *mo*: more.

61 forget-me-nots (i.e. myosotis) and remember-mes (i.e. germander speedwell) as
well.

62 humble pansies were not unaccommodated there.   63 *wote*: knows.

65 *dyvers hewe*: different colours.

67 They all seemed like one (single paving stone), to someone who knew no different.

68 *newe and newe*: continually springing (water from streams is seemingly conducted
beneath the paved floor to emerge in decorative springs).

70 That you could not imagine where it came from.

My felawshyp were comyng everichone,
So must me nede abide as for a space;
Remembryng of many dyvers cace   75
Of tyme past, musyng with sighes depe,
I set me downe and ther fil in slepe.

And as I slept me thought ther com to me
A gentilwomman metely of stature:
Of grete worship she semed for to be,   80
Atired wele, nat hye but bi mesure;
Hir contenaunce ful sad and ful demure,
Hir colours blewe, al that she had upon;
Theyr com no mo but hirsilf alon.

Hir gowne was wele enbrowdid, certaynly,   85
With sovenez aftir hir owne devise:
On the purfil hir word, by and by,
Bien loialment, as I cowde me avise.
Than prayd I hir in every maner wise
That of hir name I myght have remembraunce: 90
She sayde she was callid Perseveraunce.

73 *everichone*: every one.
74–5 So I had to wait for a time; and, thinking back over many different occurrences.
75–7 This oblique reference to past unhappy occurrences perhaps ties in with the earlier reference to the narrator's pallor (20); it seems part of a deliberate strategy of vagueness concerning her circumstances and preoccupations.
77 *set*: sat.   *fil*: fell.   79 *metely of stature*: of moderate height.
80 *worship*: worthiness.   81 *hye*: grandly.   *bi mesure*: appropriately.
82 *sad*: sober.
83 The colour blue generally signified constancy and truth; cf. the refrain to the Chaucerian poem *Against Women Unconstant* (Chaucer 1987: 657): 'In stede of blew, thus may ye were al grene'.
84 *Theyr com*: there came.   *hirsilf*: herself.   85 *enbrowdid*: embroidered.
86 *aftir hir owne devise*: in the form of her own device/in a pattern devised by her.
87 *purfil*: border.   *word*: motto.   *by and by*: repeatedly/precisely.
87–8 Items of aristocratic clothing were often embroidered with devices or texts: Charles of Orleans had the music and words of a song set in pearls on one of his sleeves (Evans 1931: i. 145) Cf. *TG* 303 n. *AL* manifests a particular concern with the importance of women's mottoes or devices; a similar concern is shown in the descriptions of women in the Rous Roll, BL Add. MS 48976, compiled in the 1480s by John Rous in honour of his patrons, members of the Beauchamp family; see Courthope 1980, intro. by Ross.
88 'very loyally', as I perceived.
89 *Than*: then.   *in every maner wise*: in every way I could.

So furthermore to speke than was I bold:
Where she dwelt I prayed hir for to say.
And she ageyne ful curteisly me told:
'My dwellyng is, and hath be many a day,   95
With a lady.' ' What lady, I yow pray?'
'Of grete astate, thus warne I yow,' quod she.
'What calle ye hir?' ' Hir name is Loiaulte.'

'In what office stand ye, or in what degre?'
Quod I to hir, 'that wold I wit ful fayne.'   100
'I am,' quod she, 'unworthy though I be,
Of hir chamber ussher in certayne.
This rodde I bere as for a tokene playne,
Lyke as ye knowe the rule in suche service
Perteyneng unto the same office.   105

She charged me be hir comaundement
To warne yow and youre felawes everichone
That ye shuld come there as she is present
For a consaile, which shuld be anone,
Or seven dayes bien comen and gone.   110
And more, she badde that I shuld sey
Excuse ther myght be none nor delay.

---

94 *curteisly*: courteously.   95 *hath be many a day*: has been for a long time.
97 *astate*: estate, rank.   *warne*: inform.
98 *Loiaulte*: Loyalty. The emphasis in *AL* (as in *TG*) on the virtue of loyalty widens its
application beyond the concerns of lovers. Most of the problems addressed in the ladies'
petitions later in the poem are of a general sort and could be relevant to relationships of
service, patronage, or family obligation.
99 *degre*: rank.
100 *wold I wit ful fayne*: I would gladly know.
102 *ussher*: door-keeper.   *in certayne*: certainly.
102–3 The usher of a household—usually a man—was responsible for the lord's food
and its service, and carried a rod as a mark of office. The special offices and responsibilities
of household servants are described in medieval courtesy books such as John Russell's *Boke
of Nurture*: see Furnivall 1868: 185–9 (usher), 189–94 (marshall), and 175–85 (chamberlain).
103 *rodde*: staff.   *bere*: carry.   *tokene playne*: clear sign.
106 *be*: by.   108 *there*: to where.   109 *consaile*: council.
110 *Or*: before.   *bien comen*: have come.
111 *more*: furthermore.   *badde*: commanded.

Another thyng was nygh forgete behynd
Whiche in no wise I wold nat but ye knewe—
Remembre it wele and bere it in your mynde: 115
Al your felawes and ye must com in blewe,
Everiche yowre matier for to sewe,
With more, whiche I pray yow thynk upon,
Yowre wordes on yowre slevis everichon.

And be nat ye abasshed in no wise,   120
As many as bien in suche an high presence;
Make youre request as ye can best devise
And she gladly wil yeve yow audience.
Ther is no grief nor no maner offence
Wherin ye fele your hert is displeased   125
But with hir help right sone ye shul bien eased.

'I am right glad,' quod I, 'ye telle me this.
But ther is none of us that knowith the way.'
'And of your wey,' quod she, 'ye shul nat mys;
Ye shul have one to guyde yow day be day   130
Of my felawes—I can no better say—
Suche on as shal telle yow the wey ful right:
And Diligence this gentilwomman hight,

A womman of right famous governaunce,
And wele cherisshed, I sey yow for certeyne;   135
Hir felawship shal do yow grete plesaunce,
Hir porte is suche, hir maner is triewe and playne;

113 *nygh forgete behynd*: nearly forgotten about.
114 Which in no way would I wish you to be ignorant of.   115 *bere*: bear.
117 *Everiche*: each one. *matier*: business, case. *sewe*: press, pursue.
119 *wordes*: mottoes. *slevis*: sleeves.   121 *As many as*: however many.
123 *yeve yow audience*: give you audience, listen to you.
129 she said: 'You won't miss your way'.
132 *Suche on as*: someone who.   133 *hight*: is called.
134 *governaunce*: conduct, well-controlled behaviour.
136 *felawship*: companionship.
137 *porte*: demeanour. The phrase 'Trewe and playne' recurs in many contexts and
virtually carries the force of a motto: cf. *TG* 446, and (signalled by Pearsall 1962, in a note
to this line) *Generydes* 4845.

She with glad chiere wil do hir busy peyne
To bryng yow there. Farwele, now have I done.'
'Abide,' quod I, ' ye may nat go so soone.'   140

'Whi so?' quod she, 'and I have fer to go
To yeve warnyng in many dyvers place
To youre felawes, and so to other moo,
And wele ye wote I have but litel space.'
fo. 39ᵛ 'Yit,' quod I, 'ye must telle me this cace,   145
If we shal any men unto us calle?'
'Nat one,' quod she, 'may come among yow alle.'

'Nat one?' quod I, 'ey, benedicite!
What have they don? I pray yow, telle me that.'
'Now, be my lif, I trowe but wele,' quod she,   150
'But evere I can beleve ther is somwhat—
And for to sey yow trowth more can I nat.
In questions nothyng may I be to large;
I medle me no further than is my charge.'

'Than thus,' quod I, 'do me til undrestond   155
What place is there this lady is dwellyng?'
'Forsoth,' quod she, 'and on sought al a lond
Feirer is none, though it were fore a kyng;
Devised wele, and that in every thyng:
The toures high ful plesaunt shul ye fynde,   160
With fanes fressh tournyng with every wynde;

138 *glad chiere*: willing manner.   *busy peyne*: utmost.   141 *fer*: far.
142 *yeve*: give.   143 *other moo*: more others.
144 *wote*: know.   *space*: time.
145 *Yit*: yet.   *telle me this cace*: explain this point.
148 *ey*: oh.   *benedicite*: (lit. = bless [the lord]) goodness me!
150 'Now, on my life, I believe only good'.
150–1 This coyness seems in line with the poem's strategy of vagueness about male conduct.
151 *evere*: still, nonetheless.   152 *more can I nat*: I know no more.
153–4 I can't be too plain-spoken in answering questions; I don't interfere beyond my instructions.
155 *do me til undrestond*: tell me.
157 *forsoth*: indeed.   *and on sought al a lond*: even if one searched a whole country.
158 *feirer*: fairer.   159 *Devised*: designed.
160 *toures*: towers.   *shul*: shall.   161 *fanes*: weather-vanes.   *fressh*: bright.

The chambres and parlours both of oo sort,
With wyndowes goodely as can be thought;
As for daunsyng and other wise disport,
The galaries right wonderfully wrought   165
That wele I wote, yef ye were thider brought
And toke goode hede therof in every wise,
Ye wold it thynk a verray paradise.'

'What hight this place?' quod I, 'now sey me that.'
'Plesaunt Regard,' quod she, 'to telle yow pleyne.'   170
'Of verray trouth?' quod I, 'and wote ye what,
It may wele be callid so sertayne.
But furthermore, this wold I wite ful fayne:
What shal I do as soone as I com there,
And after whom that I may best enquere?'   175

'A gentilwomman porter at the yaate
Ther shal ye fynde: hir name is Contenaunce.
If so happe ye com erly or late,
Of hir were goode to have som aqueyntaunce;
She can telle how ye shal yow best avaunce,   180
And how to come to this ladyes presence;
To hir wordis I rede yow yeve credence.

---

162 *both of oo sort*: both of a kind.

163 *goodely as can be thought*: as fine as can be imagined. The manuscripts of group T here read 'bay wyndowes'; as Pearsall points out, this is the first literary recorded use of the term.

164 *other wise disport*: other amusements.

165 *galaries*: partly enclosed walks along the sides of buildings.

166 That I know well, if you were brought there.

168 *verray*: true, real.   169 *hight*: is called.

170 'Plesaunt Regard', in terms of the allegory of the poem, is a feature associated with the lady's 'pleasant looks'; it may also suggest the more literal 'regard' in which Loyalty might be expected to hold those close to her (cf. Charles of Orleans 1923–7: ii. 422, French *rondeaux* 231, 'l'aumosnier Plaisant Regart').

172 *sertayne*: certainly.   173 *ful fayne*: very gladly.

175 And who best should I ask for?   176 *yaate*: gate.

177 *Contenaunce*: Good Manners.   178 *If so happe ye com*: whether you come.

180 *avaunce*: present, put forward.

182 *rede*: advise.

. 40ʳ

Now it is tyme that I part yow fro,
For in goode soth I have grete busynesse.'
'I wote right wele,' quod I, 'that that is soo,   185
And I thanke yow of youre grete gentilnesse.
Yowre comfort hath yeve me suche hardynesse
That now I shal be bold withouten faile
To do after youre avise and counsaile.'

Thus parted she and I left al alone   190
With that I sawe, as I behielde aside,
A womman come, a verray goodely oon,
And furth withal as I had hir aspied
Me thought anon that it shuld be the guyde,
And of hir name anon I did enquere.   195
Ful wommanly she yave this answere:

'I am,' quod she, 'a symple creature
Sent from the court; my name is Diligence.
As soone as I myght com, I yow ensure,
I taried nat after I had licence.   200
And now that I am com to yowre presence,
Looke what service that I can do or may
Comaunde me: I can no further say.'

I thanked hir and prayed hir to come nere
Because I wold se how she were arrayed.   205
Hir gowne was bliew, dressed in goode manere
With hir devise—hir word also, that sayde
Taunt que je puis—and I was wele apayed,

fo. 40ᵛ

---

183 *yow fro*: from you.   184 *in goode soth*: truly.
186 *gentilnesse*: courtesy.
187 *hardynesse*: confidence.   189 *avise*: advice.   190 *I left*: I (was) left.
191 *behielde*: looked.   193 *furth withal*: straightaway.   196 *yave*: gave.
199 *ensure*: assure.   200 I did not delay once I had permission.
202–3 Whatever kind of service I may be able to do, command me (to it).
206 *dressed*: decorated, adorned.
208 *taunt que je puis*: 'As much as I can'.   *apayed*: pleased.

For than wist I without any more
It was ful triew that I had herd afore.   210

'Though we toke now before a lite space
It were ful goode,' quod she, 'as I cowth gesse.'
'How fer,' quod I, 'have we unto that place?'
'A dayes journey,' quod she, 'but litel lesse;
Wherfor I rede that we onward dresse,   215
For I suppose oure felawship is past
And for nothyng I wold that we were last.'

Than parted we at spryngyng of the day
And furth we wente a soft and esy pase,
Til at the last we were on oure journay   220
So fer onward that we myght se the place.
'Nowe lete us rest,' quod I, 'a litel space,
And say we as devoutly as we can
A Pater Noster for seynt Julyan.'

'With al myn hert,' quod she, 'I gre me wele;   225
Moche better shul we spede whan we have done.'
Than taryed we and sayde it every dele.
And whan the day was fer gon after none
We sawe a place, and thider come we sone,

209 *wist*: knew.   *more*: more (evidence).
211–12 'It would be a good thing to set off now before too long', she said, 'as far as I can see'.
214 *but litel*: only a little.
215 *rede*: advise.   *onward dresse*: press on/make headway.
216 *felawship*: companions.
217 *And for nothyng I wold*: And I would not for anything.
218 *parted*: left.   219 *pase*: pace.
224 *Pater Noster*: Our Father. St Julian the Hospitaller was the patron saint of hospitality; cf. the eagle's words to 'Geffrey' in *HF* 1021–2: 'Now up the hed, for al ys wel; | Seynt Julyan, loo, bon hostel!'
225 *I gre me wele*: I completely agree.
226 *Moche better shul we spede*: we shall make much better progress.
227 *every dele*: every part.   228 *fer gon after none*: far past noon.
229 *thider*: towards it.

Whiche rounde about was closid with a wal   230
Semyng to me ful like an hospital.

There fonde I oon had brought al myn array,
A gentilwomman of myn acqueyntaunce.
'I have mervaile,' quod I, 'what maner wey
Ye had knowlache of al this governaunce?'   235
'Yis, yis,' quod she, 'I herd Perseveraunce,
How she warned youre felawes everichone,
And what array that ye shal have upon.'

fo. 41ʳ

'Now, for my love,' quod I, 'I yow pray,
Sith ye have take upon yow al this peyne,   240
That ye wold helpe me on with myne array,
For wite ye wele I wold be go ful fayne.'
'Al this prayer nedith nat, certeyne,'
Quod she ageyne, 'com of, and hie yow soone,
And ye shal se how wele it shal be done.'   245

'But this I dowte me gretely, wote ye what,
That my felaws bien passed by and gone.'
'I waraunt yow, quod she, 'that ar they nat,
For here they shul assemble everichon.
Natwithstandyng, I counseil yow anone   250
Make ye redy and tarye ye no more;
It is non harme though ye be there afore.'

So than I dressid me in myn array
And asked hir if it were wele or noo.
'It is,' quod she, 'right wele unto my pay—   255

230–1 The high wall round the dwelling suggests to the dreamer the walls that
surrounded medieval leper hospitals. Strictly the term 'hospital' might denote a building
offering hospitality not only to the sick but also to travellers and pilgrims.
232 *fonde*: found. *oon*: someone who.
234–5 'I wonder by what means you knew of all this arrangement?'
236 *Yis*: yes.   240 *Sith*: since.   *peyne*: trouble.
242 For believe me, I would like to be on my way.
243 There's certainly no need for all this pleading.
244 *com of*: come on.   *hie yow soone*: hurry up.
245 But do you know, I really fear this.
252 *afore*: beforehand.   255 *unto my pay*: to my liking.

Ye dare nat care to what place so ever ye goo.'
And while that she and I debated soo
Com Diligence, and sawe me al in bliew:
'Suster,' quod she, 'right wel broke ye your niewe.'

Than went we forth and met at aventure   260
A yong womman, an officer semyng.
'What is your name,' quod I, 'goode creature?'
'Discrecioun,' quod she, 'without lesyng.'
'And where,' quod I, 'is yowre abidyng?'
'I have,' quod she, 'this office of purchace,   265
Chief purviour that longith to this place.'

'Faire love,' quod I, 'in al your ordynaunce,
What is hir name that is the herbegyer?'
'Forsoth,' quod she, 'hir name is Aqueyntaunce,
A womman of right graciouse maner.'   270
Than thus quod I, 'What straungiers have ye here?'
'But fewe,' quod she, 'of hie degre ne lowe;
Ye bien the first, as ferforth as I knowe.'

Thus with talis we com streyght to the yaate;
This yong womman departed was and gone.   275
Com Diligence and knokked fast therate.
'Who is without?' quod Contenaunce anone.
'Triewly,' quod she, 'faire suster, here is one.'
'Whiche oon?' quod she, and ther withal she lough:
'I, Diligence, ye knowe me wele inough!'   280

41ᵛ

256 You need not worry where you go (dressed like that).
259 *right wel broke ye your niewe*: your new clothes suit you very well.
260 *at aventure*: by chance.
261 *an officer semyng*: seeming to be an officer (of the household).
263 *lesyng*: lying.   265 *this office of purchace*: this job, of purchasing (provisions).
266 *purviour*: purveyor.   *longith to*: belongs to.
267 *ordynaunce*: order of appointments, establishment.
268 *herbegyer*: official in charge of accommodation.
269 *Acqueyntaunce*: Friendship.   273 *as ferforth as*: as far as.
274 *talis*: chat.   *streyght*: straight.   *yaate*: gate.
276 *fast therate*: hard on it.
279 *ther withal she lough*: with that she laughed.

Than opened she the gate and in we goo.
With wordis feyre she sayde ful gentily:
'Ye ben welcom, iwis; bien ye no mo?'
'No,' quod she, 'save this womman and I.'
'Now than,' quod she, 'I pray yow hertily,   285
Take my chambre as for a while to rest
To yowre felawes bien comen, I hold it for the best.'

I thanked hir and furth we gon echeon
Til hir chambre without wordes mo.
Come Diligence and toke hir leve anon.   290
'Where ever yow list,' quod I, 'nowe may ye goo;
And I thank yow right hertily also
Of yowre laboure, for whiche God do yow mede.
I can nomore, but Jhesu be yowre spede.'

Than Contenaunce asked me anone: 295
'Yowre felawship, where bien they now?' quod she.
'Forsoth,' quod I, 'they bien comyng echeone,
But in certeyne I knowe nat where they be.
At this wyndow whan they come ye may se;
Here wil I stande awaityng ever among,   300
For wele I wote they wil nat now be long.'

Thus as I stode musyng ful busily
I thought to take heede of hir array.
fo. 42ʳ   Hir gowne was bliew, this wote I verily,
Of goode facion and furred wele with gray.   305
Upon hir sleve hir worde, this is no nay,
The whiche saide thus, as my penne can endite:
A moy que je voy, writen with lettres white.

---

283 *iwis*: indeed.   *bien ye no mo*: are there no more of you?
287 *To*: until.   289 *Til*: to.
291 *yow list*: it pleases you.   293 *do yow mede*: reward you.
294 *can nomore*: can (say) no more.   *spede*: help.
300 *awaityng*: looking out.   *ever among*: every now and then.
305 *facion*: cut, style.   *furred wele with gray*: well trimmed with grey fur.
306 *this is no nay*: without denying it/in truth.   307 *endite*: write.
308 *'A moy que je voy'*: 'To me what I see' (what I see is mine).

Than ferforth as she com streyght unto me,
'Yowre worde,' quod she, 'fayne wold I that I knewe.'   310
'Forsoth,' quod I, 'ye shal wele know and se:
And for my word I have none, this is trewe.
It is inough that my clothyng be blew,
As here before I had comaundement,
And so to do I am right wele content.   315

But telle me this, I pray yow hertily:
The stiward here, sey me, what is hir name?'
'She hight Largesse, I say yow surely,
A faire lady and right of nobil fame—
Whan ye hir se ye wil report the same.   320
And undir hir, to bid yow welcom alle,
There is Bealchiere, the marchal of the halle.

Now al this while that ye here tary stille
Yowre owne matiers ye may wele have in mynde;
But telle me this, have ye brought any bille?'   325
'Ye, ye,' quod I, 'or ellis I were behynde.
Where is ther on, telle me, that I may fynde
To whom I may shewe my matiers playne?'
'Surely,' quod she, 'unto the chambrelayne.'

'The chambrelayne,' quod I, 'say ye trewe?'   330
'Ye, verily,' quod she, 'be myn advise,
Be nat aferd, but lowly til hir shewe.'

309 *ferforth*: immediately.   317 *stiward*: steward.

318 *Largesse*: Generosity.

319 *right of nobil fame*: with a very worthy reputation.

322 *Bealchiere*: Hospitality. The marshal was responsible for the organization of cere-
monies, and the disposition and serving of guests.

325 *bille*: letter, petition. Cf. the *bille* presented in *TG* 317–20. Much attention is paid
here to the documents and their presentation. In legal terms, the bill stated the cause of a
complaint and requested redress. Pearsall (1962: 161) notes that 'In style as well as content
the bills of *AL* recall those of fifteenth-century law, especially those presented before the
King's Council.'

329 The chamberlain is the household officer with responsibility for the private
chambers.

331 *be*: by.

332 *aferd*: frightened.   *lowly*: humbly.   *til hir shewe*: show (yourself) to her (there
may be some grounds for emending this to *sewe*: supplicate).

'It shal be don, quod I, 'as ye devise;

But me must knowe hir name in every wyse.'

'Triewly, quod she, 'to telle yow in substaunce,   335

Without feyneng, hir name is Remembraunce.

The secretarye yit may nat be forgete,

For she may do right moche in every thyng;

Wherfor I rede whan ye have with hir met

Yowre matier hole telle hir withoute feyneng: 340

Ye shal hir fynde ful goode and ful lovyng.'

'Telle me hir name,' quod I, 'of gentillesse.'

'Be my goode soth,' quod she, 'Avisenesse.'

'That name,' quod I, 'for hir is passyng goode,

For every bille and cedule she must se.   345

Now goode,' quod I, 'com stonde where I stoode—

My felawes bien comyng, yonder they be.'

'Is it a jape or say ye soth,' quod she.

'In jape? nay, nay! I say it for certeyne;

Se how they come togyder tweyne and tweyne.'   350

'Ye say ful soth,' quod she, 'it is no nay:

I se comyng a goodely company.'

'They bien, quod I, 'suche folk, I dare wele say,

That list to love, thynk it ful verily.

And my faire love, I pray yow feithfully   355

At any tyme whan they upon yow cal

That ye wil be goode frend to theym al.'

'Of my frendship,' quod she, 'they shul nat mys

As for ther case to put therto my payne.'

334 *in every wyse*: anyway.   335 *in substaunce*: shortly.
336 *feyneng*: pretence.
337 *yit*: furthermore.   *forgete*: overlooked. The secretary's office (with responsibility for the written bills) is a predominantly clerical one.
338 *right moche*: a great deal.   340 *Yowre matier hole*: all your business.
342 *of gentilesse*: out of courtesy.   343 *Avisenesse*: Forethought, Deliberation.
344 *passyng*: extremely.   345 *bille*: written petition.   *cedule*: written document.
346 *goode*: good lady.   348 *jape*: jest.
350 *tweyne and tweyne*: two by two.
351 *it is no nay*: there is no denying it.   354 Who wish to love, believe it truly.
358–9 'They won't lack my friendship in putting my efforts into their affairs', she said.

ssembly of Ladies* 215

'God yield it yow,' quod I, 'but telle me this: 360
How shal we knowe whiche is the chambrelayne?'
'That shal ye wele knowe by hir worde, certayne.'
'What is hir worde, suster, I pray yow say?'
43ʳ '*Plus ne purroy*, thus writeth she alway.'

Thus as we stoode togydre, she and I, 365
At the yate my felawes were echon.
So mette I theym, as me thought was goodely,
And bad hem welcom al by one and oon.
Than forth com Contenaunce anon:
'Ful hertily, feyre sustres al,' quod she, 370
'Ye bien right welcom to this contre.'

'I counseile yow to take a litel rest
In my chambre, if it be youre plesaunce.
Whan ye bien there me thynk it for the best
That I gon in and cal Perseveraunce, 375
Because she is oon of youre acqueyntaunce,
And she also wil telle yow every thyng
How ye shal be rulyd of your comyng.'

My felawes al and I, be oon avise,
Were wele agreed to do as she sayde. 380
Than we began to dresse us in oure guyse
That folk shuld se us nat unpurvayde,
And wageours among us there we layde
Whiche of us atired were goodeliest,
And whiche of us al preysed shuld be best. 385

The porter than brought Perseveraunce;
She welcomd us in ful curteys manere:
'Thynk ye nat long,' quod she, 'youre attendaunce;
I wil go speke unto the herbergier

360 *yield*: reward.   364 '*Plus ne purroy*': 'I could do no more'.
367 *goodely*: fitting.   368 *by one and oon*: one by one.
378 [about] how your arrival will be organized.
379 *be oon avise*: by a single decision.   381 *guyse*: outfits.
382 *unpurvayde*: unprovided for.   383 *wageours*: bets.
388 *attendaunce*: wait.

That she may purvey for youre loggyng here, 390
Than wil I gon to the chambrelayne
To speke for yow, and come anon agayne.'

And whan she departed and was agone
We sawe folkes comyng without the wal,

fo. 43ᵛ So gret people that nombre couthe we none. 395
Ladyes they were and gentil wymmen al,
Clothed in bliew everiche, her wordes withal:
But for to knowe theyr wordis or devise
They com so thycke we myght in no wise.

With that anon come Perseveraunce 400
And wher I stoode she com streight to me:
'Ye bien,' quod she, 'of myn old acqueyntaunce;
Yow to enquere the bolder dare I be
What worde they bere eche after theyr degre.
I pray yow telle it me in secrete wise 405
And I shal kepe it close on warantise.'

'We bien,' quod I, 'fyve ladies al in feere,
And gentilwymmen foure in company.
Whan they begynne to opyne theyr matiere
There shal ye knowe her wordis, by and by. 410
But as for me, I have none verily
And so I told to Countenaunce here afore:
Al myn array is bliew, what nedith more?'

'Now,' quod she, 'I wil go in agayne,
That ye may know what ye shal do.' 415

---

392 *come anon agayne*: come straight back.
393 *agone*: gone.   394 *without*: outside.
395 So many people that we could not number [them].
397 *her wordes withal*: and with their mottoes.
399 They arrived in such numbers that we could not in any way.
403 *Yow to enquere*: to ask of you.   404 *degre*: rank.
406 *on warantise*: for certain.   407 *in feere*: all together.
409 *opyne theyr matiere*: present their case.
  413 The narrator's unwillingness to specify a motto for herself is part of the general deliberate mysteriousness surrounding her circumstances and position.

'Forsoth,' quod I, 'yif ye wil take the peyne,
Ye dide right moche for us, yif ye did so;
The rather spede the sonner may we go.
Grete cost alwey there is in taryeng,
And long to sue it is a wery thyng.'   420

Than parted she and come agayne anon:
'Ye must,' quod she, 'com to the chambrelayne.'
'We bien,' quod I, 'now redy, everichone,
To folowe yow whan ever yow list, certeyne.
We have none eloquence, to telle yow pleyne,   425
Besechyng yow we may be so excused
Oure triewe meanyng that it be nat refused.'

Than went we forth after Perseveraunce.
To se the prease it was a wonder case:
There for to passe it was grete combraunce,   430
The people stoode so thykk in every place.
'Now stonde ye stille,' quod she, 'a litel space,
And for yowre ease somwhat shal I assay
Yif I can make yow any better way.'

And furth she goth among hem everychon,   435
Makyng a wey that we myght thurgh passe
More at oure ease, and whan she had don
She bekened us to com ther as she was,
So after hir we folowed more and lasse.
She brought us streight unto the chambrelayne;   440
There left she us and than she went agayne.

f. 44^r

416–17 'Indeed,' I said, 'if you will take that on, you would do a great deal for us, were you to do so.'

418 The greater speed, the sooner may we leave.   419 *cost*: harm.

420 *sue*: plead, make petition. This observation has a weary ring of truth. The pursuit of litigation in the Middle Ages was often protracted and expensive.

429 *prease*: crowd. *wonder case*: wonderful thing.

430 *grete combraunce*: very awkward.   433 *assay*: attempt.

434 *Yif*: if.

439 *more and lasse*: great and small / one and all.

We salwed hir as reson wold it soo,
Ful humbly besechyng hir goodenesse
In oure matiers that we had for to doo
That she wold be goode lady and maystresse.   445
'Ye bien welcom,' quod she, 'in sothfastnesse,
And so what I can do yow for to please
I am redy, that may be for youre ease.'

We folowed hir unto the chambre doore.
'Suster,' quod she, 'come in ye after me.'   450
But wite ye wele, ther was a paved floore,
The goodliest that any wight myght see;
And furthermore aboute than loked we
On eche a corner and upon every wal,
The whiche is made of berel and cristal,   455

Wheron was graven of storyes many oon:
fo. 44^v First how Phillis of wommanly pite
Deyd pitously for the love of Demephon;
Next after was the story of Thesbe,
How she slowe hir self under a tre;   460
Yit sawe I more how in pitous case
For Antony was slayne Cleopatrace.

That other syde was how Melusene
Untriewly was disceyved in hir bayne;

442 We greeted her as right dictated.
443 *hir goodenesse*: for this usage, cf. her highness, her majesty.
444 In the business that we had to conduct.   446 *in sothfastnesse*: in truth.
452 *wight*: person.
455 *berel*: beryl (a form of crystal rather than a precious stone). The walls recall the materials of the temples in *HF* and *TG*, part of a tradition which goes back to the Bible, in Revelation 21: 18–21.
456 *graven*: engraved, figured. The stories of other lovers depicted here are in scope and purpose similar to those in *TG* 55–143.
458 *Deyd*: died.   460 *slowe*: slew.
463–4 Melusene, whose story circulated in versions in both French and English, habitually turned into a snake from the waist down on Saturdays. She kept this secret from her husband for many years, but he finally saw her serpent's tail as he spied on her bathing. For the English versions, see Skeat 1866 and Donald 1895.
464 *Untriewly*: faithlessly.   *disceyved*: deceived.   *bayne*: bath.

Ther was also Anelada the quene   465
Upon Arcite how sore she did complayne;
Al these storyes wer graven ther certayne,
And many mo than I reherce yow here—
It were to long to telle yow al in feere.

And bicause the wallis shone so bright   470
With fyne umple they were al over-spredde
To that entent folk shuld nat hurt theyr sight,
And thurgh that the storyes myght be redde.
Than further I went as I was ledde
And there I sawe, without any faile,   475
A chayer set with ful riche apparaile;

And fyve stages it was sette from the grounde,
Of cassidony ful curiously wrought,
With foure pomels of gold and verray rounde
Set with saphirs as fyne as myght be thought.   480
Wote ye what, yif were thurgh sought
As I suppose from this contre til Ynde,
Another suche it were hard to fynde.

465–66 Queen Anelida lamented her desertion by Arcite; her 'compleynt', in which this is voiced, is a part of Chaucer's short lyrico-narrative *A & A* (in Chaucer 1987).

468 *mo*: more.   *reherce*: recount.   469 *to*: too.   *in feere*: altogether.

471 *umple*: gauze.   472 *To that entent*: so that.

475 *without any faile*: indeed.

476 *chayer*: raised seat, throne.   *apparaile*: apparelling.   477 *stages*: steps.

477–8 The throne is placed on five steps made of chalcedony, a semi-transparent white quartz which is also one of the stones forming the foundations of the New Jerusalem described in Revelation 21: 19. In lapidaries it is a symbol of authority, as in the so-called 'London Lapidary': 'Our lord yaue swiche vertue to this stone þat he þat berith hit shal be wele spekyng of gode . . . Calcedyone berith grace' (Evans and Serjeantson 1933: 29–30).

478 Skilfully made of chalcedony.

479 *pomels*: knobs.   *verray*: completely.

480 Sapphires, as here on the rounded knobs of the throne, were thought to rival rubies as most precious of stones, and to represent truth and constancy: the 'London Lapidary' announces that 'The veray bokes tellen vs þat saphire is of þe colour of heuen', and a poem on precious stones in BL MS Add. 34360 (whose text of *AL* is followed here) writes of 'The goode Saphir, most mekest in moode . . . a stidefast stone' (Evans and Serjeantson 1933: 22–3, 61).

481–2 You know, if everywhere were thoroughly searched, from this country to India.

For wete ye wele, I was ful nere that;
So as I dursst beholdyng by and by,   485
Above ther was a riche cloth of state
Wrought with the nedil ful straungely

Hir worde theron, and thus it sayde triewly
A endurer, to telle in wordis fewe,
With grete lettres, the better for to shewe.   490

Thus as we stoode a doore opened anon:
A gentil womman semely of stature,
Beryng a mace, com out, hir self alone—
Triewly, me thought, a goodely creature.
She spak nothyng to lowde, I yow ensure,   495
Nor hastily, but bi goodely warnyng:
'Make roome,' quod she, 'my lady is comyng.'

With that anon I saw Perseveraunce
How she hield up the tappet in hir hande.
I sawe also in right goode ordynaunce   500
This grete lady withyn the tappet gan stande,
Comyng outward, I wil ye undrestande,
And after hir a noble company—
I cowde nat telle the nombre sikerly.

Of theyr names I wold nothyng enquere   505
Further than suche as we wold sue unto,

484 *wete ye wele*: believe me.
485 Looking round as much as I dared, bit by bit (I saw).
486 *cloth of state*: stately hanging; a piece of rich fabric which formed a canopy over a throne.
487 *Wrought with the nedil*: made with needlework.   *straungely*: unusually.
489 '*A endurer*': '[ever] to endure'.   490 *grete*: large.
492 *semely of stature*: of attractive bearing.
495 *nothyng to lowde*: not a bit too loud.
496 *bi goodely warnyng*: with a courteous warning.
499 *hield*: held.   *tappet*: hanging.
499–502 Perseveraunce holds aside the cloth hanging which covers the entrance or doorway, so that her lady can pass through it into the hall.
500 *ordynaunce*: order.   504 *sikerly*: certainly.
505–6 I didn't at all wish to ask their names beyond those we wanted to put our case to.

Sauf oo lady whiche was the chaunceler—
Attemperaunce sothly hir name was soo—
For us must with hir have moche to doo
In oure matiers, and alwey more and more.   510
And so furth to telle yow furthermore,

Of this lady hir beauties to discryve,
My konnyng is to symple verily;
For never yit the dayes of al my live
So inly fayre I have none sene, triewly;   515
In hir astate assured utterly,
Ther lakked naught, I dare yow wele ensure,
That longged to a goodely creature.

[And furthermore to speke of hyr aray
I shall yow tell the maner of hyr goune: 520
Of cloth of gold full ryche, hyt ys no nay,
The colour blew of a ryght good fassion;
In taberd wyse the slevys hangyng don;
And what purfyll ther was and in what wyse
So as I can I shall hyt yow devyse: 525

Aftyr a sort the coler and the vent,
Lyke as ermyn ys made in purfelyng,
With gret perles full fyne and oryent
They were couchyd, al aftyr oon worchyng

507 *Sauf oo*: except for one. The chancellor looked to the running of household and
estate.
508 *Attemperaunce*: Temperance.   512 *discryve*: describe.
513 *konnyng*: skill.   514 *live*: life.   515 *inly*: utterly.
516 *astate*: estate, nobility.   518 *longged*: was appropriate.
521 *hyt ys no nay*: there's no denying it.   522 *fassion*: fashion.
523 *In taberd wyse*: like a tabard.   *don*: down. The sleeves of the garment (probably a
surcoat) are wide and loosely hanging: see Scott 1986, plate 101 (from Germany, 1467);
'bag' sleeves and long sleeves of other kinds are depicted in other plates.
524 *purfyll*: trimming, border.
526–9 The collar and the v-shaped opening at the neck were in the same style; studded
with very fine precious pearls, all in the same design, in the way ermine is used as a trim
(the neckline and collar are trimmed with pearls and diamonds, rather than with fur and
black-tail 'powdering'; cf. Fortune's garment in *LR* 344–99).

With dyamondes in stede of pouderyng;   530
The slevys and purfyllys of assyse
They were made lyke in every wyse.]

fo. 45ᵛ   Abowte hir nekke a serpe of fayre rubies
In white floures of right fyne enemayle;
Upon hir hede sette in the fresshest wise   535
A cercle with grete balays of entaile,
That in ernest to speke, withouten faile,
For yong and old and every maner age
It was a world to loke on hir visage.

This comyng to sit in hir astate,   540
In hir presence we knelid downe echeon
Presentyng up oure billis, and, wote ye what,
Ful humbly she toke hem by oon and oon.
Whan we had don than com they al anon
And dide the same iche after in theyr manere,   545
Knelyng attone and risyng al in feere.

Whan this was don and she sette in hir place,
The chambrelayne she dide unto hir cal,
And she goodely comyng til hir apace,
Of hir intent knowyng nothyng at al,   550
'Voyde bak the prease,' quod she, 'unto the wal;

530 *in stede of pouderyng*: in the place of 'powdering' (ornamenting) with ermine tails.
531 *purfyllys*: trims. *of assyse*: to match.
533 *serpe*: ornamental chain, necklace. *LR*'s Fortune also wears a *serpe* or ornamental collar. The *cercle* is a jewelled circlet or crown; for the significance of the *balays* see *LR* 345 n.
534 *floures*: flowers. *enemayle*: enamel.
536 *cercle*: crown. *balays of entaile*: carved rubies.
539 *world*: world (of pleasure); cf. similar expressions using 'heaven' or 'paradise', such as *TC* II. 637, 'It was an heven upon hym for to see'.
540 *This comyng*: Thus coming/This (lady) having come. *in hir astate*: in state.
541 *echeon*: every one.
544 *they al*: refers to the company of other ladies, all dressed in blue, mentioned at 395.
545 *iche after in theyr manere*: each after (another) in their own way.
546 *attone*: at the same time.
549 *goodely*: courteously. *apace*: quickly.
551 *Voyde*: remove. *prease*: crowd.

Make larger rome, but loke ye do nat tarye,
And take these billes unto the secretarye.'

The chambrelayne dide hir comaundement
And come ageyne as she was bode to doo.   555
The secretarie there beyng present
The billes were delyvered til hir also,
Nat only oures but many another moo.
Than this lady with gode avise ageyne
Anone withal callid hir chambrelayne: 560

'We wil,' quod she, 'the first thyng that ye doo,
The secretary make hir come anon
With hir billes; and thus we wille also
In oure presence she rede hem everychone,
That we may take goode avise theron   565
Of the ladyes whiche bien of oure counsaile.
Looke this be don without any faile.'

The chambrelayn whan she wist hir entent
Anon she dide the secretarye calle:
'Lete yowre billes,' quod she, 'be here present: 570
My lady it wil.' 'Madame,' quod she, 'I shal.'
'In hir presence she wil ye rede hem al.'
'With goode wil I am redy,' quod she,
'At hir plesure whan she comaundith me.'

And upon that was made an ordynaunce   575
They that com first theyr billes to be redde.
Ful gently than seyde Perseveraunce:
'Reason it wold that they were sonnest spedde.'
Anon withal, upon a tappet spredde,

. 46ʳ

---

552 *rome*: room.   *loke*: see.   *tarye*: delay.   555 *bode*: bidden.   557 *til*: to.
559 *avise*: consideration.   561 *wil*: wish.   565 *avise*: advice.
568 *wist*: knew.   *entent*: intention.   570 *present*: presented.
571 *it wil*: wishes it.   575 *ordynaunce*: regulation.
576 That the bills of those who arrived first should be read first.
578 It is reasonable that they should be soonest dealt with.
579 *tappet*: carpet.

The secretarye layde hem downe everichon.   580
Oure billes first she red, oon by oon.

The first lady, beryng in hir devise
Sanꝛ que jamais, thus wrote she in hir bille:
Compleyneng sore and in ful pitous wise
Of promesse made with feithful hert and wil   585
And so broken, ayenst al maner skille,
Without desert alweys in hir party,
In this matier desiryng remedy.

Hir next felawes word was in this wise—
Une sans chaungier, and thus she did complayne: 590
Though she had bien gwerdoned for hir service
Yit nothyng, as she takith it, pleyne,
Wherfor she cowde in no wise restreyne
fo. 46ᵛ   But in this case sue until hir presence,
As reason wold, to have recompense.   595

So furthermore, to speke of other tweyne,
Oon of hem wrote, after hir fantasye,
Oncques puis lever; and for to telle yow pleyne,
Hir compleynt was grevous, verily;
For as she sayde ther was grete reason why,   600
And as I can remembre that matiere
I shal yow telle the processe al in fere:

582–707 The complaints enumerated in these lines are characterized by Pearsall (1962: 167) as 'repetitive, imperfectly distinguished, monotonous, and imprecise', altogether marking 'a low ebb in fifteenth-century verse'. Lurking in their imprecision might be an attempt to indicate the difficulty of unravelling the complexities inherent in human relationships, and a call to crucial qualities like loyalty to cut through these. Just as the relationship between the knight and the lady in *TG* represents concerns beyond those of lovers, so these complaints—of broken promises, instability, unreciprocated feelings—have a wide general relevance.

583 '*Sanꝛ que jamais*': 'Without ever [giving cause]'.   584 *sore*: sorrowfully.
586 *ayenst al maner skille*: against every kind of reason.
587 *desert*: cause, deserving.   *in hir party*: on her part.   589 *wise*: way.
590 '*Une sans chaungier*': one without changing.   591 *gwerdoned*: rewarded.
592 Yet not, as she considers it, in full.   594 *sue*: plead.   *until*: unto.
595 *wold*: would (decree).   596 *tweyne*: two.   597 *fantasye*: inclination.
598 '*oncques puis lever*': 'I can never rise'.
602 *processe*: business.   *al in fere*: altogether.

Hir bille was made compleyneng in her guyse
That of hir joye, comfort and gladnesse
Was no suerte, for in no maner wise   605
She fonde therin no poynt of stabilnesse—
Now ill, now wele, out of al sikernesse—
Ful humble desiryng of Her Grace
Som remedy to shewe in this case.

Hir felaw made hir bille, and thus she sayde   610
In pleyneng wise: ther as she lovid best,
Whethir she were wroth or ill apayde,
She myght nat se whan she wold faynest;
And wroth was she in verray ernest
To telle hir worde, and forsoth, as I wote,   615
Entierment vostre right thus she wrote.

And upon that she made a grete request,
With hert and wil and al that myght be done,
As until hir that myght redresse it best,
For in hir mynde thus myght she fynde it sone,   620
The remedy of that whiche was hir bone;
Rehersyng that she had seyd before,
Besechyng hir it myght be so no more.

And in like wise as they had don before
The gentilwymmen of oure company   625
Put up their billes; and for to telle yow more,

---

603 *guyse*: own way.   605 *suerte*: certainty.
607 *out of al sikernesse*: without any security.
608–9 Very humbly wishing that her grace (i.e. Lady Loyalty) would offer some
remedy in this matter.
611 *In pleyneng wise*: in the manner of complaint.   *ther as*: where.
612 *ill apayde*: ill pleased.
613 She might not see (the person she loved) when she most wanted to.
614–15 This plaintiff's anger seems to result from her sense that her motto, 'Entirely
yours', can have little meaning in circumstances where it is difficult for her to see her lover.
615 *wote*: know.   616 '*Entierment vostre*': 'Entirely yours'.
617 *upon*: following.   619 To her who might best put it right.
621 *bone*: request.
624–5 The distinction here is between the ladies and the gentlewomen.

One of hem wrote *Cest sanȝ dire*, verily;
Of hir compleynt also the cause why
Withyn hir bille she put it in writyng,
And what it saide ye shul have knowlachyng: 630

It sayde, God wote, and that ful pitously,
Like as she was disposed in hir hert:
No mysfortune that she toke grevously,
Al on til hir it was the joy or smert;
Somtyme no thank for al hir desert;   635
Other comfort she wayted non comyng,
And so used it greved hir nothyng;

Desiryng hir and lowly hir besechyng
That she for hir wold se a bettir way,
As she that had bien al hir dayes livyng   640
Stadefast and triewe, and so wil be alway.
Of hir felaw somwhat shal I yow say,
Whos bille was redde next after forth withal,
And what it ment reherce yow I shal:

En dieu est she wrote in hir devise,   645
And thus she sayde, without any faile,
Hir trowth myght be take in no wise
Like as she thought, wherfor she had mervaile;
For trowth somtyme was wont to take availe
In eche matiere, but now al that is goo—   650
The more pite that it is suffred soo.

627 '*Cest sanȝ dire*': 'It needs no words' / 'It goes without saying'.
630 *knowlachyng*: knowledge.   631–2 *It sayde . . . Like*: It told . . . how.
633–5 She took no misfortune seriously to heart, joy and pain were all one to her; in the
past [she had] no thanks in reward (for her devotion, and so . . .).
636 *wayted*: expected.
637 And she had been so used (for so long that) it didn't upset her.
639 *se*: contrive.   640 *As she that*: as one who.
641 *Stadefast*: steadfast.   643 *next after forth withal*: straight afterwards.
644 *reherce*: tell.   645 '*En dieu est*': in God is [my trust].
647–8 Her [true] word was not taken in any way as she meant it, which she found
incredible.
649–50 For truth formerly used to prevail in every matter, but now all that is past.

Moche more ther was wherof she shuld compleyne
But she thought it to grete encombraunce
So moche to write, and therfor, in certayne,
In God and hir she put hir affiaunce—   655
As in hir worde is made a remembraunce—
Besechyng hir that she wold in that case
Shewe til hir the favour of hir grace.

. 47^v

The thridde she wrote rehersyng hir grevaunce,
Yee, wote ye what, a pitous thyng to here,   660
For as me thought she felt grete displesaunce—
One myght wele perceyve bi hir chiere;
And no wonder, it sat hir passyng neere.
Yit loth she was to put it in writyng,
But neede wil have his cours in every thyng.   665

Sejour ensure, this was hir worde certeyne,
And thus she wrote but in litel space:
There she loved hir labour was in vayne,
For he was sette al in another place;
Ful humble desiryng in that cace   670
Som goode comfort hir sorow to appese
That she myght live more at hertis ease.

The fourth surely, me thought, she liked wele,
As in hir port and in hir havyng;
And *Bien monest*, as ferre as I cowth feele,   675
That was hir worde, til hir wele belongyng;

653 *encombraunce*: burden.   655 *hir*: her (Loyalty).   *affiaunce*: faith, trust.
658 *til*: to.
660 *Yee, wote ye what*: Indeed, you can imagine it.
661 *as me thought*: it seemed to me.   662 *chiere*: expression.
663 *it sat hir passyng neere*: it affected her very deeply.
665 *his cours*: its way. This line offers a variant of the proverb 'need has no law'
(Whiting 1968: N51).
666 '*Sejour ensure*': 'rest assured'.   669 *sette*: set [to love].
670 *humble*: humbly.
674 *port*: demeanour.   *havyng*: behaviour.
675 '*Bien monest*': 'Well advised'.   *as ferre as I cowth feele*: as far as I could make out.
676 *til*: to.   *wele belongyng*: very appropriate.

Wherfor til her she prayde above al thyng
Ful hertily, to say yow in substaunce,
That she wold sende hir goode contenuaunce.

'Ye have rehersed me these billis alle,   680
But now late se somwhat of youre entente.'
'It may so happe peraventure ye shal.'
'Now, I pray yow, while I am here present.'
'Ye shal, parde, have knowlache what I ment.
But thus I say in trowth, and make no fable,   685
The case it silf is inly lamentable,

And wele I wote that ye wil thynk the same
Like as I say, whan ye han herd my bil.'
'Now, goode, telle on, I hate yow, be seynt Jame.'
fo. 48ʳ   'Abide a while; it is nat yit my wil—   690
Yet must ye wite bi reason and bi skil,
Sith ye knowe al that hath be done afore.'
And thus it sayde without any more:

'Nothyng so lief as death to come to me
For fynal end of my sorwes and peyne.   695
What shuld I more desire, as seme ye?
And ye knewe al aforne it, for certeyne
I wote ye wold; and for to telle yow pleyne,
Without hir help that hath al thyng in cure
I can nat thynk that it may long endure.   700

678 *in substaunce*: in short.   679 *goode contenuaunce*: the ability to persevere.
     681 *late se*: let's see. Loyalty here addresses the narrator, who is at first unwilling to state
her own grievance, and whose 'bill', when eventually read, makes reference in the vaguest of
terms to the cause of her suffering (cf. her mysteriousness about men's wrongs at 151 ff.).
     682 *happe*: happen.   *peraventure*: perhaps.   684 *parde*: indeed.
     686 *it silf*: itself.   *inly*: utterly.
     689 *goode*: good lady.   *hate*: bid. The remains of St James, supposedly at Compostella
in Spain, attracted large numbers of medieval pilgrims.
     691–2 Yet it is right and appropriate that you know, since you know everything that has
happened until now.
     694 *lief*: dear.   696 *as seme ye*: might you think.
     697 *al aforne it*: everything that has happened.
     698 *I wote ye wold*: I know you would (agree).
     699 *in cure*: in her care.

And for my trouth, preved it hath bien wele—
To sey the soth it can be no more—
Of ful long tyme, and suffred every dele
In pacience and kept it al in store;
Of hir goodenesse besechyng hir therfor   705
That I myght have my thank in suche wise
As my desert deservith of justice.'

Whan these billes were redde everichone
This lady toke goode avisement,
And hem til aunswere, eche on by oon,   710
She thought it to moche in hir entent;
Wherfor she yaf in comaundement,
In hir presence to come, both oon and al,
To yeve hem there hir answere in general.

What did she than, suppose yow, verily?   715
She spak hir silf and seyde in this manere:
'We have wele sen youre billis by and by
And som of hem ful pitous for to here.
We wil therfor ye knowen this al in feere:
Withyn short tyme oure court of parlement   720
Here shal be holde in oure paleys present,

48ᵛ

701 *preved*: proved.   703 *dele*: bit.
704 *in store*: locked up, hidden.
706–7 That I might be thanked as appropriately as my cause deserves justice.
709 *toke goode avisement*: deliberated carefully.
710 *hem til aunswere*: to answer them.
711–12 She considered it in her own mind too much; for which reason she commanded . . .
712–14 Any final judgement is deferred—a common feature of poems, such as *PF*, which air debates, and part of the 'recreational irresolution' discussed by Reed 1990: 153–218. A listening audience, or a close circle of readers, might perhaps have felt encouraged to discuss the range of possible outcomes.
714 *yeve*: give.   717 *by and by*: one by one.
719 *al in feere*: all together.
720 The 'court of parlement' seems to be anticipated as a judicial assembly of some kind.
721 *in oure paleys present*: in this our palace.

And in al this wherein ye fynde yow greved
There shal ye fynde an open remedy,
In suche wise as ye shul be releved
Of al that ye reherce heere triewly.   725
As of the date ye shal knowe verily
Than ye may have a space in your comyng,
For Diligence shall bryng it yow bi writyng.'

We thanked hir in oure most humble wise,
Oure felawship echon bi on assent,   730
Submyttyng us lowly til hir servise,
For as us thought we had oure travel spent
In suche wise as we hielde us content.
Than eche of us toke other by the sleve
And furth withal as we shuld take oure leve.   735

Al sodainly the water sprang anone
In my visage and therwithal I woke
'Wher am I now?' thought I, 'al this is goon,'
Al amased, and up I gan to looke.
With that anon I went and made this booke,   740
Thus symply rehersyng the substaunce
Because it shuld nat out of remembraunce.

'Now verily your dreame is passyng goode
And worthy to be held in remembraunce,
For though I stande her as long as I stoode   745
It shuld to me be none encombraunce,

726 *As of*: as for.   727 Then you may have time to get here.
730 Each one of our company unanimously.
732-3 For it seemed to us we had exerted ourselves in such a way as to be content.
735 *furth withal*: straightway.
736 The narrator, recounting the substance of her dream to the knight or squire
encountered in the maze, here recalls for him the point at which she awoke. The water
which brought her round might have been spray from one of the water features in the
arbour where she fell asleep.
738 *goon*: gone.
740 This is the first mention that the dream has been embodied in a book: earlier
references describe it as a 'tale' (21), a 'procese' (27) and a 'matiere' (28).
742 So that it would not pass from memory.
743 The knight or squire now speaks.

I toke therin so inly grete plesaunce.
But tel me now what ye the booke do cal,
For me must wite.' 'With right goode wil ye shal:

As for this booke, to sey yow verray right   750
And of the name to tel the certeynte,
"La semble des dames" thus it hight.
How thynk ye that the name is?' 'Goode, parde!'
'Now go, farwele, for they cal after me,
My felawes al, and I must after sone.'   755
Rede wele my dreame for now my tale is done.

749 *me must wite*: I must know.
750 *sey yow verray right*: tell you absolutely precisely.
752 *'La semble des dames'*: 'The Assembly of Ladies'.
755 *I must after sone*: I must follow quickly.

John Skelton, *The Bouge of Court*

John Skelton's writings, which bridge the periods conventionally clas-
sified as 'medieval' and 'Renaissance', demonstrate the continued life of
the poetic dream vision well over a century after Chaucer's influential
experiments with the form. Skelton had read Chaucer carefully, but also
draws into his own writing the fruits of the wide scholarly reading which
qualified him in the last years of the fifteenth century for a post as tutor
to the future Henry VIII. The details of Skelton's early life are unclear,
but he seems to have come from a northern family, to have studied at
Cambridge and Oxford, and to have been awarded the title of 'laureate'
by these universities (and that of Louvain) in acknowledgement of his
rhetorical skill. During the period of his royal tutorship he lived in
London, writing in both English and Latin, and taking holy orders in
1498. From about 1503 until 1512, Skelton lived in Norfolk, where he was
rector of Diss but retained contact with Henry (who became king in
1509), and acquired the title 'orator regis' (king's orator). After this he
seems to have returned to London, where he kept some contact with
the king, and also wrote a play, *Magnificence*, on the subject of rulership
and power, and a number of satires which addressed the growing
influence of Cardinal Wolsey. During his last years he published *The
Garland of Laurel*, a dream vision about poetic fame and the relationship
between writers and their patrons, and became involved in the public
condemnation of religious heresy. He died in 1529.

BC is among Skelton's earliest surviving works, printed by Wynkyn
de Worde in 1499. The astrological details in the first stanza suggest that
it was probably composed in the autumn of 1498, although a case has
also been made for a much earlier date of 1480. Its narrator, who names
himself as 'Drede' or Fearfulness (line 77), prefaces the account of his
dream with some discussion of the moral purposes of poetry, and the
charges of ignorance or presumptuousness which are risked by those
who castigate vice under 'coverte termes'. The dream itself concerns life
aboard a splendid ship ruled by Fortune, and it opens with a scene

reminiscent of love visions, in which gentlewomen personifying the qualities of 'Daunger' and 'Desyre' are portrayed in the service of a great lady to whom the occupants of the ship pay court. These suppliants wish not for success in love, however, but for the 'bouge of court'—the allowance paid to members of a court or household—and their ability to profit from this, as Drede is told by Desyre, depends not on the quality of their service but simply on luck. The course of the sea voyage is dominated for Drede by a series of encounters with shifty individuals engaged on the chancy pursuit of this profit; their suspicions of him, and their whispered collusion, provoke such mortal fear that he moves to jump overboard, and the dream ends as this sudden impulse jolts him awake. The brief, enigmatic conclusion directs readers to make their own sense of what has been recounted.

The substance and tone of this dream define it gradually as curial satire rather than love vision. The individuals encountered by Drede personify a selection of the vicious traits necessary for speedy success at court, such as disdain for others, flattery, and the capacity for dissimulation; all are qualities which have to do with the self-presentation and self-preservation which concerned many aspiring courtiers in the medieval and Renaissance periods. Although Drede seems to begin as the desirous but fearful dreamer-narrator common in the love vision, his fears take on different aspects as the poem proceeds, comprehending both the paranoia induced by the competition for advancement and the trepidation facing the poet who feels it his moral responsibility to reveal unwelcome truths. Truth, and the possibility of reflecting it in words, seem among the central issues of *BC*: Drede's aspirations to poetic truth are mocked by the empty songs of Harvy Hafter, and one by one the characters he meets make statements (often about truth and 'plain' speaking, as at lines 214, 235, 311, and 463) which belie their actions.

The traditions of personification allegory on which Skelton draws in *BC* owe something to love visions like *Le Roman de la Rose*, but reflect also the traditions of Middle English visions of other kinds, such as *Piers Plowman* (Langland 1978, ed. Schmidt), where dream opens the way for satirical comment. The satire in *BC* turns in part around the way in which the 'favour' and 'grace' bestowed here have material rather than amorous or spiritual connotations, and permit the aspiring retainer to profit financially from his allowance and to strengthen the networks on which his prosperity depends. Those who press aboard the ship are merchants, and the poem's key words ('chaffer', 'wares, 'chevysaunce', for example) relate to trade and profit, and to coins and purses (see lines 238, 364, 395, 475, 488, 504). Relationships here are bonds which guarantee an advantageous 'affinity' (139), and even the naive Drede is aware of his need for 'acquaintance' (lines 45, 93) to smooth his way. Prosperity also depends on luck, of course, and Drede's new friends make frequent reference to games of chance with dice and cards.

Drede's encounters are intensely dramatic and give *BC* much in common with moral plays such as Skelton's own *Magnificence*, or with dramatic episodes like the procession of Sins in *The Castle of Perseverance* (Eccles 1969). The emphasis on clothing and outward representation (Favell's cloak, for example, or Riot's indecent attire, or the double-faced hood mentioned at 428) all add to the impression that the poem is comprised of a series of short dramatic scenes in which costume and props contribute to the meaning conveyed in dialogue. Other contemporary satires which may have been influential on Skelton's choice of form are the different versions of the story of the 'ship of fools', describing a vessel bearing individuals who embody different follies (Sebastian Brant's *Narrenschiff* is probably the best known). Editions of this were printed in the 1490s in Latin and German and French, many with arresting woodcut illustrations, and their existence may have alerted Skelton's early readers to his satirical purposes in *BC*.

NOTE ON THE TEXT

The text used as the basis for this edition is de Worde's 1499 printed edition (*STC* 22597), now in the Advocates' Library in the National Library of Scotland, Edinburgh (E); the textual notes make reference to variants in de Worde's edition of *c.*1510 (*STC* 22597.5), in the copy now in Cambridge University Library (C), and on occasion to John Stow's edition of Skelton's collected works, printed by Marshe in 1568 (*STC* 22608; M).

TEXTUAL NOTES

14 moralyte] C; mortalyte E
19 I] from M; not in E or C
33 me] C; my E

49 certeynte] certeynet E; certayne C
58 traves] C; tranes E
114 laugheth] C; laughed E

117 cheryssheth] C; cherysshed
   E. casteth] C; casseth E
138 etc. Hafter] Haster E C M
198 commened] C; commaunde
   E. a praty space] Dyce's
   emendation; a party spake E; a
   party space C
219 dyscure] M; dysture E and C
223 man] C; wan E
234 Me] M; my E and C
245 skan] M; stan E and C
251 what] E and C (Kinsman
   (Skelton 1969) and Scattergood
   (Skelton 1983) read 'that')
255 I] supplied from C; omitted
   in E

294 carkes] Kinsman's emendation;
   carbes E and C
298 ryghte] C; ryghce E
311 layne] C; sayne E
394 I] E and M; not in C
403 harnes] harmes E and C; armes
   M
411 curtel] M; curtet E and C
416 Unthryftynes] M; unthryftnes E
   and C
417 whome] C; home E
446 hym] supplied from C; omitted
   in E
464 to] C; te E
515 Parde] parte E C M
526 rounded] C; roynded E

FURTHER READING

Skelton's life and writings are discussed variously by Nelson (1939), Edwards (1949), Pollet (1971), Kinney (1987), Walker (1988 and 2000); there are bibliographies in Kinsman and Yonge (1967) and Staub 1988. Reliably annotated texts of *BC* are in the collected editions of Skelton made by Dyce (Skelton 1965) and Scattergood (Skelton 1983), and in the selections edited by Kinsman (Skelton 1969). The dating of *BC* is discussed by Sale (1937), Tucker (1970), Brownlow (1984), and Walker (1988: 10–15). Commentary on the poem is to be found in the standard works on Skelton cited above, and also in Larson (1962), Psilos (1976), Spearing (1976: 197–202), Kosikowski (1977 and 1982), Halpern (1986), Sharratt (1986), Torti (1991: 107–18), Dickey (1992), Simpson (1993), Barr and Ward-Perkins (1997), Gillespie (1997), Cooney (2000*a*). Winser (1970) explores the poem's dramatic potential. Putter (1997) discusses traditions of curial satire, Walker (2000) reviews Skelton's associations with the court, and Scattergood (1988) and Pompen (1925) explore the iconography of the ship of Fortune and the ship of fools. Useful discussions of courts and court life in this period are to be found in Starkey (1981 and 1987), and Green (1980); Greenblatt (1980) explores the literary implications with reference to the lyrics and satires of Sir Thomas Wyatt, edited in Rebholz (1978).

Here begynneth a lytell treatyse named
The Bouge of Courte

Aii[r]

In autumpne, whan the sonne *in Vyrgyne*
By radyante hete enryped hath our corne,
Whan Luna, full of mutabylyte,
As emperes the dyademe hath worne
Of our pole artyke, smylynge halfe in scorne   5
At our foly and our unstedfastnesse;
The tyme whan Mars to werre hym dyd dres,

I, callynge to mynde the great auctoryte
Of poetes olde, whyche, full craftely,
Under as coverte termes as coude be,   10
Can touche a troughte and cloke it subtylly
Wyth fresshe utteraunce full sentencyously—

Title. Bouge: court rations (*MED bouge* 3 [1], defined as sustenance, an allowance of food and drink granted by a king or nobleman to a member of his household or to the retinue of a guest; related to a word derived from Fr. *bouche*, a leather bag).

1 *sonne*: sun.   '*In Vyrgyne*': in the astrological sign of Virgo (from about 22 August to 22 September). A springtime opening is more usual in dream poems, but autumn or winter are invoked in e.g. *HF*, *TG*, and Skelton's own *Garlande of Laurell*. Autumn dreams were thought to be particularly troubled and foreboding; see Spearing 1976: 197, and the note to this line by Scattergood in Skelton 1983.

2 *enryped*: ripened.

3 *Luna*: the moon, symbolizing change; cf. *LR* 370–1.

4 *emperes*: empress.   *dyademe*: crown. The moon as empress has worn the crown of the northern pole, i.e. 'Ariadne's crown' or the *Corona Borealis*, visible in the north-eastern sky after sunset from mid-April until early December.

5 *pole artyke*: north pole.

7 *Mars*: astrologically, the planet Mars, but also Mars, god of war.   *to werre hym dyd dres*: prepared himself for war.

8 *auctoryte*: authority.

8–16 This view of the moral 'authority' of poets is characteristic of Skelton; see Ebin 1988.

9 *craftely*: skilfully.   10 In terms as enigmatic as might be.

11 *touche a troughte*: single out a truth; *touche* here may perhaps be a printer's error for *couche*, 'set' or 'place' (cf. confusion between lower-case *c* and *t* at 219 and 298), and it is possible that *troughte* should read *thoughte*.   *cloke*: cover.

12 *utteraunce*: speech.   *sentencyously*: meaningfully.

Dyverse in style, some spared not vyce to wrythe,
Some of moralyte nobly dyde endyte,

Wherby I rede theyr renome and theyr fame   15
Maye never dye, bute evermore endure—
I was sore moved to aforce the same.
But Ignorance full soone dyde me dyscure
And shewed that in this arte I was not sure:
For to illumyne, she sayde, I was to dulle,   20
Avysynge me my penne awaye to pulle

And not to wrythe, for he so wyll atteyne,
Excedynge ferther than his connynge is—
His hede maye be harde, but feble is his brayne—
Yet have I knowen suche er this.   25
But of reproche surely he maye not mys

Aii^v]   That clymmeth hyer than he may fotynge have;
What and he slyde downe, who shall hym save?

13 *Dyverse*: varied.   *some spared not vyce to wrythe*: some did not refrain from writing about vice.

15 *renome*: renown.

17 *sore moved*: keenly impelled.   *aforce*: attempt. The main verb of this long opening sentence is withheld until this point, perhaps in the tradition of the opening to *Gen Prol*, which provoked attempts at emulation in e.g. Lydgate's *Prologue to the Siege of Thebes* (Lydgate 1911, ed. Erdmann and Ekwall); see Pearsall 1970: 59.

18 *full*: very.   *dyde me dyscure*: exposed me.

19 *shewed*: demonstrated.   *sure*: confident.

20 I was too stupid to make (things) clear. The term *illumyne* is characteristic of the 'high style' or 'aureate' vocabulary used by Chaucer's successors of the processes of literary composition, and derives partly from Chaucer's own poetry; see e.g. the praise of Petrarch which begins the prologue to *Cl T*, *CT* III. 31–56, and for further discussion, Ebin 1988: 1–18 and Pearsall 1970: 262–3, 268–74. The narrator modestly disclaims his own poetic abilities, and follows his conventional modesty topos with a description of intellectual doubt and uncertainty which is again typical of dream visions; cf. the opening sections of *HF*, *PF*, *BD*, *LR*, and of poems outside the Chaucerian tradition such as *Piers Plowman* (Langland 1978, ed. Schmidt).

21 *Avysynge*: advising.   *awaye to pulle*: to withdraw.

22 *wrythe*: write.   *he so wyll atteyne*: for he (i.e. whoever might do this) will succeed only this much.

23 Going beyond the extent of his understanding/skill.

24 *hede*: head.   *feble*: weak.   *brayne*: brain.   25 *er this*: before now.

26–7 But he who climbs up beyond where he may keep his footing will surely not be short of reproofs. Overreaching is a vice commonly criticized in court satire: see e.g. Thomas Wyatt's poems on court life (Rebholz 1978).

28 *What and*: what if.

Thus up and down my mynde was drawen and cast
That I ne wyste what to do was beste,   30
Soo sore enwered that I was, at the laste,
Enforsed to slepe and for to take some reste,
And to lye downe (as soone as I me dreste)
At Harwyche Porte; slumbrynge as I laye,
In myne hostes house called Powers Keye,   35

Me thoughte I sawe a shyppe, goodly of sayle,
Come saylynge forth into that haven brood,
Her takelynge ryche and of hye apparayle.
She kyste an anker, and there she laye at rode.
Marchauntes her borded to see what she had lode: 40
Therein they founde royall marchaundyse,
Fraghted with plesure to what ye coude devyse.

But than I thoughte I wolde not dwell behynde:
Amonge all other I put myselfe in prece.
Than there coude I none aquentaunce fynde.   45
There was moche noyse, anone one cryed, 'Cese!'
Sharpely commaundynge eche man holde hys pece.

29 *drawen*: pulled.   *cast*: thrown.

30 *ne wyste*: did not know. As so often in poems of this kind, mental exertion induces the need for sleep.

31 *sore enwered*: very tired.   *at the laste*: in the end.   32 *Enforsed*: forced.

33 *me dreste*: prepared myself.

34–5 *Powers Keye* has been identified as a house on the quay at Harwich owned by one John Power; see the note to this line by Kinsman in Skelton 1969; and also Tucker 1970; and Walker 1988: 10–15.

36 *Me thoughte*: it seemed to me that.   *goodly of sayle*: with splendid sails. The ship may be connected with the Ship of Fools (see Scattergood 1988).

37 *haven brood*: wide harbour.

38 *takelynge*: the masts etc. of a ship.   *of hye apparayle*: with lofty rigging.

39 *kyste an anker*: cast anchor.   *at rode*: riding (at anchor).

40 *Marchauntes*: merchants.   *borded*: boarded.   *had lode*: was loaded with.

41 *marchaundyse*: merchandise.

42 (She was) loaded with pleasure to satisfy anything you might wish.

43 *than*: then.   *dwell*: remain.   44 I hurried along with all the others.

44–6 The hurrying crowd and the anonymous voice (cf. *KQ* 531; *HF* 1871) contribute to the sense of confusion in this dream.

45 Then I could find no one I knew there (Drede lacks any patronage or existing connection to smooth his way).

46 *anone*: immediately.   *one*: someone.   *Cese*: stop.

47 *holde hys pece*: be quiet.

'Maysters', he sayde, 'the shyp that ye here see,
The Bouge of Courte it hyghte for certeynte.

'The awnner therof is lady of estate,   50
Whoos name to tell is Dame Saunce-Pere.
Here marchaundyse is ryche and fortunate,
But who wyll have it muste paye therfore dere.
This royall chaffre that is shypped here
Is called Favore-to-stonde-in-her-good-grace.'   55
Than sholde ye see there pressynge in a pace

Of one and other that wolde this lady see,
Whiche sat behynde a traves of sylke fyne
Of golde, of tessew the fynest that myghte be,
In a trone whiche fer clerer dyde shyne   60
Than Phebus in his spere celestyne,
Whoos beaute, honoure, goodly porte,
I have to lytyll connynge to reporte.

But of eche thynge there as I toke hede,
Amonge all other was wrytten in her trone,   65

48 *Maysters*: masters.   49 *it hyghte*: it is called.
50 *awnner*: owner.   *estate*: high rank.
51 *Dame Saunce-Pere*: Lady Peerless. Personifications of this kind recall the allegory of
e.g. the sections of Langland's *Piers Plowman* which deal with the marriage of Lady 'Mede'
(reward); Langland 1978, passus II–IV. On personification allegory more generally, see
Frank 1953.
52 *Here*: her.   *fortunate*: brings good fortune.   54 *chaffre*: merchandise.
55 *stonde*: stand.
56 *a pace*: quickly (apace)/a crowd; the noun 'pace', understood as a 'company' (of e.g.
asses; *MED* 5[b]), and attested by usage contemporary with *BC*, seems to make good sense
here.
57 *wolde . . . see*: wanted to see.
58 *traves*: curtain, screen.   *sylke fyne*: fine silk. Dyce's note to this line (Skelton 1843: ii.
106) quotes contemporary examples of noble figures seated behind low screens or curtains.
59 *tessew*: a rich fabric, sometimes interwoven with silver or gold.
60 *trone*: throne.   *fer clerer*: far more brightly.
61 *spere celestyne*: heavenly sphere. *Phebus* is the sun, who, according to the Ptolemaic
system by which the universe was understood to function, was thought with the other
planets to revolve around the earth.
62 *goodly porte*: virtuous demeanour. *Whoos* refers back to the lady, not to Phebus.
63 *to lytyll connynge*: too little skill.   64 *toke hede*: noticed.
64–5 The logic of these two lines is clearer if 'I noticed that' is understood to link
them.

In golde letters, this worde, whiche I dyde rede:
Garder le fortune que est mauelȝ et bone.
And as I stode redynge this verse myselfe allone,
Her chyef gentylwoman, Daunger by her name,
Gave me a taunte, and sayde I was to blame   70

To be so perte to prese so proudly uppe.
She sayde she trowed that I had eten sause;
She asked yf ever I dranke of saucys cuppe.
And I than softly answered to that clause,
That, so to saye, I had gyven her no cause.   75
Than asked she me, 'Syr, so God the spede,
What is thy name?' and I sayde it was Drede.

[Aiiiᵛ]   'What movyd the,' quod she, 'hydder to come?'
'Forsoth,' quod I, 'to bye some of youre ware.'
And with that worde on me she gave a glome   80

66 *worde*: text.   *dyde rede*: read.

67 'Preserve fortune which is both bad and good' or 'beware of fortune which is both bad and good'; the advice is deliberately ambiguous, in keeping with Fortune's dual nature. Mottoes and devices of various kinds, often used practically to personalize clothing and portable effects (and often in French), can in literary contexts serve to focus meaning; cf. the devices of *TG* and *AL*, and the message brought by the dove in *KQ* 1247–51.

69 *chyef*: principal.   *Daunger*: a personification of disdain or standoffishness; a figure of the same name guards the rose-bush in *RR* 2825 ff. (*Romaunt*, 3130), and appears in other texts such as *TG* 760, 763.

70 *Gave me a taunte*: picked a quarrel with me.

71 *perte*: forward.   *to prese so proudly uppe*: to put myself forward in such a vain way.

72 *trowed*: believed.   *eten sause*: 'become saucy'. Cf. the proverbs cited in Whiting 1968: S 67; Tilley 1952: 100.

73 *of*: from.   *saucys cuppe*: sauce's cup.

74 *clause*: technically a section of discourse; here it simply seems to refer to what Daunger has just said.

75 That I had given her no reason to speak so.

76 *so God the spede*: may God speed you.

77 *Drede*: fearfulness.   78 *movyd the*: prompted you.   *hydder*: hither, here.

78–9 It is noticeable here that while Drede addresses Daunger with the polite 'you', she speaks to him with the less formal 'the'.

79 *Forsoth*: truly, indeed.   *bye*: buy.

80 *on me she gave a glome*: she gave me a sullen look.

80–3 Daunger acts in character, behaving disdainfully towards Drede.

With browes bente, and gan on me to stare
Full daynnously, and fro me she dyde fare,
Levynge me stondynge as a mased man,
To whome there came another gentylwoman:

Desyre her name was, and so she me tolde,   85
Sayenge to me, 'Broder, be of good chere,
Abasshe you not, but hardely be bolde,
Avaunce your selfe to aproche and come nere.
What though our chaffer be never so dere,
Yet I avyse you to speke, for ony drede: 90
Who spareth to speke, in fayth, he spareth to spede.'

'Maystres,' quod I, 'I have none aquentaunce
That wyll for me be medyatoure and mene.
And this an other, I have but smale substaunce.'
'Pece,' quod Desyre, 'ye speke not worth a bene!   95
Yf ye have not, in fayth, I wyll you lene
A precyous jewell, no rycher in this londe:
Bone aventure have here now in your honde.

81 *gan on me to stare*: stared at me.
82 *Full daynnously*: very disdainfully. *fro me she dyde fare*: she went away from me.
83 *stondynge*: standing. *mased*: bewildered.   84 *To whome*: i.e. to me.
85 Desyre, while familiar from love visions as the personification of the lover's desire
for his beloved, here seems to comprehend desire for material gain and advancement.
86 *Broder*: brother. *be of good chere*: cheer up.
87 *Abasshe you not*: don't be confounded. *hardely*: confidently.
88 *Avaunce your selfe*: come closer.
89 What does it matter how costly our merchandise may be?
90 *Yet*: nevertheless. *avyse*: advise. *for ony drede*: in spite of any fear.
91 He who omits to speak indeed fails to prosper. Proverbial: see Whiting 1968: S554;
Tilley 1952: S709.
92 *Maystres*: mistress. *none aquentaunce*: no contact/acquaintance.
92–4 For Drede, wealth and influential contacts are essential for advancement. Desire
suggests that luck is all one needs.
93 *medyatoure and mene*: mediator and go-between (another reference to Drede's lack
of friends and patronage).
94 *And this an other*: and for another thing. *but smale substaunce*: only small means.
95 *Pece*: be quiet. *ye speke not worth a bene*: your words are not worth a bean.
96 *lene*: lend.   97 *londe*: land.
98 *'Bone aventure'*: good luck. *honde*: hand.

'Shyfte now therwith, let see, as ye can,
In Bouge of Courte chevysaunce to make;   100
For I dare saye that there nys erthly man
But, an he can *Bone aventure* take,
There can no favour nor frendshyp hym forsake.

[Aiv^r]   *Bone aventure* may brynge you in suche case
That ye shall stonde in favoure and in grace.   105

'But of one thynge I werne you er I goo:
She that styreth the shyp, make her your frende.'
'Maystres,' quod I, 'I praye you tell me why soo,
And how I maye that waye and meanes fynde.'
'Forsothe,' quod she, 'how ever blowe the wynde,   110
Fortune gydeth and ruleth all oure shyppe.
Whome she hateth shall over the see-boorde skyp.

Whome she loveth, of all plesyre is ryche
Whyles she laugheth and hath luste for to playe.
Whome she hateth, she casteth in the dyche,   115
For whan she frouneth she thynketh to make a fray.
She cheryssheth him, and hym she casteth awaye.'

99 Have a go with it now, and show us, as best you can.

100 (How) to make a profit on your court allowance.

101–3 there's no man on earth, if he takes *Bone aventure*, who will be forsaken by favour and friendship. The syntax of these lines is loose; the translation supplied changes the active sense of the verb in 103 to a passive one.

104 *in suche case*: into such circumstances.

105 *Favoure* and *grace* are loaded words which in other contexts often have spiritual or amorous significance. Here their associations are all with influential wordly advancement.

106 *werne*: warn.   *er*: before.   107 *styreth*: steers.

108 *why soo*: why.   109 *meanes*: means.

110 *Forsothe*: truly.   *how ever blowe the wynde*: how ever the wind blows.

111 *gydeth*: guides.

111–19 In the tradition of texts such as *LR*, this description stresses Fortune's changeableness.

112 Those whom she hates will quickly go overboard (cf. 531).

113–14 Whoever she loves is rich in pleasure as long as she laughs and wishes to amuse herself.

115 *casteth*: throws.   *dyche*: ditch.

116 *frouneth*: frowns.   *thynketh to make a fray*: intends to pick a quarrel.

117 She looks after this one, and dismisses that one from her service.

'Alas,' quod I, 'how myghte I have her sure?'
'In fayth,' quod she, 'by *Bone aventure*.'

Thus, in a rowe, of martchauntes a grete route   120
Suwed to Fortune that she wold be theyre frynde.
They thronge in fast and flocked her aboute,
And I with them prayed her to have in mynde.
She promysed to us all she wolde be kynde;
Of Bouge of Court she asketh what we wold have,   125
And we asked favoure, and favour she us gave.

Thus endeth the prologue, and begynneth the Bouge of
Courte brevely compyled.

 Aiv^v]   DREDE

The sayle is up, Fortune ruleth our helme,
We wante no wynde to passe now over all.
Favoure we have toughther than ony elme,
That wyll abyde and never frome us fall.   130
But under hony ofte tyme lyeth bytter gall,
For, as me thoughte, in our shyppe I dyde see
Full subtyll persones in nombre foure and thre.

118 *have her sure*: be confident of her friendship.
120 *rowe*: row.   *martchauntes*: merchants.   *grete route*: huge crowd.
121 *Suwed to*: petitioned.   *frynde*: friend.   122 *thronge*: thronged.
123 *to have in mynde*: to remember (me).
125 She asks what we want in the way of reward at court.
125a '*brevely compyled*': concisely written down.
127 ff. The headings, indicating different speakers, are characteristic of early printed texts—a development from programmes of manuscript rubrication or annotation which often supplied speech markers.
127 *helme*: tiller or wheel (of a ship). The image of Fortune as steersman occurs elsewhere: see Scattergood 1988.
128 *wante*: lack.   *to passe . . . over all*: to overtake everything/to travel anywhere.
129 *toughther*: hardier.   *elme*: elm tree.
130 *abyde*: remain.   *frome us fall*: desert us.
131 *hony*: honey.   *lyeth*: lies.   *gall*: an intensely bitter substance. The sense here is proverbial: see Tilley 1952: H 561; Whiting 1968: H 433.
132 *as me thoughte*: as it seemed to me.
133 *subtyll*: crafty.   *nombre*: number.   *foure and thre*: clearly, seven, and different significances have been attached to the number and the form of expressing it. Seven suggests most readily the deadly sins: see Bloomfield 1952.

The fyrste was Favell, full of flatery,
Wyth fables false, that well coude fayne a tale;   135
The seconde was Suspecte, whiche that dayly
Mysdempte eche man, with face deedly and pale;
And Harvy Hafter that well coude picke a male,
With other foure of theyr affynyte:
Dysdayne, Ryotte, Dyssymuler, Subtylte.   140

Fortune theyr frende, with whome oft she dyde daunce:
They coude not faile, they thought, they were so sure.
And oftentymes I wolde myselfe avaunce
With them to make solace and pleasure,
But my dysporte they coude not well endure;   145
They sayde they hated for to dele with Drede.
Than Favell gan wyth fayre speche me to fede:

FAVELL

'Noo thynge erthely that I wonder so sore
As of your connynge, that is so excellent.
Deynte to have with us suche one in store,   150
So vertuously that hath his dayes spente.

134 *Favell*: Duplicity. *Favell* is often used as a type-name for a flatterer; see e.g. *Piers Plowman*, B ii. 6, 41 (Langland 1978), where he is connected with Meed, and B iii. 78–91, where he is associated with the deadly sins.

135 *fayne*: feign.   136 *Suspecte*: Suspicion.   *dayly*: daily.

137 *Mysdempte*: thought badly of.   *deedly*: deathly. Suspicion's physical appearance reflects his anxiety; the deadly sin of Envy is often depicted as pale (cf. *Piers Plowman*, B, v. 78; Langland 1978). For general discussion of the the physical characteristics of the different sins, see Bloomfield 1952.

138 *well coude picke a male*: well knew how to pick a purse. Harvy Hafter's name appears as *Haster* (with a long *s*) in the printed editions (see the textual notes above); the emendation seems justified since 'hafter' means sharper or trickster.

139 *affynyte*: affinity, company.

140 *Dysdayne*: Disdain.   *Ryotte*: Riot.   *Dyssymuler*: Dissembler.   *Subtylte*: Craftiness.

141 Fortune, their friend, often danced with them.

142 *sure*: sure of themselves.

143 *I wolde myselfe avaunce*: I would put myself forward.

146 *dele with*: have to do with.   147 Then Duplicity fed me with pleasant words.

148–9 Nothing on earth amazes me so much as your knowledge, which is so excellent.

150 *Deynte*: (it's a) pleasure.   *in store*: staying.

[Av^r] Fortune to you gyftes of grace hath lente:
Loo, what it is a man to have connynge!
All erthly tresoure it is surmountynge.

'Ye be an apte man, as ony can be founde,   155
To dwell with us and serve my ladyes grace.
Ye be to her, yea, worth a thousande pounde.
I herde her speke of you within shorte space,
Whan there were dyverse that sore dyde you manace:
And, though I say it, I was myselfe your frende,   160
For here be dyverse to you that be unkynde.

But this one thynge ye maye be sure of me,
For by that Lorde that bought dere all mankynde,
I can not flater, I muste be playne to the.
And ye nede ought, man, shewe to me your mynde,   165
For ye have me whome faythfull ye shall fynde;
Whyles I have ought, by God, thou shalt not lacke,
And, yf nede be, a bolde worde I dare cracke.

'Nay, naye, be sure, whyles I am on your syde
Ye maye not fall; truste me, ye maye not fayle.   170
Ye stonde in favoure and Fortune is your gyde,

---

152 *gyftes*: gifts. *lente*: provided with. Favell distinguishes between God's gifts of Grace (mental and spiritual, of which knowledge is one) and gifts of Fortune (status and wealth); gifts of Nature constituted the third traditional category. The history of the categories is briefly discussed, in relation to the qualities of the heroine of Chaucer's *Phys T* (*CT* VI. 9–29), in Chaucer 1987: 902.

153 Behold, what it is (for) a man to have knowledge!

154 *surmountynge*: surpassing.

155 You are as suitable a man as any that can be found.

158 *within shorte space*: a short while ago. Despite the need to keep counsel which is impressed upon Drede, the figures he meets report to him (and presumably fabricate) numerous conversations which they have overheard or contributed to (cf. 175, for example).

159 *dyverse*: several (people present). *sore*: grievously. *manace*: menace, threaten.

163 *bought dere*: redeemed.

164 *flater*: flatter.   165 *And*: if. *ought*: anything. *shewe*: show.

167 *Whyles I have ought*: as long as I have anything.

168 *cracke*: utter.   169 *whyles*: as long as.   171 *gyde*: guide.

And, as she wyll, so shall our grete shyppe sayle.
Thyse lewde cok wattes shall nevermore prevayle
Ageynste you, hardely; therfore be not afrayde.
Farewell tyll soone. But no worde that I sayde!'   175

DREDE

Than thanked I hym for his grete gentylnes.

[Av^v] But, as me thoughte, he ware on hym a cloke
That lyned was with doubtfull doublenes.
Me thoughte, of wordes that he had full a poke;
His stomak stuffed ofte tymes dyde reboke.   180
Suspycyon, me thoughte, mette hym at a brayde,
And I drewe nere to herke what they two sayde.

'In fayth,' quod Suspecte, 'spake Drede no worde of me?
Why? What than? Wylte thou lete men to speke?'
'He sayth he can not well accorde with the.'   185
'Twyst,' quod Suspecte, 'goo playe; hym I ne reke!'
'By Cryste,' quod Favell, 'Drede is soleyne freke!
What, lete us holde him up, man, for a whyle.'
'Ye, soo,' quod Suspecte, 'he maye us bothe begyle.'

172 *wyll*: wishes.

173 *lewde*: ignorant.   *cok wattes*: louts (more probably some sort of derogatory coinage from *cok*, male bird, and *wat*, fellow or person, than a variant of ME *cokewald*, cuck-old).   *prevayle*: win.   174 *hardely*: certainly.

175 *no worde that I sayde*: no word (of anything) that I said.

176 *gentylnes*: kindness / good breeding.

177 *ware on hym*: wore.   *cloke*: cloak. The attention paid to details of clothing in *BC* intensifies its dramatic impact (also a feature of Skelton's *Magnificence*; Skelton 1980, ed. Neuss).

178 *lyned was*: was lined.   *doublenes*: duplicity.   179 *full a poke*: a full bag.

180 *dyde reboke*: belched.   181 *at a brayde*: suddenly.   182 *herke*: listen to.

183 *spake*: spoke.

184 *Wylte thou lete men to speke*: will you prevent people from speaking?

185 *accorde with the*: get on with you.

186 *Twyst*: here possibly an exclamation (although no usage of this sort is recorded in *MED*, the use of 'twyss' as an exclamation is cited in *OED*).   *goo playe*: go and play.   *hym I ne reke*: I reckon nothing to him.

187 *soleyne freke*: an unsociable fellow.

188 *lete us holde him up*: let's accost him (or possibly 'let's string him along').

189 *begyle*: trick.

And whan he came walkynge soberly,   190
Wyth 'Whom' and 'Ha' and with a croked loke,
Me thoughte his hede was full of gelousy;
His eyen rollynge, his hondes faste they quoke,
And to mewarde the strayte waye he toke.
'God spede, broder,' to me quod he than,   195
And thus to talke with me he began.

SUSPYCYON

'Ye remembre the gentylman ryghte nowe
That commened with you, me thought, a praty space?
Beware of him, for, I make God avowe,
He wyll begyle you and speke fayre to your face.   200
Ye never dwelte in suche an other place,
For here is none that dare well other truste;
But I wolde telle you a thynge, and I durste.

'Spake he, a fayth, no worde to you of me?
I wote, and he dyde, ye wolde me telle.   205
I have a favoure to you, wherof it be
That I muste shewe you moche of my counselle—
But I wonder what the devyll of helle
He sayde of me, whan he with you dyde talke—
By myne avyse use not with him to walke.   210

'The soveraynst thynge that ony man maye have
Is lytyll to saye, and moche to here and see;

191 *Whom*: hmm. *croked*: sideways.   192 *gelousy*: jealousy.
193 *His eyen rollynge*: his eyes were rolling. *hondes*: hands. *quoke*: trembled. These physical details are again symptomatic of envy.
194 *to mewarde*: towards me. *strayte*: direct.
198 *commened*: conferred. *a praty space*: a good while (see textual note).
199 *I make God avowe*: I swear to God.   200 *speke fayre*: speak pleasantly.
203 *and I durste*: if I dared.   204 *a fayth*: in faith.
205 I know if he did you would tell me.
206 *favoure to you*: liking for you. *wherof it be*: which means.
207 *moche of my counselle*: many of my private thoughts.
210 My advice is: don't make a habit of going around with him.
211 *soveraynst*: supreme.
212 *lytyll*: little. *here*: hear. This is proverbial: Tilley 1952: M1277; Whiting 1968: H264; see also Lydgate's short poem 'See myche, say lytell' (Lydgate 1934: 800–1).

For, but I trusted you, so God me save,
I wolde noo thynge so playne be.
To you oonly, me thynke, I durste shryve me;   215
For now am I plenarely dysposed
To shewe you thynges that may not be disclosed.'

DREDE

Than I assured hym my fydelyte,
His counseyle secrete never to dyscure
Yf he coude fynde in herte to truste me.   220
Els, I prayed hym with all my besy cure,
To kepe it hymselfe; for than he myghte be sure
That noo man erthly coude hym bewreye,
Whyles of his mynde it were lockte with the keye.

'By God,' quod he, 'this and thus it is,'   225
And of his mynde he shewed me all and some.

[Avi^v]   'Fare well,' quod he, 'we wyll talke more of this.'
Soo he departed. There he wolde be come
I dare not speke; I promysed to be dome.
But as I stode musynge in my mynde,   230
Harvy Hafter came lepynge, lyghte as lynde.

Upon his brest he bare a versynge boxe:
His throte was clere and lustely coude fayne.

213 *but*: unless.   *so God me save*: may God save me.
214 I would be nothing like so open.
215 *I durste shryve me*: I dare confess myself.
216 *plenarely*: fully.   218 *my fydelyte*: of my loyalty.
219 And that I would never reveal his confidential business.
220 *fynde in herte*: find it in his heart.   221 *Els*: otherwise.   *besy cure*: diligence.
223 *coude hym bewreye*: could betray him.
224 As long as it was locked in his mind with the key.
226 *all and some*: the whole. Despite Suspycyon's avowed wish to be open with Drede,
the content of the conversation between them is carefully obscure.
228 *There he wolde be come*: where he wished to go.   229 *dome*: silent.
230 *musynge in my mynde*: thinking.
231 *lepynge*: leaping (up).   *lyghte as lynde*: light as a linden (leaf), i.e. very nimbly (a
common phrase: see the citations in *MED*, under 'linde', 1 [b]).
232 *bare*: wore, carried.   *versynge boxe*: dicing box/hurdy-gurdy.
233 *throte*: throat, singing voice.   *clere*: clear.   *lustely*: vigorously. *fayne*: (i) sing with
due regard for the accidentals of a musical score, (ii) invent a story.

Me thoughte his gowne was all furred wyth foxe;
And ever he sange, 'Sythe I am no thynge playne'.   235
To kepe him frome pykynge, it was a grete payne.
He gased on me with his gotyshe berde;
Whan I loked on hym, my purse was half aferde.

HERVY HAFTER

'Syr, God you save, why loke you so sadde?
What thynge is that I maye do for you?   240
A wonder thynge that ye waxe not madde!
For and I studye sholde as ye doo nowe,
My wytte wolde waste, I make God avowe.
Tell me your mynde: me thynke ye make a verse;
I coude it skan and ye wolde it reherse.   245

But to the poynte shortely to procede,
Where hathe your dwellynge ben, er ye cam here?
For, as I trowe, I have sene you in dede
Er this, whan that ye made me royall chere.
Holde up the helme, loke up and lete God stere: 250

---

234 *furred*: fur-trimmed—suggestive of Hervy's foxy craftiness.
235 *ever*: continuously. *Sythe*: since. *no thynge playne*: not at all clear/honest. *Sythe I am no thynge playne* (echoing Suspycyon at 214) probably refers to the first line of a popular song, although nothing with this text survives. Cf. the references to other songs at 252, 253, 254, and 360 (and see Carpenter 1955 and Fallows 1977).
236 It was very difficult to prevent him from thieving.
237 *gased*: gazed. *gotyshe berde*: goat-like beard (perhaps suggestive of lechery).
238 *half aferde*: half afraid.   239 *sadde*: serious.
240 What can I do for you?
241 It's a marvel that you don't go mad.
242 *and I studye sholde*: if I were to study.
243 *wytte*: wit, brain. *waste*: waste away.
244 *make a verse*: are composing a song/poem (possibly a jibe which relates to the narrator's allusion in lines 17–30 to his own waking attempts at writing poetry).
245 *skan*: analyse its metre. *and*: if. *reherse*: repeat.
246 *shortely*: quickly.
247 Where did you live, before you came here?
248 *as I trowe*: I believe. *in dede*: indeed.
249 *Er*: before. *whan that ye made me royall chere*: when you treated me royally (or possibly, 'showed me some high living').
250 *lete God stere*: let God direct.

I wolde be mery what wynde that ever blowe,
'Heve and how, rombelow, row the bote, Norman, rowe.'

'Prynces of youghte', can ye synge by rote,
Or 'Shall I sayle wyth you' a felashyp assaye?
For on the booke I cannot synge a note.   255
Wolde to God it wolde please you some daye
A balade boke before me for to laye,
And lerne me to synge *Re my fa sol*—
And whan I fayle, bobbe me on the noll!

Loo, what is to you a pleasure grete   260
To have that connynge and wayes that ye have!
By Goddis soule, I wonder how ye gete
Soo greate pleasyre, or who to you it gave.
Syr, pardone me, I am an homely knave
To be with you thus perte and thus bolde;   265
But ye be welcome to our housholde.

And I dare saye there is no man hereinne
But wolde be glad of your company.
I wyste never man that so soone coude wynne

251 *what wynde that ever blowe*: whatever kind of wind blows.

252 'Heave, ho, rumbelow, row the boat, Norman, row'. 'Heave ho, rumbelow' is a familiar phrase in sailors' songs (see the note to this line by Dyce in Skelton 1843: ii. 110–11). London chronicles record a song with the refrain 'Rowe the bote Norman', sung by the Thames watermen when they rowed the Lord Mayor (1453–4), John Norman, to Westminster (see Kingsford 1905: 164; Ellis 1811: 628).

253 *Prynces of youghte*: princess of youth. *TG* contains a reference to *Prynces of youghte* (at 970) which suggests that it may have been a well-known song; see Fallows 1977. '*Shall I sayle wyth you*' 254 may have been another song.   *by rote*: from memory.

254 Or can you join in to sing the parts for 'Shall I sail with you'?

255 *on the booke*: from written music.   257 *for to laye*: to put.

258 *lerne*: teach.   *Re my fa sol*: musical notes; Hervy speaks of learning to read music from the six-note scale (usually beginning with *do*) of Guido of Arezzo.

259 *fayle*: go wrong.   *bobbe*: knock.   *noll*: head.

260–1 What a great pleasure (it) is for you to have your knowledge and manners.

262 *Goddis soule*: God's soul.   *gete*: get.   263 *Soo*: such.

264 *homely*: over-familiar.   *knave*: rascal.   265 *perte*: saucy.

266 The reference to the *housholde*, like those to service (274 etc.), draws attention to the role of Drede's new acquaintants as retainers of different kinds.

267 *hereinne*: in here.   269 *wyste*: knew.   *coude wynne*: could win.

The favoure that ye have with my lady;   270
I praye to God that it maye never dy.
It is your fortune for to have that grace:
As I be saved, it is a wonder case.

For, as for me, I served here many a daye,
And yet unneth I can have my lyvynge;   275
But I requyre you no worde that I saye!
For and I knowe ony erthly thynge
That is agayne you, you shall have wetynge;
And ye be welcome, syr, so God me save,
I hope here after a frende of you to have.'   280

DREDE

Wyth that, as he departed soo fro me,
Anone ther mette with him, as me thoughte,
A man—but wonderly besene was he:
He loked hawte, he sette eche man at noughte;
His gawdy garment with scornnys was all wrought;   285
With indygnacyon lyned was his hode;
He frowned as he wolde swere 'by Cockes blode'.

He bote the lyppe, he loked passynge coye;
His face was belymmed as byes had him stounge—

---

273 *As I be saved*: As I (hope to) be saved.   *wonder case*: amazing occurrence.
274 *served*: served in the household.
275 And yet I can scarcely make a living.
276 But I must request (that) you (repeat) no word that I say.
277–8 If I hear anything on earth against you, you'll know about it.
279 *be*: are.   280 *of you*: in you.
281 *departed soo fro me*: left me in this way.
283 *wonderly besene*: strange-looking.
284 *hawte*: proud.   *sette . . . at noughte*: reckoned nothing to.
285 *gawdy*: a yellowish colour, or a fabric of this hue: appropriate for the envious Disdain (291–4).   *scornnys*: taunts.   *wrought*: embroidered.
286 *lyned*: lined.   *hode*: hood.
287 He frowned as (if) he wanted to swear 'by Cock's blood' (= by God's blood).
288 *bote*: bit (cf. 321, where the definite article is used in a similar construction). *passynge coye*: surpassingly disdainful.
289 *belymmed*: disfigured.   *as*: as if.   *byes*: bees.   *stounge*: stung.

It was no tyme with him to jape nor toye.   290
Envye hathe wasted hys lyver and his lounge;
Hatred by the herte so had hym wrounge
That he loked pale as asshes to my syghte.
Dysdayne, I wene, this comerous carkes hyghte.

To Hervy Hafter than he spake of me,   295
And I drewe nere to harke what they two sayde.
'Now,' quod Dysdayne, 'as I shall saved be,
I have grete scorne and am ryghte evyll apayed.'
'Than,' quod Hervy, 'why arte thou so dysmayde?'
'By Cryste,' quod he, 'for it is shame to saye,   300
To see Johan Dawes, that came but yesterdaye,

How he is now taken in conceyte,
This Doctour Dawcocke—Drede, I wene he hyghte.
Biiʳ   By Goddis bones, but yf we have som sleyte,
It is lyke he wyll stonde in our lyghte!'   305
'By God,' quod Hervy, 'and it so happen myghte!
Lete us, therfore, shortely at a worde
Fynde some mene to caste him over the borde.'

'By him that me boughte,' than quod Dysdayne,
'I wonder sore he is in such conceyte.'   310
'Turde,' quod Hafter, 'I wyll the nothynge layne,

290 It was never the right moment to joke or play with him.
291 *lyver*: liver.   *lounge*: lung.   292 *wrounge*: wrung.
294 *Dysdayne*: Disdain. *wene*: think. *comerous carkes*: troublesome carcase.
hyghte: was called.
298 I am treated with great contempt, and am very ill pleased.
299 *dysmayde*: surprised, put out.
300 *it is shame to saye*: it's shameful to say (it).
301 *but*: only.   *Johan Dawes*: a name used by Dysdayne contemptuously; *dawe* = fool.
302 *in conceyte*: into favour.   303 *Dawcocke*: simpleton.
304 *Goddis bones*: God's bones.   *but yf*: unless.   *sleyte*: trick.
305 *lyke*: likely. Dysdayne and Hervy are worried that Drede will 'stand in their light'
or somehow attempt to usurp their favour.
307 *at a worde*: straightaway.
308 *mene*: way.   *caste*: throw.   *borde*: ship's side.
309 *By him that me boughte*: by Christ, who redeemed me.
310 *I wonder sore*: I am very much amazed.   *in such conceyte*: so well thought of.
311 *I wyll the nothynge layne*: I'll hide nothing from you.

There muste for hym be layde some prety beyte.
We tweyne, I trowe, be not withoute dysceyte:
Fyrste pycke a quarell and fall oute with hym then,
And soo outface hym with a carde of ten.'   315

Forthwith, he made on me a prowde assawte,
With scornfull loke mevyd all in moode.
He went aboute to take me in a fawte:
He frounde, he stared, he stampped where he stoode.
I loked on hym, I wende he had be woode.   320
He set the arme proudly under the syde,
And in this wyse he gan with me to chyde.

DISDAYNE

'Remembrest thou what thou sayd yesternyght?
Wylt thou abyde by the wordes agayne?
By God, I have of the now grete dyspyte;   325
I shall the angre ones in every vayne!
It is greate scorne to see suche a hayne
As thou arte, one that cam but yesterdaye,
With us olde servauntes such maysters to playe.

312 *layde*: laid.   *prety beyte*: attractive bait.
313 *tweyne*: two.   314 *pycke*: pick.
315 *outface hym with a carde of ten*: put him out of countenance with a bluff (proverbial: see Tilley 1952: C75; Whiting 1968: C36; *a carde of ten* is not a high card).
316 Immediately, he accosted me haughtily; *assawte* is strictly an assault or attack; Disdayne's *assawte* does not seem to involve any physical violence to Drede.
317 *mevyd all in moode*: all turned to anger.
318 He did all he could to catch me out.   319 *frounde*: frowned.
320 *I wende he had be woode*: I thought he must be mad.
321 He bent his arm out proudly on his side. For similar use of the definite article, cf. 288.
322 *wyse*: way.   *gan with me to chyde*: argued with me.
323 *yesternyght*: yesterday evening. Disdayne presumably invents the previous encounter as part of his strategy to pick a quarrel with Drede.
324 Will you hold to the words still?
325 *have . . . grete dyspyte*: greatly despise.   *the*: you.
326 I'll make you angry all over (literally, 'I'll make you angry once in every vein [in your body]').
327 *greate scorne*: very contemptible.   *hayne*: (household) servant.
328 *cam*: arrived.
329 Playing at masters with us old-established serving-men.

[Bii^v]   'I tell the, I am of countenaunce.   330
          What weneste I were? I trowe thou knowe not me.
          By Goddis woundes, but for dysplesaunce,
          Of my querell soone wolde I venged be.
          But, no force, I shall ones mete with the;
          Come whan it wyll, oppose the I shall,   335
          Whatsomever aventure therof fall.

          'Trowest thou, drevyll, I saye, thou gawdy knave,
          That I have deynte to see the cherysshed thus?
          By Goddis syde, my sworde thy berde shall shave!
          Well ones thou shalte be chermed, iwus: 340
          Naye, strawe for tales, thou shalte not rule us;
          We be thy betters, and so thou shalte us take,
          Or we shall the oute of thy clothes shake!'

DREDE

          Wyth that came Ryotte, russhynge all at ones,
          A rusty gallande, to-ragged and to-rente;   345
          And on the borde he whyrled a payre of bones,

---

330 *of countenaunce*: someone who matters. *MED* 1(a) suggests 'bearing (good manners)' for *countenaunce*, but also with the connotation of pretence (a friend 'of countenaunce' is a false friend).

331 *What weneste I were*: What did you think I was?

332 *but for dysplesaunce*: were it not for the unpleasantness.

333 I would soon take revenge for my grievance.

334 *no force*: no matter. *mete with*: encounter.

335 Come when it (i.e. the occasion) will, I'll set myself against you.

336 Whatever the outcome is.

337 *Trowest thou*: do you believe. *drevyll*: drudge. *gawdy knave*: deceitful rascal.

338 *I have deynte*: it gives me pleasure. *cherysshed*: looked after, promoted.

339 *Goddis syde*: by the wound in Christ's side. *berde*: beard.

340 Then you'll be really charmed, indeed.

341 *strawe for tales*: a straw for (your) talk. *rule us*: lord it over us.

344 *Ryotte*: Riot, who typifies the 'gallant', frequently satirized in late medieval poems and plays, whose interests centre on ludicrously fashionable clothes, gambling, drinking, and foolish talk. See further Scattergood 1974 and Davenport 1983. *at ones*: at once.

345 *rusty*: shabby. *gallande*: 'gallant' (see 344 n.). *to-ragged and to-rente*: all ragged and torn.

346 *borde*: table. *whyrled*: threw round. *payre of bones*: set of dice; it was usual to have three dice in a set.

'*Quater treye dews*' he clatered as he wente.
'Nowe have at all, by Saynte Thomas of Kente!'
And ever he threwe, and kyst I wote nere what;
His here was growen thorowe oute his hat.   350

Thenne I behelde how he dysgysed was:
His hede was hevy for watchynge overnyghte,
His eyen blereed, his face shone lyke a glas;
His gowne so shorte that it ne cover myghte
His rumpe, he wente so all for somer lyghte;   355
His hose was garded with a lyste of grene,
Yet at the knee they were broken, I wene.

His cote was checked with patches rede and blewe;
Of Kyrkeby Kendall was his shorte demye;
And ay he sange, 'In fayth, Decon, thou crewe.'   360
His elbowe bare, he ware his gere so nye,
His nose a-droppynge, his lyppes were full drye;

Biii^r

347 *Quater treye dews*: four three two.   *clatered*: gabbled.
348 *have at all*: here goes. St Thomas of Kent is St Thomas Becket, who was murdered in 1170.
349 *ever he threwe*: he went on throwing.   *kyst*: cast.   *I wote nere what*: I don't know what.
350 *here*: hair.   *thorowe oute*: out through. These details suggest the proverbial feature of the spendthrift: see Whiting 1968: H22.
351 *behelde*: looked at.   *dysgysed*: done up.
352 *hede*: head.   *watchynge overnyghte*: staying up all night.
353 *eyen*: eyes.   *blereed*: watery.   *glas*: mirror.
354 *ne cover myghte*: could not cover.
354–5 Those who dressed in fashionably short and skimpy clothes were sometimes accused of failing to support the wool trade and hence the national economy; see Scattergood 1987.
355 *he wente so all for somer lyghte*: he went (about) so lightly (dressed) for summer.
356 *hose*: stockings.   *garded*: trimmed.   *lyste*: strip.
357 *broken*: torn.   *wene*: think.   358 *cote*: jacket.   *rede and blewe*: red and blue.
359 *Kyrkeby Kendall*: Kirkby, near Kendall in Westmorland, was known for its production of low-grade green woollen cloth.   *demye*: short, close-fitting garment.
360 *ay*: continually.   *crewe*: act as crew. 'Indeed, Dickon, you crew' is probably the refrain or first line of a popular song, now lost. Skelton also quotes it in *Why come ye nat to courte*, 66–7 (Skelton 1983: 280).
361 His elbows (were) bare, (since) he wore his clothes so tight-fitting.
362 *a-droppynge*: dripping.   *lyppes*: lips.   *full*: very.

And by his syde his whynarde and his pouche,
The devyll myghte daunce therin for ony crowche.

Counter he coude *O lux* upon a potte.   365
An eestryche fedder of a capons tayle
He set up fresshely upon his hat alofte.
'What, revell route!' quod he, and gan to rayle
How ofte he hadde hit Jenet on the tayle,
Of Felyce fetewse and lytell prety Cate,   370
How ofte he knocked at her klycked gate.

What sholde I tell more of his rebaudrye?
I was ashamed so to here hym prate:
He had no pleasure but in harlotrye.
'Ay,' quod he, 'in the devylles date,   375
What arte thou? I sawe the nowe but late.'
'Forsothe,' quod I, 'in this courte I dwell nowe.'
'Welcome,' quod Ryote, 'I make God avowe.'

363 *whynarde*: short sword.   *pouche*: bag, purse.

364 *devyll*: devil.   *daunce*: dance.   *crowche*: cross. Many coins were marked with a cross or *crowche*, so the term came to mean the coin itself. The line is proverbial (see Whiting 1968: D191), and means 'the devil might dance there (in his purse) without meeting a single coin'.

365 *Counter*: sing a part accompanying plainsong. *O lux*: *O lux beata Trinitas* is a phrase from the hymn *Et principalis Unitas*, usually sung at Vespers on Saturday.   *potte*: drinking pot.

366 *eestryche fedder*: ostrich feather.   *of a capons tayle*: from the tail of a castrated cock. Riot attempts a cut-price version of the fashionable touches of the day.

368 *revell route*: let revelry roar.   *rayle*: jest.

369 *Jenet*: a small horse/Janet.   *tayle*: tail/female sexual organs. Riot's jest puns on the meaning of *jenet*, which in the context of this line means 'a small horse'. But the line can also be understood to mean 'he joked about how often he'd had sex with Janet'. The humour of Chaucer's *Shipman's Tale* (*CT* VII. 1–434) similarly depends on the double meaning of 'tayle'.

370 *Felyce fetewse*: handsome Phyllis.

371 *klycked*: fastened with a latch (a further sexual innuendo).

372 *rebaudrye*: ribaldry.   373 *prate*: go on.

375 *devylles date*: = devil's name (a common proverbial phrase; see Whiting 1968: D200).

376 *I sawe the nowe but late*: I saw you only recently.

377 *Forsothe*: certainly.

RYOTE

'And, syr, in fayth, why comste not us amonge
To make the mery, as other felowes done?   380
Thou muste swere and stare, man, aldaye longe,
And wake all nyghte and slepe tyll it be none.
Thou mayste not studye or muse on the mone.
This worlde is nothynge but ete, drynke and slepe,
And thus with us good company to kepe.   385

Plucke up thyne herte upon a mery pyne,
And lete us laugh a placke or tweyne at nale:
What the devyll, man, myrthe was never one!
What, loo, man, see here of dyce a bale;
A brydelynge caste for that is in thy male!   390
Now have at all that lyeth upon the burde—
Fye on this dyce, they be not worth a turde!

Have at the hasarde or at the dosen browne,
Or els I pas a peny to a pounde!

379 *comste not us amonge*: don't you come among us.
380 *make the mery*: have a good time.   *done*: do.
381 *swere*: swear.   *aldaye*: all day.
382 *wake*: stay awake.   *none*: midday.
383 *mayste not*: may not.   *muse on the mone*: look meditatively at the moon (= spend time thinking; swot).
386 Be cheerful (proverbial: see Tilley 1952: P335; Whiting 1968: P215).
387 *placke*: Scattergood (Skelton 1983, note to this line) suggests a 'pluck', or deep draught of ale; *MED* and *OED* do not cite this usage, but do include *plakke*, a Flemish coin common in the Netherlands in the 15th c.; hence a trifle.   *tweyne*: two.   *at nale*: over the ale.
388 *myrthe was never one*: good cheer was never solitary.   389 *bale*: set.
390 *brydelynge caste*: probably the final throw made while the horses are being saddled and bridled; hence, a final throw of the dice.   *for that is in thy male*: for whatever is in your bag.
391 Now, (let's) have (a go) at everything that's on the board.
392 *Fye*: fie.   *be*: are.
393 *hasarde*: a dice-game; *the dosen browne* or 'brown dozen', may signify another game, or perhaps simply a throw at dice.
394 Otherwise I leave the game, a penny to a pound. Kinsman (Skelton 1969) understands *pas* to indicate 'passage', a dice-game, and suggests the translation 'Or else let us play "passage" and I'll give you odds'. Scattergood (Skelton 1983) explains *pas* as 'to leave the game' or 'to forgo one's opportunity to throw'.

Now wolde to God thou wolde leye money downe!   395
Lorde, how that I wolde caste it full rounde!
Ay, in my pouche a buckell I have founde;
The armes of Calyce, I have no coyne nor crosse!
I am not happy, I renne ay on the losse!

Now renne muste I to the stewys syde   400
To wete yf Malkyn, my lemman, have gete oughte.
I lete her to hyre that men maye on her ryde:
Her harnes easy ferre and nere is soughte.
By Goddis sydes, syns I her thyder broughte,
She hath gote me more money with her tayle   405
Than hath some shyppe that into Bordews sayle.

[Biv^r]   Had I as good an hors as she is a mare,
I durste aventure to journey thorugh Fraunce;
Who rydeth on her, he nedeth not to care,
For she is trussed for to breke a launce.   410
It is a curtel that well can wynche and praunce;

395 *wolde to God*: would to God.   *leye*: lay.
396 *caste it*: throw the dice.   *full rounde*: very quickly.
397 *pouche*: bag.   *buckell*: buckle.
398 *The armes of Calyce*: possibly an oath ('by the arms of Calais!'), although until the mid-15th c. some English coins, bearing the royal arms, were minted at Calais.   *coyne*: coin.   *crosse*: coin with a cross on (cf. 364).
399 *happy*: lucky.   *I renne ay on the losse*: I'm continually running at a loss.
400 *the stewys syde*: the 'red-light district' or brothels. Southwark was at this time notorious for its brothels.
401 *wete*: find out.   *Malkyn*: 'Molly' (*Malkyn* was frequently used of a woman of low class or behaviour; see Chaucer's *Introduction to the Man of Law's Tale*, CT II. 30, and the note in Chaucer 1987: 855).   *lemman*: mistress.   *have gete oughte*: has earned anything.
402 *lete her to hyre*: let her out for hire.   *ryde*: ride.
403 *harnes*: harness, 'gear'; the emendation to *harnes* (see textual note) is suggested by Kinsman in Skelton 1969. Skelton uses riding metaphors elsewhere with sexual implications: see *The auncient acquaintance*, 13–25 (Skelton 1983).   *easy*: comfortable.   *ferre and nere*: far and near.
404 *syns*: since.   *thyder*: there.   405 *tayle*: see 369.
406 *shyppe*: ships.   *Bordews*: Bordeaux.
408 *durste aventure to journey*: would dare to risk to travel.   *thorugh*: through. Gallants' tastes and fashions were often associated with France; see Boffey 1993*a*.
410 *trussed for to breke a launce*: built to break (the attack of) a lance.
411 *curtel*: horse (or other animal) with a docked tail.   *wynche*: kick.

To her wyll I nowe all my poverte lege.
And tyll I come, have, here is myne hat to plege.'

DREDE

Gone is this knave, this rybaude foule and leude.
He ran as fast as ever that he myghte.   415
Unthryftynes in hym may well be shewed,
For whome Tyborne groneth both daye and nyghte.
And as I stode and kyste asyde my syghte,
Dysdayne I sawe with Dyssymulacyon,
Standynge in sadde communicacion.   420

But there was poyntynge and noddynge with the hede,
And many wordes sayde in secrete wyse;
They wandred ay and stode styll in no stede.
Me thoughte alwaye Dyscymular dyde devyse
Me: passynge sore myne herte than gan aryse.   425
I dempte and drede theyr talkynge was not good.
Anone Dyscymular came where I stode.

Than, in his hode, I sawe there faces tweyne:
That one was lene and lyke a pyned goost,

412 *wyll I . . . lege*: I'll attribute.
413 *tyll I come*: until I return. *have*: take this. *to plege*: as a pledge.
414 *rybaude*: rogue. *leude*: ill-mannered, lascivious.
415 *as ever that he myghte*: as ever he could.   416 *Unthryftynes*: prodigality.
417 *For whome*: for whose sort. *Tyborne*: Tyburn, a place of public execution until
1783, was familiarly associated with fashionable scoundrels: cf. *Youth* 255, in Lancashire
1980: 119–20. *groneth*: groans.
418 *stode*: stood. *kyste asyde my syghte*: looked aside.
420 *sadde*: earnest, sober.   422 *in secrete wyse*: in a secretive way.
423 *wandred ay*: kept wandering about. *stode styll in no stede*: would not remain in one
place.
424 *Dyscymular*: Dissembler. *devyse*: scrutinize.
425 *passynge sore*: intensely painfully. *gan aryse*: rose with emotion.
426 *dempte*: thought (about it). *drede*: feared.   427 *Anone*: then.
428 *tweyne*: two.
428–39 Kinsman (Skelton 1969) relates these lines to proverbs such as Tilley 1952: F20,
'He carries (bears) two faces under one hood', and Tilley 1952: H 457, 'He has honey in his
mouth and the razor at his girdle'; Scattergood (Skelton 1983) compares conventional
figures of hypocrisy such as Fals-Semblant in *RR* (see Chaucer's *Romaunt*, 7417–18) and
the threatening figure depicted in Mars' temple in *Kn T*, *CT* I. 1999: 'The smylere with the
knyf under the cloke'.
429 *lene*: thin. *lyke a pyned goost*: like a tormented spirit.

That other loked as he wolde me have slayne.   430
And to mewarde as he gan for to coost,
Whan that he was even at me almoost,
[Biv^v]   I saw a knyfe hyd in his one sleve,
Wheron was wryten this worde: *Myscheve.*

And in his other sleve, me thought I sawe   435
A spone of golde, full of hony swete,
To fede a fole, and for to preye a dawe.
And on that sleve these wordes were wrete:
A false abstracte cometh from a fals concrete.
His hode was syde, his cope was roset graye;   440
Thyse were the wordes he to me dyde saye:

DYSSYMULATION

'How do ye, mayster? Ye loke so soberly!
As I be saved at the dredefull daye,
It is a perylous vyce, this envy.
Alas, a connynge man ne dwelle maye   445
In no place well, but foles with hym fraye!
But as for that, connynge hath no foo
Save hym that nought can: Scrypture sayth soo.

430 *loked*: looked.   *as he wolde me have slayne*: as if he would have murdered me.
431 And as he approached me.
432 *even at me almoost*: almost up to me.
433 *knyfe*: knife.   *hyd*: hidden.   *in his one sleve*: in one of his sleeves.
434 *Myscheve*: mischief.   436 *spone*: spoon.   *hony*: honey.
437 *fede a fole*: feed a fool.   *preye a dawe*: rob a simpleton.   438 *wrete*: written.
439 *abstracte*: abstract (idea).   *a fals concrete*: a false concrete (idea); *concrete* was a technical term used of a quality as actually found, 'concreted' or sticking to a substance.
440 *syde*: long.   *cope*: cloak.   *roset graye*: russet grey.
441 *Thyse*: these.   *dyde saye*: said.
442 How are you, sir? You have such a sober look.
443 As I (hope to) be saved on the (last) fearful day.
444 *perylous vyce*: terrible sin.
445 *connynge*: learned.   *ne dwelle maye*: cannot live.
446 Anywhere agreeably, without fools quarrelling with him.
447–8 Proverbial: Whiting 1968: C611.
448 *Save hym that nought can*: except the man who knows nothing.   *Scrypture*: the Bible (perhaps a reference to Proverbs 26: 1–12).

'I knowe your vertu and your lytterkture
By that lytel connynge that I have.   450
Ye be malygned sore, I you ensure—
But ye have crafte your selfe alwaye to save.
It is grete scorne to se a mysproude knave
With a clerke that connynge is to prate.
Lete theym go lowse theym, in the devylles date.   455

'For allbeit that this longe not to me,
Yet on my backe I bere suche lewde delynge.

[Bv^r]

Ryghte now I spake with one, I trowe, I see—
But, what, a strawe! I maye not tell all thynge.
By God, I saye, there is a grete herte-brennynge   460
Betwene the persone ye wote of, you—
Alas, I coude not dele so with a Jew.

'I wolde eche man were as playne as I.
It is a worlde, I saye, to here of some—
I hate this faynynge, fye upon it, fye!   465
A man can not wote where to become.
Iwys I coude tell—but humlery, home,

449 *knowe*: recognize. *lytterkture*: 'book-learning'.
450 *By*: from, through.   451 *malygned sore*: sorely defamed.
452 But you have the skill forever to protect yourself.
453 *It is grete scorne*: it's very contemptible. *se*: see. *mysproude*: arrogant.
454 Holding forth to a learned scholar.
455 *Lete theym go lowse theym*: let them go and lose themselves. *in the devylles date*: see
375.
456–7 For although this does not pertain to me, yet I feel on my shoulders the weight of
such ignorant behaviour.
458 *spake*: spoke. *one*: someone.
459 *a strawe*: used as an expression of contempt, meaning 'it's nothing'.
460 *herte-brennynge*: 'heart-burning', discontent.
461 *the persone ye wote of*: you-know-who. A telling use of the figure of *aposiopesis*
(sudden breaking-off in the middle of a sentence). Dyssymulation suggests obliquely that
the conversation he alludes to in some way threatens Drede.
462 *dele*: deal. Proverbial: Whiting 1968: J41.
463 *wolde*: wish. *playne*: open.   464 *worlde*: marvel.
465 *faynynge*: pretence.
466 A man can't know where to go.
467 *Iwys*: indeed. *humlery, home*: this seems to be an exclamation of impatience or
disgreement ('ahem').

I dare not speke, we be so layde awayte,
For all oure courte is full of dysceyte.

'Now, by Saynte Fraunceys, that holy man and frere,   470
I hate this wayes agayne you that they take!
Were I as you, I wolde ryde them full nere;
And by my trouthe, but yf an ende they make,
Yet wyll I saye some wordes for your sake
That shall them angre, I holde thereon a grote,   475
For some shall wene be hanged by the throte.

'I have a stoppynge oyster in my poke:
Truste me, and yf it come to a nede.
But I am lothe for to reyse a smoke
Yf ye coude be otherwyse agrede;   480
And so I wolde it were, so God me spede,
For this may brede to a confusyon,
Withoute God make a good conclusyon.

[Bvᵛ]   'Naye, see where yonder stondeth the teder man!
A flaterynge knave and false he is, God wote.   485

468 *layde awayte*: spied on.
470 St Francis of Assisi (1182–1226), founder of the Franciscan order. The reference
hints at the frequently made connection between friars and dissimulation.
471 *this wayes*: 'these ways', this behaviour. *agayne*: against.
472 *ryde them full nere*: 'ride close to them', challenge them (on the matter).
473 *trouthe*: troth, truth. *but yf an ende they make*: unless they make an end (of it).
475 *I holde thereon a grote*: I lay a groat (small coin) on it.
476 For some will think that they'll be hanged by the neck. Kinsman (Skelton 1969)
translates: 'For by the time I get through with them, they'll think that they've been shut up
for good.'
477 *stoppynge oyster*: from a proverb (Whiting 1968: O93), meaning 'something that
will stick in the throat of (and hence silence) your enemies'. *poke*: bag.
478 *and yf it come to a nede*: if it should become necessary.
479 *lothe*: reluctant. *reyse*: raise (perhaps to be translated as 'raise a stink'; the
expression is proverbial: see Whiting 1968: S413).
480 *coude be otherwyse agrede*: come to an agreement by some other means.
481 *I wolde it were*: I wish it were so.
482 *may brede to a confusyon*: give rise to a confusing situation.
483 Unless God bring it to a good end.
484 *stondeth*: stands. *the teder man*: the other man; equivalent to 't'other', and
technically the other of two. Here it is perhaps Disceyte, coming near to listen, although
in the atmosphere of uncertainty and fear created by this point in the poem, the reader, like
Drede, may well imagine it to be a further character, as yet unintroduced.
485 *God wote*: God knows.

The drevyll stondeth to herken, and he can.
It were more thryft he boughte him a newe cote;
It wyll not be, his purse is not on-flote.
All that he wereth, it is borowed ware;
His wytte is thynne, his hode is threde-bare.   490

'More coude I saye—but what, this is ynowe.
Adewe tyll soone, we shall speke more of this;
Ye muste be ruled, as I shall tell you howe.
Amendis maye be of that is now amys,
And I am your, syr, so have I blys,   495
In every poynte that I can do or saye.
Gyve me your honde, farewell and have good daye.'

DREDE

Sodaynly, as he departed me fro,
Came pressynge in one in a wonder araye.
Er I was ware, behynde me he sayde 'Bo!'   500
Thenne I, astonyed of that sodeyne fraye,
Sterte all at ones: I lyked no thynge his playe,
For yf I had not quyckely fledde the touche,
He had plucte oute the nobles of my pouche.

486 *drevyll*: drudge.   *herken*: listen.   *and he can*: if he can.
487 He'd be better off buying himself a new coat.
488 *on-flote*: 'afloat', free from financial trouble.
489 *wereth*: is wearing.   *ware*: goods.
490 *wytte*: wit.   *thynne*: thin.   *hode*: hood.
491 *ynowe*: enough.   492 *Adewe*: adieu.
493 *ruled*: advised.
494 What's now wrong may be put right.
495 *I am your*: I am at your service.   *so have I blys*: as I may have salvation.
496 *poynte*: detail.   498 *departed me fro*: left me.
499 *pressynge*: hurrying.   *one in a wonder araye*: someone amazingly dressed.
500 *Er I was ware*: before I was aware (of him).   *Bo*: boo.
501 *astonyed of that sodeyne fraye*: surprised by that sudden fright.
502 Started suddenly: I didn't like his tricks at all.
503 *fledde the touche*: fled from his touch.
504 He would have picked the nobles from my purse. A *noble* was a gold coin, that had a contemporary value of a third of a pound (6*s*. 8*d*.).

He was trussed in a garmente strayte—　　　　505
I have not sene suche anothers page—
For he coude well upon a casket wayte,
His hode all pounsed and garded lyke a cage.
Lyghte lyme-fynger, he toke none other wage.

[Bvi^r]　'Harken,' quod he, 'loo here myne honde in thyne;　　　　510
To us welcome thou arte, by Saynte Quyntyne!'

DISCEYTE

'But by that Lorde that is one, two and thre,
I have an errande to rounde in your ere.
He tolde me so, by God, ye maye truste me.
Parde, remembre whan ye were there,　　　　515
There I wynked on you—wote ye not where?
In *A loco*, I mene *juxta* B:
Woo is hym that is blynde and maye not see!

'But to here the subtylte and the crafte
As I shall tell you, yf ye wyll harke agayne—　　　　520
And whan I sawe the horsons wolde you hafte,
To holde myne honde, by God, I had grete payne;

505 He was all done up in a close-fitting garment.

506 I haven't seen anyone else's page (dressed) like that; Drede has never seen a page or household servant dressed in this way; he pursues the idea that the newcomer must be a page, hinting that the 'master' he serves must be a coffer of money.

507 He well knew how to wait upon a casket (of money).

508 *pounsed*: ornamented with eyelet holes.　*garded*: trimmed with braid or lace.

509 *Lyghte lyme-fynger*: nifty pilferer; proverbial; see Whiting 1968: L293.

510 Listen, he said, 'Here's my hand in yours'.

511 *Saynte Quyntyne*: St Quentin; cf. also *Mankind* (Eccles 1969: 153–84), 271.

513 *rounde in your ere*: whisper in your ear.

514 The *he* mentioned here, and the locations invoked, go unnamed; Disceyte continues the process which will eventually confound Drede.

516 *There*: where.　*wote ye not*: don't you know.

517 *A loco . . . juxta B* (Lat.): in place A . . . next to B. The places are named deliberately vaguely, as if to prevent any eavesdropper understanding the conversation.

519–20 To hear the cunning and the craftiness, which I'll tell you about, if you'll go on listening.

521 *horsons*: whores' sons; generally a contemptuous term, although sometimes used for comic effect.　*hafte*: cheat.

522 By God, I had great difficulty restraining my hand.

For forthwyth there I had him slayne,
But that I drede mordre wolde come oute.
Who deleth with shrewes hath nede to loke aboute!'   525

DREDE

And as he rounded thus in myne ere
Of false collusyon confetryd by assente,
Me thoughte I see lewde felawes here and there
Came for to slee me of mortall entente.
And as they came, the shypborde faste I hente,   530
And thoughte to lepe; and even with that woke,
Caughte penne and ynke, and wroth this lytyll boke.

I wolde therwith no man were myscontente;
Besechynge you that shall it see or rede,
In every poynte to be indyfferente,   535
Syth all in substaunce of slumbrynge doth procede.
I wyll not saye it is mater in dede,
But yet oftyme suche dremes be founde trewe.
Now constrewe ye what is the resydewe.

Thus endeth the Bouge of Courte. Enprynted at west-
mynster By me Wynkyn the worde

523 *forthwyth*: straightaway.   *I had him slayne*: I would have killed him.
524 Had I not feared 'murder would out'; proverbial: Whiting 1968: M806.
525 Whoever deals with rascals needs to keep an eye open.
526 *rounded*: whispered.
527 *confetryd by assente*: bound by agreement.
528 *lewde felawes*: mischievous companions.
529 (Who) came with the deadly intention to kill me.
530 *the shypborde faste I hente*: I grasped the edge of the ship tightly.
531 *thoughte to lepe*: thought I would jump (cf. the premonition at 112).   *even with that*:
at that (same moment).
532 *Caughte*: took.   *wroth*: wrote.
533 I would like no one to be dissatisfied with it.
534 *Besechynge*: begging.   *rede*: read.   535 To be impartial in every respect.
536 Since any seeming matter in it arises from sleep.
537 *mater*: of consequence.   *in dede*: actually.   538 *oftyme*: frequently.
539 *constrewe*: interpret.   *resydewe*: remainder.

[viᵛ]

Bibliography

ALAN OF LILLE (1980), *The Plaint of Nature*, trans. J. J. Sheridan, Toronto.

ALFRED THE GREAT (1899), *King Alfred's Old English Version of Boethius De consolatione Philosophiae*, ed. W. J. Sedgefield, Oxford.

—— (1900), *King Alfred's Version of the Consolations of Boethius*, trans. W. J. Sedgefield, Oxford.

ARN, M.-J. (1990), 'Poetic Form as a Mirror of Meaning in the English Poems of Charles of Orleans', *PQ* 59: pp. 13–29.

—— (1993), 'Charles of Orleans and the Poems of BL MS Harley 682', *ES* 74: pp. 222–35.

—— (2000) (ed.), *Charles d'Orléans in England (1415–1440)*, Cambridge.

Assembly of Ladies, The (1962, repr. 1980), in *The Floure and the Leafe and The Assembly of Ladies*, ed. D. A. Pearsall, Manchester; see also Pearsall 1990.

BALFOUR-MELVILLE, E. (1936), *James I, King of Scots, 1406–1437*, London.

BARR, H. (1993) (ed.), *The Piers Plowman Tradition*, London.

—— and WARD-PERKINS, K. (1997), ' "Spekyng for one's sustenance": The Rhetoric of Counsel in *Mum and the Sothsegger*, Skelton's *Bowge of Court*, and Elyot's *Pasquil the Playne*', in Cooper and Mapstone (1997), pp. 249–72.

BARRATT, A. (1987), '*The Flower and the Leaf* and *The Assembly of Ladies*: Is there a (Sexual) Difference?' *PQ* 66: pp. 1–24.

—— (1992) (ed.), *Women's Writing in Middle English*, London.

BARTHOLOMAEUS ANGLICUS (1975–88), *On the Properties of Things: John of Trevisa's translation of Bartholomaeus Anglicus, 'De Proprietatibus Rerum'*, ed. M. C. Seymour *et al.* (3 vols.), Oxford.

BAWCUTT, P. (1987), '*The Copill*: A Crux in *The Kingis Quair*', *RES* NS 38: pp. 211–14.

—— and RIDDY, F. (1987) (eds.), *Longer Scottish Poems*, i: *1375–1650*, Edinburgh.

BEADLE, R., and OWEN, A. E. B. (1977) (intro.), *The Findern Manuscript (Cambridge University Library MS Ff. 1. 6')*, London.

BENNETT, J. A. W. (1957), *The Parlement of Foules*, Oxford.

—— (1982), 'A King's Quire', in *The Humane Medievalist and Other Essays in English Literature and Learning, from Chaucer to Eliot*, Oxford, pp. 67–88.

BENSON, C. D. (1980), *The History of Troy in Middle English Literature*, Cambridge and Totowa, NJ.

BIANCO, S. (2000), 'New Perspectives on Lydgate's Courtly Verse', in Cooney (2000*b*), pp. 95–115.

BLAKE, N. F. (1972) (ed.), *Middle English Religious Prose*, London.

BLAMIRES, A., *et al.* (1993) (ed.), *Woman Defamed and Woman Defended: An Anthology of Medieval Texts*, Oxford.

BLOOMFIELD, M. (1952), *The Seven Deadly Sins*, East Lansing, Mich.

BOCCACCIO (1964–) *Tutte le opere di Giovanni di Boccaccio*, gen. ed. V. Branca, vols.: i (*Filocolo*), ii (*Filostrato* and *Teseida*); iii (*Amorosa Visione*); iv (*Decameron*), Florence.

BOETHIUS (1918, repr. 1968), *Tractates, De consolatione Philosophiae*, ed. and tr. H. F. Stewart and E. K. Rand, London and Cambridge, Mass.

—— (1969, repr. 1976), *The Consolation of Philosophy*, tr. V. E. Watts, Harmondsworth.

BOFFEY, J. (1991), 'Chaucerian Prisoners: The Context of *The Kingis Quair*', in J. Boffey and J. Cowen (eds.), *Chaucer and Fifteenth-Century Poetry*, London, pp. 84–102.

—— (1993*a*), '*The Treatise of a Galaunt* in Manuscript and Print', *Library*, 6th series 15: pp. 175–86.

—— (1993*b*), 'Women Authors and Women's Literacy in Fourteenth- and Fifteenth-Century England', in C. M. Meale (ed.), *Women and Literature in Britain, 1150–1500*, Cambridge, pp. 159–82.

—— (1996), 'Charles of Orleans Reading Chaucer's Dream Visions', in P. Boitani and A. Torti (eds.), *Medievalitas: Reading the Middle Ages. The J. A. W. Bennett Memorial Lectures, Perugia, 1995*, Cambridge, pp. 43–62.

—— and EDWARDS A. S. G. (1997) (intro.), *The Works of Geoffrey Chaucer and 'The Kingis Quair'. A Facsimile of Bodleian Library, Oxford, MS Arch. Selden. B. 24*, Cambridge.

—— and EDWARDS, A. S. G. (1999), 'Bodleian MS Arch. Selden. B. 24 and the "Scotticization" of Middle English Verse', in T. A. Prendergast and B. Kline (eds.), *Rewriting Chaucer: Culture, Authority, and the Idea of the Authentic Text, 1400–1602*, Columbus, Oh. pp. 166–85.

—— (2000), ' "Forto compleyne she had gret desire": The Grievances Expressed in Two Fifteenth-Century Dream Visions', in Cooney (2000*b*), pp. 116–28.

—— (2001), ' "Twenty thousand more": Some Fifteenth- and Sixteenth-Century Responses to *The Legend of Good Women*', in A. Minnis (ed.), *Middle English Poetry: Texts and Traditions. Essays in Honour of Derek Pearsall from the 8th York Manuscripts Conference*, Woodbridge, pp. 279–97.

BOITANI, P. (1986), 'Old Books Brought to Life in Dreams: The *Book of the Duchess*, the *House of Fame*, the *Parliament of Fowls*', in Boitani and Mann (1986), pp. 39–57.

—— and MANN, J. (1986) (eds.), *The Cambridge Chaucer Companion*, Cambridge.

BOITANI, P. and TORTI A. (1988) (eds.), *Genres, Themes, and Images in English Literature from the Fourteenth to the Fifteenth Century: The J. A. W. Bennett Memorial Lectures, Perugia, 1986*, Tübingen.

BREWER, D. S. (1955), 'The Ideal of Feminine Beauty in Medieval Literature', *MLR* 60: pp. 257–69.

—— (1960, repr. 1972) (ed.), *The Parlement of Foulys*, Manchester.

—— (1976) (intro.), *Geoffrey Chaucer: The Workes, 1532, with Supplementary Material from the Editions of 1542, 1561, 1598 and 1602*, London.

BROWN, M. (1994), *James I*, Edinburgh.

BROWNLOW, F. W. (1984), 'The Date of *The Bowge of Courte* and Skelton's Authorship of "A Lamentable of King Edward the III" ', *ELN* 22 (1984), pp. 12–20.

BURROW, J. A. (1988a), 'The Poet and the Book', in Boitani and Torti (1988), pp. 230–45.

—— (1988b), *The Ages of Man: A Study in Medieval Writing and Thought*, Oxford.

CALIN, W. (1994), *The French Tradition and the Literature of Medieval England*. Toronto.

CARPENTER, N. C. (1955), 'Skelton and Music: Roty Bully Joys', *RES* NS 6: pp. 279–84.

—— (1968), *John Skelton*, New York.

CARRETTA, V. (1981), '*The Kingis Quair* and *The Consolation of Philosophy*', *SSL* 16: pp. 14–28.

CHAMPION, P. (1907), *Le Manuscrit autographe des poésies de Charles d'Orléans*, Paris.

—— (1911), *Vie de Charles d'Orléans*, Paris.

CHARLES OF ORLEANS (1923–7), *Charles d'Orléans: Poésies* , ed. P. Champion (2 vols.), Paris.

—— (1970), *The English Poems of Charles of Orleans*, ed. R. Steele and M. Day, EETS OS 215 and 220 (for 1941 and 1946), repr. in one volume with new bibliography, London.

—— (1973), *Charles d'Orléans: choix de poésies* , ed. J. Fox, Exeter.

—— (1994), *Fortunes Stabilnes: Charles of Orleans's English Book of Love*, ed. M.-J. Arn, Medieval and Renaissance Texts and Studies, Binghampton, NY.

CHAUCER, GEOFFREY (1894), *The Complete Works of Geoffrey Chaucer*, ed. W. W. Skeat (6 vols.), Oxford.

—— (1987, UK edn. 1988), *The Riverside Chaucer* (3rd edn.), gen. ed. L. D. Benson, Boston and Oxford.

CHRISTINE DE PIZAN (1983), *The Book of the City of Ladies*, tr. E. J. Richards, London.

—— (1985), *The Treasure of the City of Ladies*, tr. S. Lawson, Harmondsworth.

CLANVOWE, JOHN, *The Boke of Cupide* (1975), in Scattergood.

CONNOLLY, M. (1998), *John Shirley: Book Production and the Noble Household in Fifteenth-Century England*, Aldershot.

COONEY, H. (2000*a*), 'Skelton's *Bouge of Court* and the Crisis of Allegory in Late-Medieval England', in Cooney (2000*b*), pp. 153–67.

—— (2000*b*) (ed.), *Nation, Court and Culture: New Essays on Fifteenth-Century English Poetry*, Dublin.

COOPER, H., and MAPSTONE, S. (1997) (eds.), *The Long Fifteenth Century: Essays for Douglas Gray*, Oxford.

COURCELLE, P. (1967), *La Consolation de Philosophie dans la tradition littéraire: antécédents et postérité de Boèce*, Paris.

COURTHOPE, W. (1980), *This rol was laburd and finished by Master John Rows of Warrewyk*; intro. C. Ross, Gloucester; 1st published London, 1845–59.

COWEN, J. (1991), 'Women as Exempla in Fifteenth-Century Verse of the Chaucerian Tradition', in J. Boffey and J. Cowen (eds.), *Chaucer and Fifteenth-Century Poetry*, London, pp. 51–65.

CUNNINGTON, C. W. and P. (1952), *Handbook of English Medieval Costume*, London.

CURTIUS, E. R. (1953), *European Literature and the Latin Middle Ages*, tr. W. R. Trask, London.

DANTE ALIGHIERI (1969), *La Vita Nuova*, tr. B. Reynolds, Harmondsworth.

—— (1980–2), *The Divine Comedy*, tr. with a commentary by C. S. Singleton (3 vols.), Princeton.

DAVENPORT, W. A. (1983), ' "Lusty Fresche Galaunts" ', in P. Neuss (ed.), *Aspects of Early English Drama*, Cambridge.

—— (1989), *Chaucer: Complaint and Narrative*, Cambridge.

—— (2000), 'Fifteenth-Century Complaints and Duke Humphrey's Wives', in Cooney (2000*b*), pp. 129–52.

DAVIDOFF, J. M. (1983), 'The Audience Illuminated, or New Light Shed on the Dream Frame of Lydgate's *Temple of Glas*', *SAC* 5: pp. 103–25.

—— (1988), *Beginning Well: Framing Fictions in Late Middle English Poetry*, London and Toronto.

DESMOND, M. (1994), *Reading Dido: Gender, Textuality and the 'Aeneid' in the Middle Ages*, Minneapolis.

DICKEY, S. (1992), 'Seven Come Eleven: Gambling for the Laurel in *The Bowge of Courte*', *YES* 22: pp. 238–54.

DONALD, A. K. (1895) (ed.), *Melusine*, EETS es 68, London.

DOOB, P. R. (1990), *The Idea of the Labyrinth, from Classical Antiquity through the Middle Ages*, Ithaca, NY, and London.

DOYLE, A. I. (1961). 'More Light on John Shirley', *M Ae* 30: pp. 93–101.

Dream of the Rood, The (1978), ed. M. Swanton (2nd edn.), Manchester.

DUNBAR, WILLIAM (1996), *William Dunbar: Selected Poems*, ed. P. Bawcutt, Harlow.

DYCE, A., *see* Skelton.

EBIN, L. (1974), 'Boethius, Chaucer, and *The Kingis Quair*', *PQ* 53: pp. 321–41.

—— (1988), *Illuminator, Makar, Vates: Visions of Poetry in the Fifteenth Century*, Lincoln, Nebr., and London.

ECCLES, M.(1969) (ed.), *The Macro Plays*, EETS os 262, London.

ECONOMOU, G. D. (1972), *The Goddess Natura in Medieval Literature*, Cambridge, Mass.

EDWARDS, A. S. G. (1983), 'Lydgate Manuscripts: Some Directions for Future Research', in D. Pearsall (ed.), *Manuscripts and Readers in Fifteenth-Century England: The Literary Implications of Manuscript Study*, Cambridge, pp. 15–26.

—— (1984), 'Lydgate Scholarship: Progress and Prospects', in R. F. Yeager (ed.), *Fifteenth-Century Studies: Recent Essays*, Hamden, Conn., pp. 29–47.

—— (1985) (intro.), *MS Pepys 2006, Magdalene College, Cambridge: A Facsimile*, Norman, Okla.

EDWARDS, H. L. R. (1949), *Skelton: The Life and Times of an Early Tudor Poet*, London.

EHRHART, M. H. (1987), *The Judgement of the Trojan Prince Paris in Medieval Literature*, Philadelphia.

ELLIS, H. (1811) (ed.), *Fabyans Chronicle*, London.

EVANS, J. (1931), *Pattern: A Study of Ornament in Western Europe from 1180 to 1500* (2 vols.), London.

—— and SERJEANTSON, M. S. (1933) (eds.) *English Medieval Lapidaries*, EETS os 190, London.

EVANS, R., and JOHNSON, L. (1991), 'The *Assembly of Ladies*: A Maze of Feminist Sign-Reading', in L. Hutcheon and P. Perron (eds.), *Feminist Criticism: Theory and Practice*, Toronto, pp. 171–96.

FALLOWS, D. (1977), 'Words and Music in Two English Songs of the Mid-Fifteenth Century', *EM* 5: pp. 38–43.

FAMIGLIETTI, R. C. (1986), *Royal Intrigue: Crisis at the Court of Charles VI, 1392–1420*, New York.

FENSTER, T. S., and ERLER, M. C. (1990) (eds.), *Poems of Cupid, God of Love*, Leiden.

FISH, S. E. (1965), *John Skelton's Poetry*, New Haven and London.

FLETCHER, B. Y. (1979), 'Some Printer's Copy for William Thynne's 1532 Edition of Chaucer', *Library*, 6th ser. 1: pp. 97–113.

—— (1987) (intro.), *MS R. 3. 19, Trinity College, Cambridge: A Facsimile*. Norman, Okla.

Floure and the Leafe, The (1962, repr. 1980), in *The Floure and the Leafe and The Assembly of Ladies*, ed. D. A. Pearsall, Manchester; see also Pearsall (1990).

FOX, J. (1969), *The Lyric Poetry of Charles d'Orléans*, Oxford.

FRANK, R. (1953), 'The Art of Reading Medieval Personification Allegory', *ELH* 20: pp. 237–50.

FROISSART, JEAN (1972), *L'Espinette amoureuse*, ed. A. Fourrier, Paris.

—— (1975), *Le joli buisson de Jonece*, ed. A. Fourrier, Paris.

—— (1979), *'Dits' et 'Débats'*, ed. A. Fourrier, Paris.

—— (1986), *Le Paradis d'amour*, ed. P. F. Dembowski, Geneva.

FURNIVALL, F. J. (1868) (ed.), *The Babees Book*, EETS os 32, London.

FYLER, J. M. (1979), *Chaucer and Ovid*, New Haven.

GEORGE, W., and YAPP, B. (1991), *The Naming of Beasts: Natural History in the Medieval Bestiary*, London.

GIBSON, M. (1982) (ed.), *Boethius, his Life, Thought and Influence*, Oxford.

GILLESPIE, V. (1997), 'Justification by Faith: Skelton's *Replycacion*', in Cooper and Mapstone (1997), pp. 273–311.

GIVEN-WILSON, C. (1986), *The Royal Household and the King's Affinity: Service, Politics and Finance in England, 1360–1413*, New Haven.

—— (1996), *The English Nobility in the Late Middle Ages: The Fourteenth-Century Political Community*, London.

GORDON, E. V. (1953) (ed.), *Pearl*, Oxford.

GOWER, JOHN (1899–1902), *The Complete Works of John Gower*, ed. G. C. Macaulay (4 vols.), Oxford.

—— (1962), *The Major Latin Works of John Gower*, tr. E. W. Stockton, Seattle.

GREEN, R. F. (1980) *Poets and Princepleasers: Literature and the English Court in the Late Middle Ages*, Toronto.

—— (1983), 'The *Familia Regis* and the *Familia Cupidinis*', in V. J. Scattergood and J. W. Sherborne (eds.), *English Court Culture in the Later Middle Ages*, London, pp. 87–108.

GREENBLATT, S. (1980), *Renaissance Self-Fashioning*, Chicago and London.

GUILLAUME DE DEGUILEVILLE (1893), *Le pèlerinage de la vie humaine*, ed. J. J. Stürzinger, Roxburghe Club, London.

—— (1895), *Le pèlerinage de l'âme*, ed. J. J. Stürzinger, Roxburghe Club, London.

—— (1897), *Le pèlerinage de Jhesucrist*, ed. J. J. Stürzinger, Roxburghe Club, London.

GUILLAUME DE MACHAUT (1875), *Le livre du Voir-Dit*, ed. P. Imbs, intro. J. Cerquiglini-Toulet (1999), Paris.

—— (1908–21), *Oeuvres*, ed. E. Hoepffner (3 vols.), SATF, Paris.

—— (1984),*The Judgement of the King of Bohemia*, ed. and tr. R. Barton Palmer, New York.

—— (1988*a*), *Le Jugement du Roy de Behaigne and Remède de Fortune*, ed. and tr. J. I. Wimsatt and W. W. Kibler, Athens and London.

—— (1988*b*), *The Judgement of the King of Navarre*, ed. and tr. R. Barton Palmer, New York.

GUILLAUME DE MACHAUT (1993), *The Fountain of Love*, ed. and tr. R. Barton Palmer (1993), New York.

—— (1998) *Le Livre dou Voir Dit* (*The Book of the True Poem*), ed. D. Leech-Wilkinson, tr. R. Barton Palmer, New York.

HADFIELD, A. (1994), *Literature, Politics and National Identity: Reformation to Renaissance*, Cambridge.

HALPERN, R. (1986), 'John Skelton and the Poetics of Primitive Accumulation', in P. Parker and D. Quint (eds.), *Literary Theory/Renaissance Texts*, Baltimore, pp. 225–56.

HAMMOND, E. P. (1911) (ed.), 'The Eye and the Heart', *Anglia* 34: pp. 235–65.

—— (1927), *English Verse between Chaucer and Surrey*, Durham NC.

HANNA, R. III (1996), 'John Shirley and British Library, MS. Additional 16165', *SB* 49: pp. 95–105.

HARVEY, J. (1990), *Medieval Gardens*, 2nd edn., London.

HEISERMAN, A. R. (1961), *Skelton and Satire*, Chicago.

HICKS, E. (1977) (ed.), *Le Débat sur le Roman de la Rose*, Paris.

HENRYSON, ROBERT (1981) *The Poems of Robert Henryson*, ed. D. Fox, Oxford.

HOCCLEVE, THOMAS (1990), *Lepistre de Cupide*, in Fenster and Erler (1990).

HUOT, S. (1993), *The 'Romance of the Rose' and its Medieval Readers Interpretation, Reception, Manuscript Transmission*, Cambridge.

JACK, R. D. S., and ROZENDAAL, P. A. T. (1997) (eds.), *The Mercat Anthology of Early Scottish Literature 1375–1707*, Edinburgh.

JAMES I OF SCOTLAND (1911), *The Kingis Quair*, ed. W. W. Skeat, Scottish Text Society, 2nd edn., Edinburgh.

—— (1939), *The Kingis Quair*, ed. W. Mackay Mackenzie, London.

—— (1973), *The Kingis Quair of James Stewart*, ed. M. McDiarmid, London.

—— (1981), *The Kingis Quair*, ed. J. Norton-Smith, Leiden.

—— (1987), selections from *The Kingis Quair* in *Longer Scottish Poems, i: 1375–1650*, ed. P. Bawcutt and F. Riddy, Edinburgh.

—— (1997), *The Kingis Quair* in Jack and Rozendaal (1997).

JANSEN, J. P. M. (1989), 'Charles of Orleans and the Fairfax Poems', *ES* 70: pp. 206–24.

JEAN DE CONDÉ (1970), *La messe des oiseaux et le dit des Jacobins et des Fremeneurs*, ed. J. Ribard, TLF, Geneva.

JEFFERY, C. D. (1978), 'Anglo-Scots Poetry and *The Kingis Quair*', in *Actes de 2e colloque de langue et de littérature écossaises (Moyen Age et Renaissance)*, Strasbourg, pp. 207–21.

KEAN, P. M. (1972), *Chaucer and the Making of English Poetry I: Love Vision and Debate*, London.

KINGSFORD, C. L. (1905), *Chronicles of London*, Oxford.

KINNEY, A. F. (1987), *John Skelton: Priest as Poet*, Chapel Hill, NC.

KINSMAN, R. S., and YONGE, T. (1967), *John Skelton: Canon and Census*, Renaissance Society of America, Bibliographies and Indexes, 4, Darien, Conn.

KOSIKOWSKI, S. J. (1977), 'Lydgate, Machiavelli and More and Skelton's *Bowge of Courte*', *ANQ*, Jan. 1977, 66–7.

—— (1982), 'Allegorical Meanings in Skelton's *The Bowge of Courte*', *PQ* 61: pp. 305–15.

KRATZMANN, G. (1980), *Anglo-Scottish Literary Relations 1430–1550*, Cambridge.

KRUGER, S. F. (1992), *Dreaming in the Middle Ages*, Cambridge.

LANCASHIRE, I. (1980) (ed.), *Two Tudor Interludes: Youth and Hick Scorner*, Manchester.

—— (1978 repr. 1995), *The Vision of Piers Plowman: A Complete Edition of the B-Text*, ed. A. V. C. Schmidt, London and New York.

LANGLAND, WILLIAM (1886, repr. 1954), *The Vision of William concerning Piers the Plowman in Three Parallel Texts*, ed. W. W. Skeat (2 vols.), Oxford.

LANGLOIS, E. (1910), *Les manuscrits du Roman de la Rose: description et classement*, Paris.

LARSON, J. S. (1962), 'What is *The Bowge of Court?*' *JEGP* 61: pp. 288–95.

LAWSON, S. *see* Christine de Pizan.

LAWTON, D. (1980), 'Skelton's Use of *Persona*', *EC* 30: pp. 9–28.

LERER, S. (1993), *Chaucer and his Readers*, Princeton.

LESTER, G. (1981), *Three Late Medieval Morality Plays*, London.

LEWIS, C. S. (1936), *The Allegory of Love*, Oxford.

—— (1964), *The Discarded Image: An Introduction to Medieval and Renaissance Literature*, Cambridge.

LEYERLE, J. (1974), 'The Heart and the Chain', in L. D. Benson (ed.), *The Learned and the Lewed: Studies in Chaucer and Medieval Literature*, Cambridge, Mass., pp. 113–45.

LIVY (1919–59), *Ab urbe condita*, ed. B. O. Foster *et al.* (14 vols.), London and Cambridge, Mass.

LYALL, R. (1989), 'Materials: The Paper Revolution', in J. J. Griffiths and D. Pearsall (eds.), *Book Production and Publishing in Britain 1375–1475*, Cambridge, pp. 11–29.

LYDGATE, JOHN (1891), *Lydgate's Temple of Glass*, ed. J. Schick, EETS ES 60, London.

—— (1906–35), *Troy Book*, ed. H. Bergen (4 vols.) EETS ES 97, 103, 106, 126, London.

—— (1911a), *The Minor Poems of John Lydgate*, i, ed. H. N. MacCracken, EETS ES 107, London.

—— (1911b, 1930), *Lydgate's Siege of Thebes*, ed. A. Erdmann and E. Ekwall (2 vols.) EETS ES 108, 125, London.

LYDGATE, JOHN (1924–7), *The Fall of Princes*, ed. H. Bergen (4 vols.), EETS, ES 121–4, London.

—— (1934), *The Minor Poems of John Lydgate, ii*, ed. H. N. MacCracken, EETS OS 192, London.

—— (1961), *Lydgate's Life of Our Lady*, ed. J. Lauritis, R. A. Klinefelter, and V. F. Gallagher, Pittsburgh.

—— (1966), *John Lydgate: Poems*, ed. J. Norton-Smith, Oxford.

LYNCH, K. L. (1988), *The High Medieval Dream Vision*, Stanford, Calif.

—— (1994), 'Partitioned Fictions: The Meaning and Importance of Walls in Chaucer's Poetry', in R. R. Edwards (ed.), *Art and Context in Late Medieval English Narrative: Essays in Honor of Robert Worth Frank Jr.*, Cambridge, pp. 107–25.

MACCRACKEN, H. N. (1908), 'Additional Light on *The Temple of Glass*', *PMLA* 23: pp. 128–40.

MCLEOD, E. (1969), *Charles of Orleans, Prince and Poet*, London.

MCMILLAN, A. (1982), ' "Fayre Sisters Al": *The Flower and the Leaf* and *The Assembly of Ladies*', *Tulsa Studies in Women's Literature* I: pp. 27–42.

MACQUEEN, J. (1977), 'The Literature of Fifteenth-Century Scotland', in J. M. Brown (ed.), *Scottish Society in the Fifteenth Century*, London.

—— (1988), 'Poetry—James I to Henryson', in R. D. S. Jack (ed.), *The History of Scottish Literature, i*, Aberdeen.

MACROBIUS (1952), *Commentary on the Dream of Scipio*, tr. W. H. Stahl, New York.

MAPSTONE, S. (1997), 'Kingship and the *Kingis Quair*', in Cooper and Mapstone (1997), pp. 51–69.

MARTIANUS CAPELLA (1971–7), *De nuptiis Philologiae et Mercurii*, in *Martianus Capella and the Seven Liberal Arts*, tr. W. H. Stahl *et al.* (2 vols.), New York.

MERTES, K. (1988), *The English Noble Household, 1250–1600*, Oxford.

MINNIS, A. J. (1987) (ed.), *The Medieval Boethius: Studies in the Vernacular Translations of 'De Consolatione Philosophiae'*, Cambridge.

—— (1995), *Chaucer's Shorter Poems* (Oxford Guide to Chaucer), Oxford.

MISKIMIN, A. (1977), 'Patterns in *The Kingis Quair* and *The Temple of Glass*', *PLL* 13: pp. 339–61.

MOORE, S. (1912), 'Patrons of Letters in Norfolk and Suffolk c. 1450, I', *PMLA* 27: pp. 188–207.

—— (1913), 'Patrons of Letters in Norfolk and Suffolk c. 1450, II', *PMLA* 28: pp. 79–105.

MORGAN, D. A. L. (1986), 'The Individual Style of the English Gentleman', in M. Jones (ed.), *Gentry and Lesser Nobility in Late Medieval Europe*, Gloucester, pp. 15–35.

NEILSON, W. A. (1899), *The Origins and Sources of 'The Court of Love'*, Boston.

NELSON, W. (1939), *John Skelton: Laureate*, New York.

NORTH, J. D. (1988), *Chaucer's Universe*, Oxford.

NORTON-SMITH, J. (1958), 'Lydgate's Changes in *The Temple of Glass*', *M Ae* 27: pp. 167–72.

—— (1974) *Geoffrey Chaucer*, London.

—— (1979) (intro.), *MS Fairfax 16: A Facsimile*, London.

OTON DE GRANSON (1941), *Oton de Granson: sa vie et ses poésies*, ed. A. Piaget, Geneva.

OVID (1914), '*Heroides' and 'Amores*', ed. and tr. G. Showerman, London and Cambridge, Mass.

—— (1916), *Metamorphoses*, ed. and tr. F. J. Miller, London and Cambridge, Mass.

—— (1931), *Fasti*, ed. and tr. J. G. Frazer, London and Cambridge, Mass.

PARKES, M. B., and BEADLE, R. (1979–80) (intro.), *Geoffrey Chaucer, Poetical Works. A Facsimile of Cambridge University Library MS Gg. 4. 27* (3 vols.), Cambridge.

Parlement of the Thre Ages, The (1959), ed. M. Y. Offord, EETS os 246, London.

PATCH, H. R. (1927), *The Goddess Fortuna in Mediaeval Literature*, Cambridge, Mass.

PATTERSON, L. (1992), 'Writing Amorous Wrongs: Chaucer and the Order of Complaint', in J. R. Dean and C. K. Zacher (eds.), *The Idea of Medieval Literature: New Essays on Chaucer and Medieval Culture in Honor of Donald R. Howard*, Newark, NJ, pp. 17–71.

Pearl (1953), ed. E. V. Gordon, Oxford.

PEARSALL, D. A. (1961), '*The Assembly of Ladies* and *Generydes*', *RES* 12: pp. 229–37.

—— (1962) (ed.), *The Floure and the Leafe and The Assembly of Ladies*, London and Edinburgh.

—— (1970), *John Lydgate*, London.

—— (1990) (ed.), *The Floure and the Leafe, The Assembly of Ladies, The Isle of Ladies*, Kalamazoo, Mich.

—— (1997), *John Lydgate (1371–1449): A Bio-Bibliography*, Victoria, BC.

—— (1999) (ed.), *Chaucer to Spenser: An Anthology of Writings in English 1375–1575*, Oxford.

PETRINA, A. (1997), *The 'Kingis Quair' of James I of Scotland*, Padova.

PHILLIPS, H. (1997), 'Frames and Narrators in Chaucerian Poetry', in Cooper and Mapstone (1997), pp. 71–98.

PIAGET, A. (1891), 'La cour amoureuse dite de Charles VI', *Romania* 20: pp. 417–54.

PICKERING, F. P. (1970), *Literature and Art in the Middle Ages*. London.

POIRION, D. (1965), *Le Poète et le Prince: l'évolution du lyrisme courtois de Guillaume de Machaut à Charles d'Orléans*, Grenoble.

POLLARD, A. W., and REDGRAVE, G. R. (1976–91) (eds.), *A Short-Title Catalogue of Books printed in England, Scotland and Ireland and of English Books printed Abroad 1475–1640*, rev. W. A. Jackson, F. S. Ferguson, and K. F. Pantzer (3 vols.), London.

POLLET, M. (1971), *John Skelton*, tr. John Warrington, London.

POMPEN, A. (1925), *The English Versions of 'The Ship of Fools'*, London.

PRESTON, J. (1956), 'Fortunys Exiltree: A Study of *The Kingis Quair*', *RES*, NS 7: pp. 339–47.

PSILOS, P. D. (1976), ' "Dulle" Drede and the Limits of Prudential Knowledge in Skelton's *Bowge of Courte*', *JMRS* 6: pp. 297–317.

PURCELL, S. (1973) (ed.), *The Poems of Charles of Orleans*, Cheadle Hulme.

PUTTER, AD (1997), 'Animating Medieval Court Satire', in E. Mullally and J. Thompson (eds.), *The Court and Cultural Diversity: Selected Papers from the Eighth Triennial Congress of the International Courtly Literature Society*, Cambridge, pp. 67–76.

QUINN, W. (1980–1), 'Memory and the Matrix of Unity in *The Kingis Quair*', *Chau R* 15: pp. 332–55.

REBHOLZ, R. A. (1978) (ed.), *Sir Thomas Wyatt: The Complete Ploems*, Harmondsworth.

REED, T. J. (1990), *Middle English Debate Poetry and the Aesthetics of Irresolution*, Columbia, Miss.

RÉMY, P. (1954–5), 'Les "cours d'amour": légende et réalité', *Revue de l'Université de Bruxelles*, 7: pp. 179–97.

RENOIR, A. (1967), *The Poetry of John Lydgate*, London.

RICHARDS, E. J. *see* Christine de Pizan.

ROBINSON, P. (1980), *Minor Poems: Bodleian Library MS Tanner 346: A Facsimile*, Norman, Okla.

—— (1981), *MS Bodley 638: A Facsimile*, Norman, Okla.

Roman de la Rose, Le (1965–70), ed. F. Lecoy (3 vols.), CFMA, Paris.

—— (1971), *The Romance of the Rose*, tr. C. Dahlberg, Princeton.

RUSSELL, J. S. (1980), 'Skelton's *Bouge of Court*: A Nominalist Allegory', *Renaissance Papers*, pp. 1–9.

RUSSELL, S. (1988), *The English Dream Vision: Anatomy of a Form*, Columbus, Oh.

SALE, H. S. (1937), 'The Date of Skelton's *Bowge of Court*', *MLN* 52: pp. 572–4.

SCATTERGOOD, J. (1974), 'Skelton's "Ryotte": "A Rusty Gallande" ', *N & Q* 219: pp. 83–5.

—— (1975) (ed.), *The Works of Sir John Clanvowe*, Totowa NJ.

—— (1987), 'Fashion and Morality in the Late Middle Ages', in D. Williams (ed.), *England in the Fifteenth Century: Proceedings of the 1986 Harlaxton Symposium*, Woodbridge, pp. 255–72.

—— (1988), 'Insecurity in Skelton's *Bowge of Courte*', in Boitani and Torti (1988), pp. 186–209.

SCHÈLER, A. (1866–7) (ed.), *Dits et Contes de Baudouin de Condé, et de son fils Jean de Condé* (3 vols.), Brussels.

SCHEPS, W. (1971), 'Chaucerian Synthesis: The Art of *The Kingis Quair*', *SSL* 8: pp. 143–65.

—— and LOONEY, J. A. (1986) (eds.), *Middle Scots Poets: A Reference Guide to James I of Scotland, Robert Henryson, William Dunbar, and Gavin Douglas*, Boston.

SCHIRMER, W. F. (1961), tr. A. E. Keep, *John Lydgate: A Study in the Culture of the Fifteenth Century*, London.

SCOTT, K. (1997), *Later Gothic Manuscripts, 1390–1490* (2 vols.), London.

SCOTT, M. (1986), *A Visual History of Costume: The Fourteenth and Fifteenth Centuries*, London.

SEATON, E. (1961), *Sir Richard Roos*, London.

SHARRATT, B. (1986), 'John Skelton: Finding a Voice—Notes after Bakhtin', in D. Aers (ed.), *Medieval Literature: Criticism, Ideology, History*, Brighton, pp. 199–222.

SIMPSON, J. (1993), 'The Death of the Author? Skelton's *Bouge of Court*', in E. Maslen (ed.), *The Timeless and the Temporal: Writings in Honour of John Chalker*, London, pp. 58–79.

SKEAT, W. W. (1866) (ed.), *Partenay or Lusignen*, EETS OS 22, London.

—— (1897) (ed.), *Chaucerian and Other Pieces: A Supplement to 'The Works of Geoffrey Chaucer'*, Oxford.

—— (1900a), 'The Authoress of *The Flower and the Leaf*', *MLQ* 3: pp. 111–12.

—— (1900b), *The Chaucer Canon*, Oxford.

SKELTON, JOHN (1843, repr. 1965), *The Poetical Works of John Skelton*, ed. A. Dyce (2 vols.), London.

—— (1969), *John Skelton: Poems*, ed. R. S. Kinsman, Oxford.

—— (1980), *Magnificence*, ed. P. Neuss, Manchester.

—— (1983), *John Skelton: The Complete English Poems*, ed. J. Scattergood, Harmondsworth.

Songe du vergier, Le (1982), ed. M. Schnerb-Lièvre (2 vols.), Paris.

SPEARING, A. C. (1976), *Medieval Dream Poetry*, Cambridge.

—— (1985), *Medieval to Renaissance in English Poetry*, Cambridge.

—— (1991), 'Prison, Writing, Absence: Representing the Subject in the English Poems of Charles of Orleans', *MLQ* 53: pp. 83–99.

—— (1993), *The Medieval Poet as Voyeur. Looking and Listening in Medieval Love Narratives*, Cambridge.

—— (2000), 'Dreams in The Kingis Quair and the Duke's Book', in Arn (2000), pp. 123–44.

SPURGEON, C. F. E. (1925), *Five Hundred Years of Chaucer Criticism and Allusion, 1357–1900* (3 vols.), Cambridge.

STAUB, S. C. (1988), 'Recent Studies in Skelton (1970–1988)', *ELR* 20: pp. 505–16.

STARKEY, D. (1981), 'The Age of the Household: Politics, Society and the Arts c.1350–c.1550', in S. Medcalf (ed.), *The Later Middle Ages*, London, pp. 225–90.

—— (1987), *The English Court from the Wars of the Roses to the Civil War*, London.

STEARNS, M. W. (1942), 'Chaucer Mentions a Book', *MLN* 57: pp. 28–31.

STEPHENS, J. (1973), 'The Questioning of Love in the *Assembly of Ladies*', *RES* NS 24: pp. 129–40.

STEVENS, J. E. (1961), *Music and Poetry in the Early Tudor Court*, London.

STEVENS, M. (1979), 'The Winds of Change in the *Troilus*', *Chau R* 13: pp. 285–307.

STROHM, P. (1982), 'Chaucer's Fifteenth-Century Audience and the Narrowing of the "Chaucer Tradition" ', *SAC* 4: pp. 3–32.

—— (1988), 'Fourteenth- and Fifteenth-Century Writers as Readers of Chaucer', in Boitani and Torti (1988), pp. 90–104.

SUTTON, A. F., and VISSER-FUCHS, L. (1997), 'The Device of Queen Elizabeth Woodville: A Gillyflower or Pink', *The Ricardian* 11/136: pp. 17–24.

TILLEY, M. P. (1952), *A Dictionary of Proverbs in England in the Sixteenth and Seventeenth Centuries*, Ann Arbor.

TORTI, A. (1986), 'John Lydgate's *Temple of Glas*: "Atwixen two so hang I in balaunce" ', in P. Boitani and A. Torti (eds.), *Intellectuals and Writers in Fourteenth-Century Europe: The J. A. W. Bennett Memorial Lectures, Perugia 1984*, Tübingen and Cambridge, pp. 226–43.

—— (1991), *The Glass of Form: Mirroring Structures from Chaucer to Skelton*, London.

TUCKER, M. (1970), 'Setting in Skelton's *Bowge of Courte*: A Speculation', *ELN* 7: pp. 168–75.

TWYCROSS, M. A. (1972), *The Medieval Anadyomene: A Study in Chaucer's Mythography*, Oxford.

UITZ, E. (1988), *Women in the Medieval Town*, tr. S. Marnie, London.

USK, THOMAS (1998), *The Testament of Love*, ed. R. Allen Shoaf, Kalamazoo, Mich.

VON HENDY, A. (1965), 'The Free Thrall: A Study of *The Kingis Quair*', *SSL* 2: pp. 141–51.

WALKER, G. (1988) *John Skelton and the Politics of the 1520s*, Cambridge.

—— (2000), 'John Skelton and the Royal Court', in J. and R. Britnell (eds.), *Vernacular Literature and Current Affairs in Early Sixteenth-Century France, England and Scotland*, Aldershot, pp. 1–15.

WALTON, JOHN (1925), *Walton's Boethius*, ed. M. Science, EETS OS 170, London.

WHITE, T. H. (1954), *The Book of Beasts. Being a Translation from a Latin Bestiary of the Twelfth Century*, London.

WHITING, B. J. and H. W. (1968) (eds.), *Proverbs, Sentences and Proverbial Phrases from English Writings Mainly Before 1500*, Cambridge, Mass., and London.

WILSON, J. (1975), 'Poet and Patron in Early Fifteenth-Century England: John Lydgate's *Temple of Glass*', *Parergon* 11: pp. 25–32.

WIMSATT, J. I. (1970), *The Marguerite Poetry of Guillaume de Machaut*, Chapel Hill, NC.

—— (1991), *Chaucer and his French Contemporaries*, Toronto.

WINDEATT, B. (1982) (ed.), *Chaucer's Dream Poetry: Sources and Analogues*, Cambridge and Totowa, NJ.

WINSER, L. '*The Bowge of Courte*: Drama Doubling as Dream', *ELR* 6: pp. 3–39.

WOOD, M. (1981), *The English Medieval House*, 2nd edn., London.

WOOLF, R. (1968), *English Religious Lyric in the Middle Ages*, Oxford.

WYATT, SIR THOMAS: *see* Rebholz.

Wynnere and Wastoure (1990), ed. S. Trigg, EETS OS 297.

Index

This is an index of proper names (excluding allegorical personages and very common proper names) and titles of works as they appear in the introduction, the headnotes, and the texts. References are to the page except in the case of texts, where they are to abbreviated titles and line numbers (e.g. *TG* 92).

Lightning Source UK Ltd.
Milton Keynes UK
UKOW051829230112

185903UK00001B/42/P

9 780199 263981